THE LONDON BOMBINGS

THE LONDON BOMBINGS

MARC SAGEMAN

PENN

UNIVERSITY OF PENNSYLVANIA PRESS

PHILADELPHIA

Published by
University of Pennsylvania Press
Philadelphia, Pennsylvania 19104-4112
www.upenn.edu/pennpress

Printed in the United States of America
on acid-free paper

1 3 5 7 9 10 8 6 4 2

Library of Congress Cataloging-in-Publication Data
Names: Sageman, Marc, author.
Title: The London bombings / Marc Sageman.
Description: 1st edition. | Philadelphia : University of Pennsylvania Press,
[2019] | Includes bibliographical references and index.
Identifiers: LCCN 2018033405 | ISBN 978-0-8122-5118-0 (hardcover)
Subjects: LCSH: London Terrorist Bombings, London, England, 2005. |
Terrorism—England—Case studies. | Terrorism—Religious aspects—
Islam. | Terrorism—Prevention—Government policy—Great Britain.
Classification: LCC HV6433.G713 L6575 2019 | DDC
363.32509421/090511—dc23
LC record available at https://lccn.loc.gov/2018033405

CONTENTS

INTRODUCTION

IN ABOUT FIFTY SECONDS London became the frontline of the Global War on Terror. On 7 July 2005, around 8:47 A.M., at the end of rush hour, three nearly simultaneous explosions tore apart the London Underground. At first, the trickling of information to both the London Underground's Network Control Center and the London Metropolitan Police Headquarters indicated mysterious fires breaking out at the same time at several different locations. At 9:14 A.M., the center ordered all trains to pull into stations and remain there. At 9:40 A.M., it ordered an evacuation of the entire network. Seven minutes later, as television showed the first blackened and bloodied victims emerging from the tunnels, an explosion in a bus in Tavistock Square confirmed that this was a terrorist operation. The British government shifted into high gear and immediately held a high-level COBRA (Cabinet Office Briefing Room A) meeting.[1]

In the first days after the explosions, speculations were rampant but the people in London did not panic: they simply carried on. Within days, four suicide bombers were identified as the authors of this carnage, which killed fifty-two innocent people and injured seven hundred more. The explosions completely shattered British counterterrorism services' assumptions about the global neojihadi[2] threat to Britain. As London Metropolitan Police Assistant Commissioner Andy Hayman stated, before the investigation into the bombings he believed that "al Qaeda was a loose affiliation of like-minded groups who shared the same ideals but had no firm leadership or control." After the investigation, he changed his view and believed that "al Qaeda has a central leadership who pull the strings. . . . Al Qaeda also has a military structure based around Osama bin Laden and Ayman al Zawahiri (who appeared on the suicide video of the 7 July leader . . . and is the chief strategist) and around its foot soldiers hiding in the mountains and caves of Afghanistan. We believe there is another layer of 'masterminds' and businessmen who oversee the campaigns in the UK and other countries."[3]

Hayman's contrasting perspectives on global neojihadi terrorism[4] in the West have strong policy implications. Was it a clash of civilizations—Islam versus the West—that was an existential threat on par with the ability of a nuclear Soviet Union to obliterate the West? Was it of such a magnitude as to force the West to adopt measures limiting civil liberties, such as freedoms of expression, of the press, of assembly, of religion, or simply to vent one's frustration against government policies, as seen in the United States, the United Kingdom, or France? What was the nature of the threat: a top-down, well-orchestrated, powerful hierarchical international organization that had established an infrastructure in the West in the form of sleeper cells, "the fruition of strategic, organizational decisions made by al Qaeda years before";[5] or a bottom-up threat, leaderless and more extensive, spontaneously self-organized clusters of violent guys disillusioned with peaceful legitimate ways to address their grievances and outraged by Western persecution of their co-religionists at home and abroad?

These are important questions to answer. Fear grows from vagueness, confusion, and ignorance, when unconnected events are blended together and appear to magnify the threat. After the devastation of the September 11, 2001, attack on the United States, Western powers tried to counter this threat by spending trillions of dollars for national security, killing hundreds of thousands in invasions of two countries and operations in several failed states, and passing harsh antiterrorism measures at home. These measures selectively targeted Muslims, alienating a large portion of this community, and increased the threat they were meant to minimize—a self-fulfilling prophecy. They also affected the rest of society, as the overestimated threat became the justification for large-scale state surveillance of all electronic communications. This overreaction violated civil rights and protection of privacy gained through centuries of political struggle. These civil rights became the essence of Western liberal democracies. Does this alleged threat justify such infringement on civil rights?

Of course, despite alarmist warnings from some scholars and journalists,[6] the answer to this question is more nuanced. This book argues that the threat is a hybrid, somewhere between an organized and a leaderless one, and the al Qaeda factor in the attacks in the West varied from tight control to a looser one to none at all.[7] In fact, Hayman's two perspectives need not be incompatible: a top-down threat can coexist with a bottom-up one.[8] These two perspectives are not just academic disputes but have real consequences in terms of strategy to counter the threat. If the threat is simply top down, the eradication of al Qaeda would eliminate the threat. On the other hand, if the threat is also bottom up in addition to being top down, the destruction of a terrorist organization abroad is not enough. Western society must prevent global neojihadi sympathizers from turning to violence. Counterterrorist measures must be empirically adapted to the actual nature of the threat but also preserve civil liberties as much as possible. The analysis of the actual nature of the global neojihadi threat to the West requires a detailed account of al Qaeda's most dangerous attacks in order to understand the worst-case scenarios against the West.

A survey of global neojihadi plots or attacks in the West in the post-9/11 decade shows that there were 66 such plots or attacks, of which 16 were directly linked to al Qaeda itself.[9] Five attacks directed at Britain in the middle of the decade, from 2004 to 2006, represent the most intensive campaign of al Qaeda violence in the West. This book analyzes in detail four of these attacks—there is not enough publicly available information on the fifth plot, called Operation Rhyme[10]—to understand the nature of the threat against the West at its worst. The British government called the investigation of these attacks Operations Crevice, Theseus (the London bombings), Vivace, and Overt respectively. Given the national trauma from these attacks and the restrictive legal countermeasures that they triggered, it is surprising that there is no in-depth account of these attacks, with one exception.[11] Furthermore, these attacks are not independent from each other, but constitute the height of a campaign of violence against the West. Analyzing them together will allow us to uncover some of the links between them. Once these links are understood, we can gauge how well Britain's security service fared in protecting its society especially in relation to potential missed opportunities for preventing the bombings—the question lingering over the Coroner's Inquests five years later.[12] The detailed accounts of these four attacks act as a reality check on many speculations about the global neojihadi threat and point to some of the ways of countering this threat with minimal disruption to civil liberties and privacy.

Methodology

Terrorism, especially after the tragedies of the 9/11 attacks, the Madrid and London bombings, and the new wave of Islamic State attacks, has captured

people's imagination and spawned an industry of books and documentaries, replete with claims of dubious reliability. Self-proclaimed "experts"
feed an echo effect by recirculating erroneous information that, with time,
acquires fake validity. This makes up the conventional wisdom, which suggests that there is a domestic infrastructure of preachers of hate brainwashing naïve young Muslims and mysterious recruiters in the shadow of
mosques sending them to train in Afghanistan to transform them into
fanatics, who return home to cause large-scale mayhem.[13] There is no one
reliable database on terrorism. Research into this topic must resort to a
process of triangulation that may answer specific questions. The method is
to use multiple sources of information because any piece of data is more or
less biased. Awareness of these systematic biases helps to compensate for
them through comparison with other sources of data and other cases of
political violence at different times and places. The ideal data collection
would of course have been a series of ethnographic participant observa-
tions. However, since terrorism is a criminal activity, this form of collection
would require an observer to become an accomplice by not alerting the
authorities of an impending crime. Instead, I had to rely on a variety of
sources, each with its own strengths and weaknesses.

To understand the nature of terrorism requires data that is both very
detailed and reliable. Given the amount of nonsense written on this subject,
one cannot escape going back to primary sources, free of "expert" or jour-
nalist interpretation. So far, the richest kind of these primary sources is
legal evidence presented at terrorist trials. I have therefore collected legal
material for this project: discovery material for these trials, transcripts of
the proceedings, notes about the proceedings from such trials, and judgments justifying sentences. In the English-speaking world, criminal jurisprudence has developed a tradition of fairness based on an adversarial
system of confrontation, whereby the prosecution case can be challenged
by the defense. Initial hysterical speculations can be refuted through the
systematic sifting of evidence in court. From this conflicting evidence, one
can better approximate what really happened.

Prosecution documents and government claims are only claims: they
need to be corroborated, which is the reason that trials test them with
challenges from defendants. Most of the time, the claims of the government
present the most incriminating scenario about defendants. Without hearing
the defendants' side of the story, they cannot be viewed as reliable. They
are only the first salvo in the long battle of evidence. Many of these claims

do not withstand scrutiny at trial when confronted with defense evidence. This is why it is so important to collect the actual transcripts to check on competing claims.

Most analysts of terrorism simply take these government claims as true and weave the most incriminating scenario, which the press amplifies. They must be treated with caution because they are really only the prosecution's case and quite one-sided. Much of the press reporting and evidence cited in online blogs come from these indictments or criminal complaints. This book relies mostly on the trial transcripts, in which defendants have a chance to present their side of the story to refute the sometimes fantastic allegations against them.[14]

Of course, not all evidence is presented at trial and how much is presented varies from country to country according to what is viewed as admissible evidence or protected information for the sake of national security. For instance, evidence from electronic intercepts, especially emails with foreign entities, was not admissible in some of the cases presented here. This limits our understanding of the international linkages between the defendants and guiding masterminds elsewhere in these cases. However, as much as possible, compensations for this inherent bias of court documents and proceedings has been complemented with informal exchanges with intelligence agencies, foreign and domestic, and local law enforcement agencies where the presence of such links was discussed along with the nature of the evidence for these links.

My former job as a member of the U.S. intelligence community or since as an expert witness at many terrorist trials was both a blessing and a hindrance. I have interviewed several defendants convicted of terrorism charges, who provided information relevant to this book. I also had access to relevant secret documents and intelligence personnel. Of course, these informed my understanding of the global neojihad in England, but I am prohibited from sharing any of this information in this book. Therefore, I have cited only documents or testimony presented to the public and hence not secret. Interviews with defendants and even classified material of course must be taken with a great deal of skepticism because they are attempts to exonerate the speaker. Likewise, the circumstances of the generation of classified reports might have tainted them—such as torture, when victims may say anything to stop the pain. This information must therefore be carefully checked with corroborative evidence to reconstruct what went on.

My experience is that both the prosecution and the defense claims are exaggerated: they both try to argue for the maximal degree of guilt or innocence of the defendants. They ignore anything that is not consistent with their maximalist arguments. Sometimes, it is easy to navigate between the two, but at other times, especially when there is no other corroborating evidence, this enterprise is very challenging. I have brought other factors, based on my background knowledge, to try to choose the narrative that makes sense and is closer to both the evidence that was presented at trial and that surfaced elsewhere, often after the trial took place.

As a scholar, I cannot take the claims of government agents or intelligence officers at face value. They are secondary sources and of sometimes suspect reliability as recent U.S. government lies about the use of torture revealed. A few years ago, I used to travel around and get briefed by foreign intelligence agencies and took their claims at face value. Over time, I have had the opportunity to check many of them personally with primary sources. The results were disappointing. I simply cannot trust governments to provide reliable information without independently checking its sources and reliability.

Testimony by defendants at trial presents a challenge. For all their flaws, defendants' testimonies are still a privileged window into their mind and cannot be totally discarded. Of course, defendants will provide self-exculpatory evidence in terms of terrorism charges. However, there is no reason to believe that the evidence they provide as to their background, their activities around the time of the alleged crime, or their links to other noninvolved individuals is faulty. The only things that must be handled with care are their actual criminal activities. Even then, their motivation for certain behavior, their political sympathies, or their attitude toward the government may be accurate. On the whole, one can make an expert judgment on the evidence presented by the prosecution and by the defense (based on extensive experience with other terrorism cases).

A second source of data was terrorist self-reports, either in captured documentary form, deliberately broadcast, or interviews. One must approach them with caution, for such evidence often degenerates into self-aggrandizing propaganda. In addition, such retrospective accounts suffer from biased recollections uttered in a specific context, which may not truly reflect what actually took place. I have no desire to resume the debate between historical truth and narrative truth in the fields of psychology and history. Aware of these potential biases, I tried to compensate for them.

A third source of data was media reporting. Evaluation of this data is especially complex because it is rife with speculation, even in the most careful and prestigious publications. For any given attack, I collected all the relevant published articles both in the English-language press (via large databases like Lexis/Nexis and Factiva) and the non-English international press (via the same two large databases and the Open Source Center).[15] I then arranged them in chronological order to generate a preliminary narrative of each investigation. Driven by the tyranny of the continuous 24-hour news cycle, journalists are often compelled to speculate about events when new facts surface about a story. In a very competitive profession, they are often forced to "shoot first and aim later" to scoop their rivals. As the investigation unfolds, later findings often refute these original speculations. These erroneous "facts" are never corrected or eliminated from the record, continue to live unchallenged on the Internet, and are often picked up in many accounts based on these secondary sources. In my chronology for each case, I corrected erroneous original information when more accurate accounts later emerged in the natural course of the investigation or at the respective trials. This is especially important in Britain, where criminal cases in litigation cannot be discussed in public lest they might prejudice due process. Violations of this *sub judice* ban on reporting on cases before the end of a trial are punished by contempt-of-court charges. This means that the British press cannot reveal crucial information about each attack until its trial comes to a conclusion.[16] Furthermore, critical new evidence sometimes surfaces later on[17] or new arrests shed more evidence on earlier plots. Therefore, it is critical to keep cross-checking and correcting the narrative of each plot even years after the events took place.[18]

All too often expert accounts of a plot are haphazard, following alleged links with other individuals, prematurely connecting dots that are not linked in reality. It is imperative to construct a complete chronology of a plot in context and to avoid getting ahead of the carefully established facts (no premature "connecting the dots"). Plots evolve: people participating at the beginning may drop out to be replaced by other people. Initial hopes are transformed over time when obstacles arise but may resume when these obstacles disappear. By collapsing time, it is too easy to postulate that there is a straight line between something that happened at one time and another several years later. In constructing their narratives, scholars must appreciate these changes and adaptations over time.

The next chapter traces the emergence of an Islamist political community in Britain in the 1990s. Chapters 2–5 tell the stories of the four global neojihadi attacks in Britain, namely the fertilizer bombing plot, the London bombings, the copycat bombing attempts two weeks later, and the liquid bomb airline plot. The concluding chapter compares the narratives of these four attacks with other scholarly versions and stresses the importance of getting the story straight.

CHAPTER 1

THE EMERGENCE
OF ISLAMIST COMMUNITIES
IN BRITAIN

THE FOUR AL QAEDA attacks in England did not come out of the blue. They simmered for a while in a political protest counterculture, percolated to the surface due to some internal but mostly external factors, and finally boiled over in short bursts of activity from November 2003 to August 2006. To understand them, it is important to first re-create the environment that fostered them.

Activation of a Muslim Social Identity

The turn to political violence for a few British Muslims emerged from a new awareness of their Muslim identity. Before the 1990s, they thought of themselves, and were seen, as immigrants and "blacks." Muslims constituted only the most recent wave of immigration to Britain.[1] Their experience of settling in Britain was similar to that of earlier newcomers. In Europe post–World War II labor shortages and reconstruction attracted huge numbers of immigrants, mostly from Muslim countries with a historical link with a European one: Algerians to France, Turks to Germany, and South Asians to Britain. South Asians in Britain expanded rapidly, from 21,000 in the 1951 census to 600,000 in 1981, to about 1,000,000 in 1991, to around 1,600,000 in 2001 (just under 3 percent of the British population), and an estimated 2,900,000 in 2010 (about 4.6 percent of the total population).[2] Far from being homogeneous as feared by Islamophobes, who lump them together into a single amorphous mass, these very diverse newcomers represent different cultural traditions. From the 2001 census, about 660,000 traced their origins back to Pakistan (mostly from the Mirpur area), 260,000 to Bangladesh (mostly from the Sylhet area), 140,000 to India, 93,000 to the Middle East, 90,000 mostly black to East or West Africa, 60,000 to the Balkans (mostly from Bosnia or Kosovo), and 36,000 to North Africa. In addition, there were about 60,000 British natives who had converted to Islam. Muslims were concentrated around London (1,000,000), the West Midlands (200,000), West Yorkshire (150,000), and Manchester (125,000). They were fairly young, with a third under 15 years of age and about half under 24. Only 35,000 British Muslims studied at universities, but their numbers were complemented by foreign Muslim students, mostly from Pakistan and Bangladesh.[3]

Their awakening as Muslims rather than workers, "blacks," immigrants, or leftists was a gradual process. They had assumed all these other social identities during the 1970s and 1980s. They had come to Britain deeply divided, partially as a result of British imperialist multicultural strategy, allowing a very small civil service to rule the immense Indian subcontinent. It was basically a "divide and rule" strategy along sectarian and ethnic lines, funneling state funds through selected local representatives for each community that would fight among themselves for these limited resources. This internal competition prevented the formation of a united opposition to British rule. When South Asians immigrated to Britain, they re-created this social structure and organized themselves in small communities, each with its own house of worship. The rapid emergence of many small diverse mosques in Britain in the 1950s and 1960s reflected these narrow parochial divisions and stymied the emergence of a united Muslim community.

When the economy contracted in the 1970s, the newcomers faced a nativist backlash from indigenous Britons who accused them of stealing jobs and formed the racist far-right National Front. The first-generation immigrants accepted this racism as a fact of life and simply continued to send money back home and provide their children with better opportunity. For protection, they re-created in Britain their local mutual help system, the *biradari*, based on a network of kin and neighbors. It insulated them in their new country, encouraged ties to their home village, and protected them in a hostile world. It also came with a tradition of honor and obligations, including arranged marriages to distant family members to keep property within small clans.[4]

The children of these immigrants did not share their parents' perspective. They had grown up in Britain, saw themselves as British, and insisted on being treated as such. They spoke English as opposed to Urdu, Punjabi, or Bengali, refused to accept their parents' menial jobs, and rejected their parents' parochial biradari customs. These obligations clashed with their very Western desire to choose whom to marry, had little relevance to the drug and crime problems they encountered in their poor neighborhoods, and lacked the cosmopolitan perspective they had picked up from their British education.

The second generation rejected the first generation's fatalism. It confronted the hostile nativist prejudice and racism in British institutions, especially in the police force. At first, native Britons lumped together all nonwhite newcomers to the British Isles and generically called them "blacks." As a result, this mass of young immigrants or children of immigrants banded together against young racist Britons. This confrontation often degenerated into gang turf warfare and culminated in the 1981 summer of riots throughout Britain. For instance, the Bradford 12, named for their Midlands town, were arrested in the summer of 1981 for making homemade bombs. At their trial, they openly admitted to the charges but argued they were acting legitimately to protect their communities against impending neofascist attacks. The jury agreed and acquitted all of them.[5]

To regain control of the streets, the British government adopted the Raj's multicultural strategy at home. It appointed representatives of the various Islamic traditions and sects throughout the country as local intermediaries. Despite the Islamic names of these councils, they were political and not religious organizations, composed of local businessmen, which tried to subdue angry young men and restore peace through pride in their culture of origin and Islam. At first, this strategy broke up the amorphous antiracist coalition into more confessional lines, with occasional incidents pitting young men of Caribbean origin against those from South Asia.[6] Over the longer term, this strategy had a more insidious effect. Since all municipal funds and welfare were channeled through these Islamic councils, any request from the community had to be addressed via a religious prism. This policy fostered the emergence of a Muslim collective identity to the detriment of any other social identity based on former national, immigrant, economic, or social class status. Gradually, second-generation

Muslim South Asians started to think of themselves as Muslims rather than Kashmiris, Punjabis, Gujaratis, Bengalis, immigrants, workers, poor people, or "blacks."

Multiculturalism did not cure the resentment of second-generation Muslims toward their host society. British politicians treated them as members of Muslim communities instead of British citizens born in Britain. Anger bred by host racism did not simply go away. The promise of a liberal democracy and equal opportunity clashed with the reality of police racism, widespread slander, and discrimination in the labor market. Nor did expectations of the ability of the political system to redress this situation match reality. Disenchantment with leftist politics that could not fit the issue of racism into its ideological constructs of class warfare and the gradual disillusionment with Communist utopias eroded the belief that change could be articulated within the context of secular, progressive, and universal values and ideologies. This large discrepancy between their political expectations and the reality of their political impotence led some disillusioned young Muslims to engage in activities intended to undermine, disrupt, or overthrow British political institutions.[7]

The Rushdie Affair accelerated this transformation of leftist activists into Muslim ones. In early 1989, Salman Rushdie published *The Satanic Verses,* a novel that painted an unflattering portrait of the Prophet Muhammad. This generated worldwide Islamist protest riots and a *fatwa* (religious opinion) by the Iranian leader Ayatollah Khomeini condemning Rushdie to death, encouraging Muslims to kill him. Secular commentators strongly defended free speech and condemned Islamist intolerance. Some Muslims interpreted these criticisms as an attack on Islam. In Britain, various Muslim political organizations competed to defend Islam and become the representative of a yet unorganized "national Muslim community." This internal competition encouraged actions that distinguished them most from non-Muslim Britons, a race to the extreme, like a public book burning in Bradford.[8] The affair activated a self-categorization of an overwhelming majority of British society which defined itself in contrast to this book burning and the Ayatollah Khomeini's fatwa. In turn, a small minority of Muslims felt attacked by this backlash and defended their faith against secular accusations. This dispute put political Islam on the agenda in Britain. It became the political awakening of many young Muslims who had never read the Quran and had barely attended mosque: "Why are we being singled out? Why are we being attacked: Why can't anyone see we are under attack? It felt very frustrating because we did not seem to be able to do anything about it."[9] In this context, Ayatollah Khomeini was a validation of Islam, allowing them to stand up for themselves as proud Muslims. Kenan Malik captured the evolution of one of his friends from Trotskyism to Southern Comfort (alcohol), sex, and Arsenal (football), to Islam: "It had also become something more than simply disaffection with radical politics. He had, he said, lost his sense of who he was and where he'd come from. So he had returned to Bradford to try to rediscover it. And what he had found was a sense of community and a 'need to defend our dignity as Muslims, to defend our values and beliefs.' He was not going to allow anyone—'racist or Rushdie'—to trample over them."[10]

Although some scholars suggest a straight line between the Rushdie Affair and the 2005 London bombings,[11] in fact, it had no direct impact on the future perpetrators, most of whom were not yet 10 years old at this time. The oldest, Mohammed Sidique Khan, a teenager, was not affected by the affair. However, it was certainly a milestone in the creation of an Islamist political protest community in Britain.

The Emergence of an Islamist Social Identity

Disillusioned with secular utopias that did not address sectarian prejudice or ethnic racism, some young Muslims turned to Islamist alternatives, like Hizb ut-Tahrir (HuT, Party of Freedom). Despite their Islamic names, these were political organizations using an Islamic lexicon to make their point, hence the adjective Islamist with its political rather than religious connotation. They modeled their utopia on the followers (*ansar*) of the Prophet, who of course covered themselves in glory by conquering a huge portion of the civilized world in a few decades in the seventh century. These organizations argued that Islam was the answer to any political or social issue and only by re-creating the society of the ansar would Muslims be able to regain the grandeur and glory of the past. These arguments did not get much traction until the Bosnian War.

The war in Bosnia was another political wake-up call for passive young British Muslims. Ahmed Omar Saeed Sheikh, who later gained notoriety as the kidnapper of *Wall Street Journal* reporter Daniel Pearl, studied at the London School of Economics and joined its Islamic society, which screened the film *The Destruction of a Nation* in November 1992. He later recalled that it "shook my heart. The reason being Bosnian Muslims were shown being butchered by the Serbs." He volunteered to go on a trip to Bosnia with a Muslim charity during his university spring break. This experience started him on his path to terrorism abroad.[12]

In essence, the Bosnian War activated an Islamist social identity especially among university students exposed to the atrocities of the war and wanting to support their victimized co-religionists. The collection of young Muslims sharing this political social identity created an imagined community[13] dispersed among many small clusters of activists, as we shall soon see. It inspired a few to volunteer to join the global neojihadi movement but did not yet turn them against Britain. They defined themselves in contrast to their enemies, Serbs and Orthodox Bosnians, but not yet Britain, which was not their enemy despite their complaints that it was not doing enough to help victimized Muslim Bosnians. That war established an imagined political protest community that eventually became more radical.

The majority of young Muslims did not take Sheikh's individualistic path to Islamist activism. Instead, they formed study groups or joined HuT, which proselytized on university campuses by showing documentaries in early 1993 depicting atrocities committed against Bosnian Muslims. Films like *The Killing Fields of Bosnia* shocked young Muslims, previously involved in local Muslim groups fighting neighborhood rivals.[14] "The first time I saw the videos, it was a shocking, traumatic experience," said one. "I was so angered by what I saw that my immediate response was a desire to go and fight in Bosnia myself. I wanted to take up arms and defend the Bosnians."[15] They realized that the parochialism of their local Muslim organizations provided no guidance on Bosnia. Nor could concerned young Muslims turn to their local imams, who completely avoided any discussion of politics.

These informal and formal groups competed for leadership of this imagined political protest community. Foremost among them was HuT. Young Muslims drifted to HuT—the videos on Bosnian atrocities were powerful recruiting tools. Their message was that Bosnian Muslims were white, blond, and blue-eyed and had coexisted with Serbs for centuries, yet Serbs massacred them in the thousands. What chance of survival did British Muslims have in Britain, where their presence had been much shorter and their appearance was so different from the rest of the population? HuT organized meetings and demonstrations to bring attention to the slaughter of Muslims in Bosnia. It inspired British Muslim students to get involved in the defense of fellow Muslims worldwide. They identified with Muslim victims in Bosnia, and later Chechnya, Kosovo, Palestine, Afghanistan, and Iraq, and this emerging sense of Islamist social identity translated into political activism on behalf of their persecuted brothers and sisters.[16]

HuT was a Middle Eastern organization, a splinter from the Muslim Brotherhood, which preached a three-part strategy to take political power. The first stage was building a political party with a core group of activists. In a second stage, the activists would challenge their country's dominant political ideology with their own. Once the general public accepted its ideology, the party would take political power, most probably in a military coup. Needless to say, it was immediately banned in every Arab country and grew clandestinely, organized in weekly study groups called *halaqas*, where members analyzed its ideology, discussed strategy, and rehearsed arguments to attract potential recruits. HuT's popularity in Britain owed much to the aggressive tactics of its leader, Omar Bakri Mohammed al-Fostoq, a Syrian who joined HuT in his homeland and studied Islamic jurisprudence in Cairo and Saudi Arabia, from where he was expelled. He arrived in 1986 in Britain and was granted political asylum four years later. He was appointed HuT leader there and captured media attention through outrageous statements like his invitation for Queen Elizabeth to convert to Islam.[17]

HuT has a radical ideology. "Radical" has many meanings but I use it in the sense that a radical rejects the normal, ordinary, traditional "commonsense" outlook that is taken for granted among competent mainstream people. Radicals interpret the world through the prism of who they are, their identity, giving them a worldview that coheres around their rejection of mainstream societal outlook. Radicals generate a counterculture that defines itself in contrast to conventional culture. In turn, society usually rejects and discriminates against radicals, and this experience of discrimination becomes an integral part of their social identity. In fact, radical groups often exploit this outside hostility against them for their own advantage, acquiring a sense of importance because if they were not important, society would not discriminate against them.[18]

Buoyed by media attention, HuT infiltrated university Islamic organizations, by addressing not only Bosnia but also other important social issues for young Muslims through talks on "Sex, Drugs and Rock 'n' Roll," "Asia: Born to Be Brown," and "Marriage: Love or Arranged?" Many Muslims at university hated the old-fashioned customs of their parents' generation, especially that of arranged marriages with cousins from the old country.

They preferred to approach their future mate directly, without parental involvement, and a few eloped to get married.[19] Contrary to Western perceptions that this form of Islam is misogynist, it was, in fact, very popular with young women, who were drawn to these groups because they encouraged women to participate in public life, pursue an education, oppose arranged marriages, and engage in political activism.[20] Many of the future terrorists in this study chose their wives in opposition to their parents' wishes. This escape from the suffocation of the biradari traditions and freedom to choose attracted both sexes to this radical community.[21]

Bakri's constant pushing the envelope for publicity finally got him in trouble with his HuT superiors. In August 1995, at a rally, he declared that Muslims would not rest until "the black flag of Islam flies over 10 Downing Street."[22] This generated concern from the worldwide HuT organization on two fronts. First, it feared that these outlandish statements might backfire and negate its gains in Britain, which allowed the party to have a voice that was suppressed everywhere else in the world. Second, its goal of regime change targeted the Middle East, where it wanted to establish a caliphate, and not Britain, which it viewed as a sanctuary. Therefore, it asked Bakri to stand down with his provocations, and when the latter refused, it stripped him of his leadership in November 1995. Omar Bakri never informed his followers of this change and instead resigned from HuT in January 1996. Three days later, he launched al-Muhajiroun (the Emigrants, commonly referred to as ALM) and quickly induced many of his followers to come over to his new group. His program was basically identical to HuT, but with a new emphasis of establishing an Islamic state in Britain.[23]

At the time of the split, HuT had nearly 300 core activists and a network of contacts nearing 4,000.[24] Both HuT and ALM continued to proselytize at universities and ventured into Muslim neighborhoods, where their members struck up friendships with Muslim gangs. In fact, their intense proselytization interfered with religious observance. "We were too tired to pray," said one; "establishing the Islamic state was more important than minor matters such as praying, reciting the Koran, giving to charity, or being kind to our parents and fellow Muslims."[25]

Londonistan

Repression of Islamist militants abroad encouraged their migration to London. Egypt, Algeria, and Saudi Arabia cracked down on internal Islamist dissenters and urged Pakistan, where they had found refuge, to expel them. Refugees trickled one by one to London, one of their last sanctuaries in the world. For Algerian refugees, the situation was aggravated by French and later Belgian crackdowns on alleged supporters of Algerian insurgents as Algeria was drifting toward civil war.

Adel Abdel Bary, an Egyptian attorney who defended many Egyptian militants, was one of the first to come from Peshawar via Saudi Arabia in September 1991. His successful stay and the fact that London was a media hub inspired some of his friends, like Hani Sebai and Yassir al Siri, to join him around 1994 and use the prominent London Arab press to become the mouthpiece of the Jihad Group of Egypt, commonly referred to as the Egyptian Islamic Jihad. After the Jihad Group consolidated its structure in Yemen and elected Ayman al Zawahiri as its emir, Ibrahim Eidarous came to London in 1997 to be its official representative.

In 1994, from Saudi Arabia came Muhammad al Masari and Saad al Faqih, whose Committee for the Defense of Legitimate Rights criticized the Saudi royal family, especially its conduct during the first Gulf War. Around 1996, al Faqih split from the committee to found the Movement for Islamic Reform in Arabia. These Saudis pioneered the use of the Internet as a medium to spread their message via their website. Like the Egyptian dissidents, their target audience was their home country and their propaganda was in Arabic. Another Saudi newcomer in 1994 was Khalid al Fawwaz, who established the Advice and Reform Committee to be the media arm of Osama bin Laden and his group in Khartoum. He was in constant contact with his boss and tried to coordinate a global neojihadi movement under the leadership of bin Laden.[26] However, these expatriates interacted only with each other, not with the local English youth, and they had a negligible influence on them.

More significant for radical Islamism in Britain was the September 1993 arrival of the Palestinian Omar Mahmoud Othman (better known as Abu Qatada al Filastini), a trained cleric who had taught sharia in Peshawar before being expelled. A year later, he was granted political refugee status and took over the editorship of *Al Ansar*, the official newsletter of the GIA (Groupe Islamique Armé, armed Islamic group), the umbrella Algerian Islamist insurgent organization. He was joined by a veteran of the Soviet Afghan War, Mustafa Setmariam Nasar, better known under his pen names Abu Musab al Suri and Umar Abdal Hakim, who had taught jihad theory in training camps in Afghanistan. Setmariam had been asked by an Afghan veteran and GIA leader to come to London and assist the GIA media cell there.[27] For Arab global neojihadis, the Algerian insurgency was the rallying cause of the day. Most of the support for the insurgency had come from France, which had by far the largest expatriate Algerian community. When French authorities cracked down on these support networks in two large waves of arrests in 1993 and 1994, supporters fled to Brussels. A Belgian crackdown in March 1995 forced them to escape to London, where they gathered around *Al Ansar*. Rashid Ramda, who later financed the GIA bombings in France in 1995, came to London around that time and was involved in the distribution of *Al Ansar*.[28] Frustrated with British tolerance for support of an insurgency condemned in France, French authorities coined the derogative name "Londonistan" for this English sanctuary.

In late 1995, the indiscriminate savagery of the GIA in Algeria under Djamel Zitouni, the murder of his popular rivals within the GIA, and the expansion of its war to France in the summer of 1995 split the Arab neojihadi community in London. Bary and Nasar condemned Zitouni, while Abu Qatada continued to support him and even issued fatwas covering the legitimacy of the GIA atrocities. However, with the slide into mass slaughter of civilian populations, even Abu Qatada ceased his support of Zitouni. By June 1996, the whole Arab neojihadi community formally condemned Zitouni and *Al Ansar* ceased publication.[29]

All the above events did not have much influence on British Muslims. The disputes were in Arabic and beyond their understanding as very few were Arabic speakers. However, the presence of Abu Qatada had an indirect effect on the British Islamist community. He set himself up as an independent scholar, unaffiliated with any political religious organization. He started to preach at a prayer hall in London called the Four Feathers and adopted the global neojihad as his core subject.[30] Among his followers were two people who would have a strong influence on British radical Islamists.

Preachers of Hate

Mostafa Kamel Mostafa (better known as Abu Hamza al Masri, sometimes spelled Misri) was an Egyptian who had come to Britain in 1979. He became a citizen in 1986 and a civil engineer in June 1989. On hajj in August 1987, he met Abdullah Azzam, the proselytizer for the Afghan jihad against the Soviets, who urged him to come and help the Afghans. In 1990, Abu Hamza and his family moved to Peshawar and Jalalabad to help rebuild Afghanistan using his skills as a civil engineer for ARCON–Afghan Reconstruction, a Saudi company. At his trial, he testified that he did not participate in combat, but he taught the mujahedin how to dig trenches that would not collapse on their heads.[31] When ARCON pulled out of Afghanistan in 1992, he returned to Peshawar and did some road work on contract for the Pakistani army. In August 1993 near Lahore, Pakistan, he was the victim of an explosive accident. He survived but lost both hands and an eye. He spent the next few months in rehabilitation and returned to England in early 1994.[32] While still recovering from his injuries, he started to raise money and humanitarian aid for Bosnian victims. When one shipment was confiscated by Croatian authorities, he was asked by the relief organization to accompany its next shipment and ensure its arrival at its proper destination. During this three-week trip in the middle of 1994, he traveled to the Mujahedin Katiba (Brigade) at Zenica. A few months later, he led a second convoy to Zenica, where he again stayed for three weeks and taught the mujahedin how to dig robust trenches. After his return to England, he started attending Abu Qatada's lectures and established Supporters of Shariah to propagate the global neojihadi ideology in English for the British media. Abu Hamza returned to Bosnia after the Srebrenica massacre and stayed there for four months, until the Dayton Accords.[33]

When Abu Hamza returned to England, he was now viewed as a hero, an alleged veteran of both the Afghan and Bosnian jihads, and his wounds gave him street credibility with young Muslims. Some Luton Muslims invited him to lead a new mosque they had built. He stayed there, giving ever more radical and popular sermons, which further fed his reputation. In February 1997, he resumed the publication of *Al Ansar* when a new leader, Anouar Zouabri, took over the GIA. However, Zouabri continued to escalate the violence in Algeria, declared the whole Algerian society apostate deserving death, and carried out waves of horrible massacres of civilians. This was too much for even Abu Hamza, who rejected him and discontinued publication of *Al Ansar* in September 1997.[34]

Back in March 1997, Abu Hamza applied for the position of *khateeb*, the preacher of the *khutba* (Friday sermon) at the Finsbury Park Mosque. The board of the mosque was split by a conflict between the original Gujarati and Bangladeshi communities in the neighborhood and the growing presence of Algerian refugees. Unaware of Abu Hamza's radicalism, the trustees hoped that, as an outsider, he would calm things down. Abu Hamza, who was on a disability pension, requested only lunch on days he gave his khutba as compensation, which sealed the deal for the board, and he became the khateeb of the mosque. Soon afterward, Abu Hamza moved into the mosque and used violent thugs, who had gathered around him, to intimidate its imam and board members through strong-arm tactics. With his new platform in London, his rhetorical style and humor quickly attracted newcomers to the mosque, first from London and progressively from the rest of the Western Muslim world. His outrageous statements made for entertaining and sensationalistic reporting, and his appearance seemed straight out of central casting for villains as he reminded audiences of Peter Pan's Captain Hook, which became Abu Hamza's press nickname. The mosque became a center for distribution of tapes of his sermons and a meeting place for international militants.[35]

Another protégé of Abu Qatada was Abdullah el Faisal, born Trevor Forrest in Jamaica, who had converted to Islam as a teenager and studied at an Islamic university in Saudi Arabia. In 1991 he came to Brixton, an immigrant area of south London that became predominantly Caribbean in the 1970s. African Caribbean converts to Islam set up a small prayer room and then a mosque and Islamic cultural center, the Brixton Mosque, in 1990. Unlike other British mosques, which reflected their founders' single ethnic origin and Islamic tradition, the Brixton Mosque encompassed all of Islam's diversity as converts came in from very different conversion experiences. The preaching of Malcolm X and Muhammed Ali resonated strongly with their Caribbean experience. The arrival of Faisal, with his Caribbean background but solid Salafi education, seemed to match the needs of the mosque. He became its imam and khateeb in 1992. Gradually, his violent message and support for global neojihad alarmed its board of elders, who took over the mosque and banned Faisal from it. Faisal continued to lead study circles for followers. His preaching became more radical and he excommunicated the mosque elders. In the fall of 1993, he announced his intention to go to the mosque the following Friday, grab the microphone by force, and preach the khutba. When Faisal came to the mosque with three dozen of his followers, the trustees cut off the electricity and prevented Faisal from being heard. Shortly afterward, they elected Abdul Haqq Baker leader of the mosque. He and his Brixton Salafis became a bulwark against radical Islamist violence.[36]

After Abu Qatada came to London, Faisal attended his preaching sessions and became his translator when Abu Qatada preached to English audiences. Faisal adopted Abu Qatada's global neojihadi philosophy and pushed it even further with outrageous statements. He became an itinerant preacher, selling tapes of his sermons, visiting colleges, and conducting study circles in south London.[37]

Abu Qatada, Abu Hamza, Faisal, and Omar Bakri appealed to different audiences. Abu Qatada, who spoke only Arabic, appealed to the radical Arab diaspora. HuT and Omar Bakri's ALM focused on universities and appealed to South Asian Muslim students there. Abu Hamza appealed to young Muslims who were not students and to North African immigrants, especially Algerians. Faisal appealed to black immigrants or converts, whose nascent radicalism was not restrained by more peaceful South Asian Islamic traditions. As they competed for the radical Islamist audience in Britain, they became strong rivals, who constantly bad-mouthed and intrigued against each other. Collectively they became known as the preachers of hate to the British public.

The vast majority of British Muslims were of South Asian origin and did not follow the preachers of hate blindly. As mentioned, shocked by the events in Bosnia, they organized themselves into small groups, which discussed political events affecting Muslims worldwide. On occasion, they went to lectures given by these famous preachers out of curiosity, especially during Ramadan. During the holy month, it was a tradition to go to another mosque to listen to the khutba and mosques invited different preachers to talk to their congregations. Sometimes, the radical ideas of these preachers resonated with them, but this did not make them devoted followers of these preachers or brainwashed into extremism. It takes more than a single visit to a mosque or listening to a lecture by one of these preachers of hate to establish strong links with them as is assumed in British tabloids. Unfortunately, some academics obsessed by social network analysis adopted tabloid claims of the existence of these strong links.[38] The significance of these links, if any, is an empirical issue, which this study examines.

The Tooting Circle: Azzam.com

The first significant cluster of British global neojihadis emerged in Tooting, south London, near Saint George's Hospital. The neighborhood included many Muslim immigrants from Bangladesh, India, and Pakistan—mostly Punjabis rather than Kashmiris, who settled more in northern England. In the late 1980s, secondary school Muslim students spontaneously formed a study circle to learn about their common heritage, have fun, and help out in the community. Most attended prestigious white secondary schools and later went on to professional careers, especially medicine as Saint George's Hospital was just a block away. They volunteered to tutor students, clean up their mosque before the Eid holidays, and sometimes organize camping trips for fun. Most were born in the mid-1970s and were too young to have been affected by either the Rushdie Affair or the first Gulf War. By 1993, the circle, which met on Friday evenings (and was called the Friday Circle, although outsiders referred to it as the Tooting Circle) at the local community center, attracted about 50 local attendees. After the meeting, the attendees socialized at the Chicken Cottage restaurant.

In the fall of 1992, most of them started university, just as the Bosnian War was reaching levels of atrocities not seen since World War II. Babar Ahmad, an 18-year-old son of double immigrants (Muslims born in India, who had first immigrated to Pakistan in 1947 and then to Britain in the 1960s), became the circle's most prominent member. He saw a news report on the Omarska death camp[39] in Bosnia on ITN and was shocked by the images of the standing living skeletons, who reminded him of images of the Holocaust. He started to collect funds for the refugees and took advantage of his Christmas school break to travel to Croatia as a relief worker. There, he volunteered to go to Bosnia to deliver food to some of the war's victims. The stories and sight of the Muslim refugees outraged him so much that he dedicated his life to support of Muslim war victims.

When Ahmad came back to London, he proselytized and raised money on behalf of the Bosnian refugees at university campuses and within the Friday Circle. He acted alone, not connected to any Muslim organizations. He showed the films *Destruction of a Nation* and *Massacres in Bosnia* to outraged Muslim audiences. He was not able to return to Bosnia as Croatia had cut off the road to that country for a year and a half. In the summer of 1994, the route was reopened and about 20 young men from London made brief round trips in three- or four-truck convoys of humanitarian aid during school vacation. At the news of the Srebrenica massacre in early July 1995, about a dozen outraged Friday Circle members immediately volunteered to go to Bosnia as soldiers to protect the Muslim community there and joined the Mujahedin Katiba in Zenica. They became the majority of Londoners who fought in Bosnia.

It was in Zenica that Ahmad first heard about Abdullah Azzam and his two short books, *Defense of Muslim Lands* and *Join the Caravan*. Ahmad was wounded and came back to London in time to resume his education. He did not blend in with the foreigners who constituted Londonistan. During Ramadan, as was the tradition, Friday Circle members went to the Four Feathers Mosque to listen to Abu Qatada, but remained unimpressed. In fact, they had a negative impression of him and his followers, whom they viewed as uneducated, ill-mannered, thieves, and crooks. Many were *takfiris*, who excommunicated other Muslims as not being true Muslims and felt it legitimate not to obey the law of the land and thus to rob its inhabitants. Many of Abu Qatada's followers were involved in credit card fraud and scams, and even defrauded some of the Friday Circle members. The British-born Islamist militants distanced themselves from the Londonistan community.

Ahmad went to *umrah* (the pilgrimage to Mecca not during its traditional annual time) with his family in early 1996 and, for the first time, heard audiocassettes there with *nasheeds*, which are noninstrumental chants in Arabic, singing the praise of martyrs. He bought some and got the idea of manufacturing them in English in time for the first anniversary of the Srebrenica massacre. He started collecting hagiographic stories about martyrs in Bosnia, some of whom he had met, to preserve their legacy. He recorded them on low-budget equipment and introduced them with excerpts from Abdullah Azzam. He called this collection *In the Heart of Green Birds* (the birds of paradise) and called his enterprise Azzam Recordings. His first run of 250 cassettes came out in July 1996 and he sold them at stalls around Britain.

After graduating from university, Ahmad went to Chechnya right after the cease-fire accord that ended what became known as the first Chechen War. The complete reduction of Grozny to rubble shocked him and he interviewed victims of and fighters in the war. Shortly after his return to London, Ahmad published a translation of Azzam's two books, which he had downloaded from the Internet, and recorded a second cassette, *Under the Shades of Swords*, which sold well at his stall. Someone suggested he start a website to promote his material and educate the public about the plight of Muslims in Bosnia and Chechnya. Azzam.com first went online in early 1997. He supervised the site but several friends from the Friday Circle provided the technical support for it.[40]

The various trial testimonies of Saajid Badat provide a good picture of the Friday Circle and its significance for Islamist militancy in Britain in the late 1990s. Badat was five years younger than the founders of the Friday

Circle, too young to have participated in the Bosnian War, and part of a younger generation looking up to their elders. He came to London as an 18-year-old in the summer of 1997 after a fight with his father. Before he left Gloucester, a friend had given him a copy of *In the Hearts of Green Birds*, which moved him and made him politically aware. In London, he toured various mosques and went twice to Finsbury Park Mosque to listen to Abu Hamza. He later recalled only that the preacher shouted a lot and had no arms. His quickly forgotten speech did not affect Badat. Instead, Badat gravitated to the Friday Circle, became a member, read Azzam's books, and helped proselytize on behalf of Bosnia and Chechnya. When later asked about the main influences in his radicalization, he replied:

> Just other youths, similar age to me, that had actually fought before. There was also various bits of literature, books, by people writing about jihad, particularly a scholar called Abdullah Azzam, who said it was an obligation on every person just like prayer and fasting. There was also an audiotape published by a company called Azzam Publications . . . *In the Hearts of Green Birds*, which depicted the final moments of people killed in Bosnia. There was also videos again about the jihad in Bosnia. . . . It made me believe that, yes, it's something I have to do too. There was also the whole emotion evoked by listening to these stories about people in their final moments and also watching their dead bodies as well on the videos.[41]

In the summer of 1998, Badat went to Bosnia with about eight other Friday Circle members "to just see the country and see how it had been affected by the war, but we went to a village where a lot of those that fought in the conflict, motivated presumably by religion, were now staying and residing. . . . We stayed there for two weeks. During that time, a Bosnian individual also came and taught us how to use certain weapons . . . but we didn't do any firing."[42] This short trip whetted Badat's appetite for training, which was now available in Afghanistan. Since the Friday Circle had not yet sent anyone to Afghanistan, he would be the trailblazer setting up the way for others to follow. Because Ahmad did not know anyone in Afghanistan at the time, he asked a former independent Saudi commander in Bosnia, who was living in London at the time, to provide an introduction for Badat. This person agreed and called via satellite phone a fellow Bosnian War veteran in Afghanistan and arranged for the latter to train Badat. Badat left England in January 1999 and arrived in Qandahar, where he met several prominent members of Jamaat al Sheikh (the Sheikh's Group, better known outside Afghanistan as al Qaeda), who invited him to train with them. Badat turned them down and tracked down his London contact's friend in the north of Afghanistan. Badat stayed in Afghanistan for two and a half years and mostly associated with Zacarias Moussaoui and Richard Reid, who had similar twisted paths to Afghanistan and only joined al Qaeda after two years in country.[43] This shows that, contrary to later beliefs, there was no clear pathway for British Muslims from the London preachers of hate to al Qaeda.[44] In fact, most of the British Islamist militants who came to Afghanistan before the summer of 2000 took their basic training at Khalden, whose alumni formed a network (the Abu Zubaydah/ Ibn al Sheikh al Libi network) rival to al Qaeda. Only when bin Laden forced the closure of all the rival camps in the summer of 2000 and achieved a hostile takeover of rival global neojihadi networks did the arriving British militants train at Farouq, an al Qaeda facility.

The Friday Circle did not go on to carry out any attack against Britain. Its members volunteered to go abroad and defend the *ummah*, the imagined worldwide Muslim community, against Serbs and Russians. They identified themselves as part of this imagined group and categorized themselves in contrast to its enemies: Orthodox Bosnians, Serbs, Russians, and later Americans because of its embargo on Iraq resulting in the death of thousands of Iraqis. They did not construct their social identity in contrast to British people, who did not participate in killing Muslims worldwide at the time. In other words, they did not consider Britain an enemy, a potential target of their violence, and therefore were not a threat to Britain. Azzam Publication books, Azzam Recording audiocassettes and videocassettes, and its family of websites, Azzam.com and Qoqaz.net,[45] encouraged young Muslims to volunteer to defend their imagined community abroad. In fact, because Russia had closed Chechnya to journalists during the Second Chechen War, which started in the summer of 1999, Qoqaz.net became the major source of information on that war for the Western press. By showing the horrors perpetuated against Muslims abroad and glorifying jihad against invaders of Muslim lands, it also helped to politicize a new generation of British Muslims on the eve of 9/11 and provide an alternative framework through which to interpret and understand the world. A few adopted the Azzam.com warrior identity as their own along with its specific martial culture that harked back to the glory days of the great expansion of

Islam in the seventh century. In their attempt to imitate the traditions of the followers of the Prophet, who gave birth to this Golden Age of Islam, they rejected mainstream British culture and became radical in relation to British society. The Tooting Circle's Azzam.com, rather than that of the preachers of hate, played a significant but largely unappreciated role in the later radicalization of a few British Muslims.

The Evolution of the Global Neojihadi Threat Against Britain Before 9/11

The emergence of a politicized and even radical political protest community is not enough to trigger domestic political violence or terrorism. As I have argued elsewhere, the turn to violence of a political protest community requires at least three conditions: the escalation of its conflict with the state, its disillusionment with peaceful ways of resolving its grievances, and moral outrage at state aggression against its imagined community. Only then will a few of its members volunteer as soldiers to defend their endangered community.[46] As we shall see, the pattern of global neojihadi attacks against Britain in the first decade of the twenty-first century fits this pattern. The first credible attack,[47] the Crevice Plot, emerged from three different clusters of local relatives and friends from Crawley, Luton, and Barkingside, respectively. Let us trace the emergence of each of these clusters and their integration into the British Islamist community up to September 11, 2001.

The Crawley Cluster

Crawley was a town of about 100,000 people, approximately 28 miles south of Charing Cross (London), which underwent dramatic economic growth in the 1960s with the opening of nearby Gatwick Airport. The availability of jobs attracted new immigrants to its leafy neighborhoods. Into this town came the family of the central character of the Crevice Plot, Omar Khyam. His was a Pakistani military family and several close relatives were still on active duty in Pakistan. Khyam's grandfather immigrated to Britain in the early 1970s and Khyam's parents later settled in Crawley, where Khyam was born in 1981. He is the oldest son, and his younger brother, Shujah-ud-Din Mahmood, was born in 1986.

Khyam's father became wealthy importing clothes to Britain and Belgium from his textile factory in Karachi. Khyam enjoyed a comfortable middle-class childhood in a secular nonpracticing household. His parents sent him to a mostly white school instead of the predominantly "Asian" school closer to home. Most of his friends were non-Muslim whites. Nevertheless, his parents insisted that he learn Arabic and study the Quran. In 1992, his parents divorced and Khyam and his two brothers stayed with their mother in Crawley while his father lived in Belgium. His grandparents and relatives lived close by and helped out.

Khyam's adolescence was devoted to sports. He played cricket for a club and became captain of his school team. On the soccer field, he met Jawad Akbar, who was born in 1983 in Pakistan, the youngest of three brothers. The family immigrated first to Italy and lived there for two years before settling in Crawley around 1992, where his father became a supervisor for a Gatwick Airport catering company. Akbar's family was not religious, although his mother prayed. Akbar preferred sports to school: he boxed at a local club and played badminton, squash, and soccer.[48] His best friend, British-born Waseem Gulzar, shared his passion for sports. Being two years younger than Khyam, Akbar and Gulzar at first just knew him from the neighborhood. They were better acquainted with Khyam's British-born first cousin Ahmed Ali Khan, who was closer to their age, shared their passion for soccer, and liked to check the latest news on his computer. Ahmed's father was a taxicab driver at Gatwick Airport.

This confusion of names shows how a bunch of guys, growing up in the same neighborhood, can evolve into a politically violent group. There was no outside recruitment or brainwashing. None was religious, but one of their older neighbors, Nadeem Ashraf, born in 1977, had become religious in the mid-1990s and was active in ALM, which began to distribute leaflets and conduct poster campaigns in Crawley around 1997.[49]

In the fall of 1998, Khyam felt drawn to the local ALM chapter and attended its discussions on Friday nights about political events that affected Muslims worldwide. He described the gatherings during his trial:

We would be shown videos from Chechnya, which would show how the Russians have razed Grozny to the ground, how they are killing innocent Muslims there, how they were destroying the houses, the mosques. You will see graphic pictures of dead bodies of Muslims, bullet-ridden buildings. . . . The videos I saw of Bosnia were even more graphic than the ones that came from Chechnya, because the aim of the Serbs was just to kill the Muslims, simple as that. That's

how it was portrayed, as a complete ethnic war, and again you
would see mosques blown up, you would see people being shot. It
was quite graphic pictures. . . . The message was to go and help
them, whether that meant going there doing humanitarian work or
going there and fighting.[50]

Along with his political awakening, Khyam became religious, and
began to pray five times a day, read the Quran, and attend the local
mosque, the Crawley Islamic Center, regularly. There, he met Waheed
Mahmood and Yasir Khan. Mahmood was an adult, born in Crawley in
1972, an engineer, married with children. He had worked for British Gas
for six years, servicing and repairing boilers in customers' homes. A very
religious man, he was involved in local Islamic politics and ALM activities
around the country. Young Muslims looked up to him because of his
reputation as an Islamic scholar and deferred to him on religious matters.
Yasir Khan was born in Pakistan's Northwest Frontier Province (NWFP)
in the mid-1970s and had immigrated to Crawley with his family at the
age of three. He became a star cricket player at the local club, turned to
religion around 1998, and displayed his new conviction on his T-shirt:
"The Final Revelation, The Final Message, The Final System, The Final
Conquest: Islam."[51]

With its military background, Omar Khyam's family often discussed the
military situation in Pakistan and the issue of Kashmir. These discussions
dominated its visits to relatives in Pakistan. In the summer of 1999, Khyam
and his family visited them on a holiday and traveled around Pakistan. This
was just after the Kargil Crisis with India that lasted from May to July 1999
and resulted in atrocities on both sides. At the popular hill resort of Murree,
Khyam saw a rally organized by Al-Badr Mujahedin, a Kashmiri guerilla
group. He was intrigued and asked one of its representatives in Urdu about
Kashmir and the possibility of receiving military training. The man gave
him pamphlets and audiocassettes on Kashmir and advised him to look like
a Muslim, with Islamic clothes and a beard, if he wanted to get some training. Elsewhere, Khyam had a similar experience when he inquired another
Kashmiri group about training. When he returned home to resume his
studies, he decided to help the Kashmiris and get military training at one
of their camps. He had grown increasingly disillusioned with ALM and left
it around that time, as its goal of establishing a caliphate in Britain appeared
unrealistic.

On 18 January 2000, Khyam secretly flew to Islamabad. He had gotten money from his mother by telling her that he was going on a school trip to France. When he landed in Islamabad, he jumped into a cab and asked the driver to take him to any "mujahedin office." After the first office he visited turned him down, a second office sent him to a camp that welcomed foreigners, who were separated from locals. His six-week training included shooting AK-47s, a TT pistol, rocket-propelled grenades (RPGs), sniper rifles, and light machine guns. The training also involved physical training, tactical skills such as crawling and climbing, reconnaissance, and political and religious discussions. He did not undergo any explosives training, which was taught by the Pakistani Inter-Service Intelligence Directorate (ISID) for selected candidates in the camp.[52]

During that time, his family became concerned about his disappearance that made headlines in the British press. His father contacted relatives in Pakistan, who eventually found him at the camp. One relative, an ISID major, took him back to his grandfather. His Pakistani relatives were very proud of him but wished he had notified them so as to avoid his family's worries. Khyam returned home in mid-March. His extended family came to greet him. As he arrived home, "some of my younger cousins were standing in two rows with flowers and, as I walked in, they threw flowers at me as if I'd just got married."[53] Of course, his mother was very upset with him, but the rest of his relatives and friends celebrated his adventure. His attendance at a Kashmiri training camp was widely reported in the press, making him quite famous among his peers. Three weeks after his return, his father took him to Belgium to help with the import business.

Khyam returned to Crawley in September 2000 to begin a preparation course for university entrance and resumed hanging out with his friends, like Waheed Mahmood, who knew Islamist militants throughout the country. In the spring of 2001, Mahmood took Omar Khyam and Yasir Khan with him on one of his visits to Luton. They visited the Islamic Center on Leagrave Road, newly created by local militants to hold study sessions and political discussions that were not welcome at local mosques. They talked about *hijra*, the duty to emigrate and live in a Muslim land. They discussed the viability of setting up a business and making a living in Afghanistan or Pakistan. At some point the discussion turned to ALM. The Luton group had only contempt for Bakri and his organization, which they considered to be a joke and a waste of time. Although the Crawley trio had already left ALM, the Luton group teased them about their past association with it. After about three hours, the three Crawley men returned home.

On 29 June 2001, Khyam returned to Pakistan to attend a friend's wedding. In Islamabad, he hung out with people from his training camp and crossed the border into Afghanistan to see the country firsthand. He had read the negative coverage of the Taliban in the Western media, but local Afghans gave him a more positive view and urged him to visit their country and see for himself. He visited Kabul, Qandahar, and Jalalabad. He was impressed that Afghanistan had become a safe, law-abiding, and Islamic society, which convinced him that the Western media was wrong and unreliable. He was inspired to immigrate there as he considered the country to be very close to an ideal Islamic society.[54] He returned to Crawley on 21 August 2001.

The Luton Lads

By 2000, Luton had become a hotbed of Islamist activity. Luton is a city of about 200,000 people, 30 miles north of London. Its economy had been based historically on manufacturing, but the expansion of the Luton Airport was rapidly shifting it to a service-based economy. The availability of jobs attracted immigrants, who soon made up more than 30 percent of the city's population. Muslims made up 15 percent of the population, far larger than the national average of about 3 to 4 percent. This ethnic mix generated some conflict between Islamists and the English Defense League.

Salahuddin Amin was born in London in 1975 of Pakistani parents and, at the age of four, returned to Pakistan, where he grew up in a nonreligious family, which rarely spoke English. An uncle owned some CNG (compressed natural gas, used as fuel for cars) stations in Kahuta and Gujar Khan, and another became a brigadier general in the army. This uncle ran the Cadet College in Kohat, NWFP, and Amin used to enjoy spending time there. Amin rejoined his father in Luton in 1991 and took GCSEs (General Certificate in Secondary Education) in four subjects. An average student, he learned English, was not religious, and behaved like a normal teenager: he drank alcohol, dated girls, got into fights, and received a conditional discharge for assault in November 1994. At school, he hung out with Aftab Manzoor, a family friend, who introduced him to his best friend, Afzal Munir. Manzoor was born in Pakistan in 1976 and five years later moved to Luton with his family. Munir was the same age but born in Luton. He and Manzoor went on to study computer science at different local universities while Amin struggled with his A-level academic courses. Amin went on to study engineering and financed his education with a series of part-time odd jobs, including driving a taxi.[55]

Manzoor and Munir became religious together, went to mosque regularly, got politically involved, and participated in Friday evening ALM meetings in Luton. They both got married, Munir to a local girl and Manzoor to a Pakistani one, with whom he quickly had a daughter. Manzoor divided his time between Pakistan with his family and Luton, where he had a variety of part-time jobs, including driving a taxi. In Luton, he got to know Mohammed Qayum Khan, who lived on the same street.

Qayum, born in the early 1960s, was much older than the two friends. He had grown up in Britain but was sent back to the ancestral village in Pakistan for misbehavior such as smoking and drinking. He later returned to Luton, got married, and had several children. He worked at an electronic company and as a taxi driver. He became very religious and politically active, raising money for ALM. He invited its leader to speak in Luton several times, but the board of the Luton Central Mosque refused to allow Omar Bakri to give a sermon there.[56] Qayum liked to pray at home and Manzoor and Munir started coming to his house for tea and religious-political discussions on Friday afternoons.

Qayum had become "fairly well known, famous, highly regarded by the community" for his independent fund-raising on behalf of Kashmir, unconnected with any groups.[57] Through his activities, he met most of the local former participants in jihad abroad. Among them were Abu Mahmoud al Filastini, a Palestinian from Jordan in his late twenties, and Abu Munthir al Maghrebi, a 26-year-old Belgian of Moroccan origin. Abu Mahmoud had lived in Afghanistan, came to Luton in the mid-1990s, and also worked as a taxi driver. He befriended fellow cabdriver Amin and they would often eat lunch together.[58] Abu Munthir, who was known as Abu Qutaiba in Luton, had studied theology in Jordan and Syria. He then went to Afghanistan in the late 1990s and came to Luton around 1999 to start a new life. His English was poor and his interactions with other Luton Islamists consisted mostly of short greetings after prayer at the mosque. During his stay in Luton, he had not engaged in proselytizing for jihad.[59] Qayum's relationship with them consisted only of greeting them at the mosque.

Meanwhile, Amin spent his summers back in Pakistan and in 1999, right after the Kargil Crisis, he visited Murree with some friends. The main road was full of stalls set up by mujahedin from the war. "I heard a lady doing a very emotional speech about how the atrocities were happening in the Occupied Kashmir, the Kashmir that was under India," he recalled at trial, "and how women were raped and kidnapped all the time and they had to move from there, Indian Kashmir, to Pakistani Kashmir. . . . She made a very emotional speech and that really, you know, affected me."[60] Amin gave her money and resolved to help the Kashmir cause.

When he returned to Luton, Amin made monthly donations to Manzoor, who collected them for the Kashmir refugees. Manzoor and Munir were fully involved in support of the Kashmir cause and had gone together to train at a Kashmir guerilla camp. Despite the fact that he still was not religious and drank alcohol,[61] Amin got closer to them. They invited him to join them at Qayum's house on Friday afternoons. Amin already knew fellow taxi driver Qayum as they sometimes chatted while waiting for fares at the train station. As Amin's relationship with Manzoor deepened, Manzoor reproached him for not praying regularly. Amin felt ashamed and started attending mosque regularly with his friends. At the mosque, he often saw Abu Munthir, but their relationship was limited to simple after-prayer exchanges due to linguistic differences.

Over time, these politically oriented men got frustrated with traditional mosques because they could not discuss political issues or have study sessions there as mosque authorities denied them permission to do so. In the spring of 2001, they decided to open their own center on Leagrave Road, where they could pray and talk freely. Abu Munthir sometimes led them in prayers. Sometimes, they watched videos on the wars in Bosnia and Chechnya, like *Russian Hell* (distributed by Azzam.com). "They showed a lot of terrible things," said Amin. "They showed a lot of young children that were dead because of bombardment, a lot of old people, of women, a lot of pregnant women. Their stomachs were cut open and even the children in their stomach were killed, slaughtered and a lot of bloodshed as well as fighting. . . . I was shocked and angry."[62] After discussions, the participants would retire to the adjacent car park and play cricket.

Manzoor, Munir, and Amin drove twice to Finsbury Park Mosque to listen to Abu Hamza. One of the sermons was about the duty to migrate to Afghanistan and support its Islamic state. During his police interview, Amin said that after hearing Abu Hamza, he made up his mind to migrate to Afghanistan. However, at trial, he testified that he had long before made up his mind to return to Pakistan at the end of his studies because he had grown up there.[63] Shortly after the Leagrave center was opened, Amin, Qayum, Manzoor, and Munir welcomed Khyam, Mahmood, and Yasir Khan from Crawley. They discussed hijra to Afghanistan or Pakistan and the viability of business opportunities there. Amin later ran into Khyam a second time. He had come to deliver some goods to Crawley and called Khyam, who had given him his phone number. They met briefly at the mosque after prayers. Shortly thereafter, Abu Mahmoud al Filastini returned to Palestine/Jordan and moved on to Afghanistan with his family and sent his address and cell phone number to Amin in a letter.[64]

In early summer 2001, Amin flew to Peshawar to attend the wedding of one of his sisters. He stayed in Pakistan for his usual two months. When he called Abu Mahmoud, his friend said he was recovering from colon cancer surgery in a hospital in Rawalpindi. Amin came to visit him there. At one point, Amin went to the local office of Jaish e-Mohammed, a Kashmiri guerilla group, and asked to visit a training camp out of curiosity. The group made arrangements for him to visit one overnight. The camp was perfectly legitimate and run by the ISID. Amin saw people engage in physical exercise like volleyball and carry AK-47-shaped wooden weapons.[65]

The Adam Family of Barkingside

London is a megacity with diverse ethnic enclaves. According to the 2001 census, it had a population of 8.25 million people, of whom 8.5 percent declared themselves Muslims. Its immigrants included 84,600 born in Bangladesh, 66,700 from Pakistan, 172,000 from India (some of whom are Muslim), and 39,000 from Turkey. This count does not include the second generation born in London.

In late 1987, the Benois family immigrated from Algeria to the Barkingside district in northeast London. The parents were not religious but imposed strict discipline on their three sons and three daughters. The three boys were Lamine, born in 1981, Rahman, in 1982, and Ibrahim, in 1986. The father owned a café in nearby Walthamstow and the brothers sometimes helped out. The neighborhood had very few other Arabs, and the brothers grew up with English, Pakistani, and black friends. Lamine and Rahman were very close, but Lamine was academically oriented and did well in school while Rahman did not care much about schoolwork, often cut classes, and did poorly on his GCSEs. He played basketball all the time after he grew to a height of six feet two inches and dreamed of becoming a professional basketball player. He had lots of friends, just hung out listening to rap music, especially 2Pac, and went out at night flirting with girls.

In the summer of 1998, the family changed its surname from "Benois" to "Adam" because the father wanted to make it more English. At college, Lamine befriended Rizwan Shamim, who was a year older and a practicing Muslim. Through Shamim's influence, Lamine also joined their college Islamic Society, developed an interest in his religion, began to read books on Islam, attended talks on Islam, and invited Rahman to come with him. His brother tagged along, not because he was particularly interested in the topic, but because he just had plenty of time and enjoyed the good food afterward. Lamine liked to ask questions and have discussions with participants. He and Shamim talked a lot about the history of the Prophet and the application of Islam to their personal life. In time, these conversations started to inspire Rahman.[66]

Their father cared about politics in his home country. Abu Hamza had developed a reputation for helping destitute Algerians fleeing the civil war. The father encouraged his sons to attend Finsbury Park Mosque in order to help these illegal refugees congregating there and hear their harrowing stories firsthand. The brothers heard Abu Hamza's sermons about corrupt Muslim regimes like Algeria persecuting their populations. Lamine was the first to echo Abu Hamza's remedies for tackling corrupt Middle Eastern dictatorships. Although Rahman was less articulate and sophisticated than his brother, he was just as passionate and emotional about injustice against Muslims by corrupt Muslim regimes. The brothers discussed international Muslim politics, especially the wars in Bosnia, Kosovo, and Chechnya. They challenged the complacency of their parents and elders and denounced establishment Islamic scholars as "dollar scholars" because they had sold out to their respective governments. Lamine enjoyed intellectual debate and lengthy discussions about Islamic practice and faith, while Rahman enjoyed risk and excitement, doing, not talking or thinking.[67]

In the fall of 1999, Rahman and his younger brother Ibrahim came to one of Lamine's college Islamic Society meetings and saw a video of the just concluded war in Kashmir. "It just showed, like, these atrocities that were taking place in a place called Kashmir," said Rahman, "and it was just the worst thing . . . little children . . . sexually abused and women. . . . I still remember it quite clear. . . . I was really, really sad, you know. I remember . . . crying and trying to hide it. . . . It was really bad. . . . I tried to hide the fact that I was crying because I didn't look around and, when I did, every-one else was—it had the same effect."[68] After watching the video, Shamim, Lamine, and Rahman asked the society president how they could help. He told them that they could raise money for the cause and gave them a goal of collecting £200. A little later, after meeting their challenge, they felt very proud of themselves. Thereafter, they continued to raise funds for Kashmir on a regular basis, joined in their enterprise by a student nicknamed "Uni-boy."[69] Rahman discovered that fund-raising was something he was good at and achieved his benchmarks almost every time. He enjoyed the new respect he gained from people around him—students, shopkeepers, busi-nessmen, and colleagues. For Muslims, charity, or *zakat*, is a religious obli-gation and not a radical or extremist activity. On the contrary, it was viewed as a good deed. Rahman believed that his good works compensated for his religious shortcomings, such as smoking, flirting with girls, and occasion-ally drinking. Over time, Lamine, Rahman, Shamim, and Uni-boy raised thousands of pounds from sales of books and religious items and solicita-tions from family and friends and at events and mosques.[70]

When Lamine finished college in 2001, he and Uni-boy went to work for the London Underground, where they met a fellow worker, Zeeshan Siddiqui. Born in 1980 in London to Pakistani and Azerbaijani parents, Siddiqui showed an early taste for adventure. At the age of 16, he flew to Istanbul alone, traveled to Beirut, and tried to get into Palestinian occupied territory in order to meet Hamas members. He returned home after being away a week. In 2000, he enrolled at the School of Oriental and African Studies in London to study economics but dropped out after a few months and took jobs at Dixons and the London Underground.

Conclusion

We come to the end of this wide-ranging chapter. Its confusion cannot be avoided for, on the eve of 9/11, the future British neojihadis who later attacked Britain were still scattered throughout the country in distinct local clusters of political activists that formed naturally based on kinship and friendship. They met only later through chance. This nonlinear emergence of each of the four networks of plotters results in a complicated picture. In this chapter, I have tried to give a flavor of this evolution by focusing on the three clusters that coalesced to form the next chapter's Crevice Plot.

It is important to keep to the facts. Most of the narratives of the global neojihad in London in the middle of the last decade postulate indoctrination by preachers of hate at mosques where al Qaeda recruiters sent naïve militants to Afghanistan for training and further brainwashing only to have them return to Britain as fanatics indiscriminately killing others and themselves. This tabloid narrative is simple, elegant, and wrong. The reality is far more complex. The perpetrators of all four al Qaeda attacks against Britain did not originate top down from staff plans at al Qaeda central. On the contrary, the four conspiracies emerged from the bottom up, coalescing from local clusters through mostly chance connections. Their leaders later linked up with a British al Qaeda intermediary in Pakistan, who took advantage of his opportunity to coordinate three attacks against his former home. There was no al Qaeda infrastructure in Britain then or later on, despite contrary claims by tabloids and alarmist scholars relying on tabloid accounts rather than reliable sources.

The preachers of hate had relatively little influence on these perpetrators. They were rejected as petty thieves by the Tooting Friday Circle and clowns by the Crawley and Luton clusters. Abu Hamza had some influence only on the Adam brothers before they got involved in a university Islamic society. There was no evidence of brainwashing or indoctrination. So, contrary to the conventional narrative, they were self-radicalized: no outside organization or preachers of hate radicalized them. The acquisition of an Islamist social identity that did not yet reject British society and culture emerged from internal group discussions among friends in Tooting, Crawley, Luton, and college Islamic societies. The images of the wars in Bosnia, Chechnya, and Kashmir had a very strong impact on the future conspirators. Through their discussions of these images, they became politically aware and wanted to help the victims of their new imagined community, the ummah. On the eve of 9/11, the four clusters described in this chapter were already politically active, proselytizing for their cause and raising money for various Muslim refugee groups. A few of the older members had undergone some sort of superficial military training either in Bosnia or Pakistan. Except for the Khalden alumni network around Abu Qatada, which was mostly confined to North African immigrants and did not plot anything against Britain, the British militants had to find their own way to these camps.

Thus, on the eve of 9/11, the eventual neojihadis who attacked Britain a few years later were still divided into small local clusters with little connection between them. The individuals within each cluster knew each other before they even became religious or political. They were relatives or friends from school or the neighborhood. They were simply a rather secular bunch of guys that collectively proceeded along a path that eventually led a few to attempt or commit mass murder in the name of the global neojihad. At the time, many were still abusing drugs and alcohol. Along their path to violence, they talked to each other, shared their feelings and beliefs about political Islam, and learned from each other. Very few had ever been members of formal Islamist organizations such as HuT, ALM, or Supporters of Shariah. None had any contact with the London al Qaeda representative Khalid al Fawwaz or even the Khalden network.

The brief descriptions of the formation of these informal bunches of guys around England in this chapter point to the importance of small group discussions among friends forming a microdiscursive community. Their constant discussions were the engine that helped them acquire political and eventually radical ideas. Before the widespread use of the Internet, these discussions took place at a physical site, which, in turn, facilitated their emergence. In the four clusters, these sites were respectively the Friday Circle in Tooting, private homes in Crawley, the Leagrave Road Islamic Center in Luton, and their college Islamic Society for the Adam brothers and their friends. These discursive hot spots were safe places to discuss controversial topics like the victimization of Muslims worldwide that mainstream mosques avoided. Such places allowed progressively more radical ideas to emerge without being challenged, as attendance was limited to self-selected like-minded people, giving to everyone present the impression that everyone else agreed with them. This of course validated these ideas for them—if all of one's friends believed them, then these ideas must true.

Before the Internet, a place to discuss political topics was a crucial step in the emergence of a scattered and amorphous Islamist community. From these constant discussions emerged a political social identity that defined itself in contrast to the same enemies of their imagined ummah. In the late 1990s, the enemies were Serbia, Russia, India, and later Israel during the Second Intifada. The West was seen as a distant enemy, propping up Serbia (by preventing Muslims from helping their attacked brothers and sisters through an unfair embargo), Russia, India, and Israel, but not yet a direct enemy. At this stage, no British Islamists imagined attacking their own country. It simply was not on their minds or even in their repertoire of legitimate political protest activities in the West.

British Islamists did not yet consider their country as their enemy. Britain had not yet carried out direct attacks against Muslims that might have led a few of them to self-categorize in contrast to their own country. Any political conflict has at least two actors. In the type of political violence commonly called terrorism, on one side are the terrorists and on the other are state agents fighting terrorists: the military, police, intelligence agencies, prosecutors, judges, legislators, and correctional officers. Up to 9/11, the British counterterrorist forces were still tolerant toward potential global neojihadis, probably as a result of their failure to quash the troubles in Northern Ireland through the use of brute repression. Although an official inquiry concluded that institutional racism toward black British citizens existed in British police services,[71] British police in the 1990s never reached the level of harassment of its minorities displayed by American police departments toward blacks and Vietnam protestors in the late 1960s[72] or the French police toward minorities in the *banlieues* at the beginning of the twenty-first century.[73] Outside of Northern Ireland, British police were constrained by the legislature and an independent judiciary. In fact, the Crown Prosecution Service directed the police to make sure that before charging a suspect, there was sufficient evidence for a realistic prospect of conviction in court. Britain had long been an asylum for political refugees of all kinds and conspiring within Britain to commit terrorism abroad was not recognized as a crime at the time.[74]

Countries targeted by individuals living in London strongly criticized Britain as sheltering terrorists and called its capital Londonistan. Indeed, Britain was accused of having concluded a covenant with Middle Eastern terrorists involving a quid pro quo of leaving them alone in Britain as long as they did not attack it.[75] However, there is no evidence that such covenant was ever made because there was no need for one. Middle Eastern Islamists self-categorized in contrast to their enemies, namely their home governments. They did not consider Britain an enemy and therefore were not likely to attack it. In fact, Britain may have been their last refuge and it would have been suicidal for them to try to eliminate it by carrying out attacks in it. Britain did arrest and eventually extradite individuals wanted on international warrants for recognized criminal offenses in countries that would not torture the deportees. Several Algerians were arrested in connection with the 1995 wave of bombing in France and an attempted attack against the 2000 Christmas market in Strasbourg and awaited extradition to France. Likewise, two Egyptians and a Saudi refugee were arrested in connection with the 1998 East Africa bombings of American embassies and awaited extradition to the United States.

With the emergence of global neojihad in the 1990s and its indiscriminate targeting of civilians in crowded places, the British authorities realized that they needed to adopt a preventive logic for counterterrorism.[76] The result was the Terrorism Act 2000, which enlarged the definition of terrorism to include serious property damage and criminalized small acts useful for the commission of terrorism offences. However, the act was clearly written with Irish terrorism in mind as all the terrorist organizations proscribed in the act were Irish. Nevertheless, many of its provisions would later be used against global neojihadis, including terrorism funding and training, possessing documents or items useful for committing terrorism, membership in a terrorist organization, failing to disclose information about a terrorist act, inciting terrorism overseas, in addition to traditional terrorist offenses such as conspiracy to cause an explosion to endanger life or property and conspiracy to murder. The act also allowed the police to arrest suspects without warrants and search their premises and to stop and search people on the street.[77]

The Terrorism Act 2000 came too late to affect the evolution of the British Islamist community before the 9/11 attacks. These attacks changed not only this community but also the way British police dealt with it.

CHAPTER 2

CREVICE

THE FATEFUL DECISION
TO ATTACK BRITAIN

THE LAST CHAPTER LEFT us with clusters of British Islamists, ready to go abroad for paramilitary training but not yet ready to attack Britain. How did they reach the decision to attack their homeland on behalf of al Qaeda? Although global neojihadis had spared Britain, some had attacked Europe or the United States from that country, as in the 2000 Strasbourg Christmas Market plot or the 2001 shoe bombers airplane plot. Apparently, Khalid Sheikh Mohammed had thought about attacking Heathrow Airport but did not carry out any acts in furtherance of this idea. The alleged "ricin" attack in 2002 (Operation Springbourne) turned out to be mostly hype at trial.[1] This changed in 2003. How did members of the Islamist community in Britain turn to domestic terrorism?

The First Wave of British Supporters for Afghanistan

The 9/11 attack upon the United States and its immediate aftermath completely changed the relationship between the Islamist community and the British state. Muslims' immediate reactions to this attack were mixed. The vast majority were horrified and condemned the attacks. Some simply did not believe that Muslims could have carried them out because Islam specifically prohibits killing noncombatants and innocent civilians. Others went on to elaborate a bizarre conspiracy by the Mossad or the CIA to blame Muslims in order to justify the invasion of Muslim lands. Most Islamists had a more ambivalent attitude.

On the one hand, they were horrified and rejected the attacks. Rahman Adam and his brothers had watched them on television at Rizwan Shamim's house. At first, he believed that it was a film. A few minutes later, they grasped the events and were completely shocked. Rahman later said that 9/11 "can never be justified from a Muslim point of view, from a moral point of view, from any view. It's just—it doesn't make sense at all to even agree with it. . . . You're killing innocent people. . . . My religion would be against it, because it's not a religion that agrees or supports anything like that."[2]

On the other hand, Omar Khyam's attitude was different: "America was and is the greatest enemy of Islam and they put up puppet regimes in Muslim countries and dictatorships through which they secure their interests in the region. . . . America had been hit because of what it represented against the Muslims, but obviously 3,000 people died in it. So there was mixed feelings. . . . They had nothing to do with the war."[3]

A very small faction of Islamists, led by ALM leader Bakri, rejoiced in the attacks. Islamists debated the legitimacy of conducting operations in the West, whether, as Khyam put it, "we should only fight occupying forces in our lands such as, for example, fighting the occupying forces in Iraq or Afghanistan, and there are some that say, yes, we should do that but also we should hit them in their countries."[4] However, they unanimously condemned the American retaliatory invasion of Afghanistan in October 2001. They simply saw it as a foreign aggression against Muslims, as portrayed in the Muslim media. Khyam testified at his trial, "Appalling stories were coming out from Afghanistan about the way they were treating the prisoners or the way daisy cutter bombs were being dropped on villages, human rights abuses, et cetera, et cetera. . . . Just the way they would be treating the people there: no regard for the culture, the religion, just generally. There were graphic pictures coming from Afghanistan . . . on al-Jazeerah. . . . They were being portrayed as a war on Islam, continually interviewing Taliban people inside Afghanistan, civilians, and what was going on on the ground, but the BBC wasn't reporting this."[5]

Since the British government supported the invasion, British Islamists' usually compatible dual social identity split into divided social identities as their Islamist social identity came into conflict with their British social identity. Khyam later remembered that "for the first time, I was hearing people saying that the UK should be attacked at home, but it wasn't a majority view at that time. . . . The . . . vast majority of British Muslims . . . were born here, so we felt some allegiance to the UK. So, those that wanted to do something went over to Afghanistan. But . . . the vast majority still didn't see the UK as a target and they would make excuses for the UK."[6]

The American invasion of Afghanistan changed the orientation of British Islamists. Almost overnight, many support networks for Kashmir switched their support to the Afghan resistance.[7] Activists organized themselves into fund-raising networks for Afghanistan, others sent medical and survival supplies for Afghan refugees, and very few traveled to Pakistan to either care for Afghans refugees or join and fight with the Taliban against the infidels. On 28 October 2001, Aftab Manzoor and Afzal Munir from Luton and Yasir Khan from Crawley were killed in the bombing of a Taliban house in Kabul. Manzoor with a foot in Pakistan and England had been with his wife and child in Pakistan on 9/11. Munir came to join him, and apparently, together they went to Afghanistan. Khan had been working at Gatwick Airport on 9/11 but was later fired when he refused to adjust his work schedule in response to the cross-Atlantic aviation stand-down the following week. Being from a prestigious Afghan tribe, he identified with his Pashtun kin and went to Afghanistan to defend them against the anticipated American invasion.[8]

On 9/11, Salahuddin Amin from Luton was also in Pakistan, as he had just finished training at a Kashmiri guerilla camp. In Rawalpindi, he saw Pakistanis celebrating the attacks and distributing sweets in the streets. He had been angry with the United States for its support of Israel's killing of Palestinians and rejoiced at the hit on the Pentagon and the huge financial loss America experienced but felt sad at the carnage and "regretted" the loss of civilian life.[9] He had already made up his mind to do hijrah, and the 9/11 attacks hardened this resolution. He returned to Luton about two weeks later to make the final arrangements. While there, he learned that Manzoor and Munir were going to fight in Afghanistan and wanted to join them.[10] His family disapproved of his plans and insisted that he first get his certificate for an engineering course he had just completed. He used this delay to obtain £21,000 through fraudulent bank loans for "home improvements" that he never intended to repay. He also claimed that he had lost his passport, got a new one, and flew to Pakistan on 25 November 2001. For the next eight months, he stayed at the house of one of his uncles in Kahuta and worked one week each month at his uncle's CNG station in Gujar Khan to meet his living expenses.[11]

Waheed Mahmood of Crawley also went to Pakistan to support Afghan fighters. He took a leave of absence from his engineer trainee job at British Telecom and flew to Pakistan in early October. His wife and small children joined him a little later. They stayed in a house on a compound owned by his extended family in Gujar Khan. His family pressured him to tone down his militancy and prevented him from making any contact with the Afghan resistance.[12]

The Lahore ALM Network

Dozens of ALM members also went to Pakistan in hopes of joining the Afghan jihad and converged on the ALM office in Lahore. Its head was 25-year-old Dutch-born Sajeel Shahid, who had a degree in computer science from England. He had become politically active in the mid-1990s and joined ALM when it broke off from HuT. In 2000, he had traveled to New York City on its behalf and met two sympathizers, Mohammed Junaid Babar and Syed Fahad Hashmi. After this trip, Bakri appointed him head of the new ALM office in Lahore.

Babar was a 25-year-old Pashtun born near Peshawar in an Afghan refugee family that immigrated to New York City when he was two years old. His family was not religious and sent him to a Catholic military academy for secondary school. "There was a great deal of racism where we lived in New York," he recalled. "I was not only the only Muslim but the only nonwhite in my school at the time, and I was ostracized. Even going out to job markets you could feel the racism." He returned to visit his relatives in Pakistan two or three times and his grandfather nurtured his feeling of alienation from American society into a Muslim social identity. "He instilled in me the idea that your loyalty is with Islam, your loyalty is with the Muslims not the Americans."[13] The first Gulf War politicized him as he opposed U.S. troops' presence in the Holy Land of Saudi Arabia and their invasion of Iraq. He became politically active, read history books, and joined discussions at meeting of Islamist groups such as the Tablighi Jamaat, HuT, and ALM that shared his opposition to U.S. foreign policy in the Middle East. However, he was frustrated with their rivalries and believed that Muslims should unite to regain their former glory. He dropped out of three different pharmacy programs in three years and supported himself in a variety of odd jobs like parking cars. His parents forced him to return to school at the State University of New York at Stony Brook, but he again dropped out after a semester. At Stony Brook, he befriended Syed Fahad Hashmi, five years his junior, who, like him, had immigrated to New York as a baby from Pakistan. They started attending meetings of the New York branch of ALM, hung out with its members, and met ALM visitors Sajeel Shahid and Zaheer Ali. Babar joined ALM in early 2001 and participated in its demonstrations at the United Nations.[14]

On 9/11, Babar's mother was working in the World Trade Center North Tower, the first one hit in the attack, but she managed to escape.[15] Instead of identifying with his mother, Babar strongly identified with the aggressors. "I can't stand by and live in America while my Muslims are being bombed. My loyalty and responsibility are towards them—now it's time to prove my loyalty."[16] He wanted to go and fight against the anticipated American invasion of his ancestral homeland. He called Sajeel Shahid, who was honeymooning in London and promised to help. Babar flew to London on his meager savings, stayed with Zaheer Ali, and had to borrow £300 from Shahid to continue his trip to Lahore, where he arrived on 26 September. Sajeel's younger brother picked him up and loaned Babar another £300. To pay them back, Babar helped them out at the Lahore office, writing leaflets and proselytizing.[17]

He was the first post-9/11 ALM militant to come to Lahore, followed a few weeks later by a flock of East Londoners headed by Kazi Nurur Rahman. Rahman was a 24-year-old Bangladeshi, who had immigrated to Britain as a baby. In college, he had joined HuT. In February 1994, he was arrested in connection with the murder of a Nigerian student for insulting Islam, but was acquitted at his trial.[18] After his release, he gravitated to ALM and gathered around him a group of young East Londoners of Bengali descent who wanted to participate in jihad. In early October 2001, he made his way to the Lahore ALM office, where he met Babar.[19] Rahman was bitter about England and had no intention of returning. With him were three friends: "Asim," born in east London of Pakistani origin, who had moved to Crawley, where he met a few of the Crawley cluster; and the brothers Tanveer and Abdul Jabber, born in Britain of Bangladeshi origin. They were all looking to get some paramilitary training so they could go to Afghanistan and fight.

In Lahore, ALM continued its media strategy of making shocking statements to bring attention to itself. Babar obligingly declared on camera, "When the American troops enter we will kill them in Afghanistan. There is no negotiation with Americans. When they're coming in with the mindset to kill my Muslim brothers and sisters, I will do the same . . . on the front line. I will kill every American that I see in Afghanistan and while I am in Pakistan." He had no intention of going back home to the United States "because . . . I'm here for this conflict in the long haul."[20] He added that "I see my struggle and life's work here. Maybe I'll miss a couple of friends from home, but I've made more friends and more brothers who are involved with me in the struggle and these people are with me for life."[21]

Since no one in ALM had any contact with any guerilla group, refuting the common claim that ALM was recruiting for al Qaeda, they made inquiries among people around them. Asim reached out to his Crawley friends Waheed Mahmood and Nadeem Ashraf to see whether they had any contacts. Ashraf had come to look for a wife and participate in jihad in Kashmir or Afghanistan and was staying in Islamabad with his uncle, who owned a marble factory. Asim also told Rahman and Babar about Mahmood and Ashraf. The Jabber brothers succeeded in making contact with a Kashmiri group and Tanveer invited Babar to join them in Jhelum, Kashmir, for "explosive training." Babar agreed but Sajeel Shahid discouraged him from going, explaining that he needed Babar in the office and did not trust Kashmiri groups, for the ISID ran most of them. As a foreigner, Babar might get into trouble if it discoverd that he was undergoing guerilla training. The Jabber brothers went through the training and immediately returned to Britain.[22] None of the enthusiastic ALM militants succeeded in fighting in Afghanistan because winter came and heavy snow closed down the mountain passes into Afghanistan. Traditionally in Afghanistan, fighting stops in winter and resumes in spring.

In January 2002, Babar got married to a female ALM member and Kazi Rahman and Asim moved next door to them. Shahid's older brother hired Babar as a project manager for a Pakistan software company to allow him to support his family.[23] Around that time, Rahman allegedly got involved in a conspiracy to assassinate Pakistani president Pervez Musharraf, who supported the American invasion of Afganistan. Rahman had acquired weapons from a Pakistani military depot for that purpose, including six to eight AK-47 assault rifles, with thousands of rounds of ammunition and a few grenades. In February, Pakistani authorities arrested Rahman's contact who had provided the weapons.[24] Although Rahman had intended to stay in Pakistan, he ran out of money and had to return to England in April. Before his departure, Babar helped him bury the weapons in a field near the campus of Punjab University.[25] Before leaving, Rahman asked Babar to show Waheed Mahmood the burial site in case he should need them for the jihad if they were both out of the country. Babar complied in mid-spring 2002.[26]

By that time, all the British militants who had come to Pakistan to fight in Afghanistan were either dead or back in Britain. Left behind by his friends, Babar still wanted to get training. A friend of Shahid from the NWFP knew a *maulana* (Muslim religious leader) who had previously fought in Afghanistan and might provide training to English-speaking militants. In July 2002, Shahid and his friend went to meet him at his *madrassa* (Islamic school) in the village of Gorque, in Upper Dir, Swat Valley, in the NWFP.[27] As Shahid spoke no Pashtu and the maulana spoke no English or Urdu, the friend translated. The maulana belonged to a local mujahedin group called Hifazi Shariati Muhammadi and had to ask his emir for permission to train British foreigners. Later, the maulana notified Shahid that his emir had refused.[28]

The Luton–al Qaeda Support Network

While the ALM militants in Lahore failed to make contact with Afghan mujahedin, the Luton lads succeeded in establishing a support network with al Qaeda, based on chance meetings with two of its Arab expatriates, who had returned to Afganistan. Abu Munthir al Maghrebi fought alongside of al Qaeda against the American invaders in the fall of 2001. After distinguishing himself in the fighting, he decided to stay in Afghanistan permanently. In 2003, the al Qaeda chief for military operations in Afghanistan and Pakistan, Abdal Hadi al Iraqi,[29] appointed him as one of his major commanders in the Shawal region.

Abu Mahmoud al Filastini was recovering from colon cancer in Mardan, NWFP. His friend Salahuddin Amin came to visit regularly to provide him with needed colostomy bags, available in Rawalpindi but not Mardan. Amin also gave Abu Mahmoud £12,000 of his own money for the cause. A Pashtun man from Kohat whom everyone called "Tariq" lived with Abu Mahmoud and helped care for him. Tariq was a committed jihadi, who also helped refugees and regularly supplied Afghan fighters.[30] In the summer of 2002, Amin's parents, having just retired in England, came back to Pakistan to live. Amin, his wife, and their children moved out of his uncle's house in Kahuta and into his parents' rented house next door. At that time, Amin still did not have any contact with any fighting groups in Afghanistan.

Early that summer, Mohammed Qayum Khan from Luton came to visit his ancestral village in Pakistan and let Amin know that he was there. Qayum by then had switched all his efforts from the Kashmir to the Afghan jihad. He raised money and material for the fighters there; this was his first trip to Pakistan since 9/11. Amin later confessed, "Qayum came down and he met me in Pakistan. . . . He told me that there are people here in UK who want to send . . . money and equipment to people fighting in Afghanistan, and he asked me if I could help him . . . give it to other people who were working in Afghanistan. It was like al-Qaeda and Taliban people. One of them . . . used to pray with us. His name—he was introduced to me as Abu Munthir . . . but while he was here [England] I knew him as Abu Qutaiba." Qayum told him that these were people "doing operations in Afghanistan against U.S. forces, coalition forces. So, my job was to just take the equipment, whatever comes, like warm clothing, boots, sleeping bags, first-aid kits. There were some GPS, laptops, all this equipment and money." Some of the money was earmarked for the families of dead mujahedin, £100 for Abu Mahmoud, and the rest for operational use and weapons purchased from the area.[31]

The actual pipeline to the mujahedin ran through Abu Mahmoud and Tariq. Qayum raised money and bought supplies in England, and then notified Amin that a courier would be coming to Islamabad with them. Amin collected the money and supplies at Islamabad Airport. He then called Abu Mahmoud, who sent Tariq to collect the money and supplies. Occasionally, Amin personally delivered them to Abu Mahmoud and went to see Abu Munthir himself.[32] "First time I saw Abu Munthir, I recognized him," Amin later said. "He recognized me. He used to pray at the same mosque as us."[33] Apparently, their prior acquaintance was enough to forge a bond of trust between them; Amin was able to go and meet Abu Munthir in the Federally Administered Tribal Area (FATA) by staying at his uncle's house in Kohat.[34] Abu Munthir gave Amin a list of critical materials he needed. Amin would buy the items he could locally and for the rest, he phoned Qayum to get them in England and send them to him.

The Crawley Cluster Gets Ready for Jihad

Like Qayum in Luton, multiple small networks of British supporters of Afghan mujahedin were busy raising funds for them. After his return from Pakistan in August 2001, Omar Khyam secured a loan of about £5,000 to pay for his tuition at the University of North London and rented a flat off campus but did not attend classes.[35] Instead, he used these funds for Afghanistan. On 24 April 2002, he flew to Pakistan to attend a friend's wedding and find out what the Pakistanis were saying about the war next door. During the trip, he visited Waheed Mahmood in Gujar Khan. After he returned to England on 19 May, Khyam moved into a flat near Uxbridge with Ahmed Ali Khan, and Waseem Gulzar, who was becoming more religious. In the fall, Khyam repeated his first year at North London University while Gulzar and Ali Khan studied at other universities.[36]

At the beginning of the school year, there were mixers for new Muslim students to meet each other. At one of them, Khyam met 20-year-old English-born Azhar Khan from Slough. They quickly became friends and Azhar regularly visited the Uxbridge flat. Khyam would sometimes drive to Slough to pick him up and hang out. Azhar's sister, Saira Tabassum Khan, had the reputation of being very pretty and shared their political and religious views. Khyam asked Azhar whether his sister would be interested in marrying him. Khyam and Saira saw each other's pictures and Azhar set up a meeting at a restaurant, where Saira came fully veiled to have a look at Khyam. They were secretly married in a religious ceremony on 19 December 2002, with Azhar's approval.[37]

In the fall of 2002, Khyam met Zeeshan Siddiqui at the prayer room at London Metropolitan University. Siddiqui had just left his job at the London Underground for medical reasons and enrolled at London Metropolitan to pursue a degee in computer science. He and Khyam hit if off immediately as they shared similar political and religious views. Khyam had the same experience when he met Lamine Adam at a mixer at East London University.[38] Lamine brought his brother Rahman to meet Khyam at a restaurant a few days later. Rahman had heard about Khyam's 2000 trip to a training camp and Khyam discovered Rahman's efficacy as a fund-raiser. They got on very well despite Rahman's lack of piety. Khyam later recalled, "If he [Rahman] went to an Islamic talk, he would be there, he would pray. Then he would go off to a nightclub, where the rest of us wouldn't."[39] The Crawley cluster—mostly Nadeem Ashraf, Khyam, Waseem Gulzar, and Ahmed Ali Khan—and the friends around the Adam brothers started hanging out with each other and visited each other's homes frequently.

Rahman Adam was starting to feel that his fund-raising activities on behalf of Kashmir were not enough and wanted to go to Pakistan for military training as well. Islam encouraged military training for self-defense.

His friends viewed as "heroes" those who had gone for training. They were highly respected and not necessarily seen as extremists. Military training did not mean that one had to go on to fight. Rahman hoped he would gain respect with such training. The Adams brothers, Rizwan Shamim, and Uniboy had gone on a few camping trips to Wales in preparation for possible military training in Pakistan. Rahman had bought camping equipment and asked some Pakistani friends to help arrange for training in Pakistan. Those who had already done it told him that this would be impossible because his white looks would cause problems for his trainers. The answer upset Rahman until he approached Khyam about this issue. Khyam was receptive and told Rahman to get a lot of money together and he would take care of the rest.[40]

In November 2002, Babar came to visit his London friends for two months. He had just resigned from his job (after stealing five computers) and wanted to raise money to finance his stay in Pakistan. In London, he stayed mostly with Kazi Rahman and occasionally with Zaheer Ali. He met with the Jabber brothers, who asked him to set up a training camp for east Londoners like themselves and promised to raise funds for the camp. Babar also contacted Asim to ask for money. Asim suggested going to Crawley to seek support. Before going there, Asim introduced Babar to Rahman Adam, Shamim, and Siddiqui at a restaurant in London. During the meal, Adam and Siddiqui told Babar that they wanted to go to Afghanistan to fight. Adam also invited Babar to his home and introduced him to Lamine.[41]

A few days later, Asim drove Babar, Rahman Adam, Shamim, and Siddiqui to Crawley. Welcoming them were Khyam and Ashraf among others. A few days after that, one of the Jabber brothers organized another fundraising meeting for Babar. Babar, Khyam, Ashraf, Kazi Rahman, Asim, and the Jabber brothers attended and saw the *wassiyas* (video wills) of some of the 9/11 perpetrators. By now, most of the London Islamists were celebrating the 9/11 attacks. At the meeting, preachers Abu Hamza and Abdullah el-Faisal made short speeches. Afterward, they collected money for Babar. However, it was not enough. When Babar returned to Pakistan, he no longer could afford a flat, and he and his wife moved in with his relatives in Nowshera.[42]

Rahman Adam also spent some time in chat rooms to meet Muslim women. One of them sent him the al Qaeda Manual as an attachment.[43] In July 2002, he had told a Canadian, Zenab, that he wanted to go for military training in Kashmir. They talked about marriage as Islamic tradition dictated that a suitor mention marriage at an early stage since there is no dating outside of marriage. They exchanged photographs of themselves but Rahman did not find her attractive and lost interest in her.[44] She continued to e-mail him regularly, but he replied to her irregularly and only out of politeness.

The Canadian Link and the Departure for Pakistan

On 27 December, Mohammed Momin Khawaja from Ottawa flew to London to visit Ashraf. They had met in an Islamist chat room and developed an online friendship. Khawaja was a 23-year-old Canadian-born Muslim, whose Pakistani father had come to study political science at the University of Toronto, married in Canada, and had five children. Young Momin identified with Ali, the son-in-law of the Prophet: "I always wanted to be a soldier, cuz when I waz like 5 yrs old: me mum and I would read story about Ali . . . how he chopped off the head of Marhab the kafir [infidel] and bout jihad and stuff. . . . I loved it even then and wud repeat that story of Ali . . . over an over again." Khawaja's father wanted to work in Muslim countries. He first moved his family to Tripoli, Libya, and Momin kept a vivid memory of sirens during the April 1986 U.S. bombing raid on the city, and of his mother trying to hide the children under the dining room table. In 1987, the family moved to Saudi Arabia, where his father became director of planning, research and development at a university. During his stay in Saudi Arabia, Momin attended American schools. At the end of 1993, the family returned to Ottawa and his father got a doctorate in social science. In 2000, the father returned to Saudi Arabia while his family stayed in Ottawa, where Momin attended school and got a diploma in computer programming in 2001. He was religious and did volunteer work at the local mosque.[45]

Khawaja later remembered, "it wasn't till later in college, the year 2000 Palestinian Intifada, when my life changed. I started studying more Islamic books, learning more of the Deen, and following the Sunnah more in my life. Then after I got out of College, the invasion of Afghanistan happened. This was a milestone which gave direction to my life, and devotion to efforts of Deen."[46] In November 2001, Momin Khawaja wrote, "I, Momin, take an oath with Allah to give my life for Allah only, as a Mujahid, upholding the banner of Islam, following the Sunnah of Muhammad (may the peace and blessings of Allah be upon him)." A month later, he quit his job to go to Afghanistan and fight against the Western invasion.[47]

On 12 January 2002, Khawaja flew to Islamabad, "when the *kuffar* amreekans invaded Afghanistan, that was . . . the most painful time in my whole life cuz I loved the . . . mujahedeen and our bros in Afghanistan so so much that I couldn't . . . stand it. It would tear my heart knowing these filthy *kaafir* dog . . . Americans were bombing our muslim bros and sisters. . . . Shaykh Usama bin laden is like the most beloved person to me in the . . . whole world. . . . I wish I could even kiss his blessed . . . hand."[48] He stayed for three months but failed to get any type of training as the Pakistani authorities had closed the camps to foreigners.

Khawaja returned to Ottawa in mid-April, found a job at a small software company that did work for the Ministry of Foreign Affairs, and got a secret security clearance.[49] When he arrived in London eight months later, Ashraf introduced him to Khyam. They discussed their desire for jihad in Afghanistan, and Khyam told Khawaja about an impending trip to Pakistan with his friends. Khawaja agreed to help finance Khyam's venture and promised to wire Khyam about £2,000 to £4,000 every few months via Western Union. They agreed on a secure method of communication, as Khyam later recalled: "Basically you just go to the actual email page, put subject in, whatever that is, and then you just write an email as normal and put it in the draft. You don't actually send the email, and he would also have access to the password. So, he would open it up and read it, check it, and then if he wanted to reply he would do it in the same way."[50] Khawaja returned to Ottawa on 30 December 2002.[51]

During the trip, Khawaja learned about Zenab. Rahman Adam e-mailed her that he was off to Afghanistan, and asked her to transfer money from a Canadian contact. When she asked for this contact, Khawaja replied and wrote that he needed the help of a woman to send money for the cause because "sisters don't get caught, brothers do." Under his instructions, she opened a bank account and sent its debit card and documents to Khawaja, who forwarded it on to Khyam. Khawaja also instructed her to wire about $5,000 in two transactions in January 2003 to Saira Khan, Khyam's wife.[52]

Nadeem Ashraf's wedding in Islamabad in February 2003 was the perfect cover for the Crawley crowd and the friends of the Adam family to go to Pakistan in search of jihadi training. Khyam told all his friends about the planned trip to try to inspire them to come along. Rahman Adam was most enthusiastic about this but knew that he was going to be on his own because he did not have any family in Pakistan. To make sure he had enough to cover any contingency, he withdrew about £8,500 from his bank account

on 5 February 2003 including an overdraft of £1,720, which he did not
intend to pay back. His brothers were supportive of his plan and he told
his parents that he was only going to go to Pakistan for Ashraf's wedding.
His father, who had never understood his son's passion for Kashmir when
he was not even of Pakistani descent, immediately realized that Rahman
would try to go to a training camp and hid his passport to try to stop his
son. Rahman got a new passport and a three-month visa for Pakistan.[53]

Waseem Gulzar, Zeeshan Siddiqui, and Ahmed Ali Khan also volunteered to come for training. They each assumed an alias for security's sake:
Omar Khyam became Ausman; Rahman Adam, Abdul Rahman; Nadeem
Ashraf, Nadz; Waseem Gulzar, Akib; Ahmed Ali Khan, Mashup; and Zeeshan Siddiqui, Imran or Immy. Later in Pakistan, Babar became Kashif or
simply Kash (Big Dawg in e-mails), Waheed Mahmood was Ishmael, Kazi
Rahman was Abdul Haleem or Tipu, and Rizwan Shamim was Riaz.

Mohammed Qayum Khan, still raising funds and material in England,
found out about Khyam's plan to go to Islamabad (but not the group's
desire for military training). He got in touch with Khyam and asked him
whether he could deliver some money and equipment to Amin, whom he
called "Khalid." Khyam accepted. This request for Khyam to become a
courier was a crucial development of the Crevice Plot for it bridged the
Luton-al Qaeda and Crawley-Barkingside support networks. It was not a
recruitment pitch but a simple opportunistic request based on prior
mutual knowledge of militancy as these separate loose clusters had briefly
visited each other in the past. Qayum provided Khyam with money,
equipment (zipped fleeces, hiking boots, mosquito nets, global position-
ing system devices, and first aid kits, all packed in suitcases), and Amin's
phone number in Pakistan. Qayum called Amin, told him that "Ausman"
and "Akib" would be coming, asked him to pick them and the equipment
up at the airport, and rent an apartment in Islamabad for a week for
them.

On 9 February 2003, the eve of Ashraf and Adam's departure to Islamabad, there was a party at Ashraf's house to send him off for his wedding.
Everyone came to celebrate. During the party, Rahman gave Khyam £7,500
to look after for him and kept £1,000 for himself. The money was for Rahman's expenses, and Rahman expected Khyam to return any leftover funds
to him. This gesture made Rahman feel special, like a hero. Afterward, he
left to party in Brighton.[54] Khyam's last preparations included taking care
of his new wife. Since his family did not know that he was religiously

married, he could not ask them to provide for her while he was away, so he gave her £3,000 from Rahman's money.[55]

The Second Wave of British Mujahedin Wannabes

The six would-be soldiers flew to Islamabad in three pairs. On 10 February 2003, Rahman Adam and Nadeem Ashraf left England. Adam started a diary of his experience, giving us a peek into his mind-set. He was moved by his best friend Shamim's emotional reaction at the airport and promised his friend he would soon be back. On the plane, Adam was far more concerned about the ban on smoking on the plane and the blonde airline attendant than about anything to do with training camp. On the flight, he listened to 2Pac music. At Islamabad Airport, Ashraf's father came the collect the young men and took them to the family house.[56]

Omar Khyam and Waseem Gulzar followed two days later. Notified by Qayum, Amin was waiting for them at the airport and recognized Khyam. Amin took them to an apartment he had rented for them in Islamabad, where Khyam gave him the money he was carrying.[57] Khyam and Gulzar later picked up Adam and brought him back with them to the apartment. From Adam's diary: "Every night was the same night repeating itself with a slight difference to the jokes and the short guy [Khyam] laughing like a mad man. But, all in all things were good. We spent a week without the final two brothers."[58]

On 14 February, Amin drove to the flat to pick up the equipment that Khyam and Gulzar had brought with them. Amin told Khyam that the money and equipment were for Abu Munthir, a lieutenant of Abdal Hadi al Iraqi, presented as the chief of Afghan operations for al Qaeda.[59] Khyam and his friends told Amin that they wanted to get explosives training and then go and fight in Afghanistan. They asked him to request from Abu Munthir permission to fight in Afghanistan.[60] Amin promised he would do so. Khyam also mentioned that a friend, Waheed Mahmoud, was living in Gujar Khan and had invited them to come and visit. Amin, who was still working in Gujar Khan, suggested they go and visit Mahmood that afternoon.

When Amin and Khyam arrived at Mahmood's compound, Mahmood and Amin recognized each other. Mahmood told them that his children had fallen ill from the local water or food and his family had just returned to England. He was thinking about going back himself.[61] In the meanwhile, he invited the entire crowd of visitors to come and relax for a few days at his mansion. Khyam accepted on behalf of the group and the two visitors returned to Islamabad. Amin left to deliver the money and equipment to Abu Munthir and ask him about the visitors' request. Later, Amin notified Qayum of their delivery and mentioned the visitors' desire to go and fight in Afghanistan. This upset Qayum, who did not want to lose them as regular couriers.

On 17 February, Ahmed Ali Khan and Zeeshan Siddiqui finally arrived and moved into the apartment. From Adam's diary: "Immy [Siddiqui] turned up in his [London] Underground uniform at the bloody airport." Siddiqui became the group idiot-clown, "the strangest person I've ever met, very weird." After staying up all night (except for Khyam, who seemed to require 10 hours of sleep), the friends went to Ashraf's wedding ceremony. "Immy [Siddiqui] was totally exhausted and falling asleep. The short guy who laughs like a psycho [Khyam] went to sleep at the beginning of the journey and Cutie [Ali Khan], well, he was sleeping as well, which left Akib [Gulzar] and I alone with a bunch of pervs," Adam wrote. At the hotel, Adam had "my hair gelled in a rough manner, Wrangler jeans, my Ben Sherman with a British flag across my chest, my crocodile shoes and my $55 sun block shades, oh, yeah, and my fags. . . . My man Nadz [Ashraf] had the hump with me because I left him a note as I went to hug him in front of the ladies and his uncles saying, 'You sell out, you're a looooza' which was signed by everyone." Afterward, the five friends left for Gujar Khan. "When we arrived at his place we were like: wow, what the hell is this? It was a massive joint with pillars, tinted windows and a dog." They had originally planned to stay there overnight on the way to somewhere else, but decided to "stay at 'Hormones' [Mahmood's] . . . mansion."[62]

Meanwhile back home, Britain was gearing up to join the United States in the invasion of Iraq. The opposition to Britain joining the invading coalition of Iraq reached its height on 15 February 2003 with "Stop the War," the largest worldwide political protest demonstration up to that time, mobilizing millions of protestors.[63] Despite the unprecedented size of this protest, the British government continued its preparation for war. Although the mujahedin wannabes missed it because they were en route to Pakistan, it hardened their disillusionment with the effectiveness of peaceful mass protest to prevent a war. "Since the war in Afghanistan, attitudes had been hardening towards, as I say, the Americans and their allies," Khyam later testified. "But the Iraq war was sort of just the final—I don't know how you can say it; that was it. After that people thought this is so blatant, you know, why they are attacking Iraq? What has Iraq got to do with it? Are they really saying Saddam is linked with al Qaeda or the Taliban? People didn't understand why they were attacking Iraq: because they were simply Muslim or because they had the second biggest reserves of oil in the world?"[64] The mujahedin wannabes now in Pakistan had defined themselves in contrast to American invaders in Afghanistan. Now that Britain was joining the United States in the invasion of another Muslim country, it also joined the United States as the enemy in the militants' minds, a legitimate target of attack in an increasingly apparent war on Islam.

The Fateful Decision to Attack Britain

During their weeklong stay at Mahmood's mansion, the mujahedin wannabes relaxed: they played badminton, wrestled, Thai boxed, did calisthenics, swam in a stream, and fished. Once they climbed a 20-meter-high termite hill. On the way down, Ali Khan grabbed Adam and asked for help as he was afraid of heights, not an encouraging sign for going through paramilitary training camp in a very mountainous region. Another time, they went swimming in a stream and Gulzar almost drowned. Siddiqui, on the shore, tried to help and threw Gulzar his rucksack as if it were a floatation device but the heavy bag sank in the stream. Eventually, Gulzar made it out, but the whole group was upset at Siddiqui, for the bag contained Gulzar's clothes, watch, two knives, and a large sum of money—and Adam's lighter.[65] Toward the end of the week, two other sets of visitors joined them.

The first visitors were Kazi Rahman and Mohammed Babar. Kazi Rahman had returned to Pakistan in February with four other East Londoners, serious about getting some explosives training and then going to fight in Afghanistan. Kazi Rahman told people his move was permanent and put out the word that he was looking for a local wife. Babar welcomed them and suggested that Mahmood might have contacts to help them. Then Babar contacted Mahmood, who invited Rahman and Babar to come to his house.[66]

When they arrived, Babar recognized Siddiqui and Adam from England.[67] During his stay, Babar said to Mahmood in private that the two groups (Khyam's and Kazi Rahman's) had the same goal of joining the jihad in Afghanistan and should work together to avoid a repeat of their past failure. They should coordinate their activites, share their resources and contacts, and pool their financial support for the mujahedin. Mahmood answered that going to Afghanistan would be difficult because the mujahedin were not accepting newcomers, only those who had been with them before 9/11. Babar also told Mahmood that Kazi Rahman and his four associates wanted to get some explosives training and asked Mahmood whether he could assist them in that matter. Mahmood replied that he would look into it and get back to Babar.[68]

After Babar and Mahmood returned to rejoin the others, Mahmood read exerpts from the book he was writing about the life of the Prophet. The group went on to discuss their disagreement with ALM, complaining that it had become a joke and its initials stood for "all mouth, no action."[69] At this point of the evening, Salahuddin Amin showed up at the house with Abu Munthir's reply to Khyam's request to fight in Afghanistan. As he later confessed to the British police, "when I asked Abu Munthir he said, 'I'll ask my chief and then I'll let you know.' So, when he asked his chief [Abdul Hadi al Iraqi], he wrote me a letter and said that we have enough people here, you know, who are fighting, but what we need is money and equipment. So, the best thing would be to go back and keep sending money and equipment, and if they really want to do something, then go back and you can do something there [the UK]."[70] Amin memorized Abu Munthir's letter and destroyed it before coming to Mahmood's house.

Abdal Hadi al Iraqi probably questioned the newcomers' ability to survive and fight in the harsh environment of Afghanistan, was suspicious of potential ISID penetration, and irritated that they wanted to come to Afghanistan when his most critical need was for equipment, money, and food rather than fighters. Their request threatened the continuity of his supply lines. His throwaway last line, "if you want to make mischief, just do it at home," seems more a sign of his irritation than any attempt to convince these wannabes to carry out terrorist operations at home. Had he wanted them to conduct operations in Britain, he would have invited them for training. His focus and mission were al Qaeda operations in Afghanistan and not external operations.

Abdal Hadi al Iraqi and al Qaeda's rejection of the British militants' request obviously disappointed them. They saw their dreams of glory as mujahedin in Afghanistan evaporate. However, Mahmood focused on the letter's throwaway suggestion of doing something at home. At first, his audience seemed cool to his ideas. Babar recalled, "Everybody . . . wished for . . . the old-style jihad where you just go and fight. . . . At this time most everybody in the room would have preferred to have gone to Afghanistan and fight."[71] This was the first time anyone had raised the subject of conducting any terrorist operations in Britain and, in ordinary times, the militants at Mahmood's house would have dismissed it. However, with their country's escalation of the conflict with Muslims in the run-up to the Iraq invasion and the disillusionment with the effectiveness of large peaceful demonstrations like the Stop the War march, they started to consider attacking Britain at home. As Khyam recalled that fateful discussion, "Whereas before, myself and others may have made excuses [for the UK], a lot of people now were just silent. When people mentioned things like the UK or the Americans need to be attacked, there would be no defending the UK anymore."[72] This quote refutes the U.S. neoconservatives' argument that "we fight them there, so we don't have to fight them here."

Because this plot emerged from a support network for al Qaeda *internal* Afghan operations, al Qaeda *external* operations staff was not aware of it and therefore did not manage it. Had this plot originated with al Qaeda, its external operations staff would have managed it from the start. The British militants, and not al Qaeda, clearly initiated this plot. In fact, the idea of attacking Britain came from al Qaeda's rejection of a more active role in Afghanistan for the British mujahedin wannabes. The last line of the rejection letter, written in irritation, opened a new horizon for them and added carrying out a terrorist operation at home into their repertoire of action.

Mahmood's enthusiasm for attacking Britain gradually overcame his audience's reluctance. The initial decision to attack Britain was not the result of a terrorist bloodlust. It was about causing maximum economic with minimum human damage as a warning not to attack Muslims in Muslim lands. Mahmood gave specific examples of the types of operations that he had in mind such as communication accidents and damage he had witnessed during the course of his work at British Telecom. He argued that if they attacked the communication network in an area, they would knock out telephone and Internet communication there, resulting in billions in damages because businesses completely relied on such communication. As Babar remembered, "He had a very detailed knowledge of how things worked . . . as far as the grid goes . . . the thing to hit . . . where . . . it was guaranteed that . . . the utility would be off—whether it be telephone . . . electric or gas. . . . He seemed to have . . . a pretty good idea . . . on exactly what to hit."[73]

Waheed Mahmood went on to address the security situation in Britain. Conditions for operations there were difficult because MI5 was monitoring Islamist militants. In fact, the British police was escalating its surveillance and arrests of Muslim refugees deemed dangerous but was still leaving British Muslims alone. Nevertheless, Mahmood suggested that only new converts, who had not come to the attention of MI5, should come to Pakistan for explosives training, return to Britain, and teach everyone else. This would be better than Islamist militants coming to Pakistan and eliciting surveillance after returning to Britain. In the brainstorming session, he also suggested injecting poison into beer at soccer games, selling poisoned food from a food truck that would then disappear, or simply advertising the number of a new take-out fast food restaurant and delivering poisoned food to people who called. This would make it hard for the police to track down. Mahmood did most of the talking throughout that fateful night but the others were silently attentive. At the end, they agreed in principle that probably the only way to stop attacks on Muslims abroad was to make British citizens unsafe at home by carrying out operations in Britain. To carry them out, the militants needed to get some explosives training.

Amin had also brought a CD video showing how to dismantle AK-47s and jihad guerilla tactics. Babar took it to make a copy for Kazi Rahman for his friends in Lahore. Babar also suggested that they get fake Pakistan government identity cards that might get them out of trouble if stopped by the local police. They took digital pictures of themselves and put them on the CD. All the guests stayed overnight at Mahmood's house.[74]

The next day, they woke up in midmorning. While the rest of the guests went fishing, Mahmood drove Babar, Kazi Rahman, and Amin to the Gujar Khan bus station. After Mahmood left, Amin told Rahman that he would have to get back to him on explosive training and left for Kohat to see the "brothers."[75] During the next day or so, the other guests returned to their rental in Islamabad. Ahmed Ali Khan was the first to return to England on 8 March 2003.[76]

Looking for Terrorist Training

The idea of attacking Britain at home might have faded but for the invasion of Iraq, which figured prominently in Adam's diary. During the next month and a half, the British wannabes searched frantically for paramilitary training for different reasons. Khyam wanted explosives training to carry out operations in Britain. Others wanted to get the training, just for the experience. Still others, like Kazi Rahman, were determined to fight in Afghanistan.

After al Qaeda closed Afghanistan to British militants, Babar and Kazi Rahman searched for other contacts to set up their own training camp and invite friends, like the Jabber brothers, to come and participate in it. They asked Sajeel Shahid to broker an introduction to the maulana, whose emir had been arrested, leaving the maulana free to make his own decisions. Shahid agreed and they all traveled to Gorque to meet him and his son Zubair. Babar who spoke Pashtu translated. The maulana told the visitors he could set up a training camp on a plateau, high above the village, but they would have to cover all expenses such as food, materiel, and shelter. Zubair would be the trainer. He estimated that the total cost might come to about £3,000 to £5,000.[77] The visitors agreed and hoped that the Jabber brothers might finance it. They returned to Lahore for Kazi Rahman's wedding.

When the lease on their Islamabad rental ran out, Khyam and his associates rented a small house in a small village. As Adam later recalled, "It was a room and a toilet and . . . a kind of courtyard in the middle," where he was confined because of his light skin color, while Gulzar and Siddiqui ventured out for short periods in the evening. Khyam was often absent, traveling to set up a training camp. When he was back, they talked not about jihad but about their experiences with girls. Khyam promised to introduce Adam to a pretty girl for marriage. Over time, their bantering degenerated to the point where they competed as to who had the most expensive clothes. Adam had his CD player and listened to Justin Timberlake, 2Pac, and A-Zeem to the disapproval of his roommates.[78]

In Lahore, Babar stayed at Rahman's apartment. Mahmood came to visit with questions from the "brothers" about their request for explosive training: How long had the potential trainees known each other? Where were they from? Which school of Islam did they follow? And so on . . . [79] Mahmood repeated that it was very difficult for foreigners to get into Afghanistan: some British brothers had trained on the border for a year and had not been able to go in. An alternative was to train with Kashmiri brothers. Rahman was unhappy with any of these options.[80]

On 15 March 2003, Kazi Rahman got married in Lahore. Babar was his witness and only three of his companions attended because Ayoub, a 20-year-old of Bengali origin, was in a hospital with hepatitis. Rahman had

invited only the visitors of South Asian descent for security reasons—
Mahmood, Khyam, and Gulzar. Adam and Siddiqui had to stay out of
sight. The guests took the train to Lahore and went to the place where they
were supposed to meet Babar. However, when they arrived, they spotted a
white reporter and worried that he was a MI5 agent. They retreated to the
train station and called Babar on his cell phone to come and meet them
there. Babar protested that he was part of the ceremony, but Mahmood
insisted it was an emergency. Babar came and, during the conversation,
they realized that they were all trying to work with Abdal Hadi al Iraqi and
al Qaeda.[81]

The visitors returned to Islamabad the next day, and Gulzar, who was
homesick and missing his wife, returned to Crawley on 19 March 2003. He
reconnected with his former best friend, Jawad Akbar, who had drifted
away when he attended Brunel University in Uxbridge: Gulzar had become
more religious while Akbar continued drinking, listening to music, and
going out clubbing. Around Christmas 2001, Akbar had met Sundeep B.,
who was a year older and a Sikh. They became very close, despite the fact
that South Asian families frowned upon dating. After Gulzar returned from
his trip to Pakistan, he encouraged his friend to pray more frequently, grow
a beard, wear religious clothes, and contribute £20 monthly to charity.
Gulzar also pressured Akbar about his girlfriend. "If you want to get serious
about Islam, you can't have the best of both worlds. You can't practice your
religion and be sleeping around as well with a woman."[82] This combination
was not *haram* (licit) in Islam. Reluctantly, Akbar broke up with Sundeep
in April 2003 because he could not marry a non-Muslim. She reacted deci-
sively. She converted to Islam on 22 April 2003, taking the name Alliyah,
and married Akbar on the same day. They did not tell either of their families about the marriage or the conversion because neither family would
approve of a love marriage.[83]

Meanwhile in Pakistan, Adam was now mostly alone with Siddiqui in
their room and they were getting on each other's nerves.[84] Adam wrote,
"Immy about 3 days ago got really angry about something, then demanded
that I wipe all the funny things I wrote about him and called my bio a
stupid waste of time. This really pissed me off but I stayed quiet. He has a
real bad temper. . . . Life is too short to hold grudges so . . . pretend like
nothing has happened."[85] Siddiqui also kept a diary, which showed him
very unhappy, suffering from diarrhea, disgusted with the bad food and the
filth of the place. He washed his hands obsessively and used lots of water;

his roommates explained to him that there was a limited amount of water in the flat. He grew distant from them. "All alone in a strange land with strange ppl [people] and a strange language," Siddiqui wrote. "I'm always constantly laughed at and ridiculed. I can trust no-one, except Allah." When he went out in the evening, he complained about local shopkeepers playing pop music, which his version of Islam prohibited. He viewed Muslims who did not share his worldview as unbelievers. Nevertheless, he viewed his ordeal as a religious test. When his health improved, he thanked Allah. "I can only repay this debt of gratitude by giving my life and blood for this cause. I just pray that Allah makes this path easy for me."[86]

At the house, Adam was surfing on the Internet for pornographic and news sites and used his computer to call his brothers and Rizwan. He followed the buildup against Iraq. On 19 March, he noted in his diary, "Tomorrow they might start attacking Iraq. How sad. . . . I sometimes feel sick to think that my own country wants to assist this war and hurt thousands over just oil. I mean, they go on about how it's us the people who decide, but yet Mr. Blair is trying to convince us that if we don't BOMB the living crap out of them we might all die. But one thing it's good to see people all around the world that they are all against the war. If it was [up] to me I will rid every weapon there is on earth so as we can't have wars but [I] am only a superstar who knows how to look good."[87]

Meanwhile, two weeks after the wedding, Mahmood called Babar to come immediately to Gujar Khan. Babar took two night buses and, when he arrived at Mahmood's mansion, Khyam was already there. Mahmood told them that one of Amin's associates had been arrested and Amin's cell phone number might have been compromised. Amin had gone into hiding in Kohat. Babar turned off his cell phone for two months. Khyam and Babar stayed at Mahmood's house and discovered that they had many things in common. When Babar left, he moved into a new two-bedroom flat with a large living room in Lahore for him and his wife.[88]

When Amin came out of hiding, he took Khyam to meet with Abu Mahmoud al Filastini and Tariq and discuss explosive training. Abu Mahmoud probably wanted to see whether Khyam was serious, for he shared Abdal Hadi's and Abu Munthir's general suspicion of pampered Westerners. By that time, Khyam had shown himself to be reliable. He had become a regular supplier for Amin and the mujahedin. From his sources in England, he was giving Amin equipment and about £3,000 to £4,000 a month for Abu Munthir. About 60 percent of that went to support women and children, and 40 percent to fighters in Afghanistan and the border area. He satisfied Abu Mahmoud and, right afterward, he went to meet Babar in Lahore. He asked Babar to invite Kazi Rahman and his associates the next day. Khyam told them he had found a contact who could give them explosives training but this was serious business as the trainers became responsible for future actions of their trainees. In order to prevent any rogue action, trainees had to swear *bayat* (loyalty) to the trainers and their chiefs and accept guidance and direction from them. This meant that Kazi Rahman would lose leadership over his companions, as they would have to swear bayat to Khyam, who had already agreed to the trainers' conditions. Kazi Rahman was not interested in losing his leadership position, declined the offer, and left with his companions. Khyam moved in with Babar, who told him that two Arabs working for Abdal Hadi needed about £5,500 to send some mujahedin families back to their home countries. Khyam got him the money the next day.[89]

Around the second week of April, Babar went to see Mahmood and asked him for money to fly to Britain so he could talk to the Jabber brothers about raising money for the Gorque camp. Mahmood gave Babar about £500 for his airfare and, in return, Babar gave him two of his stolen computers to pass on to the mujahedin. Mahmood told Babar that he also planned to return to England in the very near future and had sold his Honda Accord to Amin, who until then had traveled on a motorcycle. On 13 April 2003, Mahmood returned to England to rejoin his family.[90]

Meanwhile, holed up in their small remote village house, Adam and Siddiqui passed the time by fantasizing about sex. They were often on pornographic sites and masturbated frequently. They worried when Khyam was away for too long and were tempted to call him to make sure that nothing had happened to him. Despite the boredom, Adam continued to follow the news. "Today is a sad day for me because Iraq is being attacked," he wrote. "I have always wanted America to bust up Saddam Hussein but to go in like that, with pure brute [force] surely it can't be right. Just to think of the innocent people that are going to lose their lives. It hurts, man. Immy just can't believe it. He keeps saying, 'Man, can you believe it? They're being bombed up while we are relaxing on our long holiday.' But the reality is that we can't do shit all to help the people. All we can do is be normal and help the poor with our money. Am starting to miss home. I can't wait till I go back."[91]

During this time, Khyam asked Adam to take care of his wife in case he got killed. Adam very moved, "I never thought he would ask me what he did. I just thought he had other better people in mind. . . . It's . . . like he has trusted me with a responsibility that I'm not sure if I can deal with it correctly. But then he said like, he will be at peace with himself. So, I thought, okay, man, it's like the responsibility is massive. . . . He must have liked something about me, and this is what I can't understand. Maybe because I make him laugh a lot."[92]

Khyam arranged for training at a private location in Kashmir for his associates with Lashkar e-Taiba (LeT). In April, he returned to the village and took Adam and Siddiqui to Lahore, where they moved in with Kazi Rahman's companions. Then Khyam flew back to England on 21 April 2003 to raise more money and buy some camping gear. Babar had flown to England a few days before him and again stayed at Zaheer Ali's house for three or four weeks.[93]

Fund-Raising Trip in England

In London, Babar got an instant message from Khyam asking him to meet someone in Slough. When Babar arrived at the train station, he was surprised to see Khyam since he did not know Khyam had come back. Khyam took Babar back to his hotel room, where Ali Khan, Gulzar, and Khyam's younger brother, Shujah-ud-Din Mahmood, were waiting. Shujah, as everyone called him, was 17, five years younger than Khyam, and looked up to his brother as a father figure—he had been only six years old when their father had left home. Now Islam intrigued him. Under his brother's influence, he had stopped watching music channels on television or going swimming because of mixing with girls. He had not done well at school and required special reading classes. When Khyam was in Pakistan, he drifted to delinquency, committed acts of vandalism, got into altercations, and took drugs. He was suspended at school but never prosecuted. In Pakistan, Khyam had used his brother's bank account to add another layer of security for his operations: Ashraf deposited money in it in England and Khyam withdrew it in Pakistan.[94] When Khyam got back, he took charge of his younger brother.

After Babar arrived at the hotel, Khyam sent his brother out to get food and updated Babar on his activities in Pakistan. Khyam had succeeded in setting up a training camp in Kashmir. He was back in England to raise money and buy supplies for that camp, including hiking boots, clothing, and camping gear. Khyam wanted to send them by parcel post and needed an address in Pakistan, which Babar supplied.[95]

Nadeem Ashraf invited Babar to Crawley. At Ashraf's home, Mahmood told Babar that Khyam's LeT training camp would be free and Mahmood would select and accept only serious applicants, who wanted to go on to fight in Afghanistan. He wanted to weed out those who just wanted to get the training and go home afterward. The training would include use of firearms and explosives. Mahmood then drove Babar to the Jabber brothers, who seemed reluctant to attend the camp. One said he was too busy while the other was worried as MI5 had picked up one of his friends and showed him Babar's picture. Nevertheless, the brothers said they would get back to Mahmood with names of possible attendees.[96]

Babar also ran into Hassan Butt, whom he knew from his ALM days in Lahore. Butt had returned to Manchester and told Babar that someone in Pakistani intelligence had told him that Kazi Rahman's flat in Lahore was being monitored. Babar immediately alerted them via instant messaging and told them to leave the apartment. Three of Kazi Rahman's companions left for a training camp in Kashmir while Ayoub, still recovering from hepatitis, was too weak to go with them and simply stayed with Adam and Siddiqui at a nearby hotel.

The Kohat Explosives Training

Khyam returned to Pakistan on 7 May 2003. Babar followed him a week later, having failed to raise either money or interest for the proposed Gorque camp.[97] Adam and Siddiqui had run out of money for their hotel and moved in with Babar. They occupied one bedroom while Babar and his wife occupied the other. She was in her last trimester of pregnancy and sometimes stayed with her parents. Adam started dating a girl in Lahore. Ayoub, left behind by Kazi Rahman's companions, switched allegiance to Khyam and together they went for explosive training with Amin.[98]

Abu Mahmoud al Filastini and Tariq had arranged for it. Abu Mahmoud had asked one of his former companions from Afghanistan, who used the name Dolat, to provide the training. Dolat wanted to return home in Central Asia with his family and Abu Mahmoud had arranged for him to provide the training for the cost of his relocation. Tariq had rented a house in Kohat. Khyam had specified that the ingredients for the explosives had to be readily available in Britain. Tariq and Amin went shopping locally and had to guess whether local products were also available in England. It took a few weeks to accumulate both the equipment and ingredients such as the aluminum powder, often used in paint shops to give a shine to color. When all was ready in the second half of May, Amin notified Khyam and Ayoub.[99]

They arrived in the late afternoon at a two-bedroom house, by a river. "We three of us . . . slept in one room and the guy who was training us slept in the other room," recalled Amin. Dolat did not speak English and tried to provide his instructions in Urdu. "And his Urdu wasn't very good either. So, most of the things he couldn't explain. He would just . . . show us with his hands what we were supposed to do."[100] Amin translated for Khyam and Ayoub and took extensive notes. "I didn't have . . . [any] initial intention [to train] at that time," he later said. "I thought: let's just learn it. But then later I thought . . . if somebody else wants to learn it and we don't have anybody available, I can teach them." The complete training took less than two days, including the testing of their devices and manufacture of ricin poison.[101]

The explosive devices were ammonium nitrate or urea based, and Dolat showed them how to make three or four different kinds of small bombs, using different sets of ingredients. Each student prepared a different type of explosive device. Dolat used a common Pakistani kitchen spice grinder to grind the explosive mixture. He added other ingredients, such as sulfur, sugar, and aluminum powder in specific ratios, and poured the resulting mixture into small plastic bottles.[102] It is unclear from the testimonies what type of fuses they used to detonate their devices.

After the explosive devices were ready, Dolat taught them how to manufacture ricin poison, used "to slowly kill a person." He peeled the skin of castor oil plants, and drowned them in paint thinner, a process he repeated several times. He kept the white residue and put it in a bottle to test later at Abu Mahmoud's house in Mardan. The next day, Amin drove Dolat, Ayoub, and Khyam to a little river nearby, where they tested their respective devices. Khyam and Ayoub left for Lahore at this point, while Amin and Dolat went to Mardan, where Abu Mahmoud had bought two rabbits to test the ricin. Amin could not bear to kill the two cute rabbits and the poison was never tested. Khyam was very dissatisfied with the training, because of his difficulty in understanding Dolat's instructions in broken Urdu and the fact that some of the equipment and ingredients used were not available in England.[103]

Setting Up the Gorque Camp and Buying Ingredients
for Explosives in Lahore

When Khyam and Ayoub returned to Lahore in late May, they moved into Babar's very crowded flat, joining Adam, Siddiqui, and of course Babar and his wife. The guests all lived in one room, while the married couple lived in the other one. Now Khyam was having second thoughts about the LeT training camp. Given LeT's close relationship with the ISID, he was afraid that they would draw its attention. In addition, LeT refused to train Adam because of his light skin color. Adam started to feel that his whole trip was wasted.[104]

Babar was also discouraged. He had the agreement of the maulana to set up a camp in Gorque, but the Jabber brothers had pulled out. He approached Khyam and told him that he could set up the camp for them if they could come up with the money. Khyam readily agreed. This started a frenzy of activity setting up this training camp and collecting money for it. First, they visited the maulana, agreed again on £3,500 for the total cost of the camp, and ironed out the last details with him. Back in Lahore, Khyam notified Adam that he could participate in this new camp. Adam was elated and immediately e-mailed Lamine on 1 June 2003 to send money and camping gear, and to let their friends know that the camp would start within weeks. Then Khyam, Adam, and Babar went to Gujar Khan to borrow £3,000 to £4,000 from Waheed Mahmood's brother-in-law.[105]

On 8 June, Khyam, Ayoub, Adam, Siddiqui, and Babar took the train to Karachi to meet Rizwan Shamim, who was flying in from England with about £4,000, which he turned over to Khyam. They all relaxed at a luxury hotel for four days, used the hotel pool, went to the beach, and did some sightseeing. They flew to Lahore on 12 June and moved into Babar's flat. Lamine sent an additional £1,000 as well as camping equipment, hiking boots, sleeping bags, solar panels, solar rechargeable batteries, socks, gloves, and hats. Babar went to Gorque to deliver the money to the maulana.[106]

Khyam was worried that he might not be able to buy the right ingredients for a bomb in England. He explored ways of shipping them to England from Lahore. The most important component was of course the detonators. They were not available in Lahore but were common in the tribal areas. He discussed the problem with Amin and Tariq, who gave him seven pen-shaped detonators. They discussed how to get them to England. Khyam wanted to transport them through Europe but Amin feared that this route was too risky. Amin explained that only one was enough to trigger a large explosion, for it would ignite a charge, which in turn would ignite the rest of the material, even for a huge bomb. When Khyam returned to Lahore by bus, he placed the detonators in a bag in the overhead rack, though he was afraid that the bumpy roads of Pakistan, littered with potholes, might ignite them. At Babar's apartment, he and Babar stored the bag on top of a wardrobe, with the fan running in the room all the time to prevent the detonators from overheating and igniting accidentally. That wardrobe was also used to store chemical precursors to explosive materials—ammonium nitrate, aluminum powder, diammonium phosphate, urea, and equipment to make bombs, such as thermometers, beakers, propane stove, filters, and sieves.[107]

Khyam, Ayoub, and Babar brainstormed about how to get the detonators to England. Babar volunteered to transport them overland through Iran, Turkey, all the way to Belgium, concealed in a cassette recorder. Khyam would pick them up in Belgium. Babar and Khyam also bought a dozen packages of aluminum power at a local bazaar. To test whether they could carry these packages through airport security, Khyam surreptitiously put a package in the luggage of a friend returning home to England. He and Babar drove the friend to the Lahore Airport and waited until he cleared security. This friend was a knife collector and had packed in his luggage several that he had bought in Pakistan. The airport screener went through his luggage checking the knives but missed the aluminum powder package. Khyam was happy: "At least we know that's one ingredient that can go through the airport."[108]

Later, Amin provided Khyam with a bag of ammonium nitrate pellets. Khyam tried to mix dried fruits in with the pellets, but Federal Express told him that a shipment of food to England required a health certificate, which the conspirators could not get. They explored the possibility of sending a container of the chemical to the UK by ship and found that this would work. Khyam and Babar also experimented with urea, another oxidizing agent widely available in Britain, as a possible substitute for ammonium nitrate. One of Saira Khan's friends brought a small package from England and the conspirators tested it with nitric acid, which Babar got by pretending to be a doctor for his medical laboratory. The English urea passed the test, eliminating the need to ship ammonium nitrate to England.[109]

Originally, Khyam and Babar had planned the Gorque camp for six people, but, as their friends heard about it, they asked to join. They flew in from England and congregated at Babar's flat. Even Uni-boy, who had come to Pakistan earlier in the spring for some training with a Kashmiri group, joined them and planned to attend the camp. They engaged in joyous banter about politics and girls. Babar remembered Khyam speaking about America getting hit on 9/11 while Britain had escaped any attack despite the fact that the UK was just as responsible as the United States for what was happening in the Middle East.[110]

Khyam's brother Shujah arrived on 27 June 2003, with boots, a fleece, and digital scales needed for the precise mixing of the various chemicals.[111] His mother had been fed up with his bad behavior and sent him to Pakistan to join Khyam, the oldest male in the family. The next day, the whole group packed their camping gear, along with their bomb-making ingredients and equipment, and set off for the camp. They would buy missing necessary ingredients en route. In an attempt to motivate them, Khyam and Babar told them that those who did well would go and fight in Afghanistan: people from al Qaeda were going to watch the training camp and would select some to fight in Afghanistan.[112]

The Third Wave: The Gorque Camp

On 28 June 2003, Khyam, Shujah, Babar, Ayoub, Adam, Siddiqui, Shamim, and Uni-boy checked into the Lahore Avari Hotel for a couple of days to relax and play tourist as a cover for their expedition.[113] They rented a 12-passenger van with a sign "Avari Hotel" on its side and drove to a luxury hotel in Kalam, in the upper Swat Valley. They lived their cover as tourists, dressed in Western clothes, hiking and sightseeing, while waiting several days for the maulana's son, Zubair, to come and pick them up. Khyam had warned them not to pray in public for security reasons but Babar, Shamim, and Siddiqui were so inspired by the beauty of the Swat River that they succumbed to the temptation of praying on its banks in a secluded area. When they got back to the hotel, they mentioned this to Adam, who immediately told Khyam. Khyam reprimanded Shamim and Siddiqui and restricted them to their room.[114]

Zubair finally showed up and they all piled into the van to go to Gorque. Babar returned home to Lahore to be at his wife's side as she was about to give birth. Before he left, Khyam told him that Khawaja, a Canadian financial supporter, was coming to the camp in the near future. Khyam asked Babar to assist Khawaja and gave Babar Khawaja's e-mail address and password. The trainees continued on their way and rested at the maulana's house for three or four days in preparation for hiking up to the camp. When Uni-boy found out that the training would be mostly physical exercises with a military theme to it, "he felt it was going to be a bit rubbish" as he had already done this type of training. He left the group to get some sniper training from a veteran of the Soviet Afghan jihad.[115]

The climb to the campsite was very arduous and took about 11 hours. They had to trek at night, went to sleep for a short time, and woke up at dawn for their last big stretch of what they later called "the big long mile."[116] The "camp" was simply a field with high grass on the side of a mountain and was completely bare without any equipment. Zubair had brought three AK-47s, one light machine gun, and one RPG launcher that could not be fired until the end of their stay for fear of alerting nearby villagers. He organized the camp on a military footing and posted sentries at night with loaded firearms. He taught the trainees to strip the guns down, clean them, and put them back together. The training consisted mostly of physical exercises: jogging, star jumps, push-ups, frog jumps, sit-ups, and crawling with loaded weapons. In the evenings, they read the Quran.

The participants were disappointed. Adam later remembered, "It [physical training] was quite intensive but it was really boring." He got out of some of the activities by pretending to have hurt his knee. The camp convinced him that he was better suited for fund-raising than actually fighting. The trainees did not take the camp seriously and looked down on the trainers. Adam remembered that on night guard duty, Shamim and he just chatted and drank coffee. The trainers, who were upset at the trainees' attitude, played a trick on them. Some trainers surreptitiously got behind a large rock and stomped their feet. Another one told the friends that he thought the army was coming up. Adam remembered, "I crapped myself."[117]

Khyam left the camp just before mid-July and returned to Babar's flat. Uni-boy had finished his sniper course and told Khyam in Lahore that he wanted to do an operation in the UK with Lamine. He talked about blowing up a nightclub there but he did not know how to make a bomb and needed some training. Khyam did not take him seriously and deliberately provided him with a formula of ingredients for explosives too watered down to be effective before Uni-boy returned to England.[118]

Meanwhile, Babar communicated with Khawaja, who wrote that his father had inherited a house in Rawalpindi. It was sitting empty and his family wanted to put someone in there to prevent any looting. Babar volunteered to move in with his wife in the near future. On the evening of 15 July, Khawaja arrived at Babar's flat, sporting a long beard, which Babar and Khyam made him shave for security reasons. Khawaja had brought about £1,800, half of it for al Qaeda and half for Khyam's operations in England. Babar's wife gave birth to a daughter on 17 July. Two days later, Khyam and Khawaja left for the Gorque camp, where Khawaja was thrilled to fire one RPG round. The two returned to Babar's flat about four days later.[119]

After he returned, Khyam told Babar that he expected a couple of people coming from England to participate in the Gorque camp. They went to Islamabad on 25 July to pick up the visitors. At the airport, they ran into Salahuddin Amin, who explained to Babar that Qayum had sent him two new couriers, who wanted to know what was going on in Afghanistan and specifically whether foreigners could get into the courntry.[120] When the plane landed, the couriers Mohammed Sidique Khan ("Ibrahim") and Mohammed Shakil ("Zubair") disembarked to meet Amin while Waseem Gulzar, Ahmed Ali Khan, and Jawad Akbar ("Hamza") from Crawley came to meet Khyam. Akbar was now spending all his time with Gulzar; they prayed and played soccer together. As Akbar continued to give Gulzar £20 monthly for charity, Gulzar showed him a video of children playing at the maulana's madrassa, which Babar had filmed on a previous trip, to illustrate that his money was not going to waste. Gulzar invited Akbar to come along and see the children. Akbar agreed and came together.[121]

When the three friends from Crawley had landed, Gulzar's uncle, who worked at the airport, got them through customs without any problems. Khyam was surprised to see Akbar because he had not been a practicing Muslim when Khyam had left England five months earlier. The Crawley travelers left with their respective families after making plans to meet later.[122] Sidique and Shakil[123] gave Amin money before leaving with Sidique's cousin from Rawalpindi.

After everyone else left, Khyam, his cousin Ali Khan, and Babar went to a flat in Islamabad rented by Amin to store incoming equipment. In England, Mahmood had given Ali Khan a GPS navigation system, solar panels, and invisible ink among other things for the mujahedin. A little later, Amin showed up with Sidique and Shakil. Babar and Khyam invited the couriers to the camp, and eventually the newcomers accepted the invitation.[124]

Khawaja flew home on 28 July. That day and the next, Babar bought thermometers, beakers, propane gas, sieves, and plastic tin cups to make explosive devices at local bazaars. After he arrived home in Ottawa, Khawaja sent a draft e-mail to Nadeem Ashraf, expressing his delight about the camp experience, his plan to visit his friends in England, and his desire to get married. Ashraf replied that he had some money for their friends in Pakistan and was trying to arrange for them to pick it up.[125]

On 29 July, Khyam, Ali Khan, and Babar set out from Lahore with their equipment and met up with Gulzar, Akbar, Sidique, and Shakil in Islamabad. Early next morning, they hired a small van but their trip was stopped by a riot along their way. They spent the night in Peshawar and arrived at the maulana's madrassa late afternoon the next day. They stayed at the madrassa for half an hour before starting the 10,000-feet climb to the campsite. The locals advised them to wait till the next day, but they were in a hurry and Khyam said he remembered the way up. Gulzar, Ali Khan, and Akbar did not have the right shoes and found the climb up very difficult. Akbar got sick from the altitude. Their guide failed to show up and they lost their way in the middle of the night. It was too dark to travel any farther and they stopped. As they only had a couple of sleeping bags among them, they stayed awake for fear of dying of hypothermia during their sleep. They sang songs and talked. In the morning, Akbar had a bout of diarrhea, earning him the nickname "Abu Finished Up." One of the maulana's men going up to the camp found them and guided them the rest of the way. They arrived there at midday on 1 August.[126]

At the camp, the newcomers settled into two tents. Shamim made them do physical exercises, but Akbar was too exhausted and just fell asleep. The next day, they all participated in physical exercises, although Gulzar was quite out of shape, Ali Khan had conjunctivitis, and Akbar was miserable because he missed his wife. Khyam came to their tent that second evening and told them, "You guys have a choice. I'm going to be going down tomorrow. Now, you can stay here for another two weeks, because I can come back in another two weeks, but I won't be able to come back before that. [Or] tomorrow we can leave all together and, if we do, we can fire the weapons tomorrow." The new group took the second option, "Look, bro . . . we've got the experience; we'll just go down tomorrow." Before falling asleep, they discussed jihad and Shamim read from *The Virtues of Jihad* by Maulana Masood Azhar. They punctuated their discussion with shouts, "Let's go kill the kafir!"[127]

The next day, everyone was able to shoot AK-47s and the light machine gun, but only Adam and Shakil got to fire the RPG. Apart from the others,

Khyam, Ayoub, Adam, and Babar made two bombs with Zubair and his helper, who had ground the ammonium nitrate during the night. Aluminum powder was mixed with heated ammonium nitrate, and the blend was poured into two bottles, which were then closed. They drilled a hole in them to place a wick sticking out of it. Zubair lit one wick, came running out, and the device exploded. The other device failed to explode. After the tests, they burried the rest of the ingredients. It is unknown whether the others were aware that this subgroup had made and exploded a bomb. Babar made a video of their activities for future propaganda.[128] Around noon on 3 August, everyone climbed down to the maulana's house. They then traveled from Gorque to Peshawar together except for Shamim and Siddiqui, who stayed behind for sniper training. Mufti Babar, a friend of the maulana and Abdal Hadi al Iraqi from their Afganistan days, befriended Siddiqui during that time.[129]

After the camp, people peeled off to various destinations. Babar, Ayoub, and Shakil traveled to Lahore together to Babar's flat.[130] Adam, Khyam, and Sidique Khan took a later bus to Lahore. All reacted differently to the Gorque camp experience. Adam felt both pride in achieving the training that he had wanted to do for a long time and disappointment in the quality of the training.[131] Akbar felt more positive about the camp despite his illness. At the camp, he had met people who were different from his other Muslim friends, who swore and drank. "They were trying to help people, i.e., the charity people, and on top of that they were doing this kind of training, and some of them had discussed about going to fight in Afghanistan and stuff like that, which I thought again was a noble cause. So, to me this is where I'd say my love for the Jihad started, as a result of this camp."[132]

Overall, the experience of the Gorque camp raised the morale of the participants. They were different people when they came down, proud of themselves that they had fired weapons and done some paramilitary training. Akbar later testified, "You could see it from their faces and you could see just generally—you could just tell by the atmosphere that everyone is happy. No one was saying, 'I'm happy,' but you could just tell they were happy though by the way they spoke."[133] It also cemented their social identity as soldiers defending their imagined community, the neo-ummah,[134] and solidified some relationships into friendships.[135]

From the preceding description, I am not sure that it is fair to call the Gorque camp experience that of a real training camp. There was not much instruction about carrying out terrorist attacks in the West, mostly because

Zubair, the maulana's son, had no experience of the West and there is no indication that he had ever traveled there. He was only familiar with guerilla tactics in Afghanistan. He simply put the first participants of the camp through physical education training. Four people saw Zubair quickly demonstrate the manufacture of two explosive devices, one of which failed to explode. It did not add anything to Khyam's and Ayoub's rather sketchy understanding of how to build such devices. The demonstration certainly went over Babar's and Adam's head and they never tried to experiment with explosive ingredients on their own. So it seems that there was too little real instruction to characterize the camp as a training camp.

Contrary to common mythology about this "Malakand camp," it was not an al Qaeda camp.[136] It was an independent camp, organized and paid for by Babar and Khyam, using independent former Pakistani fighters in Afghanistan, who were not al Qaeda. There is no evidence that either the maulana or his son Zubair had any connection to al Qaeda, except for the fact that they helped some of its members escape Afghanistan in the wake of the post-9/11 U.S. invasion of that country.

Qayum Drops Out

Upon his return home, Khawaja sent £1,000 to Babar, who desperately needed it for the departure of all the British trainees. Ali Khan flew back immediately, but Babar had to change the tickets for Sidique Khan and Shakil, who returned to Beeston on 7 August. Adam also had problems: his visa had expired and Babar had to bribe someone at the airport to allow him to fly back on 11 August. Shujah went to Karachi to spend 10 days with his father before flying back home to Crawley. Gulzar and Akbar spent time with their respective families before returning to Crawley.[137]

Around this time, Amin took Ayoub and Khyam to meet Abu Munthir. Up to that point, Abu Munthir had not been aware of any plot in the UK. Khyam and Ayoub wanted to brief him on what they had in mind and, in return, get some ideas from him. At their meeting, they discussed the political situation in Afghanistan and Pakistan. Abu Munthir told them he was at the battle of Shia Koat, better known as Operation Anaconda in the West. He said there had been about 35 foreigners and 45 Afghans fighting on his side. Yet the Western press had blown that skirmish out of proportion and claimed that several hundred mujahedin had been killed. Abu Munthir warned his visitors not to trust the Western media.[138]

When Ayoub and Khyam returned to Lahore about 10 days later, they briefed Babar that Abu Munthir wanted to see everyone involved in the plot, but they were now mostly gone. Abu Munthir was particularly interested in Babar, who was a U.S. citizen and spoke with an American accent. Babar was eager to meet Abu Munthir as well. Khyam talked about doing simultaneous multiple bombings in England targeting pubs, nightclubs, and train stations.[139]

The last week of August, Mohammed Qayum Khan flew to Islamabad with his family, as he wished to do hijrah in Pakistan. In early 2003, MI5 had obtained intelligence that he was the leader of an al-Qaeda facilitation network in the UK, designated him a "desirable" target, and began an investigation into his network, which it labeled Operation Crevice.[140] When Qayum flew to Pakistan, MI5 probably alerted ISID that Qayum was a suspect. Khyam, Ayoub, and Amin came to welcome Qayum at the airport. Qayum wanted to meet Abu Munthir to get an update on the situation. When the group was driving around Rawalpindi, they spotted blatant police surveillance. Khyam emailed to Khawaja, "There is a big problem right, the spooks followed the brother and his family. . . . they had 4 cars after him, and I don't know where he is."[141] Qayum had taken refuge in his ancestral village. He and his family aborted their plan for hijrah and returned to Luton after two weeks.[142] This experience may have completely spooked out Qayum, who did very little in support of the Afghan jihad from then on.

The blatant surveillance on Qayum made Amin order a complete standdown of the group's activities and postponed Babar's trip to see Abu Munthir. Khyam and Ayoub returned to Babar's flat in Lahore. They experimented with an explosive mixture using the ratios learned in Kohat and poured it in a jar, which was tested in Babar's backyard. The jar blew apart; Khyam believed it was an explosion but Ayoub and Babar were skeptical because small lumps of mixture were scattered around without having gone through combustion. Nevertheless, Khyam and Ayoub flew back to England on 31 August, with ten packets of aluminum powder. Babar had to bribe someone at the airport to help Ayoub leave since his visa had expired.[143]

After all the British wannabes had left, Babar asked Amin for more detonators and a rescheduled meeting with Abu Munthir. Amin said that he had buried the detonators and strongly advised him to stand down on meeting with Abu Munthir until it was safer. In turn, Amin requested all the leftover gear that the trainees had used at the training camp—boots, jackets, gloves, sleeping bags, and so on—for Abu Munthir's group, which desperately needed them. Babar complied and continued to collect money for the jihad. Khyam had left left him some and Babar kept a little for his anticipated trip to transport the detonators through Europe.[144]

Back in Britain

Upon their return to England, the trainees resumed their everyday home lives and tried to make sense of their experience. Rahman Adam seemed content to just vegetate at home and hang out with his friends. "I was very, very happy, excited," he later testified. "Just the fact that I was back, I was safe, I was going to see my family and friends. . . . I had quite a long time of chill-out period. . . . I've come back, I've done what I wanted to do, and I just wanted to start kind of . . . living a normal life." He let his friends think he had undergone proper "training" and avoided giving them any details for fear that they would think it had been a "joke." His friends looked up to him, Lamine supported him financially, and Khyam still owed him about £3,000. Although he did not worry about making a living at the time, he worried about the loans he had taken out before going to Pakistan. Now that his desire for jihad was gone, he wanted to pursue a modeling career and get a girlfriend. He officially changed his name to Anthony Garcia because he believed that it was a better stage name for his career and hoped to evade the debts issued in his old name. He got a passport in his new name on 22 September 2003.[145] He went back to nightclubs and in mid-October met a young woman named Sara S., who was a nonobservant Muslim, half Egyptian and half New Zealander. Their frequent meetings suffered from a lack of privacy: he was living with his parents and she with an aunt.[146] Garcia asked Khyam for his money back and discussed resumption of his fund-raising for the Kashmiri cause. Although Khyam did not yet have the money, he told Garcia he was working on it. As Garcia spent more time with Sara, he gradually faded out of Khyam's circle.

Immediately after his return, Omar Khyam spent a week with his wife, Saira, at a motel. His priority now was to sort out his marriage. Most members of their respective families did not know about it. Her brother Azhar had informed their mother, but her father was still in the dark. Her family came from an inferior tribe and was afraid that Khyam would not look after their daughter properly. The couple decided to straighten out their marriage in the South Asian way and have his mother offer a formal marriage proposal to her family. Meanwhile his mother urged him to get a serious job now that he had family responsibility. He started but dropped out of a business course and a Certificate in English Language Teaching to Adult (CELTA) course. Instead, he went to visit his father in Brussels for a few days in October 2003.[147]

Except for Garcia, who drifted away, the trainees' common experience at Gorque forged strong bonds among them. Sidique and Shakil stayed in touch with Khyam and occasionally came down to Crawley.[148] They were proud of their achievement; Akbar summed it up: "That was wicked."[149] He got more involved in Islam, not just jihad: he dressed up in religious clothes and wanted to make hijrah. He became convinced that Muslims should live in a Muslim country and he wanted to help the children in the NWFP as their poverty had shocked him. He discussed this with Khyam, who told his friend that he also planned to return there the next year but advised Akbar to sort out his marriage beforehand. Khyam explained that this would allow his wife to live with his family after his departure. Khyam also suggested they raise as much money as possible for their trip through fraudulent loans.[150]

Akbar and his wife, Sundeep, took jobs at Brunel University. Sundeep rented a flat for them at Colley House in the town center, right next to the university. Before moving in, Akbar stayed with his 18-year-old cousin, Nabeel Hussain, who was reading politics and international affairs there. Akbar tried to involve his cousin in religion, but Hussain liked to play games on the computer and watch DVDs instead. Akbar moved into the flat on 1 October. He and Sundeep split the rent, but her parents refused to let her move out of the house and required her to return home every night. She drove in early in the morning so they could walk together to work. They had lunch together, spent time together in the flat, and she drove back home in the evening. After two weeks, her car broke down, forcing her to commute by bus, where she got hassled one evening. Akbar got upset and borrowed Khyam's car to pick her up in the mornings and drop her off in the evenings. After her evening departures, the flat became the meeting place for Akbar's Crawley friends. Khyam was often visiting Saira in London and sometimes would stay overnight at the flat or with Hussain at the dorm. Ali Khan once moved in with Akbar for a few days. On weekends, they all returned to Crawley to hang out with their friends. If Khyam was still in London, he gave them a lift back. Akbar joined the school's Islamic Society for political discussions. He continued to contribute money to Khyam, who passed it on to Garcia. Akbar also tried to get his wife more involved in Islam and introduced her to Saira in October.[151]

Meanwhile, Waheed Mahmood had earned a certificate of competence in gas safety and gas appliances, which enabled him to work as a gas engineer on domestic projects. On 23 November 2003, he joined Morrison Utility Services, a contracting company that renewed and maintained gas mains and other utility infrastructure. Morrison trained him to work alone investigating gas leaks and issued him basic equipment and a laptop loaded with sensitive information, including maps of gas mains.[152] Mahmood saw his younger Crawley friends on weekends.

Khawaja's Online Romance: A Window into the Global Neojihadi State of Mind

In Canada, Khawaja was still using Zenab's account for funding his friends' activities. At some point, she discussed her involvement with him with other friends and realized that what she had gotten into was not right. She closed her account on 23 September 2003.[153]

After his return, Khawaja had started an online romance with an Islamabad woman, Zeba K. His correspondence with her demonstrates the mindset of the militants involved in Crevice. Like Rahman Adam's diary, it was contemporaneous, not a post hoc justification of jihad or written for posterity, and expressed beliefs and feelings for a good friend. On 8 August 2003, he wrote:

> I did try leaving before, after Afghanistan happened, I left and went to Pakistan like many emotionally charged brothers, intending never to return, vowing to become the West's mortal enemies. A few months later, circumstances forced almost everyone back. After I returned, I realized the sad truth that not many people are willing to part with their Western lives for the sake of helping the cause of *Deen* [religion]. . . . People . . . show . . . concern when they hear something is happening, but at the end of the day . . . life just goes on. I was not content with . . . pretend[ing] you can't . . . change anything, while the Muslim world is in flames. I . . . met some amazing bros in the UK, who felt the same way. . . . We headed for Pakistan again, and it was the most amazing and unforgettable

experience of our lives. We went to the north tribal areas . . . and trekked to a village in the mountains. . . . *Alhumdulillah*, I made my intention then to leave the West permanently. That was two weeks ago.[154]

Zeba asked him about his goals. He replied, "My main goal is to live as a Muslim. . . . I strongly believe in . . . Hijra and Jihad. Basically, migrating to preserve and build our Deen, and supporting our oppressed brothers and sisters in any and every way possible, whether physically, financially, or morally, in deterring those who wish to destroy Islam and the Muslims."[155] She also wanted "to live and die as a Muslim, to die rather than return to ignorance and faithlessness. . . . I'm kinda looking for someone more active than I am so I can join them in Islamic Activism! (InshaAllah)."[156] Their courtship quickly progressed to the point where they started exchanging very long e-mails on a daily basis and discussed the possibility of marriage.

Khawaja outlined his intellectual journey: "when I came back here from Saudi in '93, I was a bit messed up since my parents had always sent us to American schools. The only thing I got from Saudi was Qur'anic recitation. In High School, I started to pray and read Qur'an regularly. I still wasn't 'into' deen. . . . It wasn't till later in College, the year 2000 Palestinian intifada, when my life changed. I started studying more Islamic books, learning more of the Deen, and following the Sunnah more in my life. Then right after I got out of College, the invasion of Afghanistan happened. That was a milestone, which gave direction to my life."[157]

In early September, Zeba told him that a piece of her fallopian tube was accidentally removed during a surgical operation, but she should still be able to have children. He reassured her, "I'll be sticking around."[158] On 15 September, she asked, "are you really into guns and warfare and weaponry and stuff?" She understood the necessity of fighting at times but rejected "glorifying the gore and explosions" because it "downplays the sanctity of life and the deadly seriousness of taking another's person's life" and promoted "a kind of war-like mentality that's always on. . . . Though, we . . . have in us the right to fight and defend, we shouldn't take that aspect and blow it out of proportion to the extent that we're war-mongers instead of Warriors. A war-monger uses fighting as his primary mode of doing everything, righteously or not. A warrior fights when it is necessary and correct to do so, and only when it is righteous."[159]

Khawaja replied with an impassionate defense of jihad. He was outraged by Western aggression slaughtering tens of thousands of Muslims, with whom he clearly identified:

Countless examples are there before us, to remind us of the severity of abandoning Jihad, putting down arms. From Bosnia, to Somalia, to Mazar-e-Sharif, to Algeria, each and every time we find the treachery of the Americans, the U.N., and their allies in convincing the Muslims, the *Mujahideen* in putting down their arms in exchange for "peace." Every instance the Muslims gave up arms, they were slaughtered. . . . This is the precise reason why there can be no peace, no negotiations, no deals whatsoever with the Kuffar because they are treacherous and only understand the language of death and destruction. . . . America is at war with Islam. . . . They have slaughtered tens of thousands of our brothers and sisters. The blood of the Ummah has been spilt. Who is there to stand up for us? . . . This is the precise reason for the Jihad, the training, warfare, weaponry, and war-like mentality against those who commit the acts of aggression. Islam does not permit us to be show-watchers, as how convenient that would be for us to see our own brothers and sisters being killed and not do anything?

The jihad must continue until all Muslim lands and mujahid prisoners are liberated, for doing otherwise would "mean that we have abandoned our Muslim brothers and sisters." More personally, "When the Palestinian intifada happened, I started looking into my own life and questioning myself as to why our situation was so bad. I realized that 'I' must change myself first, I must be willing to make a difference. Everyone assumes SOMEONE else is probably doing something to help, so why should 'I' bother. It's not true. No one does anything. If I want change, I have to do something about it." Khawaja was disillusioned with peaceful demonstrations. "Everyone is content with going to a few rallies, shouting slogans, 'down down Israel' 'down down U.S.A.' and that's it, we've done our part. What on earth does that do? Is this the response to mobilized armies, tanks, and missiles? Are the kuffar going to stop murdering our brothers and sisters because we raise banners and shout slogans?" If he did nothing in the face of Western aggression, his conscience would tear him apart. "It was then, by the will of Allah that I met a brother from England who was in the effort of Jihad, and part of a group of brothers who were leaving to go to Pakistan and join the Mujahideen already in Afghanistan. . . . I was able to join a few brothers and spend time at a Mujahideen training camp. It was there that we built our spiritual link with Allah, trained in the ways of Jihad, and devoted our lives to the uplifting of the *Deen* and defense of the Ummah." He concluded by asking her whether, now knowing his feelings, she wanted to withdraw from the courtship.[160] Her reply was, "I'm all in favor, just DON'T LEAVE ME BEHIND!"[161]

At the beginning of October, they decided he should come to Islamabad and ask her parents for her hand. Khawaja flew to London on 10 October and stayed with Khyam for a day. He volunteered to build a remote-control device to trigger a detonator for the attack in Britain. Khyam gave him money and material for the jihad and two SIM cards for Babar. Babar picked him up at Islamabad Airport on the morning of 13 October. Babar agreed to be his companion at the dinner with Zeba's parents three days later. Before that, they met Amin, and Khawaja gave him the money and supplies from Khyam. Amin told Khawaja that Abu Munthir needed night-vision goggles for night fighting and discussed using viruses to sabotage computers and some visualization software for a model airplane with a GPS navigation system to transform it into an explosive drone. At the scheduled dinner, Zeba's family accepted Khawaja's marriage proposal and Khawaja left the next day, 17 October.[162]

After his return to Ottawa, Khawaja wrote Khyam, "I will start on the remote devices thing right away. And will let u know once we have it ready for testing. . . . I think Kman ['Khalid,' or Salahuddin Amin] said they needed night vision goggles, and that stuff here is cheaper, so if u want we can try to get some . . . here at the cost of maybe 300 UK?" Khyam replied, "if they cheap then get them and anything else you think will be good."[163] Khawaja also continued to explain to Zeba his views of jihad. His under-standing was that Islamic jurisprudence did not allow stealing in general but permitted it for the jihad. "If a person is hungry and steals food because he cant afford it, then Islam does not punish that person for stealing. . . . Stealing from the kuffar to support the J is only done for the survival of the Ummah. . . . There is no personal gain here, because stealing for personal gain makes it actual theft." Khawaja went on to condone inadvertent civil-ian deaths as unfortunate collateral damage. He claimed that the East Africa embassies bombings thwarted a CIA plan to destroy and take over the Mus-lim countries of the region. "Yes, innocent people also died as a result, but there was no other way to stop the kuffar from plotting against the Muslims in that region. So sometimes things that seem wrong from face-value due to our lack of info or understanding . . . may in fact be very noble deeds with great long-term benefits for the Muslim Ummah." The 9/11 attacks crippled the American economy. "Imagine if there were 10 Sept. 11's, wouldn't that accurately bring America down, never to rise again? Yes, I understand that innocent human beings died, but there is absolutely no other way of achieving the same objective with the same effect. The intention was to bring down the U.S. economy, not harm innocent people."[164]

However, Khawaja's enthusiasm for Zeba quickly faded after meeting her. While she kept sending him e-mails on a daily basis, he replied about once a week. On 1 November, he wrote her, "Well, I talked to my mom, and, and we kinda hit a speed bump. I think we just need to discuss things about the wedding stuff and sort it out."[165] He finally broke up with her on 8 December: "I'm retracting my engagement proposal. With that, I ask that you not hold anything against me, and forgive me for anything and everything."[166]

Khawaja continued to work on his remote-control devices and kept Khyam informed as to his progress: "We can get the devices, the cost to make em is about 4 pounds each, remote detonation, I think the range is around 2 kilometers, it is small in size. . . . When I was in PK me and Kash [Babar] talked about Immy [Siddiqui], wats he gonna do there? We have a suggestion, to use the bro for a one-way operation to the most high. Maybe in Yahood land [Israel]. What do you think?"[167] Khyam responded, "let me know asap when u find out this is really good. . . . About imy we will need to discuss that in person." Khawaja replied, "we will try to have a few devices ready for testing give me 2 weeks, and I'll give u more details on how it works an stuff. . . . Abt Immy, we will talk in person bout that."[168] Meanwhile, Babar e-mailed Khawaja at the end of October, "Don't tell no one yeah but im planning on going back to the states via Canada yeah and wanted to know if I could borrow like 350 dollars. Ill pay you back by jan 1st insallah once I reach the states."[169]

The Purchase of the Fertilizer

Khawaja's rapid progress with the remote-control device, which he called "hifidigimonster," put pressure on Khyam to get his end of the plot organized. On 1 November 2003, he met Garcia, who came to collect money for the Kashmir cause. After giving him the cash, Khyam told Garcia that he needed him and his brother Lamine to do him a favor. Garcia agreed without knowing what it was. Two days later, Khyam called Garcia to tell him that it was for the next evening. Garcia replied that Lamine could make it, but that he had a date with his girlfriend that night. Khyam said that they were going to rent a room at a Holiday Inn near Gatwick and could book an extra one for him and his girlfriend. Garcia jumped at this invitation as he had not yet spent a night with Sara. When he told her about it, she was "pretty happy."[170]

Late on the evening of 4 November, Lamine and Garcia picked up Sara and drove to the hotel. Khyam and possibly Gulzar and Ali Khan greeted them in one room while Sara went to an adjacent room and waited for her boyfriend. Khyam talked privately with Lamine and Garcia in the corridor. He told them that the brothers in Pakistan had asked him to get some fertilizer and ship it out to them. He feared that his South Asian appearance might arouse suspicion. Lamine asked why could they not get it over there, and Khyam replied, "It's just complicated." Khyam insisted he needed it "ASAP. Tomorrow morning if you can." Lamine was working in the morning but Garcia was willing to help.[171] Khyam asked him to get a small bag so he could make sure it was the right stuff before shipping it to Pakistan. Khyam, as John, had already called Bodle Brothers, ordered a 50-kilogram bag of ammonium nitrate, and told them he would collect it in the morning. Garcia just needed to go there and get it. Khyam gave Garcia directions to the store. After the quick conversation, Garcia entered Sara's room.[172]

Garcia got up midmorning next day. Khyam had rented a car for him. He and Sara drove to Bodle Brothers. Garcia inquired about the bag. The sales clerk asked what Garcia was going to do with it, and Garcia replied that it was for some land or allotment. The clerk suggested that it would work out cheaper if he got a 600-kilogram bag that was also available. Garcia bought the 50-kilogram bag and the couple drove back to the hotel with it. Garcia told Khyam about his conversation with the clerk. He and Sara returned to London in their own car.

That evening, Khyam called Garcia and asked him whether he could exchange the smaller for the larger bag. Garcia drove back to the store the next day, returned the smaller bag, and bought the larger one for £90. He needed an open-back kind of truck or van to haul the bag away and informed Khyam about it.[173] The next day, Khyam asked Nabeel Hussain whether he could use his debit card. Hussain thought it was fine as he knew that Khyam would pay him back. Among their group, this mutual borrowing was not a cause for suspicion. Khyam told him he needed identification and Hussain got his passport.[174]

Over the weekend, someone downloaded *The Mujahideen Explosives Handbook* on Akbar's computer. Khyam found a storage place for the fertilizer, Access Storage in Ealing, and asked Garcia to check it out and inquire about prices for a few weeks. Garcia was starting to get annoyed at Khyam, for the "one-time favor" just kept dragging on. Nevertheless, the next day, Garcia drove to Ealing to see whether the storage room could accommodate the 600-kilogram bag and got a leaflet with the price information. Someone called Access Storage that afternoon and made a deposit for the storage room giving Hussain's financial details. The next day, 11 November, Khyam and Ashraf rented a van, which Garcia and Ashraf drove to Bodle Brothers to pick up the fertilizer. On the way to Access Storage, Khyam and Hussain replaced Ashraf in the van. The three then drove to Access Storage and dropped off their cargo. Storage costs were £207.45 per month. The next day, Khyam repaid Garcia the first £500 slice of his loan.[175]

The Plot Slows Down

In Pakistan, Babar picked up from Western Union Khawaja's $650 for his trip back to the United States and Khyam's £2,500 for the cost of transporting the detonators overland to Europe. Babar and his family moved in with his in-laws after carefully cleaning out his Lahore flat to erase any trace of bomb making. He got a new U.S. passport on 17 November 2003 at the U.S. consulate and filled out the paperwork to bring his wife and daughter back with him.[176]

Khawaja notified Khyam on 10 November that he had hit a snag with the hifidigimonster, "just small delay cause of fastin an all . . . hopefully we shud get somethin in a few weeks . . . its all happenin."[177] With the pressure off, the London side of the plot slowed down during the last part of Ramadan, the monthlong holiday that requires Muslims to fast during the day. The conspirators sometimes met to break the fast together in the evening. At the end of Ramadan, Mahmood started to hold study sessions on either Friday or Saturday evenings, which Khyam, Shujah, Gulzar, and Ali Khan attended regularly. Shujah was hoping to change his lifestyle through religion, praying, and studying. He became anxious when he had to write essays or make speeches and dropped out. He was not truly religious but now wanted to become a Quran reciter when he found out that recitation masters in the Muslim world were like pop stars in the West. He collected famous reciters' tapes and CDs and started imitating them. He often listened to a CD or tape when he was with his brother or would practice reciting verses of the Quran. Khyam and Akbar told him that he was very good at it, which made him proud.[178]

In December, Gulzar invited Akbar to the study circle. In December, Mahmood taught about the life of the Prophet, in connection with the book he was writing. They talked about the Hadiths, the sayings of the Prophet and their authentication process. They also talked about the political situation, jihad, and how jihad applied to the current times. Since Mahmood was the oldest and most educated one in the circle, the other members also sought him out for personal advice. Akbar gradually adopted his friends' radical views. He now viewed the invasion of Iraq and general jihad activities in black-and-white terms. It was Muslims against non-Muslims, believers against nonbelievers. He watched the news regularly and became very upset when non-Muslims were attacking Muslims.[179]

Once Ramadan was over, Khyam was ready to resume his activities. He queried Khawaja, who replied, "We still need a few weeks bro, its not as easy as we thought it would be. . . . We pray to the most high we can do this in December."[180]

After the fertilizer purchase, Garcia only saw his friends when collecting funds for the Kashmiri cause. He worked nights at Tesco's, a large grocery and general merchandise retailer, and was also very busy looking for modeling jobs. He spent his free time with Sara, as their relationship became quite serious. On 19 December 2003, he and Lamine left their parents' home when they rented a two-bedroom flat, each taking a bedroom. Lamine paid the rent and Garcia helped with the rest of the bills. Sara moved in with Garcia.[181]

In mid-December 2003, Khyam rented a flat in Slough to be able to spend more time with his wife, Saira. However, she still had to return home for the night since they were not legally married. They got a temporary job together at a company, which designed advertisements on the Yellow Pages. Saira went for hajj around 18 January 2004. A few days later, Khyam asked his brother Shujah to move in with him because he was lonely. His brother-in-law Azhar was also a frequent visitor. Khyam was bored and thinking about making hijrah to Pakistan.[182]

Babar Meets Abdal Hadi al Iraqi: Afghanistan Is Open!

During the fall, Zeeshan Siddiqui had complained to Mufti Babar that Khyam and Mohammed Babar had wasted funds for the jihad in frivolous expenses and that Babar was keeping his passport. There was also a deep rivalry between Kazi Rahman's East London group and Khyam's Crawley group. To resolve these disputes, Mufti Babar took Babar and Siddiqui to see Abdal Hadi al Iraqi around the New Year.[183] Babar wanted to meet Abdal Hadi both to meet a top al Qaeda leader and to clarify the confusing situation in England. "The differences between Ausman [Khyam] and Haleem [Kazi Rahman] had just spilled out, and it was a lot of confusion on who was working with whom, and there was a lot of back-talking going on," Babar later recalled. Babar introduced himself as Iqbal Shah and told Abdal Hadi that his mother had escaped from the World Trade Center on September 11. Abdal Hadi responded, "Glory be to Allah." When Babar asked him about Khyam, Amin, or Kazi Rahman, he confessed he had never heard of them. He confirmed that Abu Munthir was one of his deputies, and it was possible that they could be working with Abu Munthir, but he did not know them. When Babar also asked him whether British militants could come and fight in Afghanistan, he replied, "People can come but we need them to commit for at least a year." Abdal Hadi did not want people just coming out for a month's thrill, shooting off an AK-47, and going back home instead of doing their bit for the jihad.[184]

After Babar returned home, he called Khyam and told him that he had just seen Abdal Hadi and was coming to England to sort things out between Khyam and Kazi Rahman.[185]

Babar's January 2004 Visit

On one of Amin's regular supply runs around the New Year 2004, Abu Munthir asked him to try to contact a friend or relative of his in Belgium about a radioisotope bomb. Abu Munthir gave Amin the name, Abu Anas, and telephone number. Abu Munthir did not want to contact him, as he believed that communications were monitored. After returning home, Amin chatted with Abu Anas over the Internet. Abu Anas told him that he had some laptops for Abu Munthir and asked whether Abu Munthir needed fake Euros. "Abu Anas told me that they had . . . made . . . contact with the Russian mafia in Belgium and from them they are trying to buy this radio isotope bomb. . . . He told me to ask Abu Munthir what we should do about it. . . . I went back . . . [and] had a word with Abu Munthir about it, and he said he would get back to me." Adding radioactive material to a bomb creates a radioactive or "dirty bomb." Amin did not think this lead was genuine because radioactive substances were a big deal and unlikely to be available on the open market. Abu Munthir was also skeptical, but asked Amin to get more information. Amin sent his brother to Belgium to meet with Abu Anas.[186]

In mid-January 2004, Babar came to London. "I was the only one out of everybody that had actually met Abdul Hadi and I came here to clear everything up," he later said.[187] Kazi Rahman had antagonized his former followers. Mohammed Babar had initially believed his claim that Khyam had wasted money destined for jihad with frivolous hotel stays. Because he seemed to be siding with its rival, the Crawley cluster had become suspicious of Babar, but Khyam had vouched for him. Babar again stayed with Zaheer Ali, but after the latter went to Mecca, Babar then stayed with his New York friend Syed Hashmi, who was studying in London at the time. Babar first met privately with Khyam, who repeated his claim to be working for Abdal Hadi via Abu Munthir. Babar informed Khyam that Abdal Hadi now welcomed British militants to come and fight in Afghanistan as long as they were committed to stay for a year.[188]

Babar then held a series of meeting with the East London militants (the Jabber brothers, Kazi Rahman, and Ayoub), the Crawley cluster (Ashraf, Mahmood, Khyam, Shuja, Gulzar, Ali Khan, and Akbar), and the Adam family and friends. He briefed them on his conversation with Abdal Hadi, assured them that the money they had raised actually went to al Qaeda, and told them that Afghanistan was now open for committed jihadis. Some of the East London militants were still skeptical about his claims and asked him whether he could broker a meeting for Tanveer Ali and another militant, Ansar Butt, with the al Qaeda leader. Babar agreed in principle. At that point, he received a call from his wife in Pakistan telling him she was sick with diarrhea and the baby had scabies. He returned immediately to Pakistan on 3 February 2004.[189]

The opening of the Afghan front strengthened Khyam's desire to immigrate to Pakistan. He had told Babar that he planned to come in April and asked Babar to get a flat for him in Islamabad.[190] Khyam asked Shujah to come with him to Pakistan. Shujah knew that his brother was planning to go and fight in Afghanistan. Khyam and Akbar had been telling him about the rape of women and the killing of people in Afghanistan. Khyam showed him videos that outraged him and he was ready to help. He went with his brother when they made various inquiries about airline tickets and prices. They went shopping for outdoor clothing together. At the trial, Shujah said that at first, he was excited about going to fight but gradually became anxious about it. He was afraid to tell his brother about his anxiety as he thought it would make Khyam angry. He asked his brother what he could do in Pakistan and his brother told him he could go to college.[191]

Operation Crevice

Unbeknownst to the Crawley cluster, MI5 had identified Omar Khyam as a courier for the Qayum network in the Crevice investigation. This identification happened in late January 2004, and MI5 put Khyam under limited surveillance.

On 25 January, Khawaja announced to Khyam that he had made some progress on the hifidigimonster and was planning to come to Britain to show them: "Gimme a week or two. In the meantime we'll test out the stuff." Khyam responded, "I hope to see u soon nigga, so we can see it too. when u come can u bring the 1000 pounds with you?" Khawaja answered a week later that he would bring the money: "how should I bring the devices? i don't know if its safe to bring that on the plane, u think? . . . Any ideas on how I shud bring it over?"[192] Khyam responded he would let him know.

Meanwhile, several of the conspirators in England scattered to celebrate Eid with their relatives. The Adam brothers went to Spain for a week to celebrate it with cousins and returned on 6 February 2004.[193] Khyam and Shujah went to Brussels to celebrate it with their father. They returned to Stansted Airport, and underwent a thorough search on arrival. The authorities examined Khyam's laptop and telephone. Apparently, they had been watching jihadi films on them.[194]

In early February, based on new intelligence, which was probably the alarming e-mail exchanges between Khawaja and Khyam, the Security Service changed its assessment on Khyam. It now strongly suspected Khyam to be part of a bomb plot probably aimed at the UK. At this point, Khyam became one of the service's top targets and Operation Crevice became its top priority—an "essential" target. This meant that its focus was not only on preventing the plot from succeeding but also on gathering evidence that could eventually be used in court.

On 8 February, Khawaja wrote Khyam: "I'm thinking of comin down on . . . February 20th. . . . I just want to do a demo of it and show you how it works and stuff, its range, and other things . . . so we gotta find a way we can get it into UK, maybe I can courier it over. . . . We're startin to work on a few other much more sophisticated projects that can be of great benefit to the J, I'll speak to you about them when we meet." Khyam replied two days later, "20th feb shud fine nigga. . . . I think the best thing is to make one here, I think it will be too dangerous to mail or send anything." Khawaja later responded that the devices would be too hard to make in England because all his parts and equipments were at home.[195]

Probably further alarmed by this exchange, the next day, 11 February, an executive liaison group (ELG) for Operation Crevice was formed to coordinate and allocate Security Service and police work. It enables MI5 to safely share secret, sensitive, and often raw intelligence (such as electronic intercepts) with the police, and make decisions about how best to gather evidence (such as eavesdropping and surveillance) and prosecute the suspects in court. It also assessed all of the people Khyam met and spoke to see if they were involved in the plan to attack the UK. It reached an apparent triage system: some contacts were involved in criminal activity, others were in the "facilitation" part of Crevice, and a few were actively involved in the alleged bomb plot. As public safety was their top priority, MI5 and the police concentrated on those who were actually talking about a terrorist attack.[196]

The next day, Khyam called Access Storage as "Nabeel Hussain" to check whether the February 2004 payment had gone through. This was the first contact between any conspirator and Access Storage since 11 November 2003.[197] Hussain's bank account was overdrawn as his original understanding with Khyam had been that his card would just pay for one month and not ongoing payments, as was the case. Access Storage had called Hussain to say that the debit did not operate. Hussain was no longer seeing Khyam and called him to sort out this mess.[198]

The same day, Qayum, the original target of Operation Crevice, called Khyam from a public telephone to arrange a meeting. That evening, around midnight, Khyam drove to meet Qayum who got into Khyam's car. Khyam gave Qayum some money and told Qayum about his plans to go to Pakistan in a few weeks. Qayum told Khyam that it was better that they did not stay in touch in case the Security Services were watching them for fear of detection. Khyam returned home after the meeting.[199]

On 18 February, an Access Storage staff member called the police anti-terrorist hotline saying that someone had been storing a 600-kilogram bag of fertilizer there since 11 November 2003, and it seemed suspicious. This call was the result of a chance informal conversation among the staff, which realized that fertilizer could be used as an explosive material. The police visited the storage unit later that same day and got details of the rental agreement. They photographed the bag and took samples for analysis. The information obtained confirmed their suspicions that a domestic bomb attack was imminent. For them, Khyam had not only had the intent but also the capability to launch an attack.[200]

The same day, Khawaja wrote: "For the devices . . . I can courier that stuff over, otherwise we can send them over later and maybe show you some pics of what it looks like. . . . I'll bring the cash with me." Khyam replied, "about the device its better we leave it wil xplain later we will discuss it and maybe show pics at most."[201] Khawaja took pictures of the hifi-digimonster, loaded them onto his computer, and transferred them onto his Yahoo account.[202]

Back in Pakistan, Babar took Ansar Butt and Tanvir Ali separately to meet Abdal Hadi, who assured the Londoners that Babar was indeed providing money and supplies to him.[203] These two meetings eliminated any skepticism toward Babar and Khyam. As Khyam later wrote Khawaja, "a lot of the brothers that doubted us yeah they came back and apologized to us. . . . We exposed the people that were lying . . . slandering."[204]

Khyam, his brother Shujah, his brother-in-law Azhar, and three Beeston militants were planning to return to Pakistan for jihad in March.[205] Akbar had originally intended to go with them, but at the beginning of the year, he started to have second thoughts.

> I think . . . because the time was coming closer and closer . . . the reality was beginning to dawn on me. I started looking at my last experience when I went to Pakistan. And my wife, I started realizing that she didn't become a Muslim because she believed in Islam; she became a Muslim because of me, emotionally. So, she was not going to come to Pakistan with me, and I was scared to leave her here, and the fact that I would have to do a runner from my parents, because you can't tell—most Muslim parents are okay

with the resistance, but they don't want their own son to go there. So, I couldn't tell them, and I would have to finish indeed my degree, which is quite a waste because I was going to be in my final year and I would have finished it if I stayed one year more. So, these were the four main things which were beginning to shake me, if you want to call it, in not going to Pakistan.

He shared these hesitations with Khyam, who still tried to convince him to go. Akbar's relationship with his wife "was going downhill. . . . So, when I'm delivering these [jihadi] views to her . . . she finds it incredibly disgusting, sick, vile, whatever you want to call it. . . . We were just getting further and further apart."[206]

Khawaja's February 2004 Visit: The Hifidigimonster

On the morning of 20 February 2004, Khyam and Shujah picked up Khawaja at London Heathrow Airport and drove him to Khyam's flat in Slough. On the way, in the car, Khyam warned his brother and Khawaja about the need for secrecy, for keeping activities to small groups, and for using strict compartmentation to avoid detection and arrest. "We have to be professional," he said.[207] The appearance of Khawaja further alarmed MI5 and the police, who believed he was an electronics expert, advising Khyam and his associates on the construction and operation of a remote detonation device.[208]

Once inside Khyam's flat, Khyam told Khawaja that there were six militants ready to move permanently to Pakistan for jihad. They expected to leave in March. Khawaja said that he could also come, but after the third week of March. Khyam advised Khawaja to buy camping equipment and clothes in Canada first. They discussed the necessity of getting long-range night-vision goggles. Khawaja described his remote-control device. They drove to a local Internet café, where Khawaja accessed a document in his account named "hifidigimonster" and showed his hosts photographs of the device. In the evening, they went to visit Akbar at his Colley House flat.[209]

The next morning, the ELG met and discussed the discovery of the large quantity of fertilizer at Access Storage. Its summary stated: "The group agreed to establish whether the target group have purchased any further quantities of fertilizer in addition to that identified. It is a real possibility that planning for more than one device is underway. . . . SyS [Security

Service] assess that turning the fertilizer in the lock up into a viable device will be a lengthy process. 'We still have no indication of target or timing for any attack, though mid March appears to feature as a significant time period. We should seek to develop the evidence and intelligence, and consider drawing other targets into the conspiracy.' "[210]

At Khyam's flat in Slough, Khawaja and Shujah reminisced about their experiences at the Gorque camp. Khawaja issued a general invitation: "You guys should come for a few days out in Canada, go shooting and stuff, it would be fun."[211] In the evening, the trio went to Gulzar's house in Crawley, where Gulzar, Mahmood, Akbar, and three Beeston militants among others welcomed them.[212] This was probably one of Mahmood's evening study circles, which usually met at Gulzar's house.

During the course of the evening, Khyam, Shujah, and the three Beeston boys went to get some kebabs and had a conversation about their upcoming trip to Pakistan. Khyam urged them to engage in scams to finance their trip and promised them that he could help them pull off the frauds.[213] The ELG misinterpreted the talk about leaving the country as the conspirators being "jumpy." Instead of correctly assessing that they had abandoned their bombing plot a month earlier (true, they had just discovered that Khyam was storing large amount of fertilizer just then, and Khawaja was visiting Khyam to show his remote-controlled device) and now desired to go and fight in Afghanistan, it became more alarmed. It believed that Khyam "and the other Crevice plotters were heard talking about leaving the country. MI5 thought this might be an escape plan for after an attack and, therefore, that the attack might be imminent."[214]

Khyam, his brother, and Khawaja stayed at Gulzar's house overnight. They returned to Khyam's flat early the next morning, 22 February 2004. They talked about how to ship camping equipment to Pakistan. Around midday, Khyam drove Khawaja back to the airport to catch his flight back to Ottawa.[215]

The Alleged Ministry of Sound Target

The evening of Khawaja's departure, Khyam and Shujah went to visit Akbar at his Colley House flat. The long conversation was another window into their frame of mind. Small selected parts of this conversation were widely broadcast to the public to give the impression that Khyam and Akbar were targeting the Ministry of Sound nightclub to protest the decadence of lewd dancing. This of course fit the government's narrative that they were al Qaeda fanatics attacking the West because of its values. However, these excerpts were taken out of context and the government and media distorted their meaning, which can only be recovered by restoring their context.[216]

After generally discussing the situation in Pakistan, Khyam's leaving his flat "in about two weeks," and the increasingly punitive counterterrorism measures in Britain, they broached Akbar's hesitation about going to Pakistan with his friends. Akbar intended to seek Mahmood's advice the next day about going with them. They discussed the need for foreign fighters in Afghanistan. Khyam speculated on why al Qaeda had closed Afghanistan and thought it simply could not accommodate the foreign fighters who would have been sitting idle in a safe house. Akbar asked, "Do you think they do need people?" and Khyam replied, "The Jihad will always need people. . . . To me the Jihad is basically just three things: you support it physically, financially, and verbally," meaning encouraging others to go to the front.[217]

Akbar asked why, after Gorque, had the brothers returned to England and not stayed in Pakistan for jihad? Khyam complained that, while he respected and trusted Mahmood and his knowledge, he did not trust the other brothers. Akbar said, "I don't want to go there and be back in two months because I'm just screwed. . . . For me, to go, I'm going to be doing a runner from my parents . . . which will probably emotionally kill them. I'm leaving my wife, leaving things just like everyone else, leaving a lot, yeah. So, all I want to know is why would everyone come back then?" Khyam lied that Garcia was working with a different cell and sent back to raise money and so had a legitimate reason to be here. He also was in the same situation, as he had to arrange things with his family before going back. Ali Khan could not handle it and Gulzar had just wanted to come back. They had learned from it. "So now, the brothers that are going, we told them there's no coming back." Even if they cannot handle it, "this time, we're not letting them go."[218]

Khyam, who no longer came regularly to Mahmood's Friday circles, assumed that Mahmood was still pursuing his plan outlined the previous February and had recruited the participants in his circles to carry it out. Khyam thought that this strategy of infiltrating utilities companies (gas, electricity, water, alarm systems) and carrying out simultaneous attacks against them would have a huge impact on the economy: something goes wrong and the electricity goes out, alarms cut out, and so on. Akbar deplored the fact that people did not care about small explosions or the events in Pakistan or Iraq. Khyam agreed, unless "it was such a big explosion that hundreds of people died, such a big impact." He referred to the 1984 Bhopal disaster in India: "Now imagine something like that happened and bin Laden was behind it. The same news would be quadrupalized in . . . everything." Akbar cited the 9/11 attack as an example of such a large attack and added, "I only see it as a great thing now because I understand it now." He again deplored people's indifference to human suffering, especially victims in Iraq. "We were seeing babies being carried burnt yesterday, yeah, and the only person, who actually [had] tears come out of his eyes was Abdul Waheed [Mahmood]. . . . The only reason we know is because we know it's *Fard* [obligation] upon us to know what is going on about the Ummah and that's why we read the news." Something had to be the size of a 9/11 operation to affect people. When the electricity had gone down in their neighborhood in Crawley two years earlier, nothing happened. There was no panic, no terror. Khyam agreed, "unless you have this planned, what you want to do . . . the brothers need to be . . . simultaneously in different fields."[219]

Akbar returned to his theme of people going to Pakistan and coming back: "You know, when we used to do these . . . circles . . . at Friday nights and I used to say . . . why go all the way there . . . when you can do stuff here, why are we not doing it?" They now faced the same punishment if they did something abroad or at home with the Terrorist Act. "You're gonna go down for the same amount of time, so why not do something here? . . . Everyone just went quiet, and no one said anything, and Abdul Waheed just changed the topic." Khyam transitioned back to his theme of the necessity of simultaneous attacks: "Unless you know how to do it simultaneously, at a large scale . . . which needs big planning and you need to be well into your companies like (unclear) . . . worked ten years and now he's got free access."[220]

Akbar picked up on this thread, but countered, "What about stuff like easy, easy stuff where you don't need no experience and nothing? . . . You could get a job . . . [in] for example, the biggest nightclub in central London, where . . . no one can even turn around and say 'oh, they were innocent,' those slags dancing around and other things. . . . You haven't even got that thing. . . . I was thinking all nightclubs . . . dance and . . . bars. . . . If you went for the social structure, where every Tom, Dick and Harry goes on a Saturday night, yeah, that would be crazy, crazy man. Like you said, you need a lot of organizing, a lot of planning, but how do you meet people like that?" Khyam asked Akbar, "If you got a job in a bar, yeah, or a club, say the Ministry of Sound, what are you planning to do there then?" Akbar replied, "Blow the whole thing up!" Khyam approved, "That's what I'm saying . . . the resources from this country, the electricity, the gas, going into the alarm engineers, stuff like this . . . is good, get brothers in each and every field, from the gas to the electric to the water to the alarm engineers, everything."[221]

The turn of the conversation suddenly frightened Akbar: "Bruv . . . you don't think this place is bugged, do you?" Khyam reassured him, "No, I don't think it's bugged, bruv, at all. I don't even think the car is bugged." He insisted that, if the authorities knew what he was doing, they would not wait one day to arrest him unless they were playing some mad game. He returned to his theme of simultaneous attacks on the utilities infrastructure. "Unless, they're in each one of these fields, and they've been in there for let's say about five years . . . and they've got access to all areas and . . . simultaneously . . . the electricity is cut out and another brother cuts the alarms, so no back service can be called, no emergency services, and then a gas explosion or something, yeah, do you understand? . . . That's not easy, bruv, that's a lot of planning, a lot of *sabar* [patience]."[222]

They both agreed that bombing a nightclub would be relatively easy: people could go abroad for training and come back. Akbar asked, "So, why hasn't this thing been done before?" Khyam answered that England was a difficult country to get in from abroad because it was an island and it was very good at protecting itself. Akbar repeated his question of why not do it in England if one is going to go down anyway. Khyam replied, "Unless you have a proper plan, simultaneously, it's got to be big and effective. . . . To the extent where it's . . . gonna raise eyebrows . . . then do it. . . . [If] it affects a lot of people, that's really difficult to do, bro. To get them into the Ministry of Sound really isn't difficult, once you've got it inside the UK (unclear). . . . But once you've got it here, bro, that's it [meaning it would be their only opportunity to do so]." Any attack had to be carefully prepared in Pakistan, but the trainers there wanted to make sure that their trainees would actually carry out the operation. Akbar asked whether Khyam ever discussed this with Mahmood. Khyan said no.[223]

Akbar asked about Khyam's impending departure: "What are you going to do about your wife?" Khyam answered that he would wait a couple of months and then bring his wife to Pakistan.[224] Akbar promised he would discuss with Mahmood his possible trip to Pakistan. They concluded by talking about some of the verses of the Quran and both agreed that they did not have the faith to do martyrdom operations.

This lengthy conversation startled MI5 and the police, who interpreted the loose talk about the the the Ministry of Sound nightclub or the mass disruption of utilities as *possible targets of the definitive bombing plot.* Seven years later, the Security Service wrote the following assessment for the Coroner's Inquests of its contemporaneous understanding of Crevice: "On 22 February 2004, KHYAM was heard considering a number of possible targets: a. a nightclub; b. water or gas utilities; c. targets that could be accessed by extremists who were engaged as water, gas, electricity or alarm engineers."[225] The fact that it made no comment to correct its alarmist and misleading interpretation of the actual conversation is startling. To my knowledge, the full transcript of the conversation has never been released in Britain, but it was part of the discovery material in the Khawaja case in Canada.

Preparations for Departure: Fraud

Operation Crevice moved into an even more intensive phase, with round-the-clock monitoring of Khyam. During the night of 24–25 February, MI5 and the police replaced the fertilizer bag at Access Storage with an identical one containing a harmless watered-down substance. A forensic scientist examined the original content and concluded that it was potentially explosive if mixed with a fuel. To explode 600 kilograms of ammonium nitrate in one go would have required about 300–400 kilograms of aluminum powder. To become a bomb, it also needed a detonator and a device to activate the detonator. MI5 did not know whether the group had more fertilizer stored elsewhere.[226]

The day after his long discussion with Khyam, Akbar asked Mahmood for advice about going to Pakistan. Mahmood encouraged him to first finish his degree and then go: "So just in case you don't finish your degree and you've left everything here and don't get to the front, you've wasted two or three years of your life."[227]

Khyam was continuing his preparations for his upcoming departure. He had several discussions with the rest of his ready-to-travel companions about raising money by fraudulent means and disappearing with it in Pakistan. His main scheme was with his uncle Saj, who owned a few construction companies. Khyam bought an off-the-shelf construction company and applied for credit from a variety of building companies. He then got on credit some building material, which he sold at half price to his uncle. This way, Khyam cashed in half of the credit value for himself and his uncle got the material at half price. He was able to raise several thousand pounds through this scheme. Azhar Khan and the Beeston men also took part in similar fraudulent schemes.

On 28 February, surveillance observed Khyam, Shujah, and three Beeston men make a series of visits to builders' merchants. They then traveled together to an HFC Bank near Luton, where Khyam knew someone who was able to ensure the approval of his applications. The next day, he applied for a loan at HFC Bank allegedly to pay off his credit cards and buy a car. On 5 March, he received £16,000 from the bank. At the same time, he was careful to take his name off any property so that banks would not be able to either put a lien on them or seize them.[228] Surveillance also saw Khyam, Shujah, and Azhar together, going shopping for outdoor clothing and equipment. They visited Internet cafés and travel agencies, where Khyam searched for flights to Pakistan. They frequently rested at Akbar's flat.

Khyam continued to apply pressure on both Akbar and Ali Khan to come to Pakistan with him. Torn between his friend's demands and his fantasy participation in Mahmood's simultaneous attacks in Britain, Akbar returned to Crawley for the 5 March Friday circle. I suspect that he was trying to probe Mahmood's plans by asking him about the legitimacy of carrying out any attack in England. Mahmood replied strongly negatively and said that he was taking a CELTA course as he was also planning to immigrate to Pakistan. Mahmood asked Akbar about his brother who had gone to Pakistan and had a teaching job for 50,000 rupees. Mahmood also advised Akbar, "If you want to go to Pakistan, yes, go, but make sure you've got something set up." Akbar took it to mean, "Make sure you don't just go there and come back."[229]

Meanwhile, Babar permanently left Pakistan on 3 March 2004, stopped in London, and three days later arrived in New York, where he moved back in with his family.[230]

The Explosive Formula and Amin's Disappearance

For a year, Khyam had been in regular contact with Amin. Khyam constantly changed phones to make it difficult to trace his calls. He usually called Amin on the latter's landlord's landline and told him in Punjabi to come over. This was a code for Amin to go to an Internet café and access their mutual e-mail account to check for draft messages. In the last four days of February, they discussed Khyam's plans to come to Pakistan.[231] Khyam also asked Amin for the exact formula for making ammonium-nitrate-based explosives. Amin had been the note taker at Kohat. According to Amin's later recollection, "[Khyam] told me that he had 600 kilograms of ammonium nitrate. . . . I thought he would have known [the formula] . . . and he goes, 'I forget already, you know.' Basically, that training that he done was no good to him."[232] Amin promised that he would try to find out from Abu Munthir on his next run. A minor variant of this event was that Khyam sent a formula to Amin based on Khyam's recollection of his training and asked Amin to verify it with either Abu Munthir or their former trainer. Amin replied that he had burned his notes during one of his moves, and it might take time for him to check out the formula.[233]

Their communications were disrupted at the end of February 2004 when Amin got into a dispute with his landlord and had to move to a home without any telephone landline. Khyam had trouble reaching him discretely.[234] Finally around 10 March, Khyam called him on his cell phone. Amin was furious and called Khyam an idiot for compromising him. From an Internet café, Amin passed on to Khyam notes that he had made from Abu Munthir's information. He was worried because he did not know what Khyam was up to and was afraid that it would get him in trouble. He destroyed the piece of paper with the mixtures of ammonium nitrate and aluminum powder. He knew what he was doing was wrong:

> I did definitely, yeah, but on the other hand . . . he was sending money and equipment and I knew that, if I wouldn't give this information to him, he would probably stop sending the money and the equipment, which would be a big loss, and this is why I was double-minded. . . . I wasn't sure what I should do about it. On one hand, if I don't help him, then I would be losing all that money and equipment that was going towards . . . the fighting in Afghanistan, the children, women, you know. . . . My job was to . . . be a link . . . mainly for equipment and money to send to people there. . . . One thing led to another and I just got stuck into the whole situation where I had no choice but to take, you know, messages across from both sides.[235]

Very shortly after this exchange, Amin discovered that ISID was looking for him. Kahuta was a small community and most of its inhabitants were related. Some civilians came and tried to kidnap one of Amin's friends but were overpowered by the local police. On interrogation at the station, one of the kidnappers confessed to be an ISID agent trying to locate Amin. Amin panicked. His friends suggested he go and hide with his brigadier general uncle running the military college in Kohat, "because, if they [ISID] get hold of you before anybody intervenes, they will beat the crap out of you." Another friend also warned him that "if they're looking for you in Kahuta, they might be standing outside the college as well." Instead of going to his uncle, Amin called Tariq, who also lived in Kohat, and hid at his house for the next three weeks.[236]

Mahmood's Alleged Plot

To assess Mahmood's alleged plot referred to in the Khyam-Akbar 22 February conversation, we must go back to early February, when Mahmood asked Akbar to keep his Transco CDs for him. These were proprietary CDs from work that contained detailed wiring diagrams of the utilities installations grid of England. Akbar believed that they were part of Mahmood's alleged plan to attack British utilities. In Akbar's mind, this plan involved the participants of the Friday circles (which Khyam had ceased to attend regularly), namely Mahmood as its emir, Gulzar, Ali Khan, Akbar, and another friend.[237] At trial, Akbar tried to gloss over this event as an innocent request: "by this time, I was beginning to feel cold feet about going to Pakistan with Omar [Khyam], I thought, if Omar goes to Pakistan, my only contact is going to be Waheed [Mahmood], who can get me to Pakistan. So, I want to show my dedication to this guy. So, I said, 'Yeah, cool' . . . these are related to the Jihad." Mahmood gave him the disks, which Akbar viewed at home on his computer. Akbar also assumed that Mahmood's encouragement of Ali Khan to get a job at a utility company was in furtherance of this plan.[238]

Throughout the month, Akbar worried about keeping Mahmood's disks at his flat. Ali Khan advised him to get rid of them as they were something "very hot and Omar [Khyam] is coming around there—and Omar had told all of us that we were going to get raided by MI5—you shouldn't keep them there anyway until you find out what's going on with these disks." On 1 March, Garcia called Akbar to say that he was coming around at Khyam's request for they had not seen each other since early February. Akbar panicked that the presence of three people from the Gorque camp at his flat might trigger a police raid.[239] He could not remember where he had hidden the disks. Sundeep was at the flat and tried to help him. He told her they had Transco written on them. "If we get raided today, I'm finished. . . . There are two guys. Why do you think they are meeting up at my place? You don't know how many people would be arrested if we . . . I don't know where to look for it. I don't know where to start."[240] Sundeep asked him what was going on, but he fended her off by saying that the less she knew, the better. Akbar finally found them and gave them to her before Garcia and Khyam arrived. She left and kept them until she left for a holiday in India three weeks later.

Garcia came with Lamine and Khyam with Shujah. They simply relaxed, reminisced about the camp, ate, but did not talk about any attack plan or jihad. Garcia got money from Khyam and everyone left. By then, although he was still collecting money for the cause, Garcia was mostly modeling at some fashion shows and planning his next trip to Spain. His social life had taken off. He and Sara had spent a lot of time at their flat with her close non-Muslim English friend Holly. Garcia suspected that Sara had been unfaithful to him, and the relationship among the three of them became awkward. Sara moved out, and Holly stayed and became Garcia's girlfriend.[241]

On 10 March in the evening, Khyam came to Akbar's flat and had another long conversation with his friend, which clarified Mahmood's alleged plot. The court proceedings glossed over this important conversation because it did not fit into the prosecution's linear theory of a bomb plot. Nor was the defense eager to present this exculpatory evidence because it did not fit with its theory that there had been no plotting whatsoever. Therefore, all accounts of Crevice have neglected it, but this conversation is crucial for it gives a completely different perspective to the alleged plots. I found the complete transcript of this conversation in the evidence of the Canadian trial against Khawaja.

The conversation started out as a discussion about various jobs teaching English available in Pakistan for them, which brought up Mahmood, who had told Akbar that he was taking a CELTA course. Khyam started asking questions about Mahmood's alleged plot of simultaneous attacks. "So, if *you lot* [the participants in the Friday circles] are doing something, I don't know what you are doing, yeah, if that's what your plan is, you have to . . .

do it simultaneously . . . otherwise, it's a failure." Akbar said that Mahmood was the emir. Khyam rejected this attempted brush-off: "because he's your emir . . . he can't just pick up and go." Akbar agreed. Khyam praised the concept of infiltrating utilities companies for an operation in Britain but insisted, "it has to be a simultaneous operation . . . to be effective, yeah, you have to all be co-ordinated. You have to let it go for a certain amount of time, for you to do the courses, which could take years." Akbar repeated that Khyam should speak about this to Mahmood. Khyam said he was troubled by the fact that Mahmood had taken a CELTA course. Akbar admitted he was puzzled as well that Mahmood was now only talking about how much money he could make teaching in Pakistan. "If he goes, we're shafted."[242]

In essence, they believed that Mahmood's plot was the one he had suggested in February 2003 at his family compound in Pakistan. Khyam said that this complicated plot needed meticulous preparation. For instance, an attack with gas required a careful mixture of gas and air for an explosion to occur and this needed to be tested in Pakistan to know whether it could succeed. "At the moment, it's all theory," he added. They admitted their own ignorance about the utilities in England, knowledge needed to carry out an attack against them, by trying to poison the water supply for instance. Only Mahmood seemed to have that knowledge. Akbar admitted, "What I'm confused about is, you're right, bruv, yeah. Abdul Waheed [Mahmood] needs to be here, and I've got a feeling he's going to pick up very soon and go."[243]

Khyam said that "our brothers" (al Qaeda) did not know anything about Mahmood's plans because Mahmood had asked him not to tell them anything and even he did not know much. All Khyam knew was that it had to do with gas and "they want to do some testing on a car in the mountains" to see whether it would blow up. Khyam speculated that the operation might take two to three years to prepare. He maintained that just one incident would not be enough. "There was a gas explosion in Europe just a couple of months ago, a massive one, some people died as well, yeah. No-one really cared. People died in it. Because, first of all, it has to be big, yeah, has to be destructive and everything. . . . Second, it has to be combined with something to make proper . . . effect and terror."[244]

Akbar repeated that Mahmood was not going to be in England for long. Khyam said, "I'll raise it with him when I see him, but you lot definitely

. . . need to raise it with him, because, if he goes you haven't got a clue, unless you do have a clue, I don't know." He then asked Akbar what was the postoperation plan: stay and carry on as if nothing had happened or try to escape from the country. Akbar replied these were questions for the emir. Khyam insisted, "but you, as the followers, need to question this as well." Akbar confessed to his own frustration, "Yeah, but whenever you do question, you get hold of that look, 'you don't need to question more than what you need to know.'" Khyam insisted, "When you question and they say 'don't worry bruv, everything is taken of' . . . I don't think it is, bruv." Akbar admitted, "Neither do I."[245]

Khyam said he was familiar with how bomb plots were supposed to unfold, but this was not happening with Mahmood's plot. In fact, if any happened in Britain, the police were definitely going to raid Crawley and arrest all of them. He advised his friend to ask "the type of questions I would be asking in an operation, yeah. One, are you going to stay? Why are you doing the CELTA course? Yeah, and should we do it as well then? Yeah, secondly, if something goes off in this country, what is our reaction? If our brothers, or you, get arrested . . . [and] they get interrogated, what happens? Do we chip the country as soon as the attack happens?" Khyam warned, "If you do something in this country, you are getting caught, trust me, a hundred percent. Don't even think that you will get away with it. . . . This country is an island. . . . They'll ground the planes and shut the ferry ports. . . . I'm pretty sure you didn't even think about getting away, you just thought you would get away with it."[246]

Khyam said that an attack against the utilities would take years to prepare because it took that much time to earn the companies' trust and get the necessary access for the operation. They needed to get in touch with others scattered around the country to carry out simultaneous attacks throughout Britain. So far, he did not see any such preparations. Instead, he believed that "some of them are thinking, we'll do it and we'll do a runner and get out, but you ain't getting nowhere." Again, he urged Akbar and his co-conspirators to question Mahmood about these aspects of the plot. Akbar suggested that Khyam might not know enough about Mahmood's plan. For instance, Gulzar got a job with a security company. Khyam replied that Gulzar and he both applied for that job and it had nothing to do with Mahmood. He again warned his friend that a massive bomb explosion in London would dramatically change public opinion that would allow for massive arrests of Islamist militants and the use of torture, like in America or Cuba, where "human rights have gone out of the window. But if it happened here . . . (unclear) . . . any different? I don't think so." They needed to be prepared for this possibility.[247]

Khyam said he did not know of any real plan to carry out any operation in Britain. Everything was in the brainstorming stage. "This is just an idea right now. It's a good idea, I'm not denying it . . . but it's not there. It's not been put together. When you've got an idea, you need everything there: a backup plan; backup emir; if this happens, we react like this; . . . if contact breaks, then contact me this way. . . . Right now, everything is just everywhere. Friday, you get together and we just discuss this, that and the other, and everyone just goes off. That's what it looks to me, and the brothers as well." Khyam suspected that there was nothing planned. Akbar asked him why he had not talked to Mahmood. Khyam replied that he did not want to have anything to do with this plot.[248]

Akbar agreed that someone had to talk to Mahmood: "all the brothers have got a lot of respect for him. He calls a lot of shots, man. You were right . . . if he's just going to get up and go, then the morale is just going to go." That left Ali Khan, Gulzar, him, and another friend. Khyam was resentful because his Crawley friends were told it was better for them to stay in England (for the plot) and therefore refused to go to Pakistan with him, while their emir Mahmood was getting ready to go himself. Akbar asked Khyam to talk to Mahmood, but Khyam said he did not see much of Mahmood anymore because he no longer regularly went back to Crawley anymore. In addition, "I don't want to get involved in it bro, cos . . . I get to know too much about you lot. . . . I don't want to know that. If you got caught I would probably get done as well, and I haven't got anything to do with it. . . . Everyone comes out with ideas. It's doing the ideas properly, seriously, that's what it is. Otherwise, you're just like, fooling yourself."[249]

From this conversation, it was clear that Khyam had distanced himself from his former co-conspirators Akbar, Ali Khan, Gulzar, and Mahmood. He was also no longer seeing Garcia. In fact, the Mahmood plot was just a series of gratuitous bull sessions among young British jihadi wannabes with overheated imaginations. Yet this conversation, which should have reassured the Security Service that there was no imminent serious plot against Britain, further alarmed them. Instead of interpreting it as more idle talk and wishful thinking, the service provided the following summary of that conversation to the Coroner's Inquests seven years later: "On 10 March

2004, Akbar was heard discussing (with a man called Osmim [*sic*]) simultaneous attacks, targeting and gathering information on: a) Poisoning water supplies; b) Disrupting supplies of electricity and gas; c) Utilities; d) Gas installations; e) Water. Akbar said that it was only a matter of time and that something would succeed, and that they needed to prepare for arrests."[250] Again, even at that date, there was no attempt by the Security Service to correct its misinterpretation of this conversation.

The Madrid Bombings Raise the Alarm Even More with the Authorities

A few hours after the above conversation, in the early morning of 11 March, ten bombs exploded on commuter trains in Madrid, killing 191 people and wounding hundreds more. It was the largest terrorist attack ever on European soil. At first the conservative Spanish government blamed ETA, a Basque separatist terrorist group. However, within two days, the evidence was overwhelming that the perpetrators were Muslim militants, but the government persisted in blaming ETA. The government did not want to defend its policy of having joined the coalition forces in the invasion of Iraq, which was extremely unpopular with the Spanish electorate at this crucial juncture. General elections were scheduled for Sunday 14 March, and it was leading in the polls. Faced with obvious lies from the government about those responsible for the bombings, the electorate punished it and voted it out of office. The incoming Socialist government immediately promised a full and transparent investigation into the bombings and pledged to withdraw from Iraq as soon as possible. Although in the perception of non-Spaniards the bombings were seen as causing the government to fall, the defeat of the conservative government was really due to its lies and cover-up so close to the elections rather than the bombings themselves.

On 11 March, Khyam telephoned Access Storage about the failed debit card monthly payment. The police had placed an undercover officer, Amanda, there. She had asked the staff to leave a message on Khyam's voice mail telling him that the transaction on Hussain's account had been refused and requesting him to call Access Storage urgently. Khyam agreed to come the next day. That evening, Khyam, Shujah, Azhar, and Akbar were heard commenting on the Madrid bombings that had taken place earlier that day. Azhar said "the brothers" had done it and Khyam agreed "100 per cent."

The next morning, Khyam drove to Access Storage. Amanda asked how long he was expecting the fertilizer to be stored there. Khyam replied that he did not know and would speak to Hussain. He said he was simply a friend of Hussain, who had asked him to come. He paid the outstanding rental charge in £50 notes, leaving change of £42.45, which he would pick up later on. He asked to see the unit where the fertilizer was stored and Amanda went with him. He looked into the storage unit and seemed reassured. He left after about 20 minutes.[251]

That evening, Khyam, Akbar, Gulzar, Ashraf, and Ali Khan came to Mahmood's Friday evening study circle at Gulzar's house and discussed the Madrid bombings. Akbar said, "If that was done by the brothers, that is what you call wicked planning."[252] They talked about leaving for Pakistan. Someone asked Mahmood what he was doing. Mahmood replied that he was not involved in anything. He said he had children and was thinking about emigrating abroad. He had heard the rumors about a plot and denied them. "Look, stop thinking you're part of an al-Qaeda splinter cell," he told them.[253] Akbar asked him about the Transco disks. Mahmood said he did not know what he was talking about. When Akbar described the disks, Mahmood said that there must have been an error because he believed that he had given Akbar CDs of fighting in the tribal areas. He did not know that Akbar had his disks and asked him to return them. Akbar said that his wife had them and he would give them back when she got them back.[254]

The Security Service later summarized this discussion for the Coroner's Inquests in one line: "On 12 March there was discussions of the 'three' bombs."[255] It avoided telling the Inquests that its interpretation had no basis in the transcripts.

Preparations for Departure

Meanwhile, Saira Khan was adamant that Khyam settle their marriage situation before he left for Pakistan. Around 12 or 13 March, her family finally accepted Khyam's marriage proposal, effectively postponing his departure to the beginning of April.[256] After the 12 March Friday circle, Akbar told Khyam he now had decided to go with him to Pakistan. He testified at trial that he had told Khyam: "The reason why I didn't want to go to Pakistan was my wife, the main reason, and you never seem to understand that." Khyam had responded, "Look, I understand that you love your wife and you think if you leave that she's going to crack under the pressure and she's going to find it difficult and she might even leave the religion. If you . . . truly believe in God, God will look after your wife."[257]

On 14 March, Akbar called his landlord and told him he was surrender-
ing his tenancy at the end of the month. He then called Garcia to come
over to his flat that evening. During the day, undercover officer Amanda
left a few voice mails on Khyam's cell phone reminding him that he had
not collected the change due to him. He came the next day around 1 PM
and told her that Hussain kept sending him because he happened to be
working in the area. He wanted to visit the unit and went there alone with
his own key. A recording device filmed him inspecting the bag very carefully, opening the top of it, and making a mark on it. He stayed in the
locker for two and a half minutes before departing.[258]

That evening at the Colley House flat, Khyam and Shujah were relaxing
with Akbar. Khyam talked about the Spanish government's decision to
withdraw its troops from Iraq after the change of government and the
Madrid bombings. Even Shujah said, "Spain are pulling out. Spain are pulling out. That's wicked, isn't it? . . . I'm happy now it's got through to one
of them. Pulled out their troops. Coming out in June or something, end of
June. Got through to them."[259]

On 17 March, Khyam brought Hussain up to date on Access Storage.
Then Hussain called and spoke to Amanda, who explained the need for a
new contract and a fresh deposit. Khyam and he drove to the facility, where
Hussain filled out the new form and handed over the money from his own
pocket. Throughout the process, he seemed deferential to Khyam.[260] Later
that day, Hussain discussed the situation of storing a large amount of fertilizer with a friend, who told him that you could make explosives out of
fertilizer.[261]

The next evening, 18 March, at Akbar's flat, Hussain asked his cousin
Akbar, "You know, fertilization? What can you make out of it? Can you
make things out of it?" Akbar was puzzled by the question but Hussain
persisted, "You know that self-storage. . . . There's nothing dodgy, right?"
Akbar asked, "What are you talking about?" Hussain continued, "Some
questions came into my mind, doubts—I don't know—fertility [sic]. There
was someone talking about fertilization [sic]—you use it to make
explosives—and then I started thinking to myself: why is it under my
account when there are other accounts? Why has it been there for so long?
I started having doubts." Akbar lectured his cousin, "Because of that stupid
little thought, you just lost out on so much reward. . . . This might be the
reason why Allah must say it sounds a little action, but you don't know
how much danger you're putting yourself in. . . . Someone had to do it."

Hussain replied, "If I go down, I'll take everyone down with me." Akbar responded, "But it doesn't matter. You'll definitely go down. . . . You should know what you're doing. . . . Trust me." Nabeel protested, "I am just going to knock out Omar and all." Akbar said, "So you go down. Do you see what they're doing? You're taking a big risk and they're trusting you with all of this one. Allah trusts you. They trust you. . . . If it's been there for some time . . . then you shouldn't talk about it, bro."[262]

Hussain said that he had doubts because he did not know what it was. Akbar replied, "You are a lot more silly than I thought you were. What did you think these guys are involved in?" His cousin replied, "I knew they were involved, but I just never thought about it that way, until that explosive word came. . . . I never thought about this before coz I did not know what it was for." Akbar told him there was no point in talking to him because Hussain could not take anything seriously. "You're part of it whether you like it or not . . . seriously, bro, you have been part of it." His cousin protested, "Well, I don't want to do nothing wrong if it's like this. I never knew what it was for. I didn't believe it in myself. Then why should I do such a thing? . . . They say in a couple of months, it will be gone away. . . . It's a huge amount of explosives there. . . . But the point is it's in my name. So, if I get screwed, for what, not knowing?" Akbar replied, "You've told me too much. Do not tell me anymore, seriously." However, he later tried to reassure his cousin, "It's nothing dodgy. I think it's just a component that will be (unclear). It's nothing to do with bombs."[263] They talked about Hussain getting caught and Akbar added, "no-one's going to believe you that you stored something for someone and didn't ask no questions; that is just so stupid."[264]

The two cousins then talked about the recent Madrid bombings. Hussain asked, "Why just take out loads of kuffar, general kuffars, not people in power?" Akbar answered, "It's like I said, man. I could seriously go into explaining it." Hussain persisted, "So, what's the point of doing trains that people are traveling on?"[265] Akbar did not have an opportunity to find out more about the stored fertilizer from Khyam because the latter was too busy preparing for his wedding to come to his flat. Akbar asked Ali Khan about this issue and Ali Khan promised to look into it.[266]

During this month of March, MI5 felt from surveillance and eavesdropping that Khyam was becoming "jumpy." Shujah always seemed to be with him. He would frequently drive and stop by telephone kiosks to make calls, while his brother waited in the car. He and some of the other Crevice suspects talked about leaving the country. MI5 interpreted this as an "escape plan" for after an attack, and now believed that the attack was imminent.[267]

The Alleged Bluewater Shopping Center Target

Meanwhile, the Pakistani army started a widespread operation in South Waziristan to uproot the Taliban, al Qaeda, and their allies. The operation started slowly, but increased in intensity by mid-March, leading to a bloody battle around the city of Wanna. There were many casualties on both sides, and the news of the fighting in Waziristan was stirring up the British militants.

On 18 March, Khawaja e-mailed Khyam saying he might come and join him in Pakistan: "the news looks bad, so I wanted to get some advice from u. if u think it would be a good idea for me to pack up and head down with u niggas." Two days later, Khawaja continued, "I hear tense stuff about PK, man what should we do? Pakis munafiqs [hypocrites] are doing all the dirty work for the kufs. . . . Let me know when it is best for me to come over." Khyam responded, "Bro, things are bad, jus be prepared in it nigga. We will let you know in the near future nigga."[268]

On Friday 19 March, in the late afternoon, Khyam, Shujah, and Ali Khan drove to Crawley. On the way, Ali Khan asked Khyam, "Have you been to Bluewater?" (an enormous shopping mall). They did not know where it was, and Khyam made a phone call asking where Bluewater was and how to get there.[269]

They went to pray at the Crawley mosque, where they met up with Mahmood. After prayer, Mahmood joined Khyam in the latter's car. They started talking about the situation in South Waziristan. Mahmood said, "I can't handle it, mate." Khyam told Mahmood that he had a "handful of brothers" willing to go there for about a year. Mahmood mentioned about doing something to relieve the pressure on the insurgents in Pakistan and mentioned AMEC.[270] Khyam reported, "There's nothing really happening." Khyam told him about his discussion with Abu Munthir, who had described how the press had completely misrepresented the fighting. They believed that al Qaeda was fighting to the last man and that the Pakistanis were "getting their arses whipped a little bit."[271] Mahmood suggested getting all the brothers together that evening to ask them who was ready to go. Khyam said that if Amin asked them to come, they would come right away, but now he was having problems contacting Amin in Pakistan.

Mahmood continued, "[The brothers] need a big diversion either a few flipping hits in Pakistan, quick hits, yeah, diverting their attention. Like that Spain was a beautiful job, weren't it? Absolutely beautiful, man, so much impact." Khyam said that he and a few others were going to Pakistan within three weeks, and, a month later, there would be six or seven of them. Mahmood asked how many "brothers are active in this country . . . actually planning things . . . and doing them here?" Khyam replied, "No one. . . . Maybe, that group I told you about . . . that's about it." Many militants would help with finance. "But that's usually as far as it goes. When it comes to the physical side, you know, there's not a lot." Mahmood continued, "what about . . . Bluewater's only an hour walk . . . local . . . tomorrow if you want right . . . (inaudible) a little explosion . . . (inaudible) time . . . (inaudible) three days time . . . tomorrow, little one. . . . (inaudible) I don't know how big it would be. . . . But might as well do one to see what it's like. . . . Do one tomorrow if you wanted to . . . (inaudible) I don't know how big it would be . . . because we haven't tested it. . . . We know it's going to work, Insha-Allah."[272]

Khyam responded, "I don't know. . . . They're gonna get back to my house." Mahmood insisted, "No, can stock up on it first. . . . Tuesday, we could do it. . . . (inaudible) Doesn't take long to stock up on this stuff either . . . from three or four garages . . . and could stock it up. . . . They can't get rid of it off the shelves anyhow." Khyam replied, "Up to you, bro." Mahmood continued, "Eh, well, no I'm just thinking. I just wanna know there's nothing flippin planned for this place on a big scale and err, they're gonna crack down on. . . . More importantly, what about AMEC, hitting AMEC?"[273] The conversation was interrupted for a few minutes.

Mahmood resumed, "Listen, so AMEC is another one to hit . . . their depot . . . hit their office blocks . . . but I couldn't do nothing on a large scale." Khyam replied, "That's the thing, isn't it 'cos, you know the guys here, they . . . can't really advise you not to do it, they can't really say to you do it. . . . They'll probably say, yeah, bruv, you wanna do it, do it." Mahmood concluded, "Yeah. What I'm saying is all we got right is a flipping car that goes bang. . . . That's all we got right . . . and now, it might land all the way up to that lamppost, it might land flippin, it'll cause a bit of damage, right but it'll definitely put the . . . bomb scare Maidstone . . . see they evacuated the little corner of the whole town in Maidstone, you know that."[274]

This local incident gave them the idea of carrying out a false alarm, especially on the American Embassy. However, they both agreed that if al

Qaeda needed them in the tribal areas at that moment, "then forget about that discussion thingy they need us now," Mahmood said. "The tribal area is very important . . . psychologically to people. . . . You can't afford to lose that, bruv. . . . It'll kill the morale. . . . They would say. . . . Al Qaeda's been destroyed . . . [with] little remnants here and there. . . . That's what they'll say . . . right . . . and they'll splash it out on a big scale, bruv."[275]

The Security Service interpreted the above conversation as follows: "On 19 March, Waheed Mahmood and KHYAM referred to: a) Blowing up a police station; b) A few quick hits in Pakistan to act as a diversion; c) Bluewater in three days' time or tomorrow; d) AMEC offices or depot; e) A car bomb; f) A bomb hoax."[276]

Around that time, Akbar came to Hussain's dorm room to stay for the night because his wife had gone to India and he wanted to spend some time with his cousin. Before she left, his wife had returned the Transco disks to him. Akbar brought them in a white carrier bag and placed it on Hussain's desk, probably for safekeeping.[277]

On 22 March, Khyam asked Garcia to contact his uncle Saj pretending to be an MI5 officer to reinforce the message Garcia had already given to him in late January, namely that Khyam and his younger brother needed to get out of Britain and go to Pakistan. Khyam asked Garcia to peg this new intervention to the bombings in Spain and the fact that the security situation in the UK was getting more serious. Garcia accomplished his task later that day.[278]

On 25 March 2004, Omar Khyam formally married Saira Khan and they had a traditional celebration two days later.[279] The next day, Khawaja e-mailed to Khyam, "we will go full speed ahead with our projects. . . . im putting together up to 30 devices for u niggas, we will test out stuff too. . . . I'm thinking about preparing for hijra too bro. . . . I wanna get these things I mentioned done in the next 2 months and make a move. . . . u bros need anything? . . . we can get military gear . . . from here for cheap, so let me know if u need anything."[280]

From the 28 March ELG meeting summary, the 19 March Mahmood-Khyam conversation seemed to indicate the existence of a second plot of which the authorities had "no visibility" and the possibility of another planned attack. "Intensive investigation has not provided any greater visibility to the second plot and without being able to discount its existence and with no control over it in combination with intelligence regarding the intended departure of the main targets it is possible to assess that they may be planning for an attack. Public safety demands that 'we now intervene to disrupt this network because of the lack of knowledge of the second plot.' "[281] As the full transcript of that conversation showed that it was just idle venting but not a second plot, I did not find any other reason for the arrest of the Crevice conspirators the next day.

The Arrests

On 29 March in the afternoon, the Canadian authorities started the wave of arrests by detaining Momin Khawaja in Ottawa. On 30 March, a large raid arrested eight people in England. The police arrested Omar Khyam at a hotel honeymooning with his wife; Anthony Garcia at his parents' home; Jawad Akbar and Nabeel Hussain together at the Colley House flat; Waheed Mahmood at his house in Crawley; and Shujah-ud-Din Mahmood, Ahmed Ali Khan, and Azhar Khan at their respective family homes. In Hussain's dorm room, the police found the 12 Transco CDs.[282] A search of Khyam's mother's house in Crawley revealed a tin of aluminum powder totaling 160.29 grams hidden under various plastic bags behind the shed in the garden.[283] There were also three airplane tickets in the names of Khyam, Shujah, and Azhar from London to Karachi for 6 April 2004, returning from Islamabad to Heathrow on 28 June 2004. Also, in Shujah's room were a list of universities in Islamabad and a list of synagogues in England.[284]

On 3 April, Salahuddin Amin heard on the radio about the arrests of Khyam and others in England and Canada. He called his uncle, the brigadier, who asked him to come to his house in Kohat. He told his nephew that British and American authorities were looking for him in connection to his "illegal activities." The brigadier called some of his colleagues from ISID, who came to the house and negotiated the surrender of Amin. In prison, Amin learned about the arrest of Abu Munthir in Pakistan around that time.[285]

In New York, the FBI took Mohammad Junaid Babar into custody on 6 April 2004.[286] On 10 April, he was formally arrested and charged with material support to a terrorist group. He pled guilty to this charge on 3 June 2004 and was released on bail at the end of 2008.[287] He was later sentenced to only five years in prison in 2011 thanks to his cooperation with U.S. prosecutors but I do not believe that he ever returned to prison after his release.

Among those arrested in England, Ali Khan and Azhar were released without charges. The other six defendants—Khyam, Garcia, Hussain,

Akbar, Mahmood, and Shujah—were jointly charged with conspiring together and with others to cause, by an explosive substance, an explosion of a nature likely to endanger life or cause serious injury to property. Amin was extradited from Pakistan to England on 8 February 2005 and arrested on landing in London. He was later charged on the same count as the other conspirators. Khyam, Hussain, and Garcia were also charged with possessing ammonium nitrate in circumstances that gave rise to a reasonable suspicion that their possession was for a purpose connected with the commission, preparation, or instigation of an act of terrorism. Khyam and Shujah were additionally charged under the same provision with possessing a quantity of aluminum powder.

The trial of the seven defendants took place at the Central Criminal Court, Old Bailey, London. It lasted more than a year, starting on 21 March 2006. Mahmood refused to testify. On 30 April 2007, after 27 days of jury deliberations, Khyam, Garcia, Amin, Mahmood, and Akbar were convicted of conspiracy to cause explosions likely to endanger life. Shujah and Hussain were acquitted on all charges. Khyam and Garcia were also found guilty of possessing 600 kilograms of ammonium nitrate fertilizer for terrorism. Khyam was also found guilty of possession of aluminum powder for terrorism.

On the main charge, each guilty party was sentenced to life imprisonment with Khyam, Mahmood, and Garcia to serve a minimum of 20 years and Amin and Akbar to serve at least 17.5 years. All five defendants appealed their convictions on the ground that the recommended minimum term in each case was excessive. The appeals were rejected for Khyam, Mahmood, and Akbar. The minimum term for Garcia was reduced to 17.5 years, and for Amin it was reduced to 16 years and 9 months.

Momin Khawaja was indicted on 16 December 2005 on seven terrorism offenses, including developing an explosive device likely to cause serious bodily harm, possession of an explosive substance, participation in a terrorist group, and material and financial support of a terrorist group. He had an extensive bail hearing in Ottawa from 6 to 8 June, with bail being denied on 15 June 2005. He was tried at the Ontario Superior Court of Justice, starting 23 June 2008. On 29 October, he was found guilty of five charges and sentenced to ten and a half years in prison, in addition to time served.

Abu Munthir al Maghrebi vanished and seems to be free back at home in Belgium. Zeeshan Siddiqui was arrested in Lahore on 15 May 2005, deported to Britain on 9 January 2006, and put on control orders. He was diagnosed with a mental disorder and placed in a forensic mental health unit, from which he escaped in September 2006. Kazi Nurur Rahman, who was viewed as an essential priority target, was arrested in a sting operation trying to buy illegal weapons from undercover agents on 29 November 2005.[288] He pled guilty to terrorist charges in May 2006 and was sentenced to nine years in prison. Abdal Hadi al Iraqi was arrested on his way to Iraq in 2006 and is languishing in Guantanamo Bay. Syed Hashmi, Babar's New York friend who was studying in London, was arrested in June 2006 and extradited to the United States in May 2007. He pled guilty to a single count of conspiracy to provide material support to al Qaeda by agreeing to keep Babar's bag for him when Babar had visited London in January 2004. He was sentenced to 15 years in prison.

As we just saw, there was no Crevice attempt against the Ministry of Sound or the Bluewater shopping center. Through misinterpretation of wiretap evidence, British authorities talked themselves into believing there were such plots. The finding of more than half a ton of stored fertilizer was alarming, but an analysis of the conversations of the plotters should have put them at ease. Garcia had bought the fertilizer back in November. There had been a conspiracy to carry out a terrorist operation in Britain then. However, when Babar came to England in January and told the conspirators that they could go and fight in Afghanistan, it seems that Khyam abandoned his plot. Garcia moved away from his former friends and focused on sex and his modeling career. By March, Khyam no longer cared about the fertilizer and the two times he visited the storage space came after the undercover police agent there had called him to straighten out his account. Mahmood's alleged plot was just talk and fantasy.

There was no evidence of any active plot by the time of the arrests. Khyam assumed that Gulzar, Ali Khan, and Akbar were in cahoots with Mahmood in another plot targeting gas and electric infrastructure. However, Mahmood denied he had such a plot and instead, he and Khyam were getting ready to leave for Pakistan without carrying out an operation in Britain. Ironically, these suspects were arrested because there was no plot at all. Convinced that it existed despite all the contrary evidence and the fact that they could not find any evidence of any active plots, the British authorities panicked and decided to disrupt the feared plot by arresting all of Khyam's associates. After these arrests, no new evidence surfaced contradicting the fact that Crevice was an abandoned plot. Yet the authorities continue to claim that there was one, but refuse to release any information that would support or refute their claim. Defense attorneys were probably reluctant to use the transcripts of the defendants' exculpatory conversations because these same conversations showed them actively fantasizing about carrying out terrorist activities in England. This has led the public and many scholars to believe that there was a real Crevice plot.

Nevertheless, the importance of Crevice should not be underestimated: self-appointed British neojihadis took the fateful decision to attack Britain. This was an important step in al Qaeda's projection of force to Europe, even though ironically, al Qaeda had very little to do with this initial decision. Nevertheless, once the decision was taken and the militants returned to Britain, it created a precedent in the minds of other self-categorized soldiers defending their imagined neo-ummah. Al Qaeda took advantage of this new addition to the repertoire of British neojihadis.

The evidence in Operation Crevice shows that Khyam, Shujah, and Azhar were ready to go to Pakistan on April 6. Akbar and Mahmood would follow them shortly after. Two or three people from Beeston were to follow them later, but the authorities did not focus on them sufficiently. Fifteen months later, this neglect resulted in the deaths of 52 innocent victims and injuries to hundreds more in the London Bombings—the subject of the next chapter.

CHAPTER 3

THESEUS

THE LONDON BOMBINGS

UNLIKE THE INDIVIDUALS BEHIND the other three plots, the perpetrators of the London bombings killed themselves in the July 2005 attack and could not provide firsthand information about their attack at trial. I have reconstructed this attack from testimonies of their former friends at their respective trials, the transcripts of their conversations entered into evidence at the Khawaja trial in Canada, the formal parliamentary investigations into the bombings, and the 2011 Coroner's Inquests.

The Beeston Boys

Let us go back to the mysterious militants from Beeston, who had associated with Khyam in the previous chapter. Beeston is a Leeds neighborhood where another cluster of young British Islamist militants emerged. It is a largely residential, close-knit, and densely populated area with back-to-back rowhouses, often in poor condition. The population is ethnically mixed and transitory in nature. There are a number of mosques, a large, modern community center, and a large park, where young people play football and cricket. The area is relatively deprived, and in the early years of this century the average income was low—more than 10,000 of the 16,300 residents at the time had living standards that were among the bottom 3 percent nationally. But there was little to distinguish this neighborhood from many other poor areas of Britain's other big cities.[1]

The majority of Muslims in the area were Barelvis from Mirpur in Pakistan Kashmir, who had created a Kashmir Muslim Welfare Association (KMWA) in the early 1980s to help their elders, teach their youths about Kashmiri traditions and religion, and establish a mosque. The KMWA moved to a Hardy Street building, where the second floor was the mosque. However, its imams spoke Urdu and Punjabi, which the second generation had trouble understanding. Instead of their parents' tradition, some youngsters gravitated to a Salafi version of Islam, whose brochures and writings were in English, funded by Saudi money. Barelvis worship the Prophet and Muslim saints while Salafis see this type of worship as heresy—only God, or Allah, is worthy of worship. The Salafis in Beeston established their own mosque, Al Madina Mosque, on Tunstall Road.

As Beeston was experiencing a serious drug problem, the KMWA created a youth center with a gym in the basement of its building. The local youths had complained that there was no facility for them like a gym, a place to relax, or a drop-in learning center.[2] In addition, the association established two part-time positions of youth workers with council money in 1996 and hired two young Muslims from the neighborhood: Mohammed Sidique Khan[3] and Mohammed Shakil.

Sidique was 22 years old, born in Leeds into a modest Pakistani immigrant family. He was generally a quiet boy in school with occasional flares of illegal activity, such as receiving stolen goods in 1986 and assault in 1992.[4] He became interested in religion as a teenager, but still drank and smoked cannabis. After school, he worked locally for the Benefits Agency and then as an administrative assistant for the Department of Trade and Industry. In September 1996, he started at nearby Leeds Metropolitan University.[5] At the time, he was not yet a practicing Muslim and was more concerned about taking the drug problem in his neighborhood head on.[6]

Mohammed Shakil was 20 years old, born in Kashmir, where he contracted polio, resulting in his left leg being about an inch shorter than the right. He came to England at the age of five and wore leg braces in primary school. His family moved to Beeston in 1988. In secondary school, Shakil replaced his brace with a built-up shoe. He liked to dance, hopping on one leg, and acquired a reputation as a "professional hip hop dancer."[7] In 1995, he married Najma Saleem, whose family came from the same village but had moved to Beeston in 1981. Sadeer Saleem, her younger half brother, was born in England in 1980 and went to the same school as Shakil, but they did not socialize as Shakil was four years older. In 1996, Shakil's medical condition deteriorated. He was unable to walk even very short distances, developed chronic fatigue and poor sleep, and was treated for depression.[8] As he improved, he got the job at the Hardy Street youth center.

Shakil and Sidique became close friends, hung out and drank together, and visited each other's homes. In their job, they dealt with the local drug problem, urging the youth to "get off the streets" and bringing them inside the center to play pool, board games, and tennis or use the weightlifting equipment. The goal was to raise community awareness while addressing drug problems. The club attracted local boys like Saleem, Shehzad Tanweer, and Shipon Ullah. Tanweer was born in 1982 in Bradford and two years later his family moved to Beeston, where it owned a fish-and-chips shop. He did well in school and was a gifted sportsman, excelling at cricket. His father called him Kaka (the little one, but his friends called him Kaki) and he lived on the same street as Ullah, born in Bangladesh in 1983. Ullah's family moved to Beeston in 1986 but a year later both parents died. Ullah and his siblings lived with a foster family a block down from Tanweer. Ullah and Tanweer became close friends: they boxed and played football and cricket all the time. Ullah instigated fights and Tanweer came in and finished them off for him.[9]

Apparently, the club was not enough to tame the local drug problem. Sidique allegedly formed a fluid group of 15 to 20 members, "Mullah boys," who kidnapped young Pakistani drug addicts and, with the consent of their families, held them in a flat near the Salafi mosque, and forcibly cleansed them of their drug habits.[10] Shakil started to practice Islam seriously around that time.[11]

In 1997, at university, Sidique started dating his future wife, Hasina Patel, a Muslim of Indian origin, who was studying sociology.[12] They rebelled against their respective families' opposition to their possible marriage because of *biradari*—the suffocating system of honor, constraints, and mutual obligations imported from Kashmir that encouraged intermarriage among first cousins to preserve family property.[13]

In September, Shakil moved to Luton to study software engineering at the University of Bedfordshire. The move became a family affair. His parents, wife, and child moved there with him. There, his piety deepened and he prayed regularly at local mosques, where he met Mohammed Qayum Khan. Shakil and his relatives stayed for two years before returning to Leeds, where his second child was born. After his return, he became closer to Saleem: they prayed and trained together. Saleem had become more religious under the influence of a friend. Before, in college, Saleem had been drinking, smoking, and clubbing. Afterward, he grew a beard and went to mosques, where he now hung out with young pious teenagers, like Tanweer, who were serious about Islam.[14]

Acquisition of a Political Social Identity

On 26 November 1999, Shakil went to Mirpur to visit his relatives. He flew there with a local friend, who had already done some basic training at a Kashmiri camp and wanted to proceed to a more advanced level. They separated upon arrival as Shakil went to visit his family in Mirpur. While there, he decided to visit a training camp for three days. The camp organizers, aware of his disability and eventual return to England, were very accommodating. On the first day, he attended lectures on Islam, the history and politics of Kashmir, and the prohibition about attacking civilians. On the second day, he was allowed to fire guns as much as he wanted to "let off some steam" and see if he wanted to go further in his training. Shakil returned to Britain on 15 February 2000—a few months later, the police came to inquire about his trip because one of his local friends had gone missing and never returned to Britain.[15] Shakil resumed his studies in information technology by transferring to Huddersfield University.

When he returned to Leeds, Shakil reconnected with Sidique, who had got his business degree certificate the previous year. Sidique had also become more religious, although he still drank and smoked cannabis. He was also more politically conscious, paying attention to issues that affected the Muslim world and was now supportive of jihad in "illegally occupied Muslim land." He also inclined toward Salafi Islam rather than the Barelvi variant of his parents, which caused tension at home. He had come to reject the Hardy Street mosque because its imams rarely interacted with second-generation Muslims: the only time they did was when they taught their students the Quran and how to recite it—in Arabic. Salafis wrote in English and Sidique and some of his friends espoused their interpretation of Islam.[16]

In 2000, Tafazal Mohammed, the manager of the Hardy Street youth center, opened up the Iqra bookstore to meet the growing popular demand for a *dawah* (preaching of Islam) center. Naveed Fiaz was its first manager and Faisal Akhtar Khan set up its bank account. The bookstore became a magnet for many young pious Muslims like Saleem, Sidique, and Shakil, who volunteered there. At the end of 2000, Saleem was hit by a bus, leaving him unconscious with a fractured skull. He was hospitalized for two days, but suffered with various mental deficits for the rest of his life, including loss of taste, mental blackouts, poor memory, constant tardiness, a sense of vulnerability, and loss of confidence. Shortly thereafter, Saleem was on a bus with Ullah, whom he recognized from the neighborhood. Ullah had dropped out of two colleges and was drifting without a regular job. Saleem sat down next to him, preached Islam to him for about five minutes, and invited him to visit the Iqra bookstore.[17]

About three weeks later, Ullah saw that there was a long wait at his barbershop and noticed the Iqra bookstore across the street. When he popped in, Saleem welcomed him and talked to him about massacres and atrocities committed against Muslims around the world. Until that time, Ullah had not been interested in politics, but he bought a book about ethnic cleansing against Muslims in Bosnia. Saleem also mentioned videos about massacres of Muslims in Chechnya and loaned him one. Ullah took it to his best friend Tanweer's home, where they watched it. At that time, Tanweer was managing Ullah's financial situation because Ullah had always been impulsive with his expenses. Ullah later said that watching the videos was inspirational: seeing Muslims from all over the world come and defend their fellow Muslims brought him "a sense of brotherhood to a different level. . . . I thought this is beautiful." It changed him. He went to pray with Tanweer at the local mosque. They stopped listening to music and started listening to audiocassettes of *nasheed* (war songs without instrumental music) and speeches by preachers like Maulana Masood Azhar, which Saleem translated for Tanweer. Ullah got rid of his ganja plants, took down his posters of boxers and Brazilian footballers, and replaced them with posters of Arabic verses, AK-47s, and Kashmir on his wall. He now wanted to help any Muslim brother in Kashmir or Afghanistan and help liberate Muslim lands.[18]

The Iqra bookstore became the hub of a network of local Muslim activists. They trained together at the gym and organized weekend outbound paramilitary camps in Wales and the Lake District. Ullah went to one with Tanweer in the Lake District and one in Wales with Sidique and Tafazal, which came under surveillance by the West Yorkshire Police on 26–28 January 2001.[19] British counterterrorism authorities were monitoring two Islamist radicals, Martin McDaid, "Abdullah," and James Alexander

McClintock, in Operation Warlock, started around 1998. McDaid was allegedly a former Special Forces veteran and described as "middle-aged, shaven hair, beard in an Islamic style, a healthy-looking man, aggressive, very outspoken and an aggressive proselytizer. He was very, very keen to convert people to the faith of Islam." He was suspected of being an Islamic extremist and of possible involvement in jihad training. He was a frequent visitor to the Hardy Street basement gym. He and McClintock had organized this specific outing for about 45 people. This was one of several such outings.[20] McClintock left Britain in 2001.

In March 2001, Sidique started a job as a mentor at a primary school at Hillside with an annual salary of £17,000.[21] In July, he and Saleem were two of four friends who planned to attend a training camp in Kashmir for two months. Ullah learned about it and asked Sidique to take him along. As the departure approached, Saleem got "cold feet," felt "homesick," and dropped out. Sidique got very upset with his friend, but Ullah replaced him. To raise money for the trip, Ullah worked for five weeks as a packer and got £700 from his older sisters. On 29 July 2001, they flew to Islamabad, where Sidique had arranged for Harkat ul-Mujahedin members to pick them up and take them for a two-week beginner's course at a camp in Manshera. They were separated from local trainees and put in a brick house, with shower and toilet, while the locals slept in small tents. They ran in the morning and learned how to handle and fire small caliber weapons. After two weeks, they asked to see Afghanistan. A Harkat ul-Mujahedin guide took them by taxi to Jalalabad, where Ullah fell sick and got diarrhea. They continued to Kabul and Bagram, the front line with the Northern Alliance. They stayed there for a week to 10 days. Ullah's health did not improve and he stayed back while Sidique visited the front line. When they returned to Beeston on 4 September 2001, they felt they had "accomplished something."[22]

The Effects of the 9/11 Attacks

The Beeston boys reacted with puzzlement to the 9/11 attacks. An unreliable witness later claimed that the next day, at a computer shop in Beeston, Martin McDaid, Naveed Fiaz, and Tafazal Mohammed celebrated, but his claim was largely discredited at the Coroner's Inquests.[23] Ullah later testified that he saw the attacks on television and first thought it was an accident: "After a couple of days of the attack . . . people in the [Iqra] bookshop, even myself, would believe that it was a Jewish conspiracy against Muslims." They printed a leaflet, *One Minute Silence*, explaining how Jews did it. "We all, even Sidique at that time, we all used to think . . . you can't do what they did in 9/11 because it's attacking innocent people, and the use of suicide operation is strictly forbidden in Islam."[24] Shakil said at his trial that he was also shocked by the attacks and denied that Muslims could have carried them out. "Before, we were seen as good . . . working class citizens, and now we were more or less . . . in the firing line . . . of people making allegations against Muslims being terrorists and extremists."[25] However, within a few months, they accepted that the attacks had indeed been carried out by al Qaeda and Sidique, at least, approved of them.[26]

The retaliatory U.S. invasion and bombing of Afghanistan affected the Beeston activists. To them, the bombing was "indiscriminate . . . and entire villages were obliterated," Shakil later recalled, "and lots and lots of innocent lives were lost."[27] They opposed these bombings and protested the war at their respective universities. Ullah also later said, "Life is very sacred and what the brothers did in 9/11 is wrong, but what the Americans did also is equally as wrong. You cannot justify one thing and then, you know, do the same."[28] Shakil condoned British Muslims who had gone to Afghanistan to defend their co-religionists: "if they want to go, they can go, it's up to them. It's none of my business."[29]

After 9/11, the Beeston boys became more defensive and aggressive about being Muslim, probably in reaction to the suspicions put on them. Mark Hargreaves, an outdoor instructor (climbing, mountaineering, caving, and camping), whom Tafazal had hired for the youth center, remembered being a target of proselytism. McDaid and the club's organizers distributed material and showed him pictures from the Iqra bookstore to probe his feelings.

> A lot of it was about Israel and anti-Semitic, showing you horrific images of young people being murdered or bodies, carcasses, and it was designed to inflame and aggravate, and they were showing me this and saying, you know, "Do you think this is a bad thing?," "Of course, I do," I agreed, but then the premise was that I should . . . become involved with their belief systems. . . . Every opportunity to bring Islam into a conversation would be manipulated, anything at all. We . . . sat in a cave . . . it was very cold and dark, and he [Sidique] used that as an opportunity to explain to me how the light

of Islam could come into my life, and it was constant, it was just a constant barrage of these kinds of things. After a while, it became quite tiring.

Nevertheless, Hargreaves remembered Sidique as reasonable compared to McDaid, who said, "It was okay to blow people up because Allah said so."[30] Hargreaves left this job by summertime 2002, partly out of disagreement with their views.

The proselytism at the Hardy Street basement gym alarmed and angered the elders of the KMWA because it was based on a Salafi interpretation of Islam rather than their Barelvi Kashmiri traditions. In early, 2002, they asked Tafazal to move his organization out of their premises. He eventually moved to Tempest Road, where he established a gym with fighting mats and punching bags for martial arts training, and called it the Hamara Healthy Living Center.[31]

Sidique had acquired a good reputation and became well respected both at the Hillside Primary School and at Hardy Street. All the young people looked up to him. After 9/11, he became more religious and concerned with the plight of Muslims worldwide. A female fellow teacher later remembered that he used to give her a lift home but stopped doing so afterward.[32] On 22 October 2001, he married Hasina Patel in a religious ceremony despite their respective families' opposition. He and his bride moved to nearby Batley. They delayed their honeymoon and took it in the first week of April 2002 in Turkey, where they did some scuba diving.[33]

The Iqra Bookstore

Around that time, Sidique tried to persuade one of his primary school pupils, an 11- or 12-year-old, to convert to Islam. On one occasion, he took his student to the Iqra bookstore and told others that people would pay for what they've done to "Pakistan [sic]." He started to keep the accounts of the bookstore from February 2002, kept minutes of its board meeting from about April 2002, and prepared official documentation relating to its management. Iqra was a subscription bookstore and Sidique and others made regular monthly payments to it from mid-2002.[34]

The social life of the young militants in Beeston centered on the mosques, youth club, gym, and bookshop. The one-room club and gym focused on children from 13 to 19 years of age who had fallen behind or been excluded from school. It also functioned as a general social meeting site where classes, lectures, and discussions took place. The group was not associated with any of the local mosques, and members attended them all. The official parliamentary investigation concluded,

> Information about what went on in these places is mixed and incomplete. Much is hearsay. Accounts from those with more direct knowledge are conflicting. It is difficult to be sure what the facts are. Some have said the clubs, gym and bookshop were well known locally as centers of extremism. For example, that one of the gyms was known as "the al Qaida gym" because of who frequented it, and that the local bookshop was used to watch extremist DVDs and videos, access extremist websites, and for extremist lectures. Others present a very different picture. There is little evidence so far that [Sidique] Khan, Tanweer or Hussain were big internet users at home. Some who attended talks by Khan say that he focused on clean living, staying away from crime and drugs and the value of sports and outdoor activity. Others heard rumors that he held extreme views and some felt that Khan could preach aggressively.[35]

Martin Gilbertson, a computer technician, started working part time at the Iqra bookstore around June 2002. He later asserted that Tafazal, Fiaz, and McDaid were running the place. When he got there, the place was not yet fully opened, with very few books. It was still run down and being renovated to store the books. Gilbertson installed computers there and converted videos for the group. He remembered two that were related to "war zones around the world, in which [Muslim] children had been swept up and injured or killed, distressing, unpleasant photographs and documents of that time." He had agreed to do them because they highlighted the war and he was part of the Stop the War movement. However, he was distressed that they were anti-Semitic and anti-American. He recalled that the atmosphere at the bookstore was very hostile toward the West. McDaid was trying to convert him to Islam and was ranting and raving against the West. McDaid approved of the suicide bombing tactics of the Palestinians against Israel and the West. Fiaz complained, "This is what they're really doing to us. . . . They're murdering us left, right and center."[36]

Ullah used to hang around Iqra with Sidique, Shakil, and Tanweer but he was away for most of 2002 in Bangladesh, where his eldest sister forced him to marry a local woman. Shakil went to the shop as a customer and not a volunteer for he was away at Huddersfield University at the time. In the two years he worked at Iqra, from June 2002 and July 2004, Gilbertson never saw Sidique there but occasionally saw Tanweer, with whom he had pleasant conversations.[37]

Tafazal, Fiaz, and others adopted a constitution for Iqra in June 2002, which declared its purpose to be "the advancement of the Islamic faith, through lectures, study groups, literature or by such other charitable means as the trustees may from time to time determine."[38] On 19 January 2003, Tafazal, Fiaz, Sidique, Saleem, Ullah, and Khalid Khaliq applied for the shop to be registered as a charity; the application was accepted on 14 February 2003. A May 2003 list of its board of trustees added Tanweer to the list.[39] Despite his constant presence there, McDaid was not on its board. Iqra sold Islamic books, tapes, CDs, DVDs, perfume, and other paraphernalia, was a lending library of Islamic books and videos, and was also used for IT lessons, lectures, and discussions on Islam. The Charity Commission investigation later reported that although a majority of the material there was appropriate, about a fifth of it "was considered to be political, biased, propagandist or otherwise inappropriate for a charity advancing the Islamic faith."[40]

In January 2003, Iqra added Arabic and Hadith interpretations to its offering and got a teacher, who brought along one of his star students, Jermaine Lindsay.[41] Lindsay was born in Jamaica in 1985. His mother split up from his father when he was five months old and she moved with her son to live with another man in Huddersfield, England. That relationship ended when Lindsay was five and his mother started another relationship. He was close to this second man and had two younger stepsisters. Lindsay was a bright, artistic, and musical child, good in school and at sports. He regularly worked out, and practiced martial arts and kickboxing. In 2000, his mother's relationship with his stepfather ended and she converted to Islam. Her son followed suit and took the name Jamal. At school, he started associating with troublemakers and was once disciplined for handing out leaflets in support of al Qaeda. At his local mosque and in Islamic groups around Huddersfield and Dewsbury, he was admired for the speed with which he learned Arabic and memorized long passages of the Quran, showing unusual maturity and seriousness. He began wearing traditional Muslim white robes.[42]

After 9/11, Lindsay expressed strong support for the Taliban and al Qaeda, held anti-American views, and browsed extremist websites on computers in the school library. He avoided former friends and neglected his studies. At one point, he and his mother went to listen to Abdullah el Faisal. In 2002, his mother moved to the United States with another man whom she met online, leaving her son behind. This may have been traumatic for him: he left school despite a respectable number of GCSEs and went on welfare. He continued his online activity and protested the run-up to the war in Iraq. He told a friend that he wished to perform jihad before he died, fight against Americans in Iraq, or join the British Army so that he could kill his fellow soldiers.[43]

Lindsay met Samantha Lewthwaite from Aylesbury online. She was two years older than him and had also converted to Islam around 2000 after her parents had separated. She was studying religion and politics at the London School for Oriental and African Studies and was militantly against the upcoming war in Iraq. They exchanged e-mails, progressed to speaking on the phone, exchanged photographs, and finally met at a "Stop the War" march at Hyde Park, probably during the gigantic rally of 400,000 people on 28 September 2002.[44] They got married at a religious ceremony on 30 October 2002 despite her family's and friends' opposition. She took the name of Asmantara and moved into his Huddersfield home.[45]

Sidique Joins an al Qaeda Support Network

Sidique Khan and his wife went for Hajj from 26 January to 19 February 2003. After his return, he got into a dispute with Tafazal and Fiaz at Iqra over the sale of a cassette by an Islamic scholar, who was condemning suicide bombings and terrorism. Sidique wanted Iqra to stop selling his cassettes as he now approved of terrorist bombings like the recent Bali bombings. The Iqra management decided otherwise and Sidique left, never to return, and stopped his monthly contribution to Iqra.[46]

Ullah, Shakil, Tanweer, and he hoped to go and fight in Afghanistan. They prepared for their trip by doing physical training, jujitsu, and Thai boxing at the gym, and going on long walks over rough terrain. Sidique also raised money for the Afghan cause[47] and gave a three-minute lift in his car to McDaid on 14 April.[48] Sidique helped run the gym and, with Tafazal and Fiaz, organized monthly weekend outings in March, April, and May 2003.[49] Shakil walked five miles during the March outing and aggravated his condition, forcing him to stop coming to these treks. Ullah and Tanweer went on the April one in the Lake District. Tanweer changed from being a highly motivated student to becoming more religious, praying five times a day, and attending mosque regularly. He distanced himself from his secular girlfriend. In June 2003, he dropped out of Leeds Metropolitan University to work part-time for his father at their fish-and-chips shop.[50]

Meanwhile, newly married Lindsay sold cell phone accessories. He had not yet connected with this militant group.[51] Saleem got married on 1 February 2003 to a pretty but very assertive woman of Bengali origin, who occasionally came to Iqra. They moved nearby in Beeston, but Saleem had two jobs besides spending time with his wife and drifted away from his friends at Iqra.[52]

On 11 March 2003, Sidique received a call from Mohammed Qayum Khan on his cell phone, which listed Iqra's address as his own.[53] Operation Crevice had just started and this was one of the first calls authorities picked up while monitoring Qayum. It is unclear how they got in contact and whether this was their first call. Shakil had met Qayum four years before during his stay in Luton[54] and may have introduced the two. Sidique and Qayum were both involved in fund-raising for Afghanistan and may have run into each other during their activities. In any case, Qayum needed a replacement for Khyam, who wanted to stay in Pakistan. Then there was a gap of four months until the Crevice monitoring team picked up their next call in July 2003.

In late spring, Shakil was finishing his university degree when his grandfather in Kashmir died. He wanted to go pay his respect and visit his grave during the summer, so Sidique volunteered to accompany him and help him with his luggage. Sidique wanted to deliver money he had collected for the Afghan cause and perhaps fight there. He had heard that the Afghan resistance was not accepting volunteers and he wanted to see for himself whether this was true. They planned to spend about two weeks with Sidique's family in Rawalpindi and find out about Afghanistan, and two weeks with Shakil's family in Kashmir.[55]

The Crevice monitoring group picked up several phone calls between Qayum and Sidique on 13, 19, and 24 July but observed no personal meetings.[56] On 24 July 2003, Shakil and Sidique flew from Heathrow to Islamabad. Sidique paid £1,130 for the tickets; Shakil reimbursed him for his share. They were scheduled to return home on 20 August.[57]

Linking with Khyam and the Gorque Camp

Chance had it that Shakil and Sidique flew in on the same plane as Omar Khyam's friends coming to participate in the Gorque camp, as described in the previous chapter. On the morning of 25 July, Khyam and Mohammed

Babar came to the airport to pick up their friends while Salahuddin Amin came to pick up Sidique and Shakil. The three hosts had come early, saw each other, and went up to the restaurant to have breakfast. Babar later testified that Amin said that he was waiting for two men sent over by Qayum "because these two guys . . . were hearing conflicting reports on whether or not . . . guys from other countries were allowed to come in. So . . . they wanted to come for themselves and find out what the situation was."[58] Babar later spotted two young Western-dressed strangers who had just cleared customs. He asked whether they were looking for "Khalid," and, when they nodded yes, he introduced them to Amin.[59]

Sidique and Shakil met up with Amin and Sidique gave him the money. When Sidique asked about Afghanistan, Amin pointed to Khyam: "That's your man. He knows more about Afghanistan than anybody else." Sidique did not have time to talk because his uncle had come to take them home. Instead, he and Khyam agreed to meet later at an apartment rented by Amin in Islamabad. A few hours later, Amin brought them to the apartment. On the way there, Amin advised them to take aliases for security reasons. Sidique became Ibrahim and Shakil Zubair.[60]

Babar, Ali Khan, Khyam, Amin, Sidique, and Shakil discussed the situation in Afghanistan. The boys from Beeston said that "they wanted to come and fight in Afghanistan against the Americans and NATO and anybody aligned with them," Babar later recounted.[61] Khyam confirmed that Afghanistan was closed to foreigners at this time but added that he and Babar had organized a training camp at Gorque. Shakil later remembered, "They were trying to say it is training, weapons training, and I said, 'I've already done that anyway in Kashmir, I don't really need to do none of that.'" So Sidique and Shakil at first declined, but, Shakil later recalled, "Sid was a very much outward type of person and . . . he'd want to spend more time and to get to know a bit more about what's going on in Afghanistan." Khyam insisted and said, "it was going to be all English lads at the camp." This was significant for Shakil. "The last thing I wanted is a camp where there would be lots of Arab geezers . . . hanging around in a camp that's established . . . proper al Qaeda type of militant run camp, and I wasn't really interested with it. I was really scared about it. Well, he put it out as if they were just lads from back home and out here to train." Khyam said it would be only for a couple of days and Shakil finally relented: "We thought it would be a good laugh, yeah, we'd go ahead. It was only a couple of days." Khyam told them he would contact them and they all left for their respective places.[62]

Sidique and Shakil met with their fellow trainees the evening of 29 July at a luxury hotel in Islamabad. I have already described their journey to Gorque in the last chapter. On the way up, Shakil experienced difficulties with the climb and his companions and a local shepherd took turns helping him. During the climb, Sidique got to know Khyam.[63]

The "trainees" rested the next day after the climb and on the morning of their third and last day, on 3 August, all the participants were allowed to shoot small-caliber weapons. While Sidique and Shakil were doing this, the head trainer detonated a bomb for a few other trainees in another part of the camp. It is unclear whether Shakil or Sidique were aware of this experiment. During that time, they fired two magazines from an AK-47 and short bursts from a light machine gun. Shakil was chosen to fire a RPG because of his infirmity. The total amount of time that Shakil or Sidique had an AK-47 in their hands and held the light machine gun, and Shakil fired the RPG was 10 to 15 minutes.[64] After the firing, they all left the camp. Shakil had a lot of difficulties coming down: "Because of my contracture in my left leg . . . if I'm coming down, I'm putting the entire weight of my body on it, I kept falling because the leg would not hold my weight, and so I had to be carried down."[65] He also had diarrhea and an ear infection.

The whole group spent the night at the maulana's house in Gorque. They left the next morning for Peshawar and traveled onward to Lahore, where Sidique and Shakil spent the night at Babar's flat. Sidique was very concerned about Shakil's health. "My legs had swollen by now, I'd overworked my body completely," Shakil remembered. "I had got a bad ear by then. I was very very ill." Sidique insisted that they should fly back immediately. Shakil protested that he wanted to visit with his family in Kashmir, but finally relented. Babar helped Sidique change their tickets for 7 August. They hired a cab to retrieve their luggage from Rawalpindi and returned in time for their early morning flight from Lahore. After their return, Sidique e-mailed Babar, who did not bother to respond.[66] On 15 August, Sidique called Qayum.[67]

As mentioned in the previous chapter, this "camp" was not an al Qaeda camp, contrary to the mythology that arose about this so-called Malakand camp.[68]

Part of the Crevice Network

Ullah later testified that when Sidique came back from his trip, "he was happy that we've sorted out good contacts to get to Pakistan and eventually to Afghanistan." As argued in the previous chapter, the camp cemented the participants' social identity as soldiers and established the friendship between Sidique and Khyam. After their return, Sidique kept in touch with their fellow trainees and Ullah remembered that the first two times they went to meet with them, Khyam was still in Pakistan—he came back on 31 August 2003. Shakil's father gave him money at the end of September for graduating from university and he bought a car with it. He drove Sidique, Ullah, and Tanweer to Crawley at the end of September to visit Khyam and his friends for a long meal. After the visit, Khyam called Shakil on 28 September to talk to Sidique.[69]

Shortly after, Shakil watched *Saving Private Ryan* with Sidique at the latter's home. A week later, Sidique accused Shakil of having stolen some money from his home. Shakil protested and this led to a serious argument. Shakil later believed that Sidique thought "Shakil, it must have been you who did this because obviously you've taken back your ticket money because you're blaming me for not being able to go to your grandfather." Sidique further reproached Shakil for drinking, smoking, and socializing with non-Muslims, and accused him of being a Kashmiri nationalist. Their relationship never recovered.[70] From then on, Shakil parted way with Sidique and also lost contact with their friends from Crawley as they were closer to Sidique than him—Sidique was in regular phone contact with Khyam starting in October 2003.[71] Shakil occasionally saw Ullah and Saleem at the mosque. In December, he started a job as an administrator trainee in a computer business in Rothwell.

In September 2003, Lindsay and his wife moved to Aylesbury near Luton for her to be closer to her mother, with whom she had reconciled. He returned on Christmas to Huddersfield to see his Christian sister and visited his Beeston friends at the same time. He took a plumbing apprenticeship around London before finding a job as a carpet fitter.[72]

In late 2003, the gym and club moved and became the Iqra Youth Centre and Gym, not to be confused with the Iqra bookshop. Sidique remained active at the gym but kept away from the bookshop. In fact, his, Tanweer's, and Ullah's names were dropped from Iqra bookshop's board of trustees.[73] They hung out together at the gym and planned on going together to fight in Afghanistan.

Operation Crevice expanded its surveillance on Khyam at the end of January 2004 and caught Sidique calling Khyam on 28 January. On 2 February, Sidique, Tanweer, and Ullah drove to Crawley in a car registered to

Hasina Patel to meet with Khyam and his younger brother. Their respective cars were observed parked next to each other at 8:28 PM. Khyam got into Sidique's car while Ullah and Tanweer joined Shujah in the other. Khyam and Sidique drove for about 25 minutes up and down a highway and returned at 9:10 PM. All the people got out of their cars, hugged each other, got back in their respective cars and went home. The Beeston boys, with discreet surveillance behind them, stopped at a McDonald's on their way back. The surveillance team secretly photographed them there and labeled them Unidentified Males C, D, and E (UDM C, D, and E) later identified as Ullah, Tanweer, and Sidique respectively. The surveillance team saw Sidique drop off his passengers in Beeston and park in his own driveway.

Shortly after this meeting, the Security Service reevaluated Operation Crevice and upgraded Khyam and his associates from an al Qaeda support cell to a suspected terrorist cell that might conduct an attack in Britain. On 11 February, the executive liaison group was formed as a result of this rise in threat level. The investigation centered around Khyam, Qayum, and a Luton associate with a view to arresting and prosecuting them and disrupting the plot.[74]

The Party on Behalf of Khawaja

By mid-February, the three Beeston boys had decided to follow Khyam to Pakistan.[75] On 21 February, they came to Crawley for the party at Gulzar's house for visiting Momin Khawaja. At 8:49 PM, Khyam, his younger brother, and the Beeston boys got into Khyam's car and drove to a kebab shop, where they bought some food. At 9:10 PM, the car was back at Gulzar's house, but the passengers remained in the car in deep discussion until 9:34 PM, when they rejoined the party. Apparently, the surveillance team had missed the three Beeston boys in the car. They believed that only Khyam and Shujah had gone to get the food. However, the car was wired and the listening device in the car showed that there were five individuals, whose conversation went as follows.[76]

On the way to the kebab shop, they talked about their upcoming trip to Pakistan and Sidique told Khyam, "I know that it's really out of order, but I was hoping for a flat extension. . . . My wife's having a kid." On the way back, Ullah or Tanweer asked Khyam, "Are you really a terrorist?" Khyam answered, "They're working with us." The first man insisted, "You're serious." Khyam interrupted, "No, I'm not a terrorist, but they are working through us." The Beeston lad continued, "There's no one higher than you." Khyam redirected the conversation to the importance of security, especially when traveling to and from Pakistan as the authorities were watching. "Right now, I'm still Emir of the brothers. . . . They are saying that they can come, like one way . . . that's it. If you agree with that yeah it's not a problem."[77]

Since it was a one-way ticket, Khyam suggested, "you may as well rip the country apart economically as well. All the brothers are running scams. . . . I advise you to do the same . . . and you will probably walk away with twenty grand. Yeah that's really good money bruv. I can set it all up for you, you can actually go. I will get a brother to run it and I think it is a very good scheme, yeah. All the brothers that [are] leaving are doing it." Sidique asked again for the postponement of his departure. His child was due in late May, and with three weeks added to make sure that his wife and baby were fine, this postponed his departure to mid-June. Khyam agreed. Sidique then asked what he needed to buy. Khyam listed the necessary gear from the top of his head: "a 45-liter rucksack; a compact sleeping bag; special boots; and a waterproof and breathable jacket—there is no need for a Gortex one." He added that Sidique would need about £20,000 but should not take more than £2,000 through customs.[78]

As for saying good-bye to friends, Khyam advised them that he rarely met any now for their own good. He no longer lived in Crawley. When he was to leave, he would tell them. "Of course you love them bruv, you love them for the Deen. It's because we love the Deen this much that we stay away from them 'cause I know it's better for me and it's better for them."[79] Sidique told Khyam that he had found another brother "who's just coming in, from all the tests that we've done our general consensus of opinion is that he is not ready for . . . (unclear) He's about 18." Khyam suggested that perhaps they could invite him over the summer in Pakistan. Khyam stressed that Sidique should give his complete obedience to his emir when he joined al Qaeda. A house had already been set up for them. In terms of timing, Khyam said that he and his companions would be gone within the next three to four weeks, before the end of March, which gave them time to pull off a few frauds. Khyam explained his scam of buying merchandise on credit, selling it at half-price to his uncle, and never paying back the credit. He said he could help them with the credit application and selling to his uncle. He also advised them to max out on their credit cards, and even apply for new ones and max out on them as well.[80] After their 40 minutes' absence, the conspirators rejoined the party.

Involvement in Fraud

The Beeston boys took Khyam up on his offer to help set them up in various fraudulent schemes. On 28 February, Sidique drove Tanweer and Ullah to Crawley, where they had breakfast with Khyam and his brother at a McDonald's. They all went to Marshall's Builders Merchants and Jewsons. Tanweer tried to open three accounts at Howdens, but they told him he could only open one. They prayed at a mosque in Slough and then went to Khyam's apartment in the afternoon. They had dinner and went to a cell phone shop owned by a radical imam, where they stayed two hours. They went for another meal, dropped off Khyam at home, and returned to Leeds around midnight. The surveillance squad recognized UDM C, D, and E and followed the car to Beeston and Sidique's home, around 3 A.M.[81]

Three weeks later, on 20 March, Sidique arrived at Khyam's apartment in Crawley around 11:20 PM in a rented car, as his car was being serviced. Khyam and his brother got into the car, which Sidique drove around for half an hour, and they then returned to Khyam's apartment around 10 minutes before 1 A.M. Sidique and Khyam engaged in a further 10-minute conversation before Sidique returned home.[82] On 22 March, Sidique called Khyam on his cell phone. On the morning of 23 March, Sidique, Ullah, and Tanweer returned to Crawley in the same rented car and met Khyam and Shujah. Surveillance again recognized them as UDM C, D, and E from Leeds. They visited with Nadeem Ashraf and picked up Azhar Khan. The six traveled in a two-car convoy to Ilford in midafternoon: Khyam, Azhar, and Tanweer in Khyam's car and Sidique, Ullah, and Shujah in Sidique's rented car. The conversation in Khyam's car was recorded, and a contemporary Security Service summary stated, "large parts of their discussion are unclear, but they did mention the importance of being physically and mentally prepared for travelling to Pakistan."[83] However, when the conversation was later transcribed, it was found that they had discussed the Madrid bombings. One unidentified speaker (UM) said, "if there was an attack the size of Madrid in the UK, we would not be able to handle it, that would destroy everything. . . . Another UM says look on the success of the Madrid bombing, change of power."[84]

In Ilford, the six militants visited a designer store, a cash-and-carry store, and a bookshop twice, lingering for approximately one hour during their second visit. They returned to Slough around 9 PM, and Khyam and Sidique went alone to a local Internet café.[85] The intelligence summary indicated that Khyam was moving to Pakistan permanently: "The group received detailed advice from a fraud expert about raising money fraudulently, selling cars bought on credit, lying about wages in loan applications, skimming credit cards, and obtaining and defaulting on bank loans. UDM E [Sidique] also mentioned that he worked in a school counselling children, and that he had to return his . . . hire car and pick up his repaired car from the garage."[86] The visitors returned home around midnight.[87]

On 24 March, Ullah opened an account at Howdens under the name of Ships Builders for £7,000 to buy large appliances, Sidique applied for an HSBC loan of £10,000 and drew the funds two days later, and Tanweer applied for credit at a car credit company and Barclay's Bank. On 30 March 2004, Khyam and his fellow Crawley conspirators were arrested. The Beeston conspirators assumed that the police had detected them and expected to be arrested at any moment. They laid low and stopped their credit applications. On 4 April, Tanweer was arrested for a public order offense of a fairly minor kind and cautioned.[88] To throw the police off their scent, Sidique and Tanweer pretended to be "un-Islamic," by going to nonhalal restaurants and movies, and laughing out loud at jokes.[89] With the Crevice arrests, Sidique lost all his contacts with al Qaeda since Qayum had already dropped out in September 2003.

Hussain Joins the Beeston Boys

In mid-2004, several of the Leeds militants had children. In April, Lindsay had a son, Abdullah, and Sidique had a daughter, Maryam. In August, Saleem had a daughter and in September, Shakil had a son. In April 2004, after an extensive fund-raising campaign, the Hamara Centre on Tempest Road opened, offering a wide variety of activities, including arts and crafts; gym and outdoor sports activities; girls' only activities such as sewing and cooking; aerobics; and classes in information technology, cultural awareness, and self-defense. The center was very popular and acted as a conduit between politicians, police, and priests. Saleem was hired as its caretaker responsible for general maintenance and opening and closing it. Sidique, Ullah, and Tanweer came regularly to take karate classes. At one point,

Ullah accidentally broke Sidique's nose, which required a visit to the emergency room.[90] Saleem reconnected with his former friends, even though Sidique kept his distance from him.

Among the center's users was Hasib Hussain from nearby Holbeck. A big 18-year-old, born in Leeds to Pakistani immigrants, he was a quiet schoolboy, with few friends, although he had been briefly involved in some racial tension at school. His older brother was close to Sidique and played cricket with Tanweer. Hasib had first met Sidique at the Hardy Street basement around 2001, when he started attending the mosque above it. Shortly after the 9/11 attacks, he openly supported al Qaeda. He wrote, "You're next," to two students and "Al Qaida No Limits" in his religious education book, drawing a picture of planes crashing into the Twin Towers. He distributed leaflets at school to younger children in support of al Qaeda and Osama bin Laden. In early 2002, he went with his family on hajj and then to Pakistan, where his older brother got married. After this, he began wearing traditional clothing and a prayer cap on Fridays. He regularly read religious texts and prayed late into the night. In 2003, he got seven GCSEs in English, literature, mathematics, science, design technology, and Urdu, but at C grade level and below. He later got a general national vocational qualification (GNVQ) certificate in business.[91]

As there was no mosque in the vicinity of his home, Hussain came to pray at the Hamara Centre. Sidique started giving him lifts to the gym in May, and soon they, Ullah, and Tanweer hung out together all the time. Sidique got closer to Tanweer. He used to pick up first Ullah then Tanweer on his rides to the gym, but by early summer 2004, he reversed his pattern and picked up Tanweer first. In July 2004, when Hussain's parents went abroad for a long period, Sidique and Tanweer frequently came over to his home and spent a lot of time talking and praying together into the early hours of the morning.[92]

The men from Beeston had not given up on their plan to go to a training camp and fight in Afghanistan. At the gym, they would talk about their upcoming trip. Hussain and Saleem heard about it. Saleem later testified that unlike in 2001 when he hesitated, he now felt ready to go. "I had a lot of issues with my wife at home and that time I know my marriage was very bad. . . . We were even contemplating separating and stuff like that. I wanted time to get away and when I heard MSK and all these boys talking about going abroad, this is like an opportunity for me to like go with 'em, I wanted to go . . . see the place for myself, see the people and . . . do the training and whatever." He told his wife, "Listen . . . I need to go away to sort my head out."[93]

Because of the continuing grudge that Sidique held about Saleem for letting him down in 2001, Saleem asked Ullah to intercede for him. Ullah approached Sidique: "You know what, Sadeer [Saleem] wants to come along, yeah, and we should let him." Ullah later explained, "For me . . . if a Muslim wants to go and help his Muslim brother . . . it's my obligation to help him." Sidique replied, "You know what, brother, if you're going to take him, you ride with him, yeah, and on your head, be it. You take him, do whatever you want, I've no problem."[94] All five now resolved to go to Pakistan after Eid, which that year fell in mid-November.

In August, Sidique and his family got a two-bedroom council house on Lees Holm in Dewsbury but moved in later, in February 2005. In the meanwhile, the couple stayed with her parents. (Sidique probably anticipated going to Pakistan soon and she wanted to stay at her parents' house with their baby during his absence.) In September, Lindsay and his family came for a week and stayed at the empty house. His wife and Sidique's wife became friends. Lindsay hung around with Sidique and his friends, and came to a Saturday karate class at the Hamara Centre with them.[95]

Around August 2004, Sidique became upset at what Shakil was saying about him to mutual friends as they were bad-mouthing each other. Sidique called him and angrily told him to stop. On 23 August, after the late afternoon prayer, Sidique and Tanweer waited for Shakil as he came out of the mosque. Since the latter was not speaking to Sidique, Tanweer asked him to get into Sidique's car. Sidique drove toward Dewsbury, angry and silent, while Tanweer asked Shakil about his swearing at Sidique and calling him a liar. Sidique pulled over, got out, and pulled Shakil out of the car. Sidique then attacked Shakil, using "martial arts moves on me, elbows, knees, punching on the floor, the rest of it." After Shakil was visibly beat up, Tanweer dragged Sidique back into the car, and they drove away, leaving Shakil on the ground with multiple injuries to the face, neck, and abdomen. A stranger saw him and drove him to a Dewsbury hospital, where he stayed overnight. The discharge diagnosis reported, "Extensive facial bruising and strangulation marks around neck. Also bruising on stomach and back, swollen face and cuts behind ears."[96] Shakil did not report the assault to the police. Two weeks later, his son was born. He invited Ullah, Tanweer, and Hussain to the celebration but not Sidique.

At the start of the school year in the fall, Sidique was frequently absent from his job and wrote a series of sick notes explaining that his father had fallen ill. He resigned on 19 November 2004.[97] At the Hamara Centre, the karate classes stopped for Ramadan. Sidique bought a rucksack, thermal undergarments, walking boots, and other camping-type associated equipment in October. Hussain was arrested for shoplifting a hat and a pair of gloves, and was cautioned. On 26 October, Sidique recorded a short videotape at his home with his daughter, Tanweer, Hussain, and Ullah.[98]

The friends stayed at a mosque for the last ten days of Ramadan (3–12 November) praying and reading the Quran. On 10 November, Sidique got visas for Tanweer and himself, but not for Ullah or Saleem. When Ullah found out, he confronted Sidique, who made an excuse: "What's going to happen is me and Kaki are going to go out first, we're going to sort out the contacts and then we'll give you a call. Be ready to move out any time soon, yeah, and then just come over." As he later testified, Ullah was upset. "I was thinking we were supposed to get the visas together. . . . I said to myself I can get my own visas, so I went and got them [for him and Saleem] the day after." Hussain would come last on his own because his parents were so protective of him. If his parents did not accept his excuse of going to Pakistan for a two-week holiday, he should "do a runner" and his friends would pick him up in Islamabad.[99]

On the last day of Eid, 15 November, Sidique made a farewell video for his daughter, explaining to her that he was not going to come back, but he loved her. He held her in one hand, the video camera in the other, and filmed their reflection in a mirror.[100] "Sweetheart, I don't have too long to go now. . . . I'm gonna really, really miss you. . . . You've been the happiest thing in my life, you and your mom. . . . I wish I could have been part of your life, especially the next few months . . . with you learning to walk and things. . . . I have to do this thing for all our future and it will the best, insh'Allah, in the long run . . . I'm doing what I'm doing for the sake of Islam." His wife filmed another clip of him holding his six-month-old daughter and telling her to remember him and look after her mother.[101] These were clearly good-bye videos, implying that Sidique did not expect to ever come back. He also made a will and left it behind. Tanweer told his family that he was going to Pakistan to look for a school to study Islam. His family paid for his trip and provided him with spending money.[102]

Sidique and Tanweer Meet al Qaeda

On 18 November 2004, Khan and Tanweer flew to Islamabad and stayed for a week with Tanweer's uncle in Faisalabad. Little was known about their trip until May 2011 when an Austrian returning from Afghanistan named Maqsood Lodin was captured in Berlin. In his underwear, he carried a digital storage device with a report on the three British bombing plots.[103]

Its author was Rashid Rauf, born into a religious family in Mirpur, Pakistan. His family and he immigrated to Birmingham around 1982 when he was one. His father opened a South Asian bakery that became successful. Rashid as the oldest son chipped in and helped deliver bread early in the mornings. Even though Rashid went to the mosque at 5 AM before his morning rounds, his interests were working out at the gym and playing soccer. Neighbors did not remember him as particularly religious or interested in Islam or politics.[104] The Rauf family kept close to its roots and relatives in Kashmir.

Rauf's best friend was Mohammed Gulzar[105] of the same age but born in Birmingham. They met as children and stayed close until they went to university around 1999. Rauf studied accounting at Portsmouth University while Gulzar studied computers at Kingston University in London before transferring to Portsmouth in 2000 and reuniting with his friend. During that year, Rauf's father established a charity, Crescent Relief, based in East London, dedicated to education and health, especially in Kashmir. His mother set up a small study center in the back of their house in Birmingham, where she taught Quran to about 20 girls three to four times a week.[106] While in Portsmouth, the two friends became involved with the Tablighi Jamaat. Gulzar dropped out of school to "do some business." During Ramadan, Gulzar went on a Tablighi Jamaat mission for a few days. It is unclear whether Rauf accompanied him.[107]

By February 2002, the two friends tried to support the mujahedin in Afghanistan. From an Internet café in Portsmouth, they ordered a GPS map receiver and various map CDs from a U.S. aviation company using a stolen credit card. They were both arrested but released and cautioned for deception offenses.[108] In April 2002, Rashid's 54-year-old maternal uncle Mohammed Saeed was stabbed repeatedly on his way home. He staggered to the steps of his house before collapsing and dying in front of his wife and children. The main suspects were the two friends, as the attack was allegedly an honor killing about an arranged marriage. Two weeks later, Rauf and Gulzar fled to Pakistan.[109]

Little is publicly known about their lives in Pakistan. They found refuge among Rauf's relatives and their friends in Pakistan, who were supporters of Kashmiri and militant Pakistani groups such as Harakat ul-Jihad Islami,

Harakat ul-Mujahidin, and Jaish e-Mohammed. Gulzar later testified that they hid with the Tablighi Jamaat[110] but they also may have gone for training at a Kashmiri military camp. In the confusion of the times, several Pakistani militant organizations were helping foreign militants fleeing Afghanistan after the U.S. invasion. The prominent members of these militant organizations formed an informal community and intermarried: surviving men married eligible young women and widows from this community. It included al Qaeda members such as Abu Faraj al-Libi, Hamza Rabia, and Abu Ubaydah al Masri; Kashmiri militants such as Harakat ul-Jihad Islami leaders Ilyas Kashmiri and Qari Imran and Harakat ul-Mujahidin leader Masood Azhar; and foreign facilitators such as Mohammed al Ghabra.[111] The two British fugitives were introduced to this community by relatives. Qari Imran arranged for Rauf to marry his wife's sister, Saira. A third sister is married to the younger brother of Jaish e-Mohammed founder Maulana Azhar. After their marriage in May 2003, Rauf and his wife moved to Bahawalpur and had two daughters.[112] It is not known how Rauf met Abu Ubaydah al-Masri, who was a veteran of the Afghan Soviet war and had resided in Germany before becoming the leader of al Qaeda's Kabul front against the allied invasion in 2001. Afterward, he became the al Qaeda emir in the Kunar Valley. Rauf's relationship with him became operational in the summer of 2004. Abu Ubaydah became one of al Qaeda's most ingenious hydrogen-peroxide-based bomb makers. He is referred to as "Haji" in Rauf's after-action report found on Lodin.[113]

In that document, Rauf reported that he got Tanweer's uncle's phone number from one of his contacts in Britain, Umar, whom he had previously trained and dispatched home to carry out an attack. However, when Umar had tried to recruit his friends for it, they had drifted back to drug abuse.[114] Rauf waited about a week before contacting the visitors to make sure they were not under surveillance. He met them in Faisalabad, about an hour's drive from Tanweer's family home. They drove back to the uncle's home: loud music was playing to hide the visitors' piety. Sidique whispered that Tanweer's family disapproved of their jihadi intentions and the family driver was not witting. After spending some time with them, Rauf found them to have sound knowledge of Islam. Sidique and Tanweer explained to him that they wanted to fight in Afghanistan. Rauf took them to an apartment in Islamabad, where they listened to tapes of Anwar al-Awlaki, Abu Hamza al-Masri, and Abdullah el-Faisal while Rauf was making arrangements. A few days later, he took them to meet Abu Ubaydah. According to the after action report, the meeting had a "profound effect on the brothers. It took Haji just a few days to persuade the duo to conduct a suicide bombing in Britain."[115] On 25 November, Hasina Patel, Sidique's wife, wrote in her diary, "S rang, good news." The next day, she wrote again, "S rang, good news, back by Feb?" She did not tell anyone that her husband would come back, not even Ullah, Saleem, or Hussain. This was a dramatic change of plans, contrary to Sidique's video to his daughter.[116]

Many pundits describe the above process of connecting with al Qaeda as "al Qaeda recruited Sidique and Tanweer." This is misleading. From this account, it is clear that both volunteered to join al Qaeda: they were looking for the organization rather than the organization looking for them. They initiated and drove this process. However, they wanted to fight and die fighting in Afghanistan and what Abu Ubaydah did was to turn them around and send them back to Britain to carry out an attack there. The evidence is quite overwhelming, and indeed accepted by the Coroner's Inquests, that they no intention to attack Britain until the end of November, and no one except for Sidique and Tanweer was aware of this until they came back in February.[117]

The Alleged Casing Trip to London

Meanwhile in Britain, Ullah and Saleem started their fraudulent schemes to fund their trip. On 22 October, Saleem applied for large loans but was turned down. On 26 October, he opened a trade account at Howdens under the name Bads Builders and accrued a debt of £2,784 but cleared £540 from it. At the end of October, Ullah got credit for merchandise he bought at Jewsons and Howdens. He got appliances like refrigerators and cookers delivered to his sister's address, where Tanweer, shortly before he left for Pakistan, picked them up in his uncle's van and dropped them off to people who bought them. Ullah gave a cooker and washing machine to Sidique's wife. He stored some of the appliances at Sidique's empty house. He also maxed out on his credit card and, by 16 December, had accumulated about £3,900 for his trip.[118]

Ullah and Salem did not receive any communication from their friends in Pakistan. Ullah grew impatient and visited Tanweer's family's fish and chip shop. Tanweer's brother told him that Tanweer had phoned from Pakistan and left a phone number in Faisalabad. Ullah decided to proceed according to plan. From his testimony, "After I've been waiting for about three weeks, me and Sadeer . . . booked the tickets and the next time I see Nicky [Tanweer's brother] I'll tell him . . . and if the message gets across, it gets across. If it doesn't, I'll already go there." He told Tanweer's brother, " 'I'm going to Pakistan. The next time you speak to him, make sure your kid comes and picks me up.' I know Kaki would not leave us there stranded. In the worst-case scenario, if he did leave us stranded, we could always go to Sadeer's family's home in Kashmir. So, really for us, it's not really a problem." He decided to go to London to buy the tickets there and take the opportunity to visit his oldest sister, who was living there in a homeless shelter. He called Lindsay and told him he would come to London. Lindsay invited him and his friends to drop by his home.[119]

On 16 December 2004, Shakil, who had reconnected with his friends after Sidique's departure, volunteered to drive Ullah and Saleem to London. Hussain joined them. They drove to east London and bypassed Lindsay's home because Aylesbury was too far away. Ullah left to see his sister for the whole evening and rejoined his friends very late. They picked up Lindsay, who came down to London, and all of them stayed overnight at a hostel near King's Cross train station. The next morning, they visited the London Eye and the Aquarium. Ullah bought two round-trip airline tickets to Islamabad and paid about £2,000 for them.[120] (He had remembered Khyam's advice to buy round-trip tickets so as not to arouse suspicion.)

The Crown prosecutors later tried Saleem, Ullah, and Shakil for involvement in the London bombings, claiming that their trip was reconnaissance for the bombings. However, a jury rightly acquitted them of this charge. At the time, the defendants believed that Sidique and Tanweer had gone to Pakistan and Afghanistan permanently, with no plans of returning home. They had no idea that they would come back and carry out a terrorist operation at home.[121]

On Christmas, Lindsay came to visit his sister. During his visit, he met Ullah, Saleem, Hussain, and Shakil at Sidique's house and all five spent the night there. The next day, Shakil and Hussain drove Ullah and Saleem to Manchester airport for their flight to Islamabad.[122]

Al Qaeda Training in Pakistan

Tanweer and his uncle's driver picked them up at the airport and drove them to a small apartment in Faisalabad. Tanweer told them, "I've been with the brothers, with Sidique, and we've just been training and every-thing." On 28–29 December, Tanweer got a call from his contact and the three friends went to Peshawar, where two individuals from the tribal areas warned them not to speak English and took them to a "little compound," Ullah recalled at trial, "where it was a house and it had big walls. . . . It was a little hut . . . like a little barn. . . . It was pretty big . . . say, the size of this court hall, and we just stayed in there. . . . We got there a bit late, about ten o'clock. . . . We prayed, ate and went to sleep, chatted with Kaki for a bit." Ullah was disappointed: "we had a set plan . . . that we wanted to be together and everything and everything changed. . . . Kaki explained to me. . . . Because you brothers have come late, you are going to have to do the training that we have already done, and then we can link up in about 4 or 5 weeks and we will be together."[123] In the morning, Sidique picked up Kaki and they left immediately to a site nearby.

Rauf had arranged for "Marwan Suri" to provide bomb-making train-ing for Sidique and Tanweer, using an organic peroxide consisting of hydrogen peroxide mixed with piperine found in black pepper for the main charge and hexamethylene triperoxide diamine (HMTD) for the detonator. The specific design of these bombs was new in Britain. More traditionally, bombs were ammonium-nitrate-fertilizer-based devices as in Crevice. Indeed, later forensic analysis took a considerable time to identify the com-ponent of the London bombs.[124]

In its pure form, hydrogen peroxide is a colorless liquid, slightly more viscous and heavier than water, and comes in a water solution, usually at low concentration for safety. In 2005, the highest concentration available in Britain was around 18 percent, which meant that, to be used as an explosive mixture, the solution had to be concentrated to about 70 percent. This process takes advantage of the fact that water boils at 100 degrees centigrade while hydrogen peroxide boils at 150 degrees centigrade. In theory, heating a mixture of water and hydrogen peroxide would selectively evaporate the water first, leaving a highly concentrated solution of hydrogen peroxide. The reality is more complicated because hydrogen peroxide is unstable and breaks down to water and oxygen as it is heated. So the heating process has to be carried out gently at around 50–60 degrees centigrade. In theory, four liters of 18 percent hydrogen peroxide could be concentrated to a liter of 72 percent hydrogen peroxide. But this gentle heating would take hours, if not days, to accomplish. More rapid heating results in a breakdown of hydrogen peroxide and is self-defeating. The measurement of its concentration in water takes advantage of its specific density, which is 1.29 at 70 percent concentration at 20 degrees centigrade. However, a small error in the measured volume or weight can dramatically throw off measurement.

Hydrogen peroxide must be mixed with an organic substance to create an organic peroxide, which is unstable and decomposes rapidly in a self-accelerating process as the decomposition generates heat, which accelerates the decomposition of the compound. This means that a main charge made up of such a compound must be mixed at the last minute and kept cool to prevent its breakdown. The fact that the training took place at high altitude in the FATA during very cold winter temperatures affected this concentration process as well as the stability of the main charge.

To set off this main charge, Suri taught Sidique and Tanweer to use a small amount (up to 10 grams) of HMTD, a powerful high explosive but very unstable as it detonates upon shock, friction, and heat, which makes it unsafe for commercial or military use. It is relatively easy to manufacture from hydrogen peroxide and hexamine in the presence of an acid as a catalyst. This detonator is inserted into the main charge and can be ignited by the filament of a small light bulb connected to a battery. The advantage of using two types of explosives, the main charge and the initiator, is safety. Although the main charge is unstable, it is less sensitive than the initiator to detonation. All the ingredients were available in Britain at various shops. At the time, there was no monitoring of hydrogen peroxide, the main ingredients of both the main charge and detonator.

Rauf recalled that Sidique and Tanweer detonated a 300-gram hydrogen peroxide mixture in the tribal areas. "Sidique was always saying to me, 'I hope these mixtures are as good as you say they are.' After he tested the mixtures, he was very happy." Rauf spent a lot of time with the duo. They would sit and talk for long periods. He later stressed that getting to know them so well really helped later when it came to communicating with them after they returned to Britain.[125]

Meanwhile, Saleem and Ullah had a miserable time at their "camp." Saleem later remembered, "The house that we were staying in had doors, but it had no windows, had like a plastic sheet in front of the windows and in them four/five/six weeks, I hardly took my clothes off, because it was extremely cold. Even when I'm—fall asleep, you had to keep your clothes on. The only time we took the clothes off was maybe when you were—

occasional bath or something like that." They could not get out, were cooped up in the house all the time, and prepared their own food; "eating the same kidney beans every day was difficult."[126] A family next door dropped off chapatti and naan for them in the early afternoon. Saleem got homesick. Three other Pakistanis from the tribal belt, who spoke only Pashtu, trained with them. Their training consisting mainly of physical exercise, such as push-ups and crawling, mostly in the house. They learned how to dismantle AK-47s and rolled around with them, but never got to fire them so as not to alert the neighbors. They never received any instructions in explosives. Their trainer came only in the morning and finished up by one o'clock. The students were stuck in the compound by themselves the rest of the day.

After about three or four weeks, Sidique and Tanweer came one evening. "When I first saw him [Sidique]," Ullah later recalled, "I was really happy. . . . I thought we were going to be chilling together now like we initially planned. . . . But then the brothers just told me straight they are going back to England. I was really disappointed about that. . . . They told me . . . we are going to go back and do a couple of things for the brothers, you lot just lie out here and I thought this was not my plans, my plans were to stay with you brothers and to ride out this thing together. . . . [Ullah asked] 'what's going on,' because Hasib was supposed to be arriving soon . . . and they go, 'don't worry about him, he is riding with us.' So, I thought cool, whatever."[127] Sidique and Tanweer left after an hour.

The Martyrdom Videos

Sidique and Tanweer met Rauf in Islamabad. They discussed potential targets: the Bank of England, the upcoming G-8 summit in Scotland, scheduled for 6–8 July 2005, or the London Underground. Rauf and Sidique agreed on a communication plan between them for after his return. Rauf instructed them to lay low for three weeks in case British authorities might monitor them after their return. He insisted that they make a martyrdom tape and supervised its creation. Rauf was annoyed because there was no natural light in the apartment. Sidique and Tanweer were at first reluctant because of their shyness but Abu Ubaydah ordered them to do it.[128]

In his tape, which was later aired on 1 September 2005, Sidique declared,

I and thousands like me are forsaking everything for what we
believe. Our driving motivation doesn't come from tangible com-
modities that this world has to offer. Our religion is Islam. . . .
Your democratically elected governments continuously perpetuate
atrocities against my people all over the world. And your support of
them makes you directly responsible, just as I am directly responsible for protecting and avenging my Muslim brothers and sisters.
Until we feel security, you will be our targets. And until you stop
the bombing, gassing, imprisonment and torture of my people we
will not stop this fight. We are at war and I am a soldier. Now, you
will taste the reality of this situation.

Later, Sidique referred to "today's heroes like our beloved Sheikh Osama
bin Laden, Dr. Ayman al-Zawahiri and Abu Musab al-Zarqawi and all the
other brothers and sisters that are fighting."[129]
Tanweer also made a tape, which was released on 6 July 2006, on the
anniversary of the bombing:

To the non-Muslims of Britain, you may wonder what you have
done to deserve this. You are those who vote in governments, who
. . . continue to this day to oppress our children, brothers and sisters,
from the east to the west, in Palestine, Afghanistan, Iraq and Chechnya. Your government has openly supported the genocide of more
than 150,000 Muslims in Faluja. You offered . . . military support
for the U.S. and Israel in the massacre of our children in Palestine.
You are directly responsible. . . . You have openly declared war on
Islam. . . . We are one hundred percent committed to the cause of
Islam. We love death the way you love life. . . . I tell all of you British
citizens to stop your support of your lying British government and
the so called war on terror and ask yourselves why would thousands
of men be ready to give their lives for the cause of Muslims?[130]

Sidique and Tanweer returned to Britain on 8 February 2005. Meanwhile at the camp, Saleem and Ullah were getting tired of the boring routine
and the cold. After another week or two after Sidique's visit, Saleem told
Ullah, "Listen, I can't handle this, this is too difficult." Ullah felt the same:
"We were just in more like a cell . . . in a house for five or six weeks and
we were not allowed out of the house, it was really claustrophobic and I

just got sick and tired of it." They asked for the main person. "We told him that our tickets are booked for 26th February to head back to UK. . . . There were still about three weeks or four weeks left at that time—so he says to us, 'when you go back to Pakistan . . . stay in Pakistan for the . . . next couple of weeks and just behave like tourists . . . stay in hotels and go visiting sites.'" Ullah and Saleem stayed at modest hotels in Rawalpindi and Lahore, where they went to restaurants, took photographs, and enjoyed being tourists. They returned to Britain on schedule.[131]

Back Home

There is little information about the conspirators from the time of their return to the bombings. They had intentionally distanced themselves from their former friends and their actions must be reconstructed from the few traces they left behind.

As soon as he returned, Ullah went to see Tanweer.

> I've hugged him and everything . . . usually he's happy to see me. So, I go, "What's going on, man? What you guys going on about, you know, flipping heck? Let me chill with you." And he goes, "'No, bruv, you shouldn't even be here. Sid would be vexed if he found out you were here. . . ." I go, "Come on, what's going on? . . . You're not going to do nothing, innit? What you guys getting up to?" and he goes, "No, we're just chilling with the brothers, we're just going to do a couple of things with the brothers, that's it." . . . I did feel really . . . left out and sad. I was thinking what's going on here, man, I've been with the brothers for a long time and they've just dropped me like a hot potato.[132]

About a week after his return, Sidique came to Saleem's house because he was upset that Saleem and Ullah had not stayed in Pakistan for two months as he had instructed them to do. He told Saleem that since they had come back from Pakistan, they were "hot" and they should keep their distance from him and Tanweer. "I didn't really think much of it," Saleem later recalled. "I mean I started hanging around with 'em in 2004, for the only purpose to go to training camp. Before that, I weren't even hanging around with these guys."[133] After these encounters, Saleem and Ullah stayed away from Sidique and Tanweer, with rare polite greetings at the mosque.

Trying to improve his relationship with his wife, Saleem spent more time at home, which left Ullah on his own. He drifted back to his friend Kavish, who did drugs. Ullah followed suit and abused Ecstasy and cocaine. He stopped praying but couldn't resume his fraudulent activities because of his poor credit history. Hussain also kept his distance from Ullah, Saleem, and Shakil. One of them ran into Hussain at the mosque and asked him why he no longer called. Hussain explained that Sidique had given him the choice of hanging with him and Tanweer or their former group, but he could not do both. He had chosen Sidique and Tanweer.[134]

Right after his return, Tanweer contacted his former girlfriend A. They had had a secret relationship four years earlier but it had ended because one of them moved away. Tanweer texted her and mentioned he had been in Pakistan for a few months. They kept in contact by text for the next three months. In March, Tanweer's father bought him a red Mercedes.[135]

Rauf explained in his report that Sidique and Tanweer began to buy bomb components at different stores: hydrogen peroxide in garden stores, hexamine in camping stove fuel, and citric acid anywhere as it was easily available. The Coroner's Inquests showed that Hussain searched for local hydroponics stores on his computers. On 22 February, one of the conspirators bought two five-liter bottles of Oxyplus liquid oxygen and three days later bought four five-liter bottles of the same product at two different stores in Huddersfield. This was a huge quantity for this product, which contained 17.5 percent hydrogen peroxide in aqueous solution.[136] Rauf wrote that Sidique had ruled out attacking the G-8 summit because it would require too much explosive material and settled on attacking the London Underground.[137]

Around 15 March, Sidique bought three prepaid unregistered cell phones dedicated to operations, kept one, and gave the other two to Tanweer and Hussain. With them, they contacted each other, chemical suppliers, vehicle hire companies, and landlords of their bomb factories. Between 22 February and 15 June 2005, there were 41 telephone contacts between these operational phones and hydroponics outlets. At first, there was some leakage, meaning that a few calls were to friends and family, but soon the conspirators became more disciplined with their operational phones.[138]

On 18 March, Sidique called Lindsay from a nonoperational phone. It does not seem that Lindsay was part of the conspiracy at first. They had very little contact with him until Sidique called him. He did not get an operational phone in the first round and was still in contact with Shakil and Ullah. He came to visit his sister in Huddersfield for Easter, which came in late March that year. He called Ullah on 24 March: "I've come down to Leeds, do you want to meet up?" Ullah could not meet him because he had been smoking that day and Lindsay would not approve. So he kept delaying him with all kinds of excuses but finally agreed to meet at a takeaway shop. Ullah said at trial, "I think Jamaal found out . . . that I started smoking weed and everything . . . and he started giving me vibes in the sense that . . . he's going to start giving me a lecture. . . . He wouldn't say it in a rude way, but I knew he were going to start giving me one, yeah, so I had to make my exit. . . . I just said to him: 'Listen, brother, I've just got to go somewhere.' "[139] This was the last time Ullah saw Lindsay.

Shortly after that, Lindsay joined the conspiracy. He no longer saw his other friends and got a phone in the next three rounds of operational phone purchases. In total, there were 15 operational cell phones: one set of three and three sets of four. Sidique bought them all, and the conspirators switched to the new operational phones simultaneously. It seems that Sidique first stored the various chemical purchases at his new house. His neighbor later remembered, "He was taking bags out of the car boot and into the house. I thought this was strange because he was making too many trips. I saw him carrying a toolbox on one of the trips. . . . He kept opening and shutting the boot like he had something to hide. . . . The man's friends were all in the house. There were three of them." She recognized Tanweer and his red Mercedes.[140]

The First Bomb Factory on Chapeltown Road

On 10 April, Sidique rented an apartment allegedly for a student friend. The landlord later remembered, "I took him to the vacant room at . . . Chapeltown Road. . . . He asked a number of questions about who else was living in other rooms in the building. He said that his friend . . . would not like loud music and things like that disturbing him. He said that he would most likely rent the room but would need to show it to his friend."[141] The next day, Sidique came with Hussain, whom he introduced as Imran Mirza. They made the deal and "Mirza" paid the owner a deposit and three months' rent in advance in cash. The next day, Tanweer drove Sidique and Hussain in his Mercedes to the Chapeltown apartment and they unloaded material into the apartment. The three were often seen at the apartment, while Lindsay came but less frequently.[142]

During April, Sidique made repeated cash withdrawals from an account with HSBC and took out a personal loan for £10,000. Lindsay also withdrew £300 several times and made several applications for credit supported by claims that he was still working at a place he had left a long time before. He started an eBay account and with it bought wireless spy color cameras, hidden video cameras, miniature bug detectors, security alarms, gas masks, and the like.[143]

The first detected call from Rauf in Pakistan to Sidique came on 23 April 2005. Only Sidique communicated with Rauf via e-mails, phone calls, and Yahoo Messenger. They changed e-mail addresses and phone number on a monthly basis, notifying themselves of the new contact information in codes.[144]

The owner of the Chapeltown apartment returned from abroad in mid-May and was told that there was an electrical overload in the building as the main fuse box switch kept switching off. He went to investigate the source of this overload. He knocked at the apartment and there was no response. He had a spare key. "I attempted to open the door but could not get the key in because of a key in the lock from the inside. This indicated someone was inside but they did not answer the door." He called his tenant on the phone and Hussain came down from the room to talk to him outside. "He told me that he was boiling water in the room on a portable stove. I asked why he was not using the kitchen, and he said it was not as effective as the stove he had in his room. He did not seem to be bothered by it and he said he did not have anything that would cause a problem in his room other than the stove."[145] After this visit, Sidique changed the lock on the apartment.

Rauf called Sidique's operational cell phone on 9, 10, and 12 May, and nine times on 14 May.[146] In his report, Rauf wrote that Sidique began to boil down hydrogen peroxide but was unsure he had concentrated it to the correct strength. Rauf provided him with technical guidance to ensure he got the bomb mixture right. This may have been the day that this discussion took place. Rauf's phone calls continued until 2 July 2005.[147]

On 27 May 2005 in the evening, Lindsay and two accomplices were involved in an armed robbery in Luton. Lindsey brandished a handgun at a woman and her baby. They robbers got into a car, whose license plate was traced back to Lindsay. A neighbor had reported this robbery but the victim was never identified because she filed no complaint. The crime was never adequately investigated because the officer in charge went on vacation shortly thereafter and then on a training course until after the bombings. A semiautomatic pistol of the kind described in the crime was found in the trunk of Lindsay's car with his DNA and fingerprints on it.[148]

Sidique went with Tanweer and Naveed Fiaz on a white-water rafting outing in Wales on 4 June 2005. Around that time, Tanweer asked his secret girlfriend to meet for the first time in years. She later testified, "He had blond parts on his hair and eyebrows and . . . the hair on his arms." She asked him about it and he replied that it was "bleached from Pakistan." She found it strange. He told her he was working in Wales. "We just felt quite strong—obviously, we had feelings for each other, so we wanted our relationship to progress." They continued to text each other until the bombings.[149]

Second Bomb Factory on Alexandra Grove

On 15 June, Sidique arranged for Lindsay to sublease a Leeds Council flat on Alexandra Grove, whose renter had gone to Egypt. The conspirators emptied out the Chapeltown apartment and resumed their bomb making at the new Alexandra Grove flat. When the Chapeltown landlord broke into his room after the bombings, "I found the room in a mess but empty. I looked around and saw the floor was littered with rubbish and boxes. I noticed that one of the boxes was for a gas mask and one of them was for a double-ring, portable hob, similar to the ones you can buy from Argos."[150] During June, all the conspirators were working on the bombs at the Alexandra Grove apartment and were eating Chinese takeout food.

The making of the bombs would have smelled badly enough to make the room very difficult to work in. Both Tanweer and Lindsay bought face masks from shops and on the Internet. It appears that the bombs were made with the windows open but with net curtains taped to the walls to avoid being seen. The fumes killed off the top of plants just outside the windows. The mixtures would also have had a strong bleaching effect. Both Tanweer and Hussain's families noticed that their hair had become lighter over the weeks before the bombings. They explained this as the effect of chlorine from swimming pools (they and Sidique regularly swam together). They also wore shower caps at the bomb factory to protect their hair.[151]

The Perpetrators' Love Lives

On 20 June, Lindsay was practicing boxing at a community center in Aylesbury. A 17-year-old girl named Nicki noticed he was interested in her and they exchanged phone numbers. He told her his name was Tyrone. He picked her up outside her home late that evening and drove for an hour. When he dropped her off, he kissed her and arranged to meet during the day. He took her to a shopping center. He asked her whether she could get hold of a gun for him. He said "he was going to London with some of his mates to teach some people a lesson. . . . It was to do with drugs," Nicki later recalled. There was something wrong with his gun but she told him she could not help him. "We drove the rest of the way home in uncomfortable silence and he turned the music on."[152] He saw her again the next day and he read to her poems praising al Qaeda and Islam. Three days later, on 25 June, she saw him cash a check and receive a phone call, which made him very agitated. He told her that he had to go and drove her back home. "He tried to control his temper and said he needed to prepare himself. I asked him what did he need to prepare himself for, and he said 'shooting the people who need to be taught a lesson in London.'" The call was from Sidique, who had just received a call from Rauf in Pakistan.[153] Nothing more is known about it.

On 28 June, Sidique, Tanweer, and Lindsay were captured on CCTV at Luton station around 8:10 AM. They bought tickets and boarded a train to King's Cross station in London, arriving at 8:55 AM. They were photographed together again at Baker Street station around midday and again at King's Cross at 12:50 PM. They returned to Luton, arriving at approximately 1:40 PM. A chart of times taken to travel between stations was later found among Lindsay's belongings. Other tickets were also found at the bomb factory, suggesting other visits to London dating back to mid-March.[154]

The next day, Lindsay called Nicki and told her he had to lie low. He texted her that he suffered a minor wound in his back but had not fired his gun. They continued their texting and on 1 July she wrote that she did not want to lose him because she had started to have feelings for him.[155]

In the weeks before the bombings, Lindsay made a number of purchases with overdrawn checks. Bank investigators visited his home on the day after the bombings. His wife later told the authorities that he had spent less time at home lately, and when he was home, he locked himself away in the computer room. Shortly before the bombings, she had allegedly confronted him about text messages she discovered on his cell phone, apparently from a girlfriend, and threw him out of the house.[156]

Meanwhile Tanweer texted his girlfriend and asked her to spend the night with him. They went to a hotel on 1 July. They talked about themselves and their future. He seemed normal and told her he would go away for a week in Scotland and would call her when he got back. He called her three days later and told her he would call her when he got back from his trip. This was the last time she heard from him.[157]

On 4 July, Sidique took his car to be serviced. Tanweer rented a Nissan Micra and paid for four days. He ran into a friend, who noticed the discoloration in his hair. Tanweer told him it had something to do with sunlight. He had started wearing sunglasses and was now getting headaches.[158] He told his family he was going to go to Manchester to visit a cousin but left his car at home. On 5 July, a neighbor saw Sidique come out of his house and put things in the Nissan Micra: "He made two trips and was carrying a rucksack and a hold-all on one trip. I saw him put them into the boot. He also had some carrier bags. I did not see where from, and he put these into the back of the car. The man was on his own at this time."[159]

On 5 July, Lindsay texted Nicki, "I love you more than you can imagine, I want to stay with you forever. Are you going to start being more loving to me? We will do everything, we will go all over the place. Ever been to New York?" He later called her and asked her if she would like to come up to London on the evening of 6 July. He said he had been paid a lot of money for what had happened in London a few days earlier. She told him to call next morning. He called early in the morning and asked her if she was ready. "The more I thought about going," she later told the inquest, "the more I worried I got that I would get into trouble or meet the people involved in the shooting. . . . I said 'I have changed my mind, I am really tired, I need to go to sleep.' He said, 'Come on, it will be nice to spend some quality time together and we'll have some bad boy room service.' I replied, 'Seriously, I'm really tied up, I need to go to sleep.' He said, 'Okay, then.' He was fine about it. I asked him if he was busy on 14 July as it was my birthday. He said, 'I might be around then, but then again I might not.' He said he would speak to me soon, he loved me and he hung up."[160]

On 5 July at around 1:30 PM, CCTV cameras picked up Sidique taking his wife to Dewsbury Hospital.[161] Rauf wrote that Sidique's wife suffered a miscarriage just before the planned attack but he decided to proceed with the plot.[162] But he did not have any more contact with Sidique after a seven-minute telephone conversation on 2 July.

The London Bombings

Some detectives testifying at the Coroner's Inquests believed that the bombings were scheduled for 6 July. That day, at 4:35 AM, Sidique texted Lindsay,

"Havin major prob cant make time wil ring ya when I got it sorted wait at home." About one hour later, Sidique texted, "Il ring ya in afternoon twoish."[163] Around that time, Sidique and Tanweer bought 15 bags of ice at a local Asda-Walmart store to keep the explosive mixture cool.[164] Rashid Rauf had instructed him to leave the tops off the explosives-filled containers to prevent their overheating. The bombs were made at the last moment to prevent degradation and inadvertent detonation.[165] The mixture was poured into thin plastic bags but it is very reactive and tends to heat itself to the point where it will actually either just boil away or detonate. To keep the mixture cool, the ice packs were inserted into the bags along with the detonator.[166] As a further precaution, they stored the bombs in breathable Gore-Tex bags to prevent the accumulation of gas. "With the blessings of Allah I think it rained on the day of the attacks which means the weather was cooler," Rauf wrote.[167]

On the evening of 6 July, Tanweer went to the park and saw friends playing cricket. Ullah later recalled:

> Kaki is parked up and I . . . shook his hand. . . . "What's going on? How are you?" and everything. He is just saying he is fine and he's chillin out and he's cool, and I noticed . . . his red hair . . . and his beard were going a bit yellow, and I asked him: "What's going on with your hair? What have you done?" He goes: "Nothing, I've just been swimming a lot and it's the chlorine." . . . On that day, he made a bit more of an effort. . . . Over the months, when we used to play football and cricket, he'd just come and shake my hand, and that's it. He'd just carry on with the game, finish the game and he'd chip off. . . . This time, he came up to me and he chatted to me a little bit more. He was asking me: "How are you? What's going on? How have you been keeping?" I were kind of happy at that time, I was thinking, 'cos I don't want to be smoking anymore, thinking, they've done what they need to do, yeah? And, slowly but surely, we will start chilling again.[168]

On the morning of 7 July 2005, Lindsay arrived at Luton station parking lot around 5 AM and waited an hour and a half for Sidique, Tanweer, and Hussain to arrive in the Nissan Micra with the bombs. They left some smaller bombs in the Nissan. They all went to the station together, boarded a train to London around 7:40 AM, and arrived together at King's Cross around 8:23 AM. They hugged, appearing happy, even euphoric, and split up around 8:30 AM in the Underground, each going in a separate direction.

At 8:50 AM, Sidique exploded himself, killing six other people and injuring over 160 others, in the Underground near Edgware Road station; Lindsay exploded himself, killing 26 people and injuring more than 340, in the Underground between King's Cross and Russell Square stations; and Tanweer exploded himself, killing seven people and injuring more than 170 others, in the Underground between Liverpool Street and Aldgate stations. Apparently, Hussain's device malfunctioned, and he calmly exited the Underground, boarded the No. 30 bus, and detonated himself at Tavistock Square, killing 13 people and injuring over 110, about one hour after his friends. The bombers were identified over the next few days. The Alexandra Grove bomb factory was discovered on 12 July with much of the bomb-making equipment still in place. The DNA of Sidique, Tanweer, and Hussain were discovered there.[169]

On 22 March 2007, Shipon Ullah, who had just changed his name to Waheed Ali a week before, and Mohammed Shakil were arrested at Manchester Airport as they were boarding a plane for Karachi and later charged with conspiracy to attend a place used for terrorist training. Sadeer Saleem was also arrested the same day, and all three were later charged with conspiracy to cause an explosion for their mid-December trip to London, which the prosecution claimed to be a reconnaissance trip for the later bombings. They were tried on these charges from 10 April to 1 August 2008, but the trial ended in a hung jury. They were retried on 13 January 2009. On 28 April 2009, a jury acquitted them of the conspiracy to cause an explosion, but convicted Ali (Ullah) and Shakil of conspiracy to attend a terrorist camp. Saleem was immediately released. On 29 April 2009, Ali and Shakil were each sentenced to seven years in prison.

Lindsay's wife, Samantha Lewthwaite, became the "White Widow" and was allegedly connected with terrorist activities in Nairobi about a decade later.

Two weeks after the London bombings, another set of conspirators tried what was essentially a copycat attack.

CHAPTER 4

VIVACE

THE FAILED COPYCAT
LONDON BOMBINGS

EXACTLY TWO WEEKS AFTER the London bombings in July 2005, four would-be suicide bombers tried to duplicate them, but the bombs did not detonate because of the conspirators' incompetence. A fifth one lost his nerve and got rid of his bomb. The government's investigation of this failed copycat London bombings is called Operation Vivace. While the suicide of the London bombers prevents us from viewing the bombings from an insider's perspective, the survival of all the failed bombers leads to a multiplicity of accounts. At trial, three of them obviously coordinated their account while a fourth one refused to cooperate with the trial and stayed silent. The fifth one turned against his comrades, providing a second account. An accomplice arrested abroad denied any knowledge of the plot in a third account. A former friend of the bombers offered a fourth account and character witnesses provided differing accounts. From a totality of the evidence, they all lied about crucial aspects of the plot to exonerate themselves. The prosecution insisted on a fifth account to try to implicate all the defendants. After the verdict, the judge, who listened carefully to the proceedings, came up with a sixth account. In this chapter, I incorporate this complex *Rashomon* story with evidence from subsequent trials and Rashid Rauf's report (a seventh account) into an eighth account.

Osama bin London

Unlike the three other attacks in this book, which arose from al Qaeda support networks composed mostly of second-generation Pakistani immigrants, this attack came from a cluster of first-generation East African immigrants to London that emerged from a study circle that Mohammed Hussein Hamid organized in Hackney. He was born in 1957 in Tanzania in a Gujarati Muslim family and immigrated to England when he was five years old. When he was 12, he dropped out of school and embarked on a career of petty criminality and short incarcerations. He drank, smoked marijuana, and dressed sharply. He married at 20 and, after another short prison stay, settled down as a car mechanic. He separated from his wife after 10 years of marriage and kept the children. Three years later, he was addicted to crack cocaine and his habit left him destitute. His brother gave him money to go to India to kick his habit and, as soon as he landed there, he felt clean overnight and became a pious Muslim. He married a local woman and, at the age of 35, returned to London with her. They had four children and lived in a council house at Almack Road.

Around 1996, Hamid opened up the Al Quran Islamic Book Centre, on Chatsworth Road, close to his house. His store sold all things Islamic—perfumes, gowns, hats, and books. In the back, he set up some chairs for a dawah center for discussions about Islam and a crèche where children could learn about Islam. The popularity of this learning center grew, leading him to hire a teacher twice a week, he recalled at trial, "and after we finish our classes . . . somebody used to run to the kebab house or pizza house and we used to sit down there and eat and have a laugh and a joke." This was the origin of the Friday gatherings, which were irregular because they stopped during his frequent travels. He regularly went back to India, and camping all over Europe was his passion. Over their nine-year duration, these Friday gatherings drew over 300 people and Hamid acquired the nickname "Al Quran" from his bookstore.[1]

Many people came to Al Quran as it was the only Islamic bookstore in the area. A blond, blue-eyed woman from Bosnia with a small child came to the store. She had been well integrated in her country and not religious, Hamid recalled, but "her husband was dragged out of the house, taken away and never to be seen. Some of her members of her family were killed and she had to run out with her children . . . into some forest and escape . . . out of the country." From other visitors, he learned about atrocities in

Kashmir and "heard stories about Chechnya . . . about two or three children dying every day in the refugee camp."[2] This sparked his interest in world politics.

The 9/11 attacks further politicized Hamid. He refused to believe that they were caused by Muslims and instead adhered to sinister conspiracy theories that American forces carried them out to give them an excuse to invade and oppress Muslim countries. He became involved in support of the flood of Afghan refugees created by the Western invasion of their country. Across the street from Al Quran was the office of the Islamic Medical Association (IMA), which collected medical supplies, clothes, and food for them.[3] "I'm right opposite it," Hamid later recalled, "and . . . the guy opposite asked me . . . to give out these leaflets. . . . I knew him from when he opened the shop. . . . He asked me . . . to drive a van to Kingston Hospital, other hospitals to . . . collect hospital equipment." Hamid invited the IMA volunteers to his house for a meal, where they discussed world events. Eventually, they collected enough to fill out seven 40-foot containers, which they shipped by sea to Pakistan.[4]

In early January 2002, Hamid flew to Karachi to clear the containers with customs and transfer the supplies onto small trucks. He hired a small escort and traveled with the convoy to massive refugee camps, where he distributed food, shoes, and warm clothing and blankets. He also delivered medical supplies to hospitals in Spin Baldak, Qandahar, and Qalat, where the convoy came under small-arms fire. Hamid wanted to fire an AK-47 from his escort guards, but they refused, he later remembered, "because the noise is so loud . . . people are going to panic . . . and might start fighting . . . thinking they're being attacked." He flew back to England on 21 March 2002.[5]

Not much is known about Hamid for the next year and a half. He gathered around him a few young politicized Muslims, who came to Al Quran and helped him. The store was not a financial success and Hamid had to rely on charity and volunteers. One of the first to volunteer was 15-year-old Shakeel Ishmael, a local boy who ran the store when Hamid was away. To proselytize beyond his store, they set up a dawah stall around mosques in London, where he gave out free pamphlets and books on Islam and asked for contributions. They also participated in Stop the War demonstrations and went to Speakers' Corner, Hyde Park, where Hamid disputed the conventional wisdom about the 9/11 attacks. His political protests provoked different reactions. A few people were interested in what he was saying and engaged him in discussion while others felt offended by his appearance—long beard and Muslim gown—and zealous defense of assertive Islam. They accused him of being a "Taliban" and called him "Osama bin Laden." With his provocative sense of humor, Hamid told them that his name was "Osama bin London."[6]

The East African Immigrants

During Ramadan 2003, which was in November, two friends, Muktar Said Ibrahim and Yasin Hassan Omar, came over to Hamid's stall at Edmonton Mosque. Hamid recognized Omar, who had previously bought some perfume at Al Quran.[7] Ibrahim was a 25-year-old born in Eritrea, whose family had fled the Ethiopian-Eritrean War and come to London as refugees when he was 12. He spoke Arabic at the time. When he was 15, in June 1993, he and a friend molested a girl in an alleyway. They held her up against a wall and fondled her breasts. Ibrahim rubbed his groin against her body. He later pled guilty to indecent assault and received a supervision order for a year. He smoked marijuana and left school at the age of 16 with two GCSEs. In April 1995, he robbed a 77-year-old woman. A month later, while still on bail, he and five others robbed and beat up two men. He pled guilty to conspiracy to rob and was sentenced to three years for the first offense and an additional two years for the second one. He was released from prison in September 1998.[8] He then lived on government benefits, supplemented them with work at restaurants, and got a council flat at Farleigh Road in January 2002. He was still not religious.[9]

Ibrahim had befriended two Eritrean brothers, Siraj and Abdu Ali, who had immigrated around the same time he did and been placed in foster care. In 1994, when the older Siraj became 18 and too old to stay in foster care, the council placed the two brothers in a flat, 65 Curtis House. After his release from prison, Ibrahim frequently came to visit them.[10] There, in 2000, he met their neighbor, 19-year-old Yasin Omar, born in Somalia, who had come to Britain in 1992 with two sisters and a cousin as refugees from the Somalian Civil War. He was placed with the same foster family as the Ali brothers and Omar lived with them for two years until they moved to Curtis House. When Omar turned 18, he too moved to Curtis House, into flat 58.

At school, Omar had become inseparable from Matthew Dixon, who was born in South Africa to a South African father and an English mother. Dixon's family moved to London during his childhood. Omar also met

Adel Yahya Ahmed at a bowling alley. He was born in Ethiopia and lived in Yemen before he and his sister came to London to live with relatives in 1991. He had bad knees that eventually required three surgical operations. At school, Yahya had befriended an English classmate, Stephen Bentley. Soon, the two pairs of friends from different schools—Omar and Dixon; Yahya and Bentley—grew very close and were occasionally joined by a Jewish schoolmate. They used to go out to nightclubs and cinemas.

After graduating in 1998, the four boys went their separate ways. Dixon and Bentley went away to different universities and became progressively more distant from their East African friends, seeing them only on holidays. Yahya, with seven GCSEs, enrolled in a local computer course. Omar, with two GCSEs, studied science, including chemistry, and experimented with hydrogen peroxide, but dropped out in the fall of 1999. Around that time, he started praying five times a day and went to mosque regularly. Bentley, who had converted to Islam, and Yahya also turned more religious. Omar and Yahya became closer and prayed at three different mosques: the nearby Edmonton Mosque, the large and prestigious Regent's Park Mosque, and the Finsbury Park Mosque, where they listened to Abu Hamza and got books. When Bentley and Dixon came back in London, they would occasionally accompany their friends. Omar became a supporter of the Palestinians and the Taliban rule in Afghanistan, which he considered a "true Islamic state."[11]

In April and May 2000, respectively, Ibrahim and Omar were granted indefinite stays in Britain. Omar eventually introduced Ibrahim to Yahya and, at the time of the 9/11 attacks, they were 20, 23, and 19 years of age respectively. Omar did not believe that Osama bin Laden had conducted the attacks because Abu Hamza claimed to know bin Laden and that bin Laden did not carry them out. Nevertheless, Omar told his friends that they were a "good thing" and he supported them. He participated in the 30 September 2001 Al Aqsa National Demonstration on the first anniversary of the Intifada in solidarity with the Palestinians and out of "respect for the martyrs" killed by Israeli bombs. He, Yahya, and Ibrahim participated in the Stop the War Campaign. Gradually, Omar got disillusioned with large legitimate protests because they did not have any effect on Prime Minister Tony Blair. There is very little known about Ibrahim in the year after the attacks except that he continued to draw unemployment benefits. In September 2002, Yahya started a two-year college computer practitioner course.[12]

In January 2003, Ibrahim went to the Sudan for two months. He financed his trip by renting out his council flat. This trip is shrouded in mystery. A prosecution witness later testified that Ibrahim boasted to him that he had undergone jihadi training and learned how to fire an RPG. At trial, Ibrahim denied he ever went for training or fired an RPG and claimed instead to have relaxed and visited relatives, in Khartoum, in the south, and on the border with Eritrea. However, his older sister testified that she had never even met these relatives and they had never been close to them. She also did not know at the time that her brother went to the Sudan.[13]

By 2003, al Qaeda had left the Sudan seven years earlier. In view of the ongoing skirmishes between Eritrea and Ethiopia, it is possible that Ibrahim met with some Eritrean militants at the border and might have fired an RPG. But it is very unlikely that he ever got any neojihadi military training, as no such organization had any camps there at the time.

After his return, Ibrahim started wearing a traditional Muslim gown and selling shoes, handbags, nightgowns, and African artifacts (imported from Thailand) at a small shop five days a week for about £35 a day. On weekends, he sold them at Sunday markets.[14] He reconnected with Omar and Yahya. Although Omar prayed at the Finchley Mosque and Ibrahim at the Turkish-run Azizi Mosque, they occasionally went to pray in the street outside the locked Finsbury Park Mosque to listen to Abu Hamza. They also listened to his tapes as well as those of Sheikh Abdullah al-Faisal at home and discussed the situation in Iraq, Chechnya, and Afghanistan.

Mohamed and Hamdi

When Ibrahim and Omar met Hamid at his dawah stall during Ramadan 2003, Omar recognized Hamid and asked him whether he was the "guy at the bookshop." Hamid confirmed that he was, and Ibrahim and Omar bought Islamic gowns from him. Hamid also recognized them from their frequent soccer games at a nearby park and invited them to come to the Friday evenings at his house.[15] They came occasionally and met his assistant Ishmael as well as others like Ramzi Mohamed, who had met Hamid at Speakers' Corner.

Mohamed was a 22-year-old, born in Somalia, who came to England in 1998 and was put in social services with his younger brother, Wahbi. The next year, Mohamed turned 18 and had to move out into council housing in Hayes, leaving his brother behind. He was granted a definite leave to stay in Britain for four years.[16] In Hayes, he met 21-year-old Hamdi Sherif, an

Ethiopian immigrant who had come to England three years earlier under the false identity of Hussein Osman from Somalia.[17] He had immigrated to Italy in 1992 to join an older brother living there before moving to Britain four years later. At the end of 1997, he started dating Yeshi Girma, another Ethiopian immigrant, who had also previously lived in Italy. Mohamed and Hamdi became close friends, chased girls in clubs and at house parties, and smoked marijuana. Girma got pregnant and at first wanted to get an abortion but Hamdi asked her to keep it. Their son, Imran, was born in 1999 and, shortly thereafter, she moved to a council flat at Blair House. Girma had begun to follow Islam but Hamdi continued his secular lifestyle. Despite being cold to Girma, he came regularly to visit his son. Meanwhile, Mohamed also impregnated his girlfriend, Azeb, from Sweden. Their son, Adam, was born three months premature in 2000 and Azeb returned to Sweden for extensive medical care for her son. Mohamed's bother, Wahbi, became more religious around this time and influenced his brother and Hamdi to visit local mosques.[18]

In 2001 and 2002, Mohamed worked at bars and lived with Azeb and their son in Elephant and Castle. Hamdi started dating a Christian Ethiopian woman, Almaz, in mid-2002. He still visited his son once a week and Girma, determined to get him back and marry him, got pregnant during one of these visits. He again wanted her to have an abortion and took her to an abortion clinic, but once inside she told the staff that she wanted to keep the baby. He stopped seeing her but resumed when their second son, Marwan, was born in May 2003.[19]

By that time, Mohamed and Hamdi had become politically active and religious. They participated in the huge 15 February 2003 Stop the War march and went to Speakers' Corner. Mohamed quit the bar job and worked at a bagel place and then a merchandising company. In July 2003, he moved out of the flat he shared with Azeb because she was not Muslim and moved in with his brother Wahbi. She gave birth to their second son, Malik, three months later. Mohamed returned to see her every day to help her with some of the household chores.[20]

Likewise, Hamdi changed overnight, went to the mosque in Brixton, shaved his head, grew a beard, and completely stopped listening to music. Almaz remembered,

> Toward the end of our relationship he used to read a lot of books and watch videos. . . . He used to talk about Iranian [I believe she meant Iraqi] people. They were abused . . . [and] killed in Iraq and

it was America's fault. . . . All Muslims are brothers and sisters, even
if you don't know them and they are killed, it will affect you. He
watched the films . . . every day. He thought the Americans were
responsible for the abuses of the Middle East countries. He used to
read religious books because he didn't know anything about his culture. . . . He had to start learning "my religion and stuff because I
am behind, I should know this stuff by now, but look at me, I am
old enough but I don't know most of them so I have to catch up."

He now approved of the 9/11 attacks. She broke up with him because she
could not see herself converting to Islam. Devastated, Hamdi returned to
Girma, who consoled him by conceiving another son in early 2004. Their
relationship improved. He went to the mosque every day in the afternoon,
and the rest of the time, he prayed at home. He worked as a night shift
delivery driver and hung out with the Mohamed brothers.[21]

The Emergence of a Martial Social Identity

During the winter of 2003–2004, Mohammed Hamid hosted Shakeel,
Ibrahim, Omar, and Mohamed at his house on Friday evenings for talk,
food, and laughter. Their presence at these gatherings later gave rise to the
accusation that Hamid radicalized them there. The participants of course
protested that these were innocent discussions about food, religion, and
everyday life. However, a wiretap planted in Hamid's house in September
2005, after the failed London bombings, showed that the gatherings were
deeply political and glorified British foreign fighters. The participants dis-
trusted the mainstream media and discussed what was really going on in
Iraq and Afghanistan. They were very security conscious, had to hand in
their phones to Hamid during the sessions, and were urged not to talk
about their discussions to anyone outside the group, including their wives.
Since the probe became active after September 2005, it is not known
whether the same security measures or discussions were already in place
two years earlier.

It might be easy to dismiss these discussions as fantasy because of Hamid's great exaggerations and blatant lies, such as claiming that he had been
acquitted nine times by British juries, hosted Mullah Omar, the head of the
Taliban, at his house for two months, and sent many people to fight in

Afghanistan.[22] The discussions, though, facilitated the emergence and hardening of a politicized social identity among the participants, who imagined themselves as part of a political community protesting against British government's policies toward Muslims at home and abroad. Furthermore, the violence of the discourse opened the possibility of violent forms of protests against the British state and society.

Around that time, Hamid closed Al Quran to save on its £150 monthly rent. He had shifted his proselytism to his dawah stall where Shakeel and he handed out Islamic literature, invited people to Islam, and solicited charity contributions. In March 2004, he went to India for about a month to visit friends and relatives. Shakeel asked Ibrahim to help him at the dawah stall. When Hamid came back from India, he and Shakeel moved the stall to Green Wood and eventually Marble Arch. Ibrahim joined them and gave up his job to devote his life to dawah full time. Omar came to help very occasionally.[23]

Hamid also organized weekend outings for his followers after his return from India. He had identified a year-round camping site in Cumbria. These outings were an opportunity for him to show off and for his young followers to pretend to be soldiers and prove how tough they were, capable of withstanding the rugged geography of Afghanistan. One such outing took place on the 2004 May Day Bank Holiday weekend at a cost of £50–60 for each participant. Shakeel invited Ibrahim and Omar, who in turn asked Yahya to come along. Mohamed came as well and invited his best friend, Hamdi, who brought his five-year-old son to play with Hamid's children. The whole group of about 28 people, including about eight children, drove up from London in two minibuses and two cars. This outing was significant because Ibrahim, Omar, and Yahya met Mohamed and Hamdi for the first time, after which they continued to see each other occasionally at Hamid's Friday evening gatherings.

In Cumbria, a local constable on his morning jog noticed them and returned later with a colleague to take pictures. "The people were . . . rolling forward and then jumping back up again and sort of rolling out of my sight and then appearing further down," the constable later testified at Hamid's trial. "Some of them actually were holding branches of sticks. . . . My impression was that it was as if they were practicing weapons."[24] The prosecution called these pretend outings "weapons training" camps that "provided instruction or training in the use of firearms wholly or partly for the purpose of preparing for terrorism."[25] Three former Special Forces soldiers testified that they had observed the campers run around with twigs in their hands, pretending they were weapons, jumping around streams, and running up and down hills, and making gestures of throwing imaginary hand grenades during soccer games. Hamid of course denied that these outings had anything to do with weapons training, but later surreptitious wiretaps during them caught him saying, "those who want to train, can train. Those who don't want to train, don't train." They could climb a mountain or carry 35-kilogram loads. "Everybody is going to get up early in the morning and come jogging. . . . [Some may] do some leopard crawling." He rejected complaints that he did not provide them with enough hard training.[26]

The irony is that the authorities took them seriously. The notion that a bunch of immature men, hopping around in mud while making weapons' noise, is the equivalent of a real terrorist or military training camp is too ridiculous for further comment. Those who call these sophomoric pretend weekend camping sessions training camps are obviously not familiar with either military boot camps or real terrorist training camps as they existed in Afghanistan a decade before. The participants never learned anything about fighting. Nevertheless, these outings were important subjectively because they hardened the participants' martial social identity that they were mujahedin, soldiers of God, defending their imagined community. But calling them "terrorist training camps" misleads and frightens the public into believing that there was a network of trained terrorists capable of devastating British society.

Enter Asiedu

Around that time, Omar met the last of the conspirators, Sumaila Abubakari, at a Turkish restaurant near the Finchley Mosque. Everyone called him by his Islamic name of Ishmail. He was a happy-go-lucky 26-year-old illegal immigrant from Ghana, whose parents had converted to Islam. He was pleasant and always smiling, earning him the nickname of Smiler. After graduating from school, he worked at his father's construction business, learning painting, decorating, and gardening. His dream was to immigrate to Britain to become rich and raise a family. Because he believed it would be impossible for him to get a visa as a Muslim, he bought fake documents allowing him to get a six-month visa on 24 September 2003. After raising money for the plane fare, he arrived in London in December 2003 wearing traditional Ghanaian clothes and with £100 in his pocket. A cabbie from

Ghana recognized the clothes and sheltered him for a few days at his home. Ishmail went to the local mosque, Finchley Mosque, to ask for help and work. He volunteered to clean the mosque on a regular basis and got cleaning jobs at local supermarkets. He tried to get British citizenship by joining the British Army but was told that he needed three months left on his visa at the time of his formal interview. He returned to Ghana to renew his visa but was unable to do so and flew back to London before its expiration. In order to work, he took the identity of another Ghanaian, Manfu Asiedu, who had left his documents behind at the cabbie's house when he was hospitalized for mental problems. With them, he got a Construction Industry Scheme card under the name Asiedu.[27]

On an early April afternoon, Ishmail met Omar, dressed in a traditional Muslim gown, at a local Turkish shop. It was time for prayers and they went together to Finchley Mosque. Afterward, Omar invited Ishmail to a local kebab house, where they talked about themselves and the state of affairs in Africa. They later saw each other in the neighborhood and played soccer at Finchley Mosque on weekends. After a two-month absence for a job to paint another mosque, Ishmail returned to Finchley and mentioned to Omar that he was looking for a place to stay. Omar invited him to move in with him, which Ishmail did in June or July 2004. Omar already had another lodger, a 30-year-old Indian Muslim, who had a laptop computer and printer. Omar, who was not working, charged them each £30 weekly to stay in his living room.

Ishmail got to know Omar's friends, who came to visit the flat: Ibrahim, Yahya, and Dixon. Ibrahim would come with books from the dawah stall and bought two tracksuits for Ishmail from his peddling business. Omar and his friends discovered that Ishmail recited the Quran in the *warsh* style, one of the seven recognized recitation styles, commonly practiced in Africa, and they often asked him to do so at their prayer sessions.[28]

The Split Between Hamid and Ibrahim

On 11 July 2004, Yahya flew to Sana'a, Yemen, to marry an 18-year-old Yemeni through an arranged marriage. His sister had given him £2,500 for his dowry; about a thousand people came to his wedding. The newlyweds honeymooned in Ethiopia for a month, arriving on 15 September 2004. They stayed with one of Yahya's rich uncles in Addis Ababa and went swimming and to restaurants and discotheques.[29]

Meanwhile, back in London, Ibrahim was granted British citizenship on 30 July and now regularly manned the dawah stall with Shakeel and Hamid. Shakeel ordered books for it and Hamid continued to organize outings.[30] The stall attracted the attention of the police. A constable later testified that, on 5 October, Hamid "was tending a bookstall . . . [at] Marble Arch. . . . The stall was a trestle table full of books on religion based on the faith of Islam. He also had tapes under the table. He assured me that the books were for free and he was not selling them. He did however have a donation box, which I asked him to remove and warned him of [a] street trading offense."[31] The constable noted that he was on a hotel property but Hamid assured her he had the manager's permission, which the constable later found out was false.

On October 12, Ibrahim, Hamid, and Shakeel were at Marble Arch again and moved their table under a nearby canopy of a retail outlet when it started to rain. As one constable later recalled, they

> were distributing literature from the stall and shouting out religious references. . . . It was causing a large number of people to gather, causing people to walk on to the road. . . . They needed to move because they were causing such a disturbance. . . . At first, they [said] that it was their right to put the stall here . . . to distribute this literature and they just didn't listen to me. I tried to explain the law relating to obstruction of the highway, but . . . they continued distributing literature shouting out phrases. I warned them . . . to no avail. And in the end, I explained, look, if they didn't move, they were going to be arrested and, at that point, they became quite abusive. They started making comments about my Hindu background and how I was a Hindu traitor and they started making comments towards my colleague . . . , who is of Afro-Caribbean descent . . . called him a black pussy hole, which was extremely offensive to him of course.[32]

Hamid at his trial said he was complying with the constables' requests as he was packing up and blamed the incident on Shakeel, who called the constable of Indian descent a "cow worshipper." They resisted arrest. Ibrahim tried to run away but was tripped up by a passerby and caught. The female constable wrestled Hamid to the ground as he was about to flee. As the police were dragging him into the van, he shouted, "I've got a bomb and I'm going to blow you all up." Hamid later testified that, at the police station, "the sergeant asked me, 'What's your name and address?' so as a joke, I . . . said, my name is Osama bin London and I live at Tora Bora."[33] Ibrahim, Shakeel, and Hamid were all charged with a minor public order offense, released on bail, and told to return for their hearing in the Magistrates' Court on 18 December.

This incident split up Ibrahim and Shakeel from Hamid. As Hamid later recalled, "After being arrested, there was a big argument between Muktar [Ibrahim], Shakeel and myself. We all blamed each other for what had happened." After suspending their activities for Ramadan (15 October to 13 November 2004), Ibrahim and Shakeel started their own stall. Omar tried to patch things up between them but failed. "They decided to go their way," Hamid remembered, "and I went mine. . . . On occasion, they tried working at Marble Arch, but I told them it was my patch and they left."[34] Ibrahim and Shakeel never socialized with Hamid again.

Hamid's theatrics attracted the attention of BBC assistant producer Nasrin Suleaman, who was working on a documentary *Don't Panic, I'm Islamic*, examining discrimination against Muslims. At trial, Suleaman recalled, "I came out of the tube station at Marble Arch. . . . Mohammed [Hamid] has a stall there and I . . . [started] talking to him and . . . found him amiable and articulate and quite a character which are . . . prerequisites if you are making a television documentary. . . . So, I started talking to him about the possibility of appearing in the programme." She talked to her producer Phil Rees, who liked his sense of humor and his larger-than-life personality. "I went to see him at Speakers' Corner," she added, "where he again was on his soapbox and was robustly discussing political issues of the day with passers-by so I felt he was a man who, yes, had certain theatrical tendency perhaps, but as we say in the business was good copy, would make good television." Rees and Suleaman met with Hamid, who agreed to participate in the documentary. She remembered, "Mr. Hamid certainly felt victim to certain of these prejudices in the way he told us. He said that he may as well call himself Osama bin Laden because in his opinion most people passing the street would simply glance at him and would equate him with Osama bin Laden. He coined a phrase 'Osama bin London' . . . which I ran in the film. . . . It may not suit everybody's sense of humor but I took it as a humorous comment." Rees and she talked about how they were to present him in their documentary and decided, she testified, "that paintballing would be a very fun way of

introducing him." They paid for the paintballing trip and gave Hamid
£300 for his troubles.[35] The segment with Hamid was filmed in November-
December 2004 and broadcast on the BBC in May 2005.

Going for Jihad in Afghanistan

During the fall of 2004, Ibrahim and Omar shared their respective disillusionment with nonviolent protests that failed to stop the killings of many
Muslims in Iraq and Afghanistan. Omar later testified, "I spoke to Ibrahim
and told him there's going to be some demonstration and Ibrahim looked
at me and just laughed and said to me, 'you're still on that. Don't you get
the message? The government is not interested and forget it.' So, at the end,
I said to him, 'But we have to somehow get the attention of the government
and the public . . . [to] put some pressure on the government.'" In his
testimony, Ibrahim recalled that he told Omar, "Don't bother, they [the
politicians] don't listen." Omar testified that he responded, "What if we do
something that will stand out? . . . Carrying out a demonstration that would
make people think there had been or were going to be some sort of explosion . . . something like fireworks or firecrackers, something that will make
noise and . . . cause panic." Ibrahim backed up his co-defendant's testimony. He claimed that around November, at an Internet café, browsing
the Web for news and dawah material, he stumbled upon a site, tadjeed.net,
where he saw a video with "a person, who was speaking Arabic and wearing
[a] balaclava and he was teaching how to make home-made explosive in
detail. . . . He called it peroxide-based explosive. . . . I told Omar that we
could use this for our demonstration, but I was thinking at that stage only
to use a detonator. . . . Omar had a CD in his bag and so we downloaded
the video on to the CD."[36]

Their testimonies introduce the theory of their defense, namely that
they just engaged in "hoax bombing" to bring attention to the Western
massacre of Muslims abroad. Like the jury and judge at their trial, I am
very skeptical about their claims. While videos on how to make bombs
were available on the Internet at the time, the bombs were not hydrogen-
peroxide-type bombs. As mentioned in the previous chapter, this type of
bomb design was new for Europe. In his direct examination, Ibrahim
implied that he already seemed familiar with bomb making as he spoke
about detonators and boosters. Furthermore, no one except Ibrahim and
Omar ever saw the CD, which they allegedly destroyed right before their

bombing attempt despite the fact that they did not destroy any of the other far more compromising material at Omar's flat. Finally, the revelations of Rashid Rauf that surfaced after the trial disclosed that al Qaeda taught Ibrahim how to make this specific type of bomb in Pakistan in the winter of 2005, contradicting Ibrahim's account. Despite his and Omar's lies, I believe that their disillusionment with peaceful demonstrations against the war was genuine. Their conclusion that something more had to be done is consistent with all that we know about the evolution of this plot.

Meanwhile, Yahya left his bride in Yemen in mid-October and flew back to London on 16 October. At school, he befriended 22-year-old Saudi "Michael Bexhill" (an alias), of Yemeni descent. Bexhill and his family had visited their ancestral home several times, where, like other young teenagers, he learned to handle an assault rifle. As a teenager, he had stabbed an older man in his home allegedly in self-defense. In September 2001, he came to Britain on a student visa and, funded by his father, studied at various universities without ever finishing any of his courses. He was involved in a fight at school, for which he was taken to the police station but never charged. In June 2004, he moved to London. Yahya and he quickly became friends. Bexhill told Yahya that he needed a place to stay. Yahya suggested that he move in with Ibrahim for £60 a week, which he did at the end of October 2004.[37]

As Bexhill turned prosecution witness at trial, his five-week stay at Ibrahim's Farley Road flat gives us a window into the internal dynamics of this group. His version is partially corroborated by Ishmail, who also turned on his co-defendants midway through the trial. Their political radicalism was not in dispute because of the mountain of evidence found at their respective flats. Instead, they accused each other of introducing these books, pamphlets, audiocassettes, videos, CDs, and DVDs into their respective flats. The defendants accused Bexhill of being a fanatic and introducing this radical material to them, while Bexhill accused them of trying to brainwash him. All agreed that Ishmail did not share their radical views. Bexhill's memory gaps about the timing of events and his obvious attempts to exonerate himself marred his account. The evidence suggests that he was just as radical as his friends at the time.

Bexhill described Ibrahim as a "fanatic, radical. . . . He used to speak about jihad . . . be against those people who doesn't [sic] like people doing jihad . . . watch a lot of movies, jihadi movies, and . . . listen to Abu Hamza tapes and Abdullah Faisal tapes." The movies were about fighting in Bosnia,

Chechnya, Afghanistan, and Iraq. Ibrahim told Bexhill that he had been to the Sudan, trained there, and learned to fire an RPG.[38]

Bexhill met Shakeel, Omar, and Yahya, who occasionally came to visit and stay overnight. He described Omar as a fanatic, who tried to convince him to engage in jihad and carry out a suicide bombing. Ibrahim would also take Bexhill along to Omar's flat and they sometimes stayed there overnight. Overall, he saw Ibrahim, Omar, and Yahya almost every day. They all shared the same radical views. They watched jihadi videos together and talked about going abroad for jihad. Ibrahim and the visitors boasted that they had gone to a camp in the north to do some training, but without weapons, in order to prepare themselves to go for jihad in Afghanistan or Iraq. Bexhill, in turn, boasted that "all his friends . . . went to Iraq to fight and . . . he regretted that he didn't go and he still intended to go."[39]

Soon reality dampened their enthusiasm to fight abroad against Western coalition troops. Omar complained that his bad back prevented him from lifting anything heavy as would be required during jihad. Likewise, Yahya's bad knees prevented him from going on long walks. So Ibrahim asked Bexhill to take Omar and Yahya with him to Yemen, as he was familiar with the country and could get there without a visa, for them to learn how to use weapons, which were ubiquitous in that country. Omar and Yahya seemed interested in going and Yahya even asked Bexhill whether they could go together to fight in Iraq. Bexhill became noncommittal and said he first wanted to check with his family in Saudi Arabia before embarking on jihad. He gave Ibrahim his father's cell phone number as a Saudi contact for Ibrahim to call and facilitate his trip to Pakistan. This was clearly a one-way trip as Ibrahim did not expect to return to Britain.[40]

Shakeel and Rizwan Majid agreed to go with Ibrahim to fight in Afghanistan. Majid was a 21-year-old of Pakistani origin, born in Walthamstow. He used to hang around Al Quran and had participated in some of Hamid's weekend outings. He also occasionally came to Ibrahim's flat and Bexhill remembered him as an amusing fellow. As Ibrahim was preparing for his trip, he bought camping equipment and rented his flat to a Turkish couple, who paid two months' rent in advance, or £800, which Ibrahim used to pay his back rent. Bexhill moved out of Ibrahim's flat and into Yahya's flat for two days before returning to Saudi Arabia for vacation. He came back to Ibrahim's flat to collect his belongings. Omar answered the door but did not invite him to come in and asked him to wait outside. Peeking past Omar, Bexhill saw 8 to 12 South Asian Muslims, dressed in traditional gowns and wearing long beards, holding a good-bye party. He recognized Shakeel and Majid among them. Ibrahim came out with Bexhill's belongings and gave him a ride back to Yahya's flat. Bexhill later recalled that, in his good-bye, Ibrahim "said that if we did not meet up again in this world, we will meet up in paradise." As a parting gift, Ibrahim gave Bexhill two jihadi videos, one about Afghanistan and the other about 9/11. Bexhill flew back home on 8 December.[41]

On 11 December 2004, a two-car convoy led by an Iraqi immigrant cab driver drove Ibrahim, Shakeel, and Majid to Heathrow Airport. The cabbie, who was a known collector of funds for the insurgency in Iraq, allegedly knew that this was a terrorism-related trip.[42] The travelers had gotten their Pakistani visas the day before and their £520 round-trip plane tickets had a return date of 8 March 2005. They had shaved their beards and wore Western garments to appear inconspicuous but still underwent a comprehensive screening at the airport. Ibrahim carried in excess of £2,000 in cash. He had antimalarial medication and vitamin supplements, a first aid kit, a cold weather sleeping bag, and a brand-new video camera. Majid was carrying £2,200 in cash along with a sleeping bag, cold weather outfit, military first aid kit, and a first aid manual covering ballistic injuries. Shakeel had approximately £3,000 cash on him and a first aid manual annotated with notes relating to injuries inflicted by bullet or blast.

They were interviewed for four hours. They claimed they were going to Pakistan for Majid's wedding but admitted they did not know the bride. They were going to be housed by Majid's family and intended to stay in Pakistan for about 20 days. Ibrahim downplayed his piety and said he did not attend mosque regularly. "When I asked how it was that an unemployed man was so bereft of time," recalled an airport security official, "he again made light of the question in such way as to suggest that he is in regular, gainful employment. A little more probing about the extent to which his faith was important to him revealed a sensitive streak about the singling out of Muslims for security examinations, such as one that he was being subjected to." The interviews or the questioning at trial never clarified how unemployed people like them raised so much money for their trip to Pakistan. I suspect that one of the purposes of the send-away party at his flat was to raise money from their militant friends. The interviews caused them to miss their flight and they flew out the next day.[43]

Ibrahim's Training with al Qaeda in Pakistan

The three friends stayed at Majid's family home in Pakistan. Rashid Rauf, the al Qaeda intermediary, waited for about two weeks before contacting them. It is not known how Rauf got the phone number of Majid's family. However, right before their departure, Ibrahim received a phone call from Abdulla Ahmed Ali's brother. As reported in the next chapter, Ali was already in Pakistan at the time and had already met Rauf. Ali's family and Majid's family were friends in Walthamstow.[44]

This time, Rauf's caution paid off as British police had notified the ISID, which came to Majid's family home and questioned them shortly after their arrival. When Rauf contacted them, they told him about the police scrutiny. Rauf instructed them to behave as if they were about to attend a wedding, consistent with their cover story. They wanted to train and fight U.S. forces in Afghanistan. They did not want to ever return to Britain because they believed they had been detected by British authorities and hoped to die as martyrs in Afghanistan.[45]

After another interval, Rauf picked them up and, after careful surveillance detection that lasted several days, took them to the tribal areas of Pakistan to meet his boss, Abu Ubaydah al Masri. They did not attend the same camp as the London bombers and got a different instructor. Their instructions on how to build a bomb were quite different from those of the London bombers. Instead of a hydrogen peroxide-black pepper mixture, their main charge was a hydrogen peroxide-chapati mixture. Instead of a HMTD detonator, they learned to build one using triacetone triperoxide (TATP). However, the overall design of the respective improvised explosive devices was the same. The tricky part of the manufacture process was the same: the concentration of the hydrogen peroxide to 70 percent so that a detonator containing five to eight grams of TATP could ignite it. Again, the British students had to learn the process of concentrating the hydrogen peroxide at altitude, in the mountains of the FATA, in very harsh winter conditions and very low humidity. These three elements—atmospheric pressure, temperature, and humidity—affect the evaporation of hydrogen peroxide and the stability of the explosive mixture. The conditions in London are very different than in the FATA.[46]

Toward the end of their training, the students tested two small devices they had manufactured, just as the London bombers had done, but something went wrong. As Shakeel and Majid went to put the devices down for testing, the bombs exploded prematurely, killing them. Ibrahim had stayed behind at a distance with Abu Ubaydah. He was deeply affected by the deaths of his friends. Before, he had been reluctant to conduct an operation in Britain, but, after their deaths, Abu Ubaydah was able to persuade him to carry out "operational work" there.

Rauf liked Sidique more than Ibrahim and spent more time with the former than the latter. This was to have very important consequences. After Ibrahim's training, Rauf met him back in Islamabad. As with Sidique, he spent time with Ibrahim creating a secure communication plan, using code words and different modes of communication. Ibrahim recorded his wasiya (martyrdom tape) just as the London bombers did. Rauf quizzed him on what he had learned and found out that Ibrahim had not quite mastered the bomb-making techniques. However, it was too late to fill his knowledge gaps because of his scheduled return to Britain. Delaying him further might have triggered more suspicion from British authorities. Rauf blamed his lack of preparation on the quality of Ibrahim's instructor.[47]

Ibrahim's lack of expertise was compounded by his lack of bonding with Rauf. When Ibrahim got back to Britain, he called Rauf immediately after landing, telling him he was safe. However, this was his last call and there was no further contact between them. Rauf later sent an intermediary[48] to contact Ibrahim, who promised he would soon get back to Rauf. But he never did. This lack of communication prevented Rauf from telling him about the types of problems that the London bombers had experienced, especially about the difficulty of measuring the concentration of hydrogen peroxide. As a result, Ibrahim never compensated for this decrease in concentration in the main charge, leading to its failure to detonate. Rauf concluded, "It was their lack of technical knowledge that caused the problem."[49] But we are getting ahead of our account.

At his trial, Ibrahim claimed that Majid, Shakeel, and he played tourists during three months and, at the end, his two friends stayed behind while he returned to England. He did not keep in touch with them, did not know where they were, and denied they ever attended a terrorist training camp.[50] This rings hollow in view of subsequent events and Rauf's report.

Meanwhile in London

Hamid showed up for the hearing on 18 December at the Magistrates' Court, but since Ibrahim and Shakeel were absent, the hearing was postponed to 19 January 2005. Hamid called Ibrahim's phone three days before that date and a stranger responded not to call up that number again. The next day, Hamid texted and tried to call Omar but got no response. Hamid went to Shakeel's house and Shakeel's father told him that his son had gone on hajj. Hamid told the court that he had lost touch with his co-defendants and was convicted of the minor public order offense but did not receive any prison time. On 14 February, the court sent a letter to Ibrahim at his flat telling him to turn himself in before the police came for him. On 28 February, a second letter urged to him "come to us before we come for you."[51]

In Saudi Arabia, Bexhill told his father about his new friends and their political views. His alarmed father told him not to associate anymore with them and sent him to Saudi scholars, who told him that his friends' ideas were wrong and followed the ideology of al Qaeda, Abu Hamza, and Omar Abdel Rahman (the blind sheikh). They told him that these people were against Islam and recommended that he listen instead to the lectures of Sheikh Abdal Aziz bin Baz, the most respected Saudi cleric, and Sheikh Yusuf al Qaradawi, an Egyptian preacher on al Jazeera. They both condemned suicide bombings and attacks on civilians, but supported Palestinian fighters against Israel and, for Qaradawi, resistance to Western occupation in Iraq.[52]

In London, Mohamed and Hamdi introduced their respective partners to each other, who became close friends. Mohamed had reconciled with Azeb when she converted to Islam, started praying, and began wearing conservative Muslim attire. They were planning on getting married. He moved into a council flat at Dalgarno Gardens in early 2005 while she kept her place.[53] After a short trip to Saudi Arabia, Hamdi was back with Girma in December 2004 when she gave birth to their third son. At trial, Girma attempted to distance herself from her partner. She claimed that he had gotten married in Saudi Arabia, which made her very upset and caused a rift between them. However, there was no evidence that Hamdi ever called Saudi Arabia after he came back. He was constantly listening to audiocassettes by the radical preachers Anwar al Awlaki, Abdullah al Faisal, and Abu Hamza and viewing videos about 9/11, Osama bin Laden, fighting in Afghanistan, Iraq, and beheadings. Girma denied that she knew anything about them, but her trial demonstrated that they tried to get rid of this large amount of material bearing both of their fingerprints by taking it to a friend's flat the night before the bombing attempts. At her flat, a tape was left in her player entitled *The Rules of Jihad*. Her computer contained documents calling on Muslims to fight the jihad in Palestine and Afghanistan and discussing martyrdom and the Beslan massacre in Russia.[54]

The large collection of material found at their friend's flat included books by Abu Hamza, dozens of cassettes containing lectures by Anwar al Awlaki, 30 by Abu Hamza, and even more by Abdullah al Faisal.[55] One of al Faisal's lecture entitled *History Repeats Itself* was summarized at her trial: "The only way forward for Muslims is martyrdom operations. Describes democracy as the devil's religion used to combat Islam. . . . In reference to 9/11, a member of the audience says, 'all the people killed were homosexuals, adulterers and rapists and needed to be killed anyway. How can we help the Taliban, shall we go and fight?' Speaker states he should go and fight. He then goes on to say that many people worry about kafir kids being killed in explosions but explains that it is a mercy for them to die as, if they lived to be adults, they would grow to be drug dealers, takers, prostitutes and homosexuals. . . . 'The only holiday for a Muslim is to go [to] jihad training.'"[56]

Hamdi's collection of extremist material was by far the largest of all the people involved in this case. His fingerprints on it left no doubt that this was his collection and indicated that Hamdi was perhaps the most dedicated radical of the defendants. In fact he was the only defendant at the trial who refused to give evidence on his own behalf, which counts against the defendant in England, unlike in the United States. Girma tried her best to distance herself from him, claiming he did not live with her, despite the fact that he was always at her flat and had his possessions and clothes there, and they socialized together as a family. Her denials sounded hollow and she was eventually convicted at her separate trial.

Bexhill returned to England on 6 January 2005 and disobeyed his father by renting a room from Yahya for £60 a week. Omar, Ishmail, and occasionally Dixon would stop by. Omar still did not believe that the 9/11 attacks had been carried out by Muslims and Bexhill showed him a video with bin Laden and some of the hijackers to prove to him that al Qaeda had done it. After his return, Bexhill became assertive in defending his understanding that terrorist attacks were not permitted in Islam and referred Omar to bin Baz and Qaradawi. Omar responded with a tape by Abdullah Faisal, *The Devils of the Saudi Salafists*, rejecting these preachers as dollar scholars. Bexhill still strongly supported the Afghan and Iraqi fighters against the allied troops and simply disagreed with his friends about al

Qaeda's ideology and suicide operations in the West. Nevertheless, they did not let these differences get in the way of their friendships, and they never discussed jihad in front of Dixon at Omar's request.[57]

Omar's support for suicide bombings surfaced in an altercation he had with the imam of the Finchley Mosque. In early 2005, the imam condemned suicide bombings at a Friday sermon after the news of a suicide bombing in Palestine. Omar waited for the imam afterward and, when he passed by, shouted, "Don't mislead the people!" The imam just continued to walk without answering. A week later, Omar apologized: "Imam, it was very inappropriate of me, and I'm very sorry about that. Please, forgive me."[58]

By mid-March, Bexhill failed his exams and was suspended for not paying his tuition.[59] He immediately enrolled at another school. This was his pattern: he enrolled in courses, paid the first slice of tuition and then stopped paying, dropped out, and enrolled in another course elsewhere to maintain his visa status and parental financial support.

Ibrahim's Return

Ibrahim returned to England on 12 March 2005 but avoided his flat for fear of getting arrested for skipping his court appearance and moved in with Siraj Ali, a floor above Omar's flat.[60] As a result, Ibrahim was constantly with Omar. One day, they went to visit Yahya, where Bexhill was very surprised to see Ibrahim alive as he had expected him to die in Pakistan or Iraq. Ibrahim was going to tell Bexhill about his adventures but Omar signaled to him not to say anything. Bexhill asked Ibrahim about Shakeel and Majid but got no answer. Yahya later told him that the missing men had been killed. This was the last time Bexhill saw Ibrahim.[61]

Bexhill was no longer a trusted member of the group. Ibrahim no longer came to Yahya's flat. Bexhill was no longer invited to come to Omar's flat despite the fact that Yahya spent much of his time there. Within two weeks, Yahya got rid of him. Yahya reproached him for having been in his bedroom to watch a jihadi DVD on his DVD player. Bexhill protested that he paid rent and could do what he liked, but he later apologized. Yahya then told Bexhill that he was going to store large boxes in his room and someone else would come and share his room, and finally that he was going to raise his rent. Although Bexhill later made a few phone calls to his former friends, he never saw them again.[62]

The telephone records show that Ibrahim and Omar reconnected briefly with Hamdi. Ibrahim and Omar lived at Curtis House in North London while Hamdi lived in South London, almost an hour away. At the beginning of April 2005, they frequently called each other and were collocated in the same place.[63] After hearing the evidence, the judge at the trial concluded, "Mohamed and Osman [Hamdi], I have no doubt, became involved soon after Ibrahim returned from Pakistan. The telephone records provide a compelling picture in this regard and I reject the contradictory evidence I heard from some of the defendants as regards supposed visits to a community centre or restaurants that were by coincidence close to Osman's home. It is my finding that those visits to Osman's home and those telephone calls were all part of their early involvement in this conspiracy."[64]

I do not share the judge's conviction. After a short flurry of calls and three meetings between Ibrahim, Omar, and Hamdi in early April and two more between Omar and Hamdi later in the month, there was absolutely no communication between Hamdi and Omar or Ibrahim for two and a half months. This communication silence is simply not how amateur conspiracies evolve. They simply do not have the discipline to maintain this silence for such a long period. Contrast this silence with the frequent communication between the four conspirators living in North London. In the six weeks between the end of March and early May 2005, Ibrahim, Omar, and Ishmail lived in the same Curtis building while Yahya was not far away. Their phone records show very frequent communications between them: 85 calls between Ibrahim and Omar, 103 calls between Ibrahim and Yahya, 171 calls between Omar and Yahya (522 calls for the longer period between 10 November 2004 and 11 June 2005), 88 calls between Omar and Ishmail, and only 21 calls between Ibrahim and Ishmail. This shows very poor communication security and discipline among the conspirators, and establishes Omar and Yahya as the main link between the two pairs of conspirators—exchanging almost four calls a day—and the fact that Ibrahim was not a close friend of Ishmail. Hamdi and Mohamed were in contact with each other 93 times between February and July 2005 and were in the vicinity of each other's flat for half of the days in the six months prior to the attacks. In contrast, there were only 30 calls between Omar and Hamdi clustered around the beginning and the end of April.[65] Furthermore, Hamdi never visited Omar's flat until four days prior to the attack in July. This pattern is more consistent with Ibrahim reconnecting with Hamdi and telling him about his experience in Pakistan, and then

Hamdi's positive reaction to his adventures but no involvement on the part of Hamdi's in Ibrahim's and Omar's activities until mid-July.

While we are on the telephone records, there is a puzzling series of calls starting on 6 May between Ibrahim's cell phone and four cell phones registered to Abdulla Ahmed Ali and Ali's family. Although Ibrahim became friendly with Ali when they were in prison together, he denied he had ever met or known Ali before his arrest. He claimed he did not remember the calls but explained that someone from Walthamstow had probably tried to call him to inquire about Rizwan Majid's disappearance. Although this explanation is plausible, the calls occurred about two months after Ibrahim's return, when Majid's family had already been notified of his death and, since Ibrahim had been to Majid's house at least once before their trip, the family could have chosen someone at least acquainted with Ibrahim, such as Hamid, rather than rely on a complete stranger to Ibrahim at the time. I suspect that the calls might be something else altogether. In his report, Rashid Rauf wrote that he lost contact with Ibrahim after Ibrahim's return to London. To reestablish contact, Rauf tried to contact Ibrahim by a messenger.[66] Since Ali was in contact with Rauf at the time, as we shall see in the next chapter, it is more probable that Ali was Rauf's messenger, urging Ibrahim to resume contact with his al Qaeda intermediary.

Buying Hydrogen Peroxide

At his trial, Ibrahim testified that, after his return, he saw on the Internet a letter from an Iraqi woman, who was raped several times by her captors in Abu Ghraib Prison, and this outraged him so much that he was determined to carry his scheme of a fake explosion to protest British participation in that war.[67] Omar confirmed this during his testimony. I share the jury's and judge's skepticism about this account of a hoax to protest the war.

After lying low for a few weeks, Ibrahim and Omar proceeded with the most crucial step in their plot, the buying and concentrating of the hydrogen peroxide. Ibrahim searched for other uses of hydrogen peroxide on the Internet and found out that it could be used for bleaching wood and wallpaper stripping. Omar's roommate, Ishmail, was an ideal buyer for this product because he was a painter and decorator in the construction business. Omar told him that he was getting married and needed to decorate his flat and strip the wallpaper there. Ibrahim showed him a printout downloaded from the Internet detailing its use for paint stripping and displaying a picture of workingmen in protective overalls and masks. Ibrahim gave Ishmail money to buy a big bottle at a pharmacy. For such a large quantity, the pharmacist directed Ishamil to a beauty supply shop. He bought a liter of 18 percent hydrogen peroxide for £2.98 on 27 April at Sally's, a hair and beauty shop in Finchley. He called Omar to tell him he had bought it but Omar was upset: "Why are you telling me on the phone? Why can't you bring it to the house?" The next day, at Maplin's, Ibrahim bought bomb components such as small bulbs, lamp holders, electric holders, electric components, transistors, small batteries, bell wire, and a light switch.[68]

On the evening of 7 May, Ishmail was cautioned for smoking marijuana in the park where he played soccer and basketball. When he got back to Omar's flat, Ibrahim asked him to buy more hydrogen peroxide. Ishmail returned to Sally's and bought their entire stock of 14 liters for £13.82 on 9 May and asked the store to order some more.[69] Now that Ibrahim and Omar were ready to concentrate the hydrogen peroxide, they chose to do it in Omar's flat, converting it to a bomb factory. But first, Omar needed to get rid of his tenants and he told them that he wanted them to leave because he was about to redecorate his flat since he was getting married. At trial, Ishmail testified that he was ready to leave because he felt they were disrespectful to him by constantly calling him "African man." Ishmail told them they were also African but they replied that they were half Arab and half African, but Ishmail was the real African.[70]

However, Ishmail later pleaded guilty and admitted that he had agreed "to take part in making bombs by buying the hydrogen peroxide; he was reluctant but did as asked; he appreciated that any explosion of the bombs would be likely to endanger life."[71] His Indian roommate was probably not aware of the plot. They moved into a small flat in the neighborhood, on Ballards Lane. The Indian Muslim took his computer with him: it had been the only computer in the flat.

Concentrating Hydrogen Peroxide and Buying Some More

As soon as the tenants were out, Ibrahim started concentrating the hydrogen peroxide. He first used a saucepan but this process took too long and he switched to a pot to boil down the chemical four liters at a time. To protect himself from the toxic steam, he wore goggles, opened the window of the kitchen, and closed its door. He calculated the specific gravity and concentration of his solution with a set of Salter electronic scales. It took about two and a half to three hours to boil the original four liters down to about 400 milliliters of estimated 70 percent hydrogen peroxide, a ten-to-one ratio. He found the weighing of the solution along the way too laborious and simply assumed that the resulting solution was a 70 percent concentration. He bought a plastic measuring jug to measure 400 milliliters and stopped checking the specific gravity of his final product. For storage, he poured the concentrated product back into the original empty hydrogen peroxide bottles, which he carefully marked with the number "70."[72]

The forensic experts at trial agreed that concentrating hydrogen peroxide is a tricky business because heating it too fast breaks it down into water and oxygen. Through experimentation, they found that heating the hydrogen peroxide at 60 degrees centigrade was the optimal temperature to prevent this breakdown, but the duration of this process took much longer than a few hours to reach the target of 70 percent. Duplicating Ibrahim's method, they obtained a mixture of only 58 percent.[73] Ibrahim's faulty manufacture process resulted in the failure of main charge to detonate at this weak concentration of hydrogen peroxide.

Ibrahim also manufactured TATP, the main ingredient of the detonator. For this he bought a small bottle of 24.5 percent hydrogen peroxide and acetone, the main component of nail varnish remover, at a pharmacy. To catalyze this reaction, he bought sulfuric acid from a B&Q chain store. He described the process at trial, "First, you put the hydrogen peroxide and then you put the acetone, bit by bit, and mixing at the same time . . . [then] put it in the fridge . . . to cool it before you put the acid because the acid makes it hot." Using a tea bag, he filtered the resulting crystals, rinsed them with tap water and stored the crystals in a mouthwash bottle.[74] Forensic experts at the trial testified that the recovered sample of TATP was 90 percent pure.

To make tens of liters of concentrated solution, Ibrahim needed a lot more hydrogen peroxide. Omar called Ishmail, who was now living on his own and more reluctant to do favors for his former landlord. Omar insisted and Ishmail reluctantly agreed. He ordered more hydrogen peroxide from the nearby shop. Omar said he should also buy some from Hairways in Tottenham. Ishmail protested that this was too far and he did not have a car. Omar suggested he call Dixon to help him. Ishmail called Dixon, who agreed to help in principle. On 18 May, Omar and Dixon drove to his flat, but Ishmail told them he was just too tired after a long day's work. He felt that Omar was abusing their friendship with these demands. Ishmail later testified that Omar told him, "Stop, don't talk. Don't give me long stories. . . . It's only once. If you don't get this opportunity, that's it." Ishmail agreed to do it the next day and meet Dixon at Omar's flat. Omar and Dixon were upset to have wasted their time.[75]

The above paragraph reflects Ishmail's version in court. Right after the prosecution's evidence and Ibrahim's direct testimony, Ishmail turned on his fellow co-defendants, arguing that at first he did not know what the hydrogen peroxide was for, and when he found out, he was very reluctant to participate in Ibrahim's and Omar's schemes. As a result, his version was not challenged by prosecution evidence or Ibrahim's examination. Omar, who testified later, insisted that Ishmail knew from the very beginning that they would use the peroxide for a "hoax" bombing. "[He] got involved since he was staying with me, me and him would talk about everything, whatever I was doing I would talk to him and Ibrahim was talking to him and was telling him that . . . we're going to demonstrate about Iraq and what's happened, the oppression there and . . . he was keen to help."[76] On cross-examination, Omar insisted that Ishmail never complained about buying the hydrogen peroxide.[77] It appears that both are stretching the truth. Ishmail later admitted knowing about the bomb making and not a hoax, as Omar claimed.

On 19 May in the afternoon, Dixon and Ishmail drove to Hairways. The salesperson later remembered that Ishmail asked her for 70 percent hydrogen peroxide.

> I explained that peroxide, some people refer to it as 18 percent, but 18 percent is also sometimes called 60 volume . . . thinking he meant 70 volume. . . . I remember him insisting that it was 70 percent, not 70 volume. . . . I explained . . . the highest we are able to get is 18 percent peroxide. He then asked for something like 48 gallons of . . . 18 percent liquid peroxide and we don't have anywhere near them sort of quantities in stock at all. . . . It was at this point I felt I needed to pass the request to my manager . . . because I did not really know what to do in that situation, ordering such a large quantity of stuff we wouldn't be able to sell. I wasn't sure if we needed to take a deposit or anything, so I passed it on to her.[78]

Ishmail and Dixon ended up buying all the stock in the store,[79] namely 12 one-liter bottles and one four-liter bottle of 18 percent hydrogen peroxide for just under £35 in cash. At trial, neither Ishmail nor Ibrahim had any explanation for Ishmail's request for 70 percent concentrated hydrogen peroxide.

From Dixon's recollection, at Hairways, "the man on the counter did express a concern that the stuff was quite volatile and said to be careful. Ishmail said, 'There's no worries. I'm a professional, I know what I'm doing.' . . . When the lady asked . . . what the bleach was for, Ishmail seemed a bit reluctant to answer and so I answered and just said it was for stripping walls. She was quite surprised. . . . I just assumed she was getting concerned because she hadn't heard of it being used in that process. . . . When we got into the car, Ishmail said that they didn't have enough at that address and he needed to get some more and he knew another hair place in Finchley." They drove to Sally's to buy 18 more one-liter bottles for £17.77. They then drove back to Curtis House, where Dixon helped Ishmail take them into Omar's flat. "Ishmail dropped one bottle," Dixon recalled. "It rolled off the top of the box. The container split and a man picked it up for him. Ishmail said, 'Be careful with that,' and took it off him."[80] Ishmail gave Dixon £5 for gas and his trouble.[81]

A few days later, Omar called Ishmail for more hydrogen peroxide and Ishmail ordered some more from Sally's. On 1 June, he and Omar picked up 42 one-liter bottles from Sally's and paid £48.86 in cash. They ordered another batch of 42 liters from the store, but the store clerk transposed the digits by mistakes and ordered only 24 liters. Omar wanted to take a taxicab back to the flat, but Ishmail suggested that they take a bus that stopped at the corner and went directly to the Curtis House, which is what they did.[82]

During that period, Yahya was studying for his year-end exams and was planning to fly to Yemen to see his wife and then go with her to Ethiopia for a vacation. He came to Omar's flat at least every other day according to the telephone geolocation records.[83] Ibrahim and Omar tried to shield their friend by testifying that he was not aware of their concentrating hydrogen peroxide as they stopped doing it before he would come over. However, Ishmail testified that there was a strong smell from the cooking process in the flat even when it was not going on.

In fact, Yahya was involved in the peroxide buying spree. Around 20 May, he inquired about hydrogen peroxide at PAK Cosmetics Centre in Finsbury Park. The salesperson remembered, "[Yahya] asked me for peroxide and he asked me . . . for . . . the maximum percentage we can get in and . . . I told him I would contact our suppliers. . . . At a later stage, I asked him [why he wanted strong peroxide] and he said they are carpenters and they use it for washing some wood and stuff." Yahya told him he wanted to buy in large quantity. The salesperson gave Yahya his business card. Yahya returned a week or two later and the salesperson said that the most he could get was 18 percent. Yahya said at first he was interested in about 50 liters, but asked whether he could get a larger discount for 100 liters. The salesperson told him he was not sure if he could get this large quantity from his supplier and said he would check the prices at that quantity. Yahya told him his name was Yousef and gave him Ishmail's phone number. The salesperson called Ishmail on 8 June and asked for Yousef. Ishmail seemed confused and when the salesperson told him it was about a hydrogen peroxide order, Ishmail said he was Yousef's friend and the salesperson asked him to tell Yousef to call back and place an order.[84]

At the trial, Yahya claimed he did not know what the hydrogen peroxide was for and confessed he might have been a bit naïve about his friends' using him. The prosecutor refuted his air of innocent naïveté by showing that Yahya got the money for his trip to Yemen by defrauding his university and getting financial aid by claiming that he was disabled, had no water and electricity at his home, and had to borrow money from friends to survive. He submitted false documents in support of his application, including a falsified bank statement. In fact, he was living on benefits and withdrew £2,800 from his bank account on 20 May and repaid his sister £1,500 for the dowry money she had loaned him the previous year. His university paid him £532 in June.[85]

Yahya asked Ishmail to help get him a cheap return ticket to Yemen. Ishmail got him one for £467 and Yahya gave £50 to Ishmail for his troubles on 10 June.[86] On 11 June, Yahya flew to Yemen to meet his wife and together they flew to Ethiopia on 18 July.

The Final Push on the Bomb Making

On 14 June, a fire burned Ishmail's flat and he and his roommate lost all their possessions. The police sheltered Ishmail at a bed-and-breakfast for a night. He spent the next two nights hanging out at a Turkish shop until it closed and slept on a bench in a park. The Finchley Mosque imam made an announcement about his predicament at services. Omar, who was there, invited Ishmail to move back with him rent free, which Ishmail did on 17 June.[87]

At trial, Ishmail testified that he was rarely in the flat after his return but his cell phone records contradict him. Omar and Ibrahim again asked him to buy more hydrogen peroxide. Ishmail claimed he did not ask any questions and complied because he felt obligated to return the favor for his rent-free living. Ibrahim was also planning to buy a van—he and Ishmail leafed through a catalogue of minivans, looking at their prices—and was scheduled to take his test for a driver's license that June.[88]

On 18 June, Ishmail and Ibrahim went to PAK Cosmetics to follow up on Yahya's inquiry. They told the salesman they were friends of Yousef, who was busy at work. He told them that he could give them a trade price for a four-liter bottle of hydrogen peroxide of £5.40 a bottle in large quantity, but he needed a 50 percent deposit before he put in an order. Ishmail, who did most of the talking, said they would come back with it. On 21 June, Omar and Ishmail went to Sally's to pick up his order but found out that the clerk had ordered only 24 one-liter bottles. They bought them for a little less than £28 pounds and placed an additional order for 120 liters. Later that day, Ishmail and Ibrahim returned to PAK Cosmetics and asked what kind of discount they could get for 200 liters. The salesman quoted them a final price of £5.20 a bottle. They placed an order for 200 liters and gave him a £100 deposit. The salesman asked them how they were going to use this much peroxide and they told him they would use it to wash wood and break it down into smaller bottles to supply some pharmacies. He promised to contact them as soon as he got delivery and placed the order with his supplier the next day. On 30 June, Ibrahim and Ishmail picked up from Sally's 120 one-liter bottles for £139.59 in Abdu Ali's Volkswagen. On 5 July, they picked up from PAK Cosmetics 52 four-liter bottles (totaling 208 liters) for an additional £170. The CCTV footage from the store showed them to be all smiles as they stood at the counter paying for their purychase.[89]

This last frenzy of purchases raised the total amount of 18 percent hydrogen peroxide for this plot to 443 liters, with one liter spilled during transportation. This was an enormous amount of concentrated hydrogen peroxide. To put it in perspective, their 219 liters from Sally's, a nationwide chain store, amounted to 41 percent of its total national sales that year and this was less than half of what the conspirators bought in total.[90]

Where did the money for these purchases come from? They totaled £557 for the hydrogen peroxide alone. The trial left this mystery unsolved. Ibrahim testified that he funded these purchases by himself. He claimed that he returned from Pakistan with about £700 and did not have any expenses since he was living with friends.[91] Prosecutors did not press him on this issue, but he did not lack for money during the duration of the plot and was even talking about buying a van. He might have received some money from Yahya, who withdrew a very large amount of unaccounted-for money in May, or Rashid Rauf might have given him money.

As soon as Ibrahim, Omar, and Ishmail got their two large deliveries, they started concentrating the hydrogen peroxide 18 hours a day. A two-week rotation schedule was later found at 58 Curtis House showing Ishmail taking the shift from 5 AM to 11 AM, Omar from 11 AM to 5 PM, and Ibrahim from 5 PM to 11 PM. This amounted to 252 hours. Using Ibrahim's calculation that it took him about two and half to three hours to concentrate four liters of 18 percent hydrogen peroxide to 70 percent, they could have easily have concentrated their last purchases of 328 liters during this period. The first half of July was a period of intense activity as reflected in Omar's higher electric bill.[92] In the end, the conspirators filled 38 one-liter bottles labeled "70."

In his defense statement, Ibrahim suggested that he had used only the oldest bottle of peroxide but the peroxide bought from PAK Cosmetics contained a high level of tin impurity, which was recovered in the main charges of the bombs. This indicates that he had used the last batch of peroxide. At trial, he also claimed that his original plan was to leave six to eight rucksacks unattended looking like real bombs (that is, with a real main charge make up of 70 percent hydrogen peroxide, but without a battery) to protest the wars in Iraq and Afghanistan.[93] As three liters of concentrated hydrogen peroxide are required for each fake bomb, this amounts only to 18 to 24 liters of concentrated liquid. Given the trouble they went to in order to concentrate hydrogen peroxide, it is surprising that they overshot the maximum required by so much by making 38 liters. This does not make sense.

I do not believe that Ibrahim originally wanted to carry out suicide attacks. He testified at his trial that he was going to leave the bombs at some site, unattended. This was quite different from what Rauf expected since he had made Ibrahim record a martyrdom video in Islamabad, so I wonder whether Ibrahim's break in communication with Rauf was due to the fact that he had decided not to carry out a suicide attack. But this still leaves the problem of the large quantity of concentrated hydrogen peroxide unresolved. The mention of a minivan that Ibrahim was shopping for in June is intriguing. I wonder whether Ibrahim planned to build a minivan bomb, which he intended to fill in with about 150 pounds of explosive material.

The hypothesis of a minivan bomb may also explain the puzzle of Yahya's disappearance from the plot, Ishmail's ambiguous status in it, and the absence of Hamdi and Mohamed from it for a long time. Up to that point, the plot actively involved only Ibrahim and Omar in all its phases. They could manufacture the larger bomb by themselves, but needed large quantities of concentrated hydrogen peroxide without triggering undue suspicion. They asked their friends, Yahya and Ishmail, to help in the purchase of a large quantity of it. Yahya, a radical like them, was a willing participant, but was no longer needed after the purchases if the plot was a minivan bomb. He could therefore go to see his wife in Yemen. I cannot imagine him abandoning his friends had he been needed to participate in coordinated suicide bombings. Ishmail was not a radical, but he had the perfect cover story of being a painter and decorator with his trade card to make the purchases. He was clearly doing a favor for his friends, and after buying the chemicals did not expect to be part of the plot. The fire at his flat and the necessity of moving back with Omar pulled him back into the plot, and his phone put him at the flat when the concentrating was taking place. By that time, Ishmail certainly knew that the large amount of concentrated hydrogen peroxide was for a bomb. He is not as naïve and stupid as he claimed to be at trial. At trial Ibrahim had tried to cover for him in his direct examination, which gave Ishmail an opportunity to change strategy when his turn to testify came and distance himself from his former comrades.

Hamdi and Mohamed were as radical, if not more so, as Ibrahim and Omar, but were not needed at all for a minivan bomb plot and were not part of it. The minivan bomb hypothesis makes far more sense than the hoax bomb excuse the defendants used at trial and ties up loose ends that are otherwise difficult to explain. Nevertheless, Omar and Ibrahim could not reveal this plan in their own defense because attempting to carry out a minivan bomb in the middle of London is just as bad as trying to carry out simultaneous suicide bombings in that city.

Last-Minute Change of Plans

By early July, Mohammed Hamid and his wife returned from their trip. He resumed his Friday evening gatherings at his house and organized a paintball game in Kent attended by Mohamed and Hamdi on 3 July.[94]

The London bombings of 7 July 2005 took everyone by surprise. Hamid received a call from a friend advising him not to set up his dawah table at Marble Arch as usual. Hamid ignored it. "Everyone was grumpy," he later recalled, "angry and the majority of them throwing racial abuse at me, shouting at me, 'You're a terrorist, you're this, you're that,' all the names under the sun, some people were spitting. . . . I said, 'Listen, how can you blame me? I'm here. I'm standing here. I haven't done anything wrong. Why are you blaming me?' . . . One of the officers . . . says to me, 'I advise you to go today.' . . . So, I say, 'I think you're right, I am packing up.'" Hamid left for home and thought about Muslims in Britain. "They're going to be scared of a backlash. . . . They're frightened of being arrested. They're frightened of racial attacks, they're frightened of abuse."[95] He texted a message to his friends: "Assalam bro, we fear no one except Allah. We will not change our ways. We are proud to be a Muslim and we will not hide. 8.00 pm Friday at my place, be there, food and talk. Al-Quran." The next evening, he held the Friday evening gathering, to which Hamdi, Mohamed, and Phil Rees of the BBC came.[96]

Ibrahim probably had not known about the London bombings beforehand. Rauf may have given him a general direction to conduct a set of bombings during the summer, which may explain the rush to make bombs in early July. Both Ibrahim and Omar testified that the London bombings changed their plans. Ibrahim noted that despite the horrors of the London bombings, "it got Britain and the politicians talking about their role in Iraq. . . . My aim is to cause maximum disruption and . . . maximum publicity and then get maximum debate about the war in Iraq, so I thought I told Omar this is the right time to put pressure on the government by making a fake suicide mission, but . . . obviously without killing innocent people."[97] Omar's testimony backed Ibrahim: "It changed the first idea of unattended [devices] and we thought if we could do the same thing, a copy-cat, fake suicide mission, we could attract a lot of media attention and this in turn was the right time to put pressure on the government. . . . We thought, if we could do this demonstration, this will make it clear how people are against this illegal war and how the people of this country, the majority of them, do not agree with this war, and we hope that the government would change its foreign policy and stop throwing bombs in Iraq. . . . Whether innocent people die here or Iraq, it's still innocent people so our aim was to stop anything happening in Iraq."[98] Ishmail may have been privy to these discussions because his phone record shows that he was at Curtis House daily from 10 to 16 July.[99]

The problem with the above tirade is that it is just wishful thinking because right after the London bombings, people rallied round Blair's government and refused to be intimidated by terrorists. The issue of Iraq was not debated to any significant extent and instead there was an overwhelming condemnation of the bombings by all the people, including Muslims and their leaders. This is not consistent with both defendants' justification for their copycat attempt.

Ibrahim and Omar testified that their original plan was to leave unattended fully operational bombs, for realism's sake, but without a battery to ignite their detonation. In view of the London bombings, their new plan now called for ignition of the detonator for the sake of an effect but without exploding the main charge. Ibrahim and Omar testified that in order to make sure that the make-believe charges would not explode, Ibrahim diluted the 70 percent concentrated hydrogen peroxide by mixing it with an equal volume of tap water to reduce it to 35 percent concentration.[100] The prosecution refuted this claim of dilution with testimony about differing isotope profiles.[101] After the trial, it was found that prosecutors knew this testimony to be false when they introduced it at trial.[102] In any case, this testimony was not really needed because it was clear that the hydrogen peroxide had been diluted not by Ibrahim's intent but by his incompetence.

Like the jury and judge, I reject the defendants' claim that they were planning a hoax bombing. The London bombings had indeed changed their plans. These suicide bombings raised the bar for terrorist attacks in the West. The London bombers had now become the prototype for global neojihadis. Their behavior became the new norm. Suicide bombers replaced simple bombers as the new heroes. Now, an unattended car bomb was simply not good enough for an attack. It had to be a suicide bombing to catch the imagination of other potential neojihadi fighters. Omar and Ibrahim simply decided to duplicate the exploits of their dead comrades.

Omar and Ibrahim claimed that they then tested a full bomb with the main charge mixture of diluted 35 percent hydrogen peroxide at Omar's flat around 14 July to ensure that it would not explode. They claimed that they knew that the small amount of TATP was not powerful enough to detonate this weak explosive mixture. According to them, Ibrahim mixed the diluted hydrogen peroxide with chapati flour in a 6.25-liter plastic bucket and inserted a detonator in it. The TATP detonator was ignited by a small electric bulb filled with TATP when connected to a battery. As expected, the detonator made a popping sound and the main charge did not explode.[103] Omar said that he wiped out the mess with a T-shirt and flushed it down the toilet. This rag with main charge residue was later found at Omar's flat. I am skeptical of this account, and Ishmail, as we shall see, had a different explanation for this rag.

Bringing Hamdi and Mohamed into the Plot

Now that Omar and Ibrahim planned to conduct a copycat attack, they needed at least two more people to copy the London bombings. Omar immediately suggested Hamdi. "Osman [Hamdi] was always against the war in Iraq. . . . Osman's the kind of person who will do demonstrations." They met him at a park in the vicinity of his home late on 14 July. Ibrahim gave him a political pitch, saying that demonstrations against the war had not worked and more had to be done. Hamdi agreed to participate and volunteered his friend Mohamed, who was just as worked up about Iraq as Ibrahim and Omar. Hamdi would speak to his friend.[104]

The next evening, Ibrahim and Omar met again with Hamdi at the park. Hamdi had earlier gone to Hamid's Friday evening gathering.[105] Mohamed was working in Reading and got back to London very late when Hamdi called him. He met Ibrahim, Omar, and Hamdi, who explained the deal to him, and Mohamed agreed to take part in it. Omar and Ibrahim invited their two new partners to come to Omar's flat to talk some more and see parts of the bombs. They drove to the flat in Mohamed's car and arrived early in the morning.[106]

At Omar's flat, they talked about their plans. Ibrahim demonstrated how a little TATP flashed in a teaspoon. They agreed to imitate the London bombers with the use of rucksack bombs. They decided to initiate the attacks from Mohamed's flat because he was the only one who lived alone as Omar planned to get married the next day. Mohamed had to buy a rucksack for himself and agreed to buy enough chapati flour necessary to make the main charge. At around 4 AM, the four conspirators woke up Ishmail, who was sleeping in the living room. Ishmail led them in prayer and went back to sleep. Hamdi and Mohamed left at daybreak, taking along 21 bottles of concentrated hydrogen peroxide with them. Later that day, Ishmail went to Ikea to buy electrical supplies.[107]

Omar's Wedding

Also on 16 July, Omar finalized the agreement for his marriage to Fardosa Abdullahi. He had met her four months before and her mother took a liking to him. They negotiated the dowry down to £3,000.[108] She was a 17-year-old girl, born in Somalia, who had immigrated to England when she was six. She had a history of mental disorder that required long hospitalizations. She later claimed she felt pressure by her family to acquiesce to the marriage within weeks of leaving the hospital.

On Sunday 17 July, Omar married her in a religious ceremony presided over by the Finchley Mosque imam. Of course, she was not at the ceremony, but her stepfather represented her interests.[109] Ibrahim and Abdu Ali were there for Omar, but Ishmail, who was cleaning the mosque at the time, later complained that he had not been invited. After the ceremony, Omar saw Ishmail at the flat and told him, "I'm a married man and my wife is coming soon, sort yourself out." Abdu Ali invited him to come and sleep at his flat upstairs at 65 Curtis House.[110] Omar later testified, "When I got married, from the 17th until the 20th, I stayed with Fardosa in the house. Ibrahim and Asiedu [Ishmail] stayed upstairs, but when I was sleeping one of them could come to the other room but as soon as I got up they [would] have to go upstairs, so Asiedu used to come in the mornings, I used to see him sometimes in the mornings to come and have shower . . . but as soon as I got up they would go upstairs."[111]

That Sunday, Hamdi, his son, and Mohamed went to Covent Garden market. Mohamed bought his rucksack and Hamdi bought some stuff for his family. Mohamed also bought the chapati flour.[112] At 65 Curtis House, Ibrahim talked to Ishmail about getting involved. "He didn't say in terms, 'I'm going to join,'" Ibrahim testified, "but he was agreeing with me that something has to be done and he was strongly against the war and agreeing with what I was saying . . . I was under the impression that he agreed and he wanted to join."[113]

On Monday 18 July, Ishmail went to work painting the whole day with someone from the mosque. The next day, he did some gardening and got locked out of the flat in the evening, as Abdu Ali was not home. Omar saw Ishmail on the staircase that evening. "On the 19th," he later said, "I spoke to Asiedu [Ishmail] . . . and Asiedu was willing to come, I told him what the plan was going to be because me and Asiedu are more closer than to Ibrahim. . . . He said anything to help, and I said to him, 'There's no pressure on you, it's up to you. If you want to do it, you can do it. If you don't want to do it, it's up to you.'" Ishmail fell asleep on the staircase until Abdu Ali came and invited him to finish the night at his flat.[114]

The Failed Bombings

On the evening of 19 July, Ibrahim and Hamdi went to Mohamed's flat at Dalgarno Gardens around midnight. Ibrahim told them that the demonstration would take place on 21 July. They experimented with weaving electric wires from inside their rucksacks through their clothes and into their pocket, where they connected the wires to a snap connector to a nine-volt battery. They talked until the 4 AM Fajr prayer before Ibrahim borrowed Hamdi's car to return to 65 Curtis House. Afterward, he went downstairs to Omar's flat as the latter had gone to his in-laws early that morning and fell asleep on the couch till early afternoon.[115]

Ishmail later claimed that Ibrahim left a booby-trap bomb in a sideboard at 58 Curtis House to explode when the police opened it after the attack. Ibrahim allegedly did this when he was by himself in Omar's flat that afternoon. This explains the manufacture of just one bomb at that flat. When Ishmail returned to Omar's flat after the failed attempted bombings, he allegedly discovered the booby-trapped bomb and flushed it down the toilet himself as well as the rest of the concentrated hydrogen peroxide and tried to get rid of compromising evidence at the flat.[116]

At Omar's flat, when Ishmail got back from work in the early evening, Ibrahim told him that the operation would take place the next day. According to Ibrahim, "he didn't say no, only, he didn't say, yes." Ibrahim got the impression that Ishmail was going to participate.[117] Ishmail's recollection at trial was of course different but he confirmed that Ibrahim told him that the operation was the next day and asked him to come along. He admitted that "I didn't just say 'yes,' but I didn't say I'm not going with them." He tried to excuse his decision to go with them by claiming that he was homeless and "felt very, very depressed" and could not focus. On the same day, Hamdi and Mohamed spent the day together praying at the mosque, playing Play Station, and just waiting for the evening at Hamdi's flat.[118]

In the evening, Omar returned to his flat, where Ibrahim and Ishmail were waiting for him. Ishmail later recalled that Omar told him that his wife loved him very much and he started tearing up. He wiped his tears and said, "This is from Sheitan [Satan]." Omar denied this at the trial. Just before all three left Omar's flat, Ishmail remembered Ibrahim adjusting the sideboard. They packed their rucksacks with all they needed for the next day—the 6.25-liter plastic tubs, the electrical wiring, the electric scales, the TATP, thermometer, and masking tape—and drove to an Internet café where Ibrahim typed a short e-mail by himself around 11 PM.[119] This mysterious e-mail may have been for Rauf, but the latter was probably hiding in the FATA after the successful London bombings and not in e-mail contact.

The three conspirators met with Hamdi and Mohamed near Hamdi's place, transferred the materiel into Mohamed's car, and drove off to Dalgarno Gardens after a quick stop at an open chicken shop. They ate and Ishmail drifted off to sleep until Fajr prayers when his co-conspirators woke him up to lead them in prayers. At trial, he claimed he went back to sleep[120] but the other four defendants said he was awake when Ibrahim made the five detonators. Ibrahim first made a hole in small light bulbs and filled them with TATP. He then rolled some paper around a pen, filled it with TATP, put a modified bulb in it, and attached wires to the bulb. Each detonator contained about five to eight grams of TATP, enough to ignite a main charge composed of 70 percent hydrogen peroxide, but not enough to do so with one having only a concentration of 58 percent.

At trial, Ishmail testified that, at this point, he allegedly started to appreciate the reality of the suicide operation: "I just left the room . . . like automatic, so I went into the toilet and I started crying. I cried for some time." He was terrified. He claimed that Omar, who had seen him crying, tried to reassure him, but all the other defendants rejected his version at the trial. On direct examination, before Ishmail turned on him, Ibrahim testified that Ishmail told him he was not going to go ahead with the demonstration. Ibrahim told Ishmail, "Okay, you can do whatever you want, just don't rock the boat. Don't tell the others." Ibrahim did not want the others to feel discouraged.[121]

Mohamed went out to buy five sets of transport cards for the conspirators and his brother Wahbi came around 8 AM to repair his computer and take Mohamed's will for his fiancée and their two children. After Wahbi's departure, all five conspirators spread plastic bin liners over the floor and mixed the main charge of three liters of concentrated hydrogen peroxide with chapati flour slowly so as not to generate much heat and bubbles. They poured the mixture into the plastic tubs, where a hole covered by tape had already been made. Ibrahim inserted the detonator into the tubs from the bottom and sealed it, with the detonator wires hanging out. He cut holes in the rucksacks so as to thread the wires through them and into the participants' pockets, where the wires were connected to a snap. They secured screws, nails, bolts, and metal washers as shrapnel around the plastic tubs with some tape and inserted them into the rucksacks, with their lid still off to let off the gases. They waited until the last minute to close the lids.[122] They shaved their hair and beards in order to blend in with the crowd. They were now ready to carry out their attacks.

The conspirators made their final selection of targets: Ibrahim was to go to the Bank Underground station; Omar, to Warren Street; Mohamed, to Oval; Hamdi, to Shepherd's Bush; and Ishmail, to White City. Since their targets were spread out over the city, the conspirators left in two teams. One consisting of Ibrahim, Omar, and Mohamed traveled to Stockwell Park in Mohamed's car and waited. They called Hamdi back at Mohamed's flat to signal for him and Ishmail to get going to their respective sites. They closed the lid on their bomb containers, put on their rucksacks, and went into the Underground. Between 12:30 and 1:00 PM, four of the conspirators tried to detonate their respective bombs, but the main charges did not explode. Ishmail abandoned his bomb in a nearby shrub, where it was found two days later.[123]

All the conspirators fled from their respective crime scenes. Ishmail returned to Omar's flat, where he cleaned up most of the compromising evidence. He went to the police on 26 July and was arrested. Omar escaped in one of his wife's burkas and fled to Birmingham, where he was arrested on 27 July. Ibrahim and Mohamed hid at Mohamed's flat, where they were arrested on 29 July. Hamdi's wife helped him escape to Brighton and then Rome via the Eurostar. He was arrested in Rome on 29 July and extradited to England on 22 September. Yahya was detained in Ethiopia on 29 November 2005 and interviewed by the British police. He returned to Britain on 20 December 2005 and was arrested at Gatwick Airport.

Ibrahim, Omar, Osman, and Mohamed were charged with conspiracy to murder; Asiedu was charged with conspiracy to cause an explosion likely to endanger life; and Yahya was charged with collecting or making a record of information of a kind likely to be useful to a person committing or preparing an act of terrorism. Their trial started on 11 January 2007 at Woolwich Crown Court. On 9 July 2007, a jury convicted Ibrahim, Omar, Hamdi, and Mohamed, who were each sentenced to life imprisonment, with a minimum term of 40 years. The jury was unable to reach a verdict for Ishmail and Yahya. On 5 November 2007, Yahya pled guilty to his charge and was sentenced to six years and nine months imprisonment. On 9 November 2007, Ishmail pled guilty to his charge and was sentenced to life imprisonment, with a minimum term of 33 years and recommended deportation.

Over a dozen more people were also arrested and convicted in connection to this case for helping the suspects escape arrest. In addition, Mohammed Hamid and a half dozen more were later arrested for violating the new Terrorism Act of 2006.

CHAPTER 5

OVERT

THE TRANSATLANTIC AIRLINES
LIQUID BOMBS PLOT

AT THE TIME THAT Rashid Rauf was organizing the training of the Theseus and Vivace leaders, he was also organizing the training of leaders of a third plot, whose investigation and prosecution the British authorities later named Operation Overt. Like Crevice and Theseus, this one emerged from a network of protest against British foreign policy and support for Kashmiri and then Afghan refugees and fighters.

The Walthamstow Cluster

Abdulla Ahmed Ali, Ahmed to his friends, was born in Newham in October 1980. His parents came to Britain in the 1960s from Jhelum, in the Punjab Province of Pakistan. His oldest brother, Dawood Khan, born in 1972, became an IT consultant and was politically active in the Stop the War movement. Another older brother, Umar Khan, became a property developer and had a part-time job in the Underground. A younger brother became a probation officer with the Home Office. Shortly after Ali was born, his whole family migrated back to Jhelum, where Ali spent the first seven years of his life before returning to Walthamstow, London, in 1987.[1]

Ali met Arafat Khan in primary school. Arafat was six months younger, born in Gujranwala, Pakistan, and his family immigrated to Walthamstow in 1982. His father, a lawyer in Pakistan, had first come to Britain alone and worked for Customs and Excise in Leeds. He went back to Pakistan to get married and take care of his ailing mother. When the family returned to Britain, he worked as a bookkeeper. He strongly believed in integration and the family was secular. They gave Christmas presents to neighbors and ate turkey on Christmas.[2]

Ali and Arafat met Oliver Savant in secondary school. Savant was their age and born in England of an Indian father and English mother. His father had immigrated to England in the 1960s, became an architect and photographer, and married a Church of England bookkeeper. The three teenagers were often together and shared an interest in football, rap music, and going out.[3]

The paths of the three friends diverged when they went to college. At 15, Ali became religious from a cultural perspective: a book on Islam lying around his house had kindled his interest. A little later, a group from the Tablighi Jamaat visiting his mosque invited him to go to another mosque for a three-day weekend, which he found a good spiritual experience. He also became politically aware at that age listening to the news. "I remember the Gulf War," he later recalled, "the first one. I must have been about 12 then. . . . When I was 15 or 16, I think the Bosnian War was going on and I can remember the images of concentration camps, of people looking like skeletons . . . and I was aware they were Muslims." About a year later, his family got the Internet, which opened a new world of information for him. Although he spoke English, Urdu, Punjabi, and a little Arabic, he could only read English, but he did not confine himself to the British press. "I've known from a young day not to believe everything the press say[s] so I've always tried to see the other point of view and understand . . . be objective about things. . . . I would just read and read and read about it until I felt satisfied I understand what's going on."[4] He became politically active at university, where he eventually got a degree in computer systems engineering, but did not join any political or religious groups.

Savant went on to study product design but quickly lost interest. He went into debt—about £800—and dropped out after a year in 1998. He converted to Islam and took Ibrahim as his first name. His conversion brought him closer to Ali, who gave him £400 to cover some of his debts. Savant moved back home and worked in retail at department stores.[5] He received a police caution for possession of a small amount of cannabis in 1999.

While at college, Arafat met Tanvir Hussain, who was the same age, and introduced him to Savant and Ali. Hussain was born in Blackburn of Pakistani immigrants, who had moved to London in the late 1980s. He was an average student, who liked to play sports. He studied information technology and got a GNVQ in it. When Arafat was studying for his A-levels, his father died of a heart attack in Pakistan. He went to the funeral and did poorly on his exams when he returned. He found it hard to cope and started taking drugs. He hung out with the wrong crowd and got two convictions, one for possession of drugs and another for car theft.[6] In the late 1990s, Arafat, Savant, and Hussain played soccer together, drank, smoked, got into drugs, and went out to clubs to chase girls.[7] They had part-time jobs and were not interested in politics or religion like their friend Ali.

IMA Charity Work

September 11, 2001, was a watershed for Ali and his friends. The U.S. invasion of Afghanistan in October 2001 created a flood of refugees in Pakistan. Several Muslim organizations that had up to then focused on Kashmiri refugees switched to providing humanitarian aid to the new Afghan refugees. Mohammed Patel, one of the organizers of the Islamic Medical Association, handed out leaflets at Friday prayers asking for collection for clothing, goods, blankets, tinned food, and milk. Patel was a 39-year-old self-employed car mechanic, who had emigrated from Gujarat, India. He was married and had a 12-year-old son, Abdul Muneem Patel. He was involved in charitable work on behalf of Kashmiri refugees and became the head of the UK office of the IMA, which was located on Chatsworth Road, right across the street from Hamid's Al Quran bookstore.[8] By 2002, it ran an ambulance service for two refugee camps near Chaman on the Afghan border. Around March 2002, Patel left for Pakistan to run the charity in the field.

Dawood, Ali's older brother, knew Patel from before and encouraged Ali to volunteer for the charity during the Afghan crisis. Ali had time on his hand. "In the evenings," he testified at trial, "we would go to the charity shop and we had to organize and sort out all the clothes, so you had to separate men's clothes from the women's clothes and if they come in suit— trousers, top—put them together, take out the rubbish people are throwing out . . . then put them in polycarbonate bags and then stitch them up ready to be put in a container."[9]

Ali dragged his friends Arafat, Savant, and Hussain to the IMA office and proselytized on its behalf, designing leaflets and a website, collecting charity at the mosque, and writing letters. The four friends became more religious and also politically active in the Stop the War movement. They prayed at the neighborhood fundamentalist mosque on Queen's Road, where they met Waheed Zaman, a devout teenager from a Kashmiri military family and about three years younger than them, who lived across the street from the mosque and prayed there every evening. He did poorly in school but was an avid soccer player and often played with Savant.

The High Wycombe Duo

Ali also briefly met future fellow co-conspirators Assad Sarwar and Umar Islam at the IMA office. Both were from High Wycombe, about 30 miles northwest of central London. Sarwar was Ali's age; his parents had immigrated to England in the 1970s from Kashmir. His uneducated father worked as a laborer but pressured his children to get a good education. Sarwar was a shy student, who got homesick when he went away to Chichester University. In early 2001, he became religious and started praying regularly at the local mosque and attending lectures at its Muslim education center. There, he befriended Umar Islam, as they had both recently embraced Islam.[10]

Umar Islam was born Brian Young and was two years older. His Caribbean immigrant parents were devout Christians and forced their children to attend church, Sunday school, and church events. He did well in school and obtained a GNVQ in business studies and finance in 1996. By that time, he had become a Rastafarian. The lyrics of reggae songs describing the past transatlantic slave trade made him politically aware. He started dating a girl his age, who already had a son. His father did not approve of the relationship and threw him out of the house. Young moved in with her, fathered a son in 1998, worked a few odd jobs, and hung out with an older Caribbean couple, discussing spiritual matters and smoking a lot of marijuana. In 1999, he, his girlfriend, and her children moved to Barbados to learn more about Rastafarianism. They grew disillusioned with it and came back to High Wycombe in early 2000. When he came back, his older Caribbean friend, who had been a heavy smoker and very disorganized, had straightened out his life by converting to Islam. Young was impressed and followed in his friend's steps. He broke up with his girlfriend, converted to Islam in March 2001, and took the name Umar Islam. It took him a couple of months of wean himself from marijuana before attending the local mosque, where he met Sarwar. They attended the same study circles to learn the rituals of their religion.[11]

In the fall of 2001, Sarwar studied sports science at university but, after three months, felt it was too competitive and switched to earth sciences before dropping out altogether in March 2002. This was a blow to his self-confidence. Two local friends volunteering at the IMA encouraged Sarwar and Islam to volunteer there. IMA was recruiting people to drive its ambulances in Chaman. Both Sarwar and Islam volunteered: they took an ambulance first aid course in the summer and flew to Pakistan in early November 2002 to drive the IMA ambulances. The misery of the camps greatly affected them. Islam recalled, "It opened my eyes a lot. It made me more grateful for the luxuries that I had basically back in England. It saddened me that . . . so many millions of people had to suffer just because of the actions of a few people."[12]

Ali did not confine his proselytism to the IMA. He went to conferences and demonstrations, participated in the million people Stop the War march (15 February 2003) and distributed leaflets protesting the impending invasion of Iraq. "It felt good . . . to know that you're doing something," he later recalled, "you're getting your voice heard, but more than that what I liked about it was that there was just so many people there from all walks of life, nationalities and colors. . . . That just impressed upon you that people are all the same really, regardless of their differences."[13] Ali also protested the new security legislation, which included detention without trial, and he wrote petitions to members of Parliament. His brother Dawood encouraged him to go to websites and to print letters, get members of the community and mosque to sign them, and send them to the home secretary.

Dispensing Charity to Refugees in Chaman

Around December 2002, Patel temporarily returned to England from the field. He was planning to go to Gujarat, India, to take a relative about half his age as his second wife. His first wife in London was upset and refused to speak to him. Savant had grown close to Patel during his work at the

IMA. He had volunteered to go to Pakistan as an ambulance driver, but the IMA trustees turned him down because he had no relative there, his family had objected, and his asthma had flared up. Knowing that Savant would stay behind, Patel left him a hard drive to keep for him.[14]

It took the IMA volunteers about a year to fill up a 40-foot container. Ali volunteered to deliver it to the camps and drive an IMA ambulance in Pakistan and, on 26 February 2003, flew to Karachi, where he met Mohammed Altaf, the project manager for Doctors Worldwide, who was the IMA contact person in Pakistan, and Umar Islam, whom Ali had come to replace. Islam briefed him on the nature of the job for a week before returning to England.[15]

A few days after Islam's departure, Ali and Altaf flew to the Quetta IMA office, which consisted of an office, a storeroom, two ambulances, and some equipment. Sarwar was still there as an ambulance driver and overlapped with Ali for about two weeks before going to his ancestral village in Kashmir. Ali delivered IMA goods to the refugee camps and the sight of their misery affected him: "There's loads of people everywhere. It's so mucky, smelly, loads of kids running 'round crying, really like appalling conditions. Lots of arguing, kind of chaotic. . . . I don't think anything can prepare you for something like that. . . . Emotionally it was very straining. Physically, it was hard." Ali felt guilty about being lucky enough to have water, food, and warmth. "I had a good couple of jumpers and a nice warm jacket and these refugees were pretty much in rags and torn up pieces of clothes." He later recalled, "When you're there, in front of them, and you see the immense suffering they're going through, it's painful. . . . It's always the kids crying and running around and the women fighting over. . . . You're trying to help them and at the same time they're trying to, like, stampede you just to get some of the stuff you got; and on the one hand you're giving them but, on the other hand, you're kind of like trying to stop yourself from being grabbed and having things yanked off you. . . . The smell is really bad because they don't have proper toilets." The refugees' physical conditions were atrocious. "Some were maimed, some had their legs blown off, some had bits of their fingers missing, scars, burn marks, skinny, rugged, rough-looking faces. . . . There were lots of deaths in these camps, daily. . . . It's mostly kids that were dying, children, young children . . . seeing the mothers going through pulling their hair out." It made Ali cry a lot when he was by himself. Both Sarwar and he blamed Britain and the United States for this suffering.[16]

On one of Ali's trips to Chaman, his group was ambushed by bandits, who took his money and passport. He got a new passport in Pakistan. At the end of his trip, he went for a few weeks to see relatives in Jhelum and flew back to England on 22 April 2003. After his return, he relaxed at home for about a month. Sarwar returned to England on 29 May 2003.[17] They continued to volunteer at IMA and went together to evening political lectures. Sarwar joined Umar Islam as a mailman in High Wycombe and also volunteered for another local Islamic charity. Ali did a few odd construction jobs for his brother Umar Khan, peddled cell phones and computers, and got married to Cossor Anwar in July 2003. She moved in with him at his mother's council house. Ali later portrayed his marriage as full of love and mutual support, but his wife, at her separate trial, distanced herself from her husband. She claimed that moving in with her in-laws was a "culture shock." She had grown up in a moderate Muslim household, but her husband insisted that she wear a veil. When she refused, he gave her a "love bite" on her cheek so she would not forget to cover her face. She also described him slapping her face so hard that she spun around and his hand left an imprint on her. She ran back to her parents and they complained to the police station, but she declined to press charges against him.[18]

The Radicalization of Ali

At the beginning of 2004, Mohammed Patel temporarily returned to London. He had not been able to bring his new wife to England and was on his way to South Africa to be with her. His first wife had divorced him. His teenage son, Abdul Muneem Patel, had become Savant's friend. Before leaving, Patel left Savant two sealed boxes and his car, an Audi TDI 80. In June, after he left, Abdul Muneem gave Savant about £4,000 to wire to his father to help him open a car repair shop in South Africa. When Savant got married a month later and moved, he came across these boxes and opened them by curiosity. They contained an improvised explosives manual, correspondence in a foreign language, videotapes of mujahedin fighting, and a stun gun.[19]

Meanwhile, Ali went on hajj in January 2004 with his younger brother and some friends, including Hussain, who was becoming more devout and Ali's best friend.[20] Ali left his pregnant wife behind at her parents' house. Shortly after returning from hajj, he wrote a will in March 2004 stating, "We know with full certainty that we are going to die so let us aim high and strive for the best death, i.e. *shahada* (martyrdom), and let us do the most pleasing deed to Allah and make the greatest sacrifice, fight with our life, tongue and wealth in the path of Allah."[21]

Ali was not forthcoming at his trial and put the date of his radicalization two years later, in the spring of 2006 after the devastation of the 8 October 2005 earthquake in Kashmir. However, his testament suggests that he was already radicalized by the time he wrote it. He was disillusioned with both charity work and the political process. He testified that having

> been on demonstrations, protests, constantly reading the news, human rights reports . . . seeing both sides of the story . . . I became less enthusiastic and confident in things like protests and marches. We had the biggest march ever, 1 million people, and it didn't seem to do anything. We knew now the war was illegal in Iraq and it wasn't a secret no more. It was a lie. It was just deceit. It was a criminal war. In my eyes that made the government criminals because it was a criminal act what they did and obviously they weren't listening to the people and I felt that aid work, as good as it was, is very limited in how far it's going to go. For every two people you help, another 100 are going to be coming into the refugee camps. So, to sum it up, basically I though the root problem was not dealing with refugees and protests, these are just dealing with the symptoms. The root problem was the foreign policy and that's something that should be tackled.[22]

His feeling about the futility of mass protest to prevent coalition forces from invading Iraq fits the 2003–2004 time frame better than the spring of 2006. Notes later recovered from his house indicated he was listening to taped lectures by Anwar al Awlaki in December 2003: "Obviously I like this lecturer. . . . The way he explains and talks, is really good." From them, he learned a lot about the history of the classical period of Islam and jihad. "I watch the news and stuff and it's impossible to read up on the Afghan War or the Iraq War or any war in the Muslim world without this word cropping up and obviously lots of things are said about it, but . . . my aim is to try and get the most authoritative original sources and study them. Because this work is considered the most authoritative, I thought it the best way to understand this topic."[23]

Ali's wife gave birth to a premature baby boy suffering from Edward's Syndrome, leading to his death a few weeks later in April 2004.[24] The couple became very depressed over this loss. Cossor was always crying and Ali supported her as much as he could. To console her, he suggested they go to Pakistan for a holiday and visit her sick grandmother. They left in September 2004. His will seems to indicate an additional motivation: fighting for jihad. They stayed with a cousin in Karachi for a week, went to Jhelum for a while before visiting Cossor's grandmother.

At his trial, Ali testified that he then called up Altaf, the Doctors Worldwide project manager. In his testimony, Sarwar also pointed to Altaf as the man who introduced him to a Kashmiri militant, who taught him how to make bombs. Since throughout the trial, they both tried to protect al Qaeda members, Altaf was probably not their intermediary to Rashid Rauf. Instead, I suspect that it was more likely Mohammed Patel, who had clear jihadi sympathies and a manual on how to manufacture explosives and knew Ali, Sarwar, Gulzar, and al Ghabra. More on this soon.

Explosives Training with al Qaeda

Rashid Rauf's report tells another story. He met Ali during this trip, around the same time that Mohamed Sidique Khan, Shehzad Tanweer, and Muktar Ibrahim were training. It is unclear how the contact was made, but when they met, Ali wanted to fight and die as a mujahed in Afghanistan. Rauf wrote, "He was a very clever, patient brother and a natural leader." Rauf introduced Ali to Abu Ubaydah al Masri, who convinced Ali to conduct a terrorist operation in Britain. According to Rauf, as a result of his training, "a big change came over his temperament when he first came and when he left."[25]

After his training, Ali returned to England with his wife in January 2005. After their return to England, Ali occasionally worked for his brother Umar and sold cell phones and laptops with his best friend Hussain. He and his wife moved into a council flat. After a miscarriage, she became pregnant again in the spring of 2005. During that time, Ali may also have acted as Rauf's intermediary to Muktar Ibrahim as Ali's cell phone called Ibrahim's cell phone several times in May.[26] Ali also resumed contact with Sarwar, who had quit his job at the Royal Mail in February 2005 and survived on a few odd jobs selling martial arts DVDs on the Internet and cell phones. He went on to work as a contractor for British Telecommunication during that summer, between 18 July and 27 September.[27]

Ali returned to Pakistan on 6 June 2005 for more advanced training. At his trial, he claimed that he went there to see relatives and start a business with Altaf. His explanation is not convincing since he presented no evidence for any business dealings on that trip. A more plausible motivation is suggested in Cossor's diary when he left. She wrote that she was becoming "more and more attached to the cause for which you are striving . . . and the reason for which we are apart. I hope and pray Allah grants your wish and gives you the highest level of shahada."[28] This suggests that he left to fight and die and that she was supportive of his enterprise despite her later denial and acquittal at her separate trial.

On his trip, Ali was accompanied by 18-year-old Adam Osman Khatib, whose father was Mauritian and mother British. Khatib was a close friend of Ali's younger brother and had a history of driving offenses. His newly adopted radical Islamist views and anti-Semitic outbursts in the classroom had alarmed his teachers. He had signed a school assignment "Adam Osama bin Laden." He started wearing traditional Islamic attire and hanging out with friends dressed like him, whom his parents refused to allow in the house. Khatib worked in a factory after he left school and Ali quickly became his mentor.[29]

Rauf wrote that, in Pakistan, Ali underwent extensive training with Abu Ubaydah while Khatib went through basic training. They were training at the time of the London bombings. Rauf believed that the success of the bombings would make it difficult for Ali to get hydrogen peroxide and Abu Ubaydah taught him to how to make explosive devices with gas. Sarwar flew to Pakistan on 1 October 2005 to join them. Sarwar later testified that he had met Altaf, who had introduced him to a militant named Jamil Shah, a fictitious character to hide the true identity of Rashid Rauf. While Ali and Khatib wanted to become martyrs, Sarwar wanted to participate in the operation but did not want to kill himself. Therefore, Sarwar was tasked to support the others and stay behind in England to conduct further operations. He had a good sense of security and was taught to keep his work compartmented from the others. With Sarwar's arrival, Rauf and Abu Ubaydah changed their mind and decided that their best plan was to continue with hydrogen peroxide bombs, which raised the problem of procuring liquid hydrogen peroxide in England or smuggling it into the country.[30]

Around that time, Mohammed Gulzar, Rauf's best friend in Birmingham, joined the conspiracy.[31] At the trial, Gulzar testified that after Rauf and he fled England in May 2002, they first hid with the Tablighi

Jamaat in Raiwind, then he went alone to his paternal ancestral village in Kashmir until his grandmother died in December 2003, and he went finally to his maternal ancestral village in Punjab. On the advice of a relative, he went to Johannesburg, South Africa, on 19 June 2004 and opened an electronics store in Heidelberg with two other Pakistani immigrants. He got fake identity documents under the name of Altaf Ravat, which enabled him to get a South African identity card and finally a passport in August 2005. He befriended Mohammed Patel in South Africa. When Patel was diagnosed as suffering a thyroid condition aggravated by tuberculosis and pneumonia, Gulzar took care of him and took him to his medical appointments. Patel's mother and son, Abdul Muneem, came to visit him in the summer of 2005 and met Gulzar. Gulzar successfully tested his new passport by going to Botswana for a day on 13 September 2005 and returned to Pakistan on 28 September 2005.[32] Apparently, Gulzar came to visit Rauf, Ali, and Sarwar at their training site. They overlapped for over two months in Pakistan. He became skilled in explosive manufacturing, as later e-mails show.[33]

Back home, Cossor hoped that her husband would choose her "over the *hoors*" (*hoorees*, the black-eyed virgins promised to martyrs in paradise, meaning he would decide to come back to her rather than sacrifice himself in Afghanistan). She read books about Muslim warriors and noted, "I am even happier with what you are doing. It makes me eager to join you on your quest." When Ali notified her that he would come back after all, she was delighted. "I think I am going to make myself slimmer *inshallah* [God willing] as it will be good for me and I think you will be happier. I am going to start doing exercises on a daily basis and when we are together, I want you to do fighting training with me. . . . I miss my soulmate, husband, lover, comforter and companion." This contradicts her testimony at her trial that she hated her husband. She also wanted another child, besides the one in her belly. "I hope that when you attain shahada, I will have at least one small child and will be pregnant with another or at least be pregnant with a healthy baby at the least, inshallah."[34]

Searching for Peroxide

In Pakistan, Ali received a call that his wife had gone into labor and he rushed home to be at her side. He and Khatib flew back on 5 December 2005 but missed the birth of his son, Saad, by one day. He took on a few odd jobs such as selling cell phones or delivering food for an Indian takeout restaurant on weekends while receiving government benefits for unemployment. He also brought his best friend, Hussain, into the plot. Hussain traveled to Pakistan on 19 February 2006, underwent training on hydrogen peroxide by Rauf and Abu Ubaydah, and met Gulzar at the training site.[35]

Sarwar returned to High Wycombe on 14 December 2005. He and Ali resumed seeing each other. Ali's testimony at trial that they decided to make a documentary to protest the Afghan and Iraqi wars and scare the public by exploding small devices is simply not credible.[36] They and Khatib were constantly text-messaging Rauf. They searched for potential targets and bomb-making material on the Internet. At that time, Rauf and Abu Ubaydah had not yet decided to target airplanes. From his previous work as a contractor for British Telecommunications, Sarwar had acquired a hard drive with the electric and energy grid of Britain. He also carefully examined the Bacton terminal of the Belgium-UK gas pipeline and gas refinery at Canary Wharf. He created a file on it on 22 February and last accessed it on 16 March.[37] In March, Khatib researched the properties of hexamine peroxide—an ingredient of HMTD for the detonator. In his notes, he warned his fellow plotters to "be extremely careful: the powder is extremely volatile and any contact could cause an explosion."[38] At the same time, he continued his impulsive behavior that brought him to the attention of the police, which issued him a community order for driving while disqualified. When Rauf found out, he cautioned Khatib via coded e-mail on 2 April 2006: "hi babe . . . keep out of trouble cos u will give my dad a heart attack!!!!!!!!!!!! . . . I think the wedding will be quick especially now dad is ok with it!!!!! so pls keep out of trouble my dad hates trouble makers he will never let me get married to one!!!!!!"[39]

Hussain returned to London on 1 April. When he landed, he underwent a secondary investigation by Scotland Yard and MI5 for a few hours. They asked him about his background, education, work, political views, religious practices, and mosque. They showed him pictures of his friends and asked for information about them. He concluded that he and his friend had been under surveillance, but a relative who was an immigration officer reassured him that airport authorities commonly stopped traveling Muslims.[40]

Sarwar tried to solve the problem of obtaining peroxide without alerting the authorities. He searched on the Internet for stores selling it in faraway places. On 25 April, he ordered hydrogen peroxide at a pharmacy in Carmarthen, south Wales, under an alias. Two days later, he drove there and bought two liters of 35 percent hydrogen peroxide along with a few other items not to arouse suspicion. He placed an order for another three liters. The total price amounted to £226. On his way home, he was photographed speeding on the highway. Shortly thereafter, Ali and Hussain tested a hydrogen-peroxide-based explosive substance in a wooded area near their home, but the experiment failed. Ali reported it to Sarwar and Rauf, who recalled him to Pakistan.[41]

New Plan: Liquid Bombs for Airplanes

Rauf and Abu Ubaydah's planning had evolved in a new direction. They had first explored ways to smuggle liquid peroxide via carry-on or checked luggage by air. "We analyzed the various machines that were used for checking baggage and persons at airports," Rauf reported. "We found it was very difficult to detect liquid explosives." They settled on using rosewater bottles that were resealed to look unopened. "After analysis that it would be possible to take concentrated hydrogen peroxide on board, the thought came to our mind: would it be possible to detonate the hydrogen aboard an airplane?" This idea became the origin of the Transatlantic Airlines Liquid Bombs Plot. Over the next months, while the English conspirators were back in England, Abu Ubaydah and Rauf experimented with the construction of various devices in order to smuggle them onto a plane. As Rauf's report stated, "The discovery that hydrogen peroxide could be colored without losing its explosive properties was a major breakthrough." They "practiced how to open a drink bottle, empty it, and replace it with hydrogen peroxide, to make it seem unopened." Through trial and error, they discovered that half a liter of the liquid explosive—the size of a regular soft drink bottle—would be enough to destroy an airplane.[42]

To keep with this theme of soft drinks, they manufactured a main charge from a mixture of concentrated hydrogen peroxide and Tang, a dissolvable, high-sugar-based product that is used in the making of soft drinks. This combination creates an energetic mixture that can be detonated. It could be disguised in half-liter bottles of Oasis or Lucozade soft drinks and carried on board an aircraft. Ali was trained to drill a small hole at the bottom of unopened soft drink plastic bottles, drain them of their content, inject the concentrated hydrogen peroxide–Tang mixture with a syringe and seal the hole with Superglue to make the bottle appear untouched.[43]

The detonators initiating the main explosive charge would be disguised as AA batteries. The batteries would be cut open at the bottom end, emptied of content, and filled with HMTD. Batteries in Pakistan were cheaply made and easily pried open, while the ones in Britain were sealed properly and too difficult to modify. Batteries would have to be imported from Pakistan. An electric element, such as a subminiature light bulb or filament connected to a disposable camera battery, could ignite the HMTD, which would set off the main charge.[44] On the plane, the bombers would insert their battery-detonator into the bottle for the final assembly of their device in the bathroom and detonate it in the air.

In mid-May, Ali returned to Pakistan with his father allegedly to visit his sick uncle. Apparently, Ali's multiple trips to Pakistan, in the immediate post–London bombings era, made the Security Service suspicious. It questioned Ali upon his departure at Heathrow Airport about his religious views and his background and asked ISID to keep an eye on him in Pakistan. Ali's cousin came to pick him and his father up at Islamabad Airport and they were stopped by a police car on the way to Jhelum. The police also conducted discreet inquiries about Ali in the village. One of his cousins, who was friendly with a police officer, told Ali that ISID had requested the search of their car.[45]

Rauf waited for a week before coming to Jhelum to pick up Ali, who told him about the incident. Rauf and Abu Ubaydah worried about it and hoped it was just a routine check. Abu Ubaydah trained Ali on their new devices. Rauf noted, "We trained (him) quickly, and wanted him to leave ASAP. He was also told to do anti-surveillance measures when he got back and only start work when he was comfortable that everything was clear."[46] Ali's mission was now to conduct simultaneous midair bombings of multiple airplanes targeting flights heading for the United States. The details of the plan and the devices continued to evolve through constant experimentation and were not completely worked out until July 2006, requiring Ali and Sarwar in England to be in constant communication with Rauf in Pakistan.

The conspirators settled on a division of labor. Ali was to recruit the other bombers, prepare them for their mission, and, with Hussain, modify AA batteries into detonators and prepare the explosive devices for final assembly on the planes. Sarwar was to manufacture the explosive substances for both the main charge and the detonator, and transfer these mixtures to Ali clandestinely. This process of concentration of hydrogen peroxide to about 70 percent was the most time consuming and delicate part of the operation, as we have seen in the previous two plots. Abu Ubaydah had learned from the failure of the Vivace case and the near failure of the Theseus case that the method for estimating high-level concentrations was inaccurate and had worked out another more accurate formula.[47] Ali and Sarwar compartmentalized their respective tasks and avoided being seen together since Sarwar would stay behind to carry out further operations.

Sarwar was also recalled for training on these new techniques. He flew to Pakistan on 19 June, after burying the hydrogen peroxide he had bought in a wood near his house. He overlapped with Ali for four days as the latter returned to London on 24 June. Ali had taken notes on the new manufacture process and overall plan in a diary:

> Clean batteries. Perfect disguise. Drinks bottles, Lucozade, orange, red. Oasis, orange, red. Mouthwash, blue, red. Calculate exact drops of Tang, plus colour. Make in HP. . . . Check time to fill each bottle. Check time taken to dilute in HP. Decide on which battery to use for D. Note: small is best. Get bags, keyrings, electrics for battery, toothbrush, toothpaste, aftershave. . . . Select date. Five days B4. All link up. Prepare. Dirty mag to distract. Condoms. One drink used, other keep in pocket maybe will not go through machine, put keys and chewing gum on D in the elec device. Keep ciggies. Camera cases. The drinks that you drink should be dif flava. . . . Lucozade, red, 1.5 drops, one teaspoon Tang, one teaspoon orange, 12 drops. Oasis, red. On red dye. Orange, two times mango.[48]

When Ali returned to England, British agents were ready and surreptitiously opened his luggage in a back room. They found two packs of 30 AA Toshiba batteries and a large quantity of Tang powder packets in four different flavors.[49] This was enough to convince the Security Service that Ali was planning to make a bomb with them. It started a full field investigation on him, including intensive surveillance of his activities and communications. Unaware of this new scrutiny, Ali e-mailed to Rauf two days after his arrival, "im cool I got back from holiday everything went fine I didn't get any problem at all . . . im just getting settled it will takea few days then ill start trading. Ill send you my new no as soon as I get it. Tariq is cool I saw

him and he is ready to trade aswell."[50] I suspect that Tariq is a code name
for Hussain.

The South African Nonconnection

Meanwhile Gulzar returned to South Africa on 20 March 2006, reported
his passport lost, and applied for a new one to erase any trace of his trip to
Pakistan. A new passport was issued on 19 April 2006.[51] He reconnected
with Mohammed Patel, whose health had greatly improved. In London,
Patel's son, Abdul Muneem, who had just turned 17, married a Muslim
woman, seven years his senior. The newlywed couple came to see Patel for
their honeymoon and met with Gulzar. Another visitor from England
around that time was Mohammed al Ghabra, a source of much speculation
as a terrorist mastermind in the press and counterterrorism literature. The
reality seems more prosaic.

Al Ghabra was a 26-year-old Syrian immigrant to Forest Gate, London,
who had become a British citizen. According to the U.S. Treasury notice
designating him as supporting al Qaeda, he originally went to Pakistan
probably to fight in Kashmir and had undergone guerilla training at one of
the many Kashmiri camps. He was in Pakistan during the post-9/11 invasion of Afghanistan and helped foreign militants fleeing Afghanistan relo-
cate elsewhere. In his new mission, he became part of the radical Islamist
community in Pakistan.[52] It is unknown whether he ever met Rashid Rauf
during this time but they traveled in the same circles. At that time, as we
saw in Crevice, insurgents in Afghanistan needed special equipment like
night-vision goggles to fight a modern guerilla war and it is likely that al
Ghabra became a middleman for them. The U.S. Treasury suggests that his
main contact was Abu Faraj al Libi. Abu Faraj was hiding in Pakistan with
his family for the first 10 months of 2002. In October 2002, Abdal Hadi al
Iraqi asked Abu Faraj to work for him in Peshawar organizing the purchase
of supplies for fighters, including medicine, equipment, food, and clothing.
In 2003, Osama bin Laden directed Abu Faraj to take on the responsibility
of collecting donations, organizing travel, and distributing funds to al
Qaeda families in Pakistan.[53] It was probably in this logistical capacity that
al Ghabra helped Abu Faraj, by getting from his British contacts equipment
difficult to find locally. Al Ghabra seems to have had a strictly logistical
support role and not one involved in operations either in Afghanistan or
in the West.

Al Ghabra returned to London in mid-2003 and was arrested in October 2003 on charges of fraud and possession of a document or record that could be useful to terrorists. He was acquitted on 19 April 2004 of those charges and released. Despite his release, the Security Service kept him under surveillance. One of his acquaintances from Forest Gate, an Iraqi refugee, drove Muktar Ibrahim, Rizwan Majid, and Shakeel Ismail to Heathrow Airport on 11 December 2004, which turned out to be their trip to meet Rashid Rauf. Nothing could be pinned on al Ghabra but this did not stop the press from speculating about his role.[54]

In mid-April 2006, al Ghabra flew to South Africa, where he visited Mohammed Patel and met with Gulzar. His friends called him "Gabs," and the alleged purpose of his visit was to set up the sale of imitation leather biker jackets. Gulzar met him several times and put down about £650 for 70 jackets. Al Ghabra's stay in South Africa overlapped with Abdul Muneem's visit and he returned to London in late May. After his return, he changed his appearance, shaved his unkempt beard, took on a more Western appearance, and assumed a low profile.

Coincidentally, either Abdul Muneem or al Ghabra brought a laptop computer to either Mohammed Patel or Gulzar. The laptop had been stolen in Birmingham and sold to Sarwar, who uploaded some software on it on 29 March 2006 at his home in High Wycombe. Sarwar later testified that he sold the laptop to someone from al Ghabra's neighborhood. In any case, Gulzar ended up with it and first accessed it on 7 June. Gulzar used it to investigate the disappearance of an Islamist extremist in South Africa and the killing of Abu Musab al-Zarqawi in Iraq, which occurred around that time. Gulzar continued browsing for similar news until 25 June, when the recorded log stopped. Apparently, there was something wrong with the software because Gulzar reinstalled a Windows operating system on 27 June but without success. He later took the laptop with him to London.[55]

The prosecutors and scholars writing about Overt postulated a South African connection to this plot, namely Gulzar. They argued that he was intentionally dispatched to be the "superintendent of this plot" in the field because he was a close friend of Rauf and bomb-making expert.[56] However, the Rauf document, which is so detailed on all the other aspects of the plot, completely fails to mention him. I strongly suspect that Gulzar's participation in Overt was accidental due to an unanticipated development: Gulzar fell in love.

Earlier on 20 March, when Gulzar was leaving Islamabad, he met a woman at the departure lounge when Pakistani authorities conducted a secondary screening on them. After a brief conversation, she gave him her name and phone number before they boarded their respective planes. She was Zora Saddique, a recent divorcee, four years his senior, living alone with two daughters, and working in a menial job at a hotel in Brussels. She had been born in London to a Pakistani father and a Philippine mother. She was raised in London, briefly in Pakistan, and in the Philippines, where her father died. She was a Christian like her mother; she got married as a teenager and went with her husband to Belgium, where they divorced in early 2006. She made a quick trip to Pakistan to sort out property left from her father and was eager to find a way out of her financial and social situation, as her former husband was harassing her.[57]

Two days after their meeting, Gulzar texted her. At trial, the prosecutor portrayed her as "an extremely vulnerable woman" cynically manipulated by mastermind Gulzar and "prepared to do and say anything for the man that had repeatedly lied to her, but who she loved and was . . . prepared to sacrifice all in order to be with him."[58] On the contrary, the evidence presented in court was that Saddique was Gulzar's relentless pursuer. Not only did she respond immediately, but within two weeks, she spoke to him every day from local international call shops. She testified in court that she did "all the talking . . . all the running and the moving in this relationship."[59] Two months later, they agreed to marry as he was a religious Muslim and Muslims could not date casually. He wanted her to come and live in South Africa and she agreed for she did not want to spoil the relationship. In reality, she really wanted to go to England with her two daughters to get away from her former husband. Unbeknownst to him, she applied for a job at the London branch of the hotel chain she was working for. The marriage was supposed to be either in Belgium or South Africa, but Gulzar's application for a Belgian visa failed because his fake birth certificate was not adequate for an international birth certificate. This obstacle did not deter Saddique's resolve and she decided to come to South Africa for the marriage. "Now I know you love me, I'm not letting you go," she texted him. She cautiously booked a round-trip flight to Johannesburg for 29 June, with a return date of 15 July "because I was not so sure it was going to work out so I always had a return ticket to go back."[60] She cashed in all her savings, £500, and arrived on 30 June. Gulzar picked her up at the airport, dropped her off at the hotel, and went to the mosque to get married in a religious ceremony. She acquiesced to the marriage by phone, and he returned to her hotel room a few hours later as her husband. They went to city hall two days later for the civil ceremony and their certificate was issued on 10 July. They planned to take their honeymoon in Mauritius.

However, the mutual deceptions they had carefully woven for each other quickly unraveled. Although he had assured her he would respect her appearance, he ordered her to cover up and wear Islamic clothes immediately after the marriage. She felt stuck in a foreign country and agreed. They visited the Belgian Consulate to straighten out his visa but in vain. She suggested going to England to live, but he refused and had 101 excuses for not going or else changed the subject. She told him she was a British citizen, wanted her daughters to grow up there, and had a job lined up there as well. As she later testified, "my mind was always back with my daughters, so I wanted to come here and we had fights about that too because I thought when I came to South Africa he agreed to everything and it was a total opposite [from] what I expected, the way he made me dress, he . . . wanted me to stay in South Africa." She became suspicious that his reluctance to go to England and his lack of family in South Africa seemed to hide something far more serious. She believed that he was lying to her but was too scared to confront him "in the middle of nowhere."[61]

On 14 July, they went to a travel agent to confirm her seat. The plan now was for her to sponsor him from Belgium as her husband. They had a fight and he told her he did not want her to go. At the agency, she changed her plans. She later testified, "I said in the agency, 'I want my ticket going to the United Kingdom. You come with me or not' because I was afraid I get stranded in South Africa. I had no money. He had no money, so I already knew at this point I was accepted [for work in England] so we had a fight. I said, 'Take it or leave it, I'm going. If you want to come with me, come. If not, then stay here.'" He caved in and decided to come along to the country where he was wanted for murder. Now, reconciled, they decided to take their honeymoon in Mauritius after all. She would use her return ticket to fly to London via Mauritius and he bought a round-trip ticket to London via Mauritius on that day, with a return date of 1 August. He said he would arrange for the accommodations in London.[62]

The couple flew to Mauritius on 15 July. During their honeymoon, Gulzar called Abdul Muneem to tell him that he was coming to London with his new wife and asked him to find a place for them. The newlyweds flew to Heathrow on 18 July, arriving late in the day. Abdul Muneem and his wife welcomed them and drove them to his in-laws' flat, where they spent two nights in a small spare bedroom. Abdul Muneem gave Gulzar two SIM cards for his cell phones. Gulzar activated a card the next day and texted Rauf in Pakistan that he was now in London.[63]

The trial evidence, especially Saddique's compelling testimony backed by a long chain of texts to her fiancé, suggests that the South African connection was a red herring. Gulzar's participation in the plot was both accidental and opportunistic. Neither Rauf, Ali, nor Sarwar knew that he was coming to London.[64]

Ali Recruits the Last Bombers

Meanwhile, Sarwar was in Pakistan learning new bomb-making techniques and Ali was assembling his team of suicide bombers from trusted long-term friends, who shared his political views, had participated with him in political activism, and had worked at the IMA. It is actually difficult to accurately identify all the conspirators in Overt. The plot was evolving all the time and depended on recruitment by Ali in England sanctioned by Rauf and Abu Ubaydah. The arrests of the conspirators were premature and interrupted this evolution: the manufacture of the main charge for the bombs had not even been started. To add to the confusion, the participants had various roles: the trainers in Pakistan, who directed the plot from far away; the suicide bombers, who would board the planes with their bombs; the bomb manufacturers and the logistics personnel, who stayed behind. In England, the active core of the plot was of course Ali and Sarwar, assisted by Hussain and Khatib.

The easiest way to identify the potential suicide bombers was through their acts in furtherance. As the plot was reaching its conclusion, many of them had reported their passports lost and applied for new ones to erase any compromising trip to Pakistan. They also applied for student loans to get money that they knew they would not repay, as Hussain did on 5 July at Barclays Bank for £8,000, the maximum amount.[65] More damning, they recorded wassiyas for explanation and propaganda purposes. Six had recorded their video by the time of their arrest. Khatib had not but was clearly another volunteer martyr, for a total of seven. Rauf claimed that two potential martyrs were not arrested because he had not yet reached out to them at the time of the arrests.[66]

There were four clear conspirators, who had all trained in Pakistan: Ali, Sarwar, Khatib, and Hussain, who had become Ali's lieutenant. On 4 July, Ali sent Rauf a coded e-mail asking him when Sarwar was coming back with guidance and giving him an update on the recruitment. "My mate half guggie one he is up for the gig aswell is it ok if we put him in. he has sorted his looks out he no longer looks like a junkie. I believe he is ready to be promoted." Ali continued, "I spoke to fatty and explained to him he has to move his office within 1 month and start fresh. He is doing well he keeps his head down he dont link the junkies anymore. He did not get any probs on his last journey." These may be references to Ibrahim Savant, also known as "Ibo," and Arafat Khan, "Aro," respectively. Ali reported that he approached someone else, who decided not to participate: "Fatty is looking for some one else to go now." He ended, "my black mate said he is cool with the (rehearsal) trial run. Ill send him soon to the club for the weekend." The only black defendant was Umar Islam, also known as "Omar B." Apparently, Islam was already part of the conspiracy, probably through his friend Sarwar, as Ali did not have to propose him as a conspirator. The next day, Rauf approved: "Nice to hear fatty's in good shape! Half gugie seems ok too. But I will confirm and let u know, but I don't think it should be a prob."[67]

Let us therefore return to Umar Islam, Arafat Khan, and Ibrahim Savant, the new members of the conspiracy, and look at their respective evolution since we left them. Islam was of course the Caribbean convert, Sarwar's friend, who went with him to Pakistan as an IMA ambulance driver. He was greatly affected by this experience and got married in October 2003 to an older pious and politically active Muslim woman of Pakistani origin. They went on hajj in January 2004 but this trip cost Islam his job at the Royal Mail because it did not authorize such a long-term absence so soon after getting the job. He found another job at Transport for London (he was checking whether people on buses had tickets), and moved there with his wife and two sons. He socialized with Ali and his friends—Ibrahim Savant and Waheed Zaman, with whom he took martial arts classes. They prayed together at the neighborhood Tablighi mosque. When Ali left for Pakistan in June 2005 and Cossor returned to her parents, Islam and his family temporarily moved into their vacant flat, rent free. Islam tried to go to Pakistan in October 2005 to join Ali and Sarwar, but a clerical error about his birthday on his new passport prevented him from leaving the country.[68]

In January 2006, Islam's wife tried to introduce Sarwar to a prospective bride, whose parents had rented a restaurant for the occasion. Sarwar got confused about the date and did not show up, embarrassing Islam and his wife. This led to a falling out between the two friends until their arrests in August.[69] Islam had switched from hanging out with Sarwar to doing so with Savant, Zaman, and Ali in Walthamstow. It is not clear when he joined the conspiracy but his attempt to go to Pakistan in the fall of 2005 and the way he was referred to in the e-mails suggest that he had agreed to participate by the spring of 2006. He seems to have been the one designated to test airport security by going on a rehearsal flight to the United States with bomb materials.

The second recruit, Arafat Khan, was Ali's oldest friend from primary school and a close friend of Savant and Hussain. He had also volunteered at the IMA. By June 2006, he had become engaged, traveled to Pakistan to visit his family, and stayed in close touch with his friends. A possible indication of his early involvement was the fact that, on 3 July, he applied for an £8,000 career development loan from Barclays Bank, which was granted a week later. On the day that surveillance on Ali started, 5 July, Ali and Arafat were seen together in Ali's Citroen car.[70]

The third recruit, Ibrahim Savant, was Ali's second oldest friend from secondary school and also a close friend of Arafat and Hussain. He had also volunteered at the IMA and kept stuff for Mohammed Patel after the latter left England. He got married in July 2004 and went on *umrah* with his in-laws in October. In 2005, he spent time with Islam and they attended Islamic lectures and took martial arts with Zaman. In January 2006, he gave Mohammed Patel's boxes to his son, Abdul Muneem, when lack of money forced him to move in with his in-laws. He grew a long beard and wore traditional Muslim clothes, but his in-laws did not approve of his new appearance and kicked the young couple out of their house. At the end of June 2006, three men attacked Savant, beat him up, and put chewing gun in his beard. To avoid further aggression, Savant shaved his beard and reverted back to Western appearance—hence Ali's e-mail reference to his change of look.[71] It also made him blend into the crowd.

After getting Rauf's approval, Ali approached Savant, who claimed that the meeting happened in mid-July, but the fact that he reported his passport lost on 7 July seems to put the date 10 days earlier.[72] According to Savant, Ali and he talked near a playing field in the early evening:

He began to speak about his first-hand experience in Pakistan, how
he helped the refugees after the invasion of Afghanistan. He related
to me as I had experience helping them in some way or form at the
charity shop itself. He also was saying its futility, how he would help
one or two people, but there's so many people behind in the line.
He also spoke briefly about politics and how the voices of many
people who marched upon London had fallen upon deaf ears against
the wars of Iraq and Afghanistan. . . . Ahmed was basically defining
the source of the problem and he was saying that basically it's got
nothing to do with religion or Islamic fundamentalism or radicalization, but it's the foreign intervention of the U.S. and unfortunately
the British.[73]

Of course, Savant testified that Ali asked him to participate in a sham explosion, but the description of the recruitment pitch sounds right. Savant said
that he agreed to participate partly because Waheed Zaman had done so.

Zaman was the last of the known suicide bombers. He was the pious
mosque-goer in the vicinity of the IMA, who had met the volunteers in
2002. He was an avid soccer player and regularly played with Savant, who
became a close friend. He later also befriended Islam, who joined their
martial arts class. In October 2002, Zaman started biomedical studies at
London Metropolitan University and was very active in venting his moral
outrage at the illegal invasion of Iraq, the humiliation of Muslims in Abu
Ghraib, and the raping of Iraqi women. In 2005, he was elected the president of his university Islamic Society. In July 2006, Zaman was again upset
at the 2006 Israeli invasion of Lebanon and the devastation it caused, com-
paring it to Iraq or Afghanistan. One evening, Ali and he went for a walk.
Ali talked about the Western invasions of Iraq, Afghanistan, Palestine, and
especially Lebanon and the Israeli use of British cluster bombs. Ali argued
that all the political protests, petitions, and demonstrations did not work
and asked Zaman to participate in the alleged sham bombing and propaganda videos. Zaman agreed, but wanted to write his own speech. Ali gave
him some CDs to watch so he could study the words and manners of
mujahedin. Despite his mediocre school record, Zaman was viewed as the
intellectual of the group.[74]

While waiting for Sarwar's return, Ali and Hussain bought some tools
for the manufacture of their bombs on 6 July. A week later, they bought
some glassware for their project and examined the seals and caps of soft

drink bottles at a Tesco.[75] Throughout the month, they were in constant telephone contact and often met with their fellow conspirators as well as other close friends,[76] who seemed aware that something important was going on—but including them in this narrative would needlessly complicate it without adding much to it. They all shared at the very least a great deal of sympathy for al Qaeda and Islamist radicalism as demonstrated by the books and tapes found at their respective homes when they were arrested.

On 8 July, Sarwar came back to England with his own set of notes: "Get block HP. Make 80 HP. Send K&S. Get more HP. Get Ace. Get hold of Nav . . . Jameel. Practice batteries. Invest in Bact. TH, Coryton. Fawley. Kingsbury and Haven. N. . . . Get hold CD changer. Get talks, Documentaries. Get hold Prices of phones. Practice notes bell. [e-mail addresses]. . . . Talc powder H. Moisturising cream AP, Lynx Spray AC, Brut Spray. Aftershave, all types, HP. Get GPS, CD changer, price list for phones." In a stunning violation of clandestine tradecraft, he wrote the meaning of the code words in the same notebook: "Talc powder: hex musk. Moisturising cream: AL. Aftershave HP. (Price is per cent). Lynx: acet, Brut: prop." He also wrote the formula for encoding numbers: "minus 2 from L4."[77]

Sarwar's notes require some explanation because of their opacity. The 80 HP meant 80 percent hydrogen peroxide, Ace was accessories or laboratory equipment, and Nav or Jameel were code for Hussain and Rauf respectively. The rest is more obscure; as previously mentioned, Sarwar had acquired a hard drive with the diagrams of the gas and electricity grid for the major facilities in Britain. Since he was going to stay behind, he was to investigate large energy facilities: Bacton was the previously mentioned Belgium-UK gas pipeline terminal; TH was Telehouse; Coryton, an oil refinery; Fawley, another oil refinery; Kingsbury, a gas terminal; and Haven, Milford Haven, another oil refinery. They were possible targets after Overt. DC changer was a voice changer; talks, documentaries were the suicide videos; and prices were the percentage concentration of the hydrogen peroxide. Talc powder meant hexamine, moisturizing cream was aluminum powder, aftershave was hydrogen peroxide, Lynx was acetone (to make TATP if necessary), and Brut spray was propane gas.[78] The last item was to remind him to write down phone numbers in code by subtracting two from the last four digits of the number.

Sarwar e-mailed Rauf four days after his arrival: "no phone call from you yet. Are you OK. My number is. . . . Have you spoke with abdul yet. I can send someone to abdul but you first need to speak to him and let him know that I need to get in touch with his friend." Abdul was probably Abdulla Ali, and the e-mail indicates that there had been difficulties with Rauf's ability to communicate with his operators in England. On 13 July, Rauf had tried to text Ali: "your friend can go for his rapping concert rehearsal. . . . Make sure he goes on the bus service which is most common over there." In other words, Rauf gave Umar Islam the green light to go on a trial run using an American carrier. The next day, Rauf finally got through to Ali, who still did not know that Sarwar was back: "I have been unable to get through to u so here is my no. and you can get in touch with me. . . . Also regarding your friend that is coming, can you get in touch with nabil and he can sort the rest." Nabil seems to be Sarwar, also known as "Nabs." Ali replied immediately, "my number does work but my phone was mashed up so it took a while to get a new one. But it should be ok now. Anyway ill call u soon. I cant get hold of nabz tell him to get in contact with me asap. Tell him to call me on the no I gave you. It should be ok now. Give me a email via nabeel to give to the camera dude . . . kid and tariq give their love." The two names referred to Khatib and Hussain respectively.[79]

Sarwar and Ali finally made contact and met in Lloyd Park in Ali's neighborhood, lying on the grass, facing each other to make sure no one else could hear the conversation. Neither was forthcoming about the conversation at the trial. They must have updated each other on the new developments—directions and guidance from Rauf and Abu Ubaydah, new recruits as suicide bombers, their respective division of labor, Ali's imminent acquisition of a flat to build the devices, the concentration of hydrogen peroxide, the purchase of equipment and chemicals, and the making of the suicide videos. After the meeting, the two went to a restaurant and then to a mosque. They separated after about three hours together.[80]

Except for Sarwar, who needed to stay away from them, the rest of the conspirators spent a lot of time together, playing soccer or tennis in the early evening. Ali and Hussain reported their passports lost.[81] On 18 July, Ali notified Rauf, with whom he still had problems communicating: "there ar a few lads who wanno join up. We have about four lads."[82] Now that all seven volunteers (Ali, Hussain, and Khatib as the original ones, plus Islam, Arafat, Savant, and Zaman) had agreed to be suicide bombers, their most pressing need was to have a locale to house their equipment, build the explosive devices, and record their wassiyas.

The Bomb Factory

The bomb factory came by way of Ali's older brothers. Dawood Khan owned a flat, which he had hoped to occupy with his family, but his wife did not like it. He sold it in early April 2006 for about £236,000 and turned the sum over to his brother Umar Khan, a part-time real estate developer, to invest it. Umar decided to buy a vacant repossession property and flip it for a profit after fixing, cleaning, and painting it. On 20 July, he bought one on Forest Road for £138,000 and gave the keys to Ali to fix, clean, paint, and decorate it before putting it back on the market.[83] This flat became the bomb factory for the next three weeks.

That afternoon, Ali went to the Spy Shop, an electronics store, to ask about intruder detection cameras but did not know what he wanted. He was advised to return after getting his exact requirements. The next day, Ali reported to Rauf that he finally had a place and at night he and Hussain brought some of their equipment there.[84]

Meanwhile Sarwar was searching for the best prices on hydrogen peroxide at different concentrations and checked with Rauf, who was micromanaging these purchases from Pakistan. On 19 July, Rauf e-mailed specific guidance to Sarwar, who did some calling the next day and then advised Rauf of his results. Rauf agreed and Sarwar summed it up on the 22nd: "The following order should be ready for delivery by next Saturday: 40–100ml (CK ONE); 30–100ml (POLO SPORT); YES . . . BOTH AT £80."[85]

Meanwhile, Gulzar called al Ghabra on July 20 on a number provided by Abdul Muneem. A little later, the teenager picked him up to see al Ghabra, who gave some money to the desperate Gulzar. When he returned home, his wife confronted him, accusing him of lying to her. Since they lived in a small cramped room in a stranger's flat, they went out to the park, where Gulzar confessed his real name and being wanted for murder. His wife reacted, "At that moment, I was scared and did not want to leave him. . . . I really love him and I just said that, you know, 'let's get out of the country' . . . if he's on the run, I run with him."[86] They decided to move into the living room of her aunt's flat for a few days before moving again into a small vacant flat given them by her aunt.

On 22 July, Ali bought six large glass jars at Tesco. Later at the mosque, Zaman handed him a prepared handwritten draft statement for his wassiya, which Ali took for review. The next day, Ali bought some more equipment at Tesco. In the early afternoon, he met with Sarwar again in a quiet section of Lloyd Park for about half an hour. Sarwar was ready to buy hydrogen peroxide in large quantity but needed help to buy laboratory equipment. He asked Ali to buy syringes, measuring cylinders, conical flasks, and thermometers. Ali gave him money for the hydrogen peroxide and promised he would help with the rest of the purchases.[87]

After Sarwar's departure, Ali met a friend and, as they talked on a bench, they believed they detected possible police surveillance. They spotted a man with sunglasses watching them. They stared at him for a moment and the man walked away. As they walked away, they turned back to see whether anyone followed them. Later that day, Ali told Hussain that he believed he was being followed, but Hussain replied that he was probably being paranoid. However, later in the evening, Ali believed a small car was following him as he was going home. He made a sudden turn and was followed by the small car. He then did a U-turn and noticed in his rearview mirror that the small car also did a U-turn, confirming his suspicion.[88]

On 24 July, Ali alerted Rauf from an Internet café and his fellow conspirators by phone. In the afternoon, he met Hussain in a park to be able to talk securely.[89] Sarwar also e-mailed Rauf, "met cha cha [Ali] and said he got a wedding film that he needs to give me. Shall I take it off him?"[90]

On 25 July, Rauf decided to use Gulzar as an adviser to Sarwar, who was having problems carrying out his mission. Rauf e-mailed Sarwar, "ny friend that would like to see you is arif. You have met him before. He is good friends with abdil and jameel so you don't need to worry bout that he can help them. He knows about the dates and he knows his aftershaves very well as he had a cosmetic shop before. But because his shop was bankrupt he is a bit out of touch about the new desighber aftersahvees [sic]. So you could update him about the ones you were shown by me it would be helpful cos h [sic] needs to show Jameel afterwards." In response to Sarwar's question the previous day, he replied, "take cha cha wedding film off him. Also can you show Arif how to make a film cos he is not very good and he wants to make one for his sisters wedding."[91] Later that day, Sarwar drove back to the pharmacy in south Wales to buy 20 half-liter bottles of 35 percent hydrogen peroxide for £343. He then drove to Bristol to a hydroponics shop to buy two five-liter containers of 17.5 percent hydrogen peroxide for £80.[92] The same day, both Ali and Hussain telephoned the passport office to expedite their passport applications. They were given fast-track appointments in person for 2 August in the early afternoon. Ali also called the Barclays Bank Career Development Loans Department for an application. He later met with Umar Islam at his home and then played tennis with Hussain. Afterward, Hussain bought several Oasis and Luco-zade soft drinks at Tesco.[93]

On 26 July, Sarwar poured the 20 liters of hydrogen peroxide into four five-liter bottles of emptied mineral water, placed them in black bin liners, and the next day hid them in an isolated spot in Fennel's Wood, not too far from his home. Ali returned to the bomb factory with two large heavy bags. He dispatched Arafat to John Bell & Croyden in the West End to pick up needed medical supplies, including glass cylinders, beakers, measuring cups, syringes, and needles. Hussain bought large surgical needles at several pharmacies while Ali bought a satellite navigation system.[94]

The Martyrdom Videos

On 27 July, Ali and Hussain bought more supplies, including a glass jar, and went to a hardware store, where they examined tools, utensils, jars, flashlights, screwdrivers, batteries, and electrically operated toothbrushes. They bought two disposable cameras, felt protector pads, and bum-bags. They then picked up Savant in late afternoon and drove to the bomb fac-tory.[95] They spent some time there and recorded their respective wassiyas with a Sony 8mm videocassette camera.

In his wassiya, Ali explained that he was becoming a martyr for entrance to Jannah [paradise] and "to punish and to humiliate the *kuffar* [non-believer], to teach them a lesson that they will never forget. It's to tell them that we Muslim people have pride . . . we are brave. We're not cowards. Enough is enough. We've warned you so many times get out of our lands, leave us alone, but you have persisted in trying to humiliate us, kill us and destroy us. Sheikh Osama warned you many times to leave our lands or you will be destroyed." An off-camera voice asked him, "What about innocent people? Surely, just because the kuffar kill our innocent does not mean that we should . . . kill theirs?" Ali replied, "You show more care and concern for animals than you do for the Muslim ummah. . . . I have the desire since the age of 15/16 to participate in jihad in the path of Allah. I had the desire since then to punish the kuffar for the evil they are doing. . . . Leave us alone. Stop meddling in our affairs and we will leave you alone. Otherwise expect floods of martyr operations against you and we will take our revenge and anger."[96]

Hussain lectured, "We're not targeting innocent civilians. We're target-ing economic . . . and military targets. They're the battlegrounds of today

. . . and collateral damage is going to be inevitable and people are going to die. . . . For many years . . . I dreamt of doing this, but I didn't have no chance of doing this. . . . I only wish I could do this . . . again and again until people come to their senses and realize . . . don't mess with the Muslims. Stop supporting the puppets and helping our enemies. If you do this, we're going to leave you alone. If you don't, you're going to feel the wrath of the mujahedin, Inshallah."[97]

Savant stressed similar points:

> As for the lovers of life and haters of death, you will class my case as a case of suicide. I say, argue your case with the Most High, and as he has said, and never think [of] those who have been killed in the cause of Allah as dead, rather they are alive with their Lord. . . . Muslims . . . remove yourself from the grasp of the kuffar before you are counted as one of them. Do not be content with your council houses and businesses and Western lifestyles. So, we also say that if you are among the polytheists whilst they are attacked, we are free from you whatever may befall you. . . . Obviously after this beautiful operation they will accuse us brothers of all sorts of things and most of the things they will accuse us of is killing for the sake of killing, hating freedom, hating the West, being fed up with our lives.[98]

Late that evening, Ali met Sarwar, gave him the laboratory equipment he and Arafat had bought, and alerted him about possible police surveillance. Sarwar was skeptical and Ali tried to prove it to him by driving around and going to an isolated lane in a graveyard to see whether anyone was following. No car came and Sarwar told him he was paranoid.[99]

On 28 July, Sarwar made about 84 calls to hydroponics companies. In the evening, Ali and Zaman went to the bomb factory where Zaman recorded a suicide video. Arafat Khan joined them shortly thereafter.[100] Zaman declared,

> I could have lived a life of ease but instead chose to fight for the sake of Allah's *deen*. . . . All of you so-called moderate Muslims, there's only one way in which to solve this crisis, the problems will not be solved by means of campaigning, big conferences, peaceful negotiations with the disbelievers. The only solution . . . is by fighting jihad . . . until the enemy is fully subdued and expelled from our

lands. America and England have no cause for complaint for they are the ones who invaded and built bases in the land of the Muslims. They are the ones who supply weapons to the enemies of Islam, including the accursed Israelis. I'm warning these two nations and any other country who seeks a bad end, death and destruction will pass upon you like a tornado and you will not feel . . . any security or peace in your lands until you [stop] interfering in the affairs of the Muslim completely. . . . Remember, as you kill us, you will be killed and as you bomb us, you will be bombed. . . . I have not been brainwashed. I have been educated to a high standard. I am old enough to make my own decisions.[101]

Arafat recorded his video after Zaman's departure. Apparently, Ali must have felt that Arafat's effort was inadequate and he asked him to do it again at a later time.

On 29 July, Sarwar drove to meet Gulzar near his flat. They went to an Internet café, where Sarwar e-mailed Rauf, "I am with arif, didn't thought it would be him. Top dude!" Sarwar then drove Gulzar to another part of London, where they entered adjacent telephone kiosks to make calls— Sarwar's call was to Ali. After prayer at a mosque and lunch at a pizza restaurant, they went to a park for a secure talk before Sarwar drove Gulzar back home.[102] Neither one was forthcoming in their respective testimonies as to the nature of this three-hour meeting. After the meeting, Gulzar delayed his departure for South Africa, probably to help Sarwar in manu-facturing the explosive charges.

After the meeting, Sarwar drove to Walthamstow for a quick talk with Ali in his car. He informed Ali about Gulzar's unexpected arrival and Ali probably advised him to hide any compromising material in his possession for security reasons. They went to an Internet café to create new e-mail accounts to communicate with each other. Sarwar then dropped Ali off before returning to High Wycombe. Ali, Hussain, and Arafat played tennis together that evening.[103]

On 30 July, Ali further increased his security precautions. He bought four new cell phones, each dedicated to specific groups of people. One was to call Rauf and another for Sarwar. A third phone was to call Hussain, Savant, Khatib, and other friends. The last phone was used just to receive calls and texts but not to make any outgoing calls.[104] Sarwar surveyed another wooded area near his home for hiding the compromising material in his possession. He continued to look for more laboratory equipment and kept in telephone and Internet contact with Ali, Rauf, and Gulzar.

In the afternoon, Ali and Arafat, carrying heavy bags, went to the bomb factory, where Arafat recorded his second wassiya, in which he berated "the bootlickers who stand shoulder to shoulder with kuffars in condemning these beautiful operations and the mujahedin. In particular, I'd like to address the scholars to whom Allah has given knowledge which they concealed . . . to please the kuffar, to save themselves from their disapproval. What a miserable deal! Pleasing the kuffar all, while just pleasing Allah; fearing them instead of fearing Allah."[105]

In the evening, when Ali, Hussain, Arafat, and Savant played tennis and went to dinner together, MI5 surreptitiously broke into the bomb factory and planted a listening device in it.[106]

Conversation at the Bomb Factory

On 31 July, Rauf sent an e-mail to Ali inquiring about the surveillance, "How is the skin infection you were telling me about? Has it got worse or is the cream working?"[107] Savant set up an appointment for a fast-track passport application for 9 August.

In the morning, Sarwar bought a thermometer, three subminiature halogen bulbs, and some battery clamps at one store; a 30-inch expandable trolley suitcase at another; and a spade at another. He made phone calls from a nearby kiosk and later walked in King's Wood carrying a bulky green plastic bag. He emerged half an hour later without the bag and drove home. He later testified that he marked a tree to identify a spot to bury the suitcase of the compromising laboratory equipment.[108]

In later afternoon, Ali and Hussain came to the bomb factory with some supplies and worked on the small batteries to make detonators. Hussain said, "Yeah, that's good. Are you sure? That's boom, that's boom, mate." Ali replied, "We've got our virgins." They worked on the soft drink plastic bottles and one of them said, "take the juice out." They went on to discuss the number of bombers. Hussain said there were six, but Ali corrected him, "seven." Hussain listed them, "one, two, Adam, Ibo, Arrow, Omar B, Waheed" (Ali, Hussain, Khatib, Savant, Arafat, Islam, Zaman). They talked about another group that might have five bombers. While drilling a hole in a plastic bottle, Ali said, "We can't all take the exact same thing. . . . It will be different terminals. . . . No-one's going to get the same," referring to different soft drinks and flavors at different airline terminals. After draining a bottle of its content, Hussain said, "It's ready, waiting for the HP." Ali responded, "He's got to boil it down . . . enough for this mission." They discussed the targeting of the operation. One said, "You need sound places like New York, Washington, D.C., California, Miami, Philadelphia. . . . Find out from a travel agent the ten most popular places where British . . . people [are] going." They rehearsed what they would say at airport security when asked who they would be visiting. They'd reply that they were single, visiting a girlfriend and mention they had a condom in their bag. Finally, they concluded, "Batteries are done, bulbs are done." They left the bomb factory after four hours, carrying three plastic bags. Along the way, Ali dropped one bag into a rubbish bin and put the other two in the trunk of his car. Police officers fished the discarded bag from the rubbish and noted that it contained two empty Lucozade bottles and one empty Oasis bottle and latex gloves with black substance from the batteries on them.[109]

On 1 August, around 4 or 5 AM, before surveillance came to his home, Sarwar went into King's Wood with his spade to dig a hole and hide the new suitcase filled with laboratory equipment. The ground was too hard for him to dig. After half an hour, he abandoned the effort, leaving his spade behind. He returned home to take a nap. In late morning, he went to the post office and mail-ordered measuring cylinders, a glass beaker, and a flask from a wine store in Devon. He bought small boxes of citric acid (the catalyst for HMTD) at three different pharmacies, a box of 50 latex gloves, and a bag of "Homebase Easy Dig Soil Cultivator," which he had learned about on the Internet earlier that day. In early afternoon, he went to an Internet café to open up a new account from notes he pulled out of his pocket. After lunch, he called Ali and Gulzar respectively from adjacent telephone kiosks. Ali spent the day with his family at a shopping center. Hussain applied for an additional £8,000 loan. In the evening, Ali socialized with Arafat and Zaman.[110]

On 2 August, again before surveillance arrived in the morning, Sarwar returned to King's Wood. He poured his soil cultivator and water on the soil, but it stayed hard. He gave up, returned home, and went back to sleep. After he woke up, he tried to contact Ali from various public phone booths, punctuated with calls to Rauf and Gulzar. In the afternoon, he went to King's Wood and left a small package. Since he could not dig a hole, he looked for an alternative place to hide the suitcase. He came across a fallen tree with a large cavity at its base, where he could hide the suitcase. He marked the spot and left.[111] Meanwhile, Ali and Hussain went to their interviews at the passport office in central London. Barclays Bank notified Savant of its approval of his application for a £10,000 loan for the purchase of a car. In the evening, Ali and Hussain played tennis with some of their friends.[112]

The next day was a very busy day. In the early morning, Sarwar hid the suitcase in the identified tree in King's Wood without being detected. Ali e-mailed Rauf from an Internet café, "Listen, it's confirmed, I have fever. Sometimes when I go out in the sun to meet people, I feel hot. . . . By the way I set up my music shop now. I only need to sort out the opening time. I need stock."[113] So despite detecting surveillance, Ali informed Rauf that he had set up the bomb factory and was waiting for the explosive charge from Sarwar.

Sarwar called Gulzar, bought Oasis and Lucozade soft drinks, and drove to Gulzar's flat. He went in with two bags, including the soft drinks, and came out two hours later with just one. Sarwar later testified that he had brought Gulzar a home-cooked meal for lunch, but surveillance saw him going to a restaurant for a meal right after leaving Gulzar. The prosecutor, and I agree, suggested instead that Sarwar met with Gulzar to demonstrate the latest in the construction of the explosive devices because, though Gulzar was an explosive expert, he was not familiar with Abu Ubaydah's new design. After their session, Sarwar took away the compromising bomb-making material. Afterward, Gulzar called South Africa from a public phone booth.[114]

That afternoon, Ali and Hussain went to the bomb factory for five and a half hours to work on their devices. They drilled holes in the bottles. The radio was on, making it very difficult for the listening device to pick up their conversation. Some of the shreds of conversation revealed discussion about the possibility of taking camera or camcorder batteries on the plane and exploration of pretexts to go to the toilet with a toilet bag. They left in the evening with Ali carrying an electric drill set in a black plastic bag. They allegedly went to an isolated graveyard area to check if anyone was following them. They saw someone there and there was no reason for him to be there. "After that, I thought, 'I'm finished,'" Hussain said at trial. "I didn't do anything regarding making the device or anything after that. I stopped." This excursion to a graveyard is not documented in the surveillance record and may not be true.[115]

On 4 August, Ali went to an Internet café to check for Rauf's response.[116] Rauf first inquired about the wassiyas: "Regarding the camera

dude why are u still seeing him???? Pass him on to nabs." Rauf then asked
for details about the surveillance to brief Abu Ubaydah and decide
whether to abort the mission. "Your skin infection is contageous dont it
spreading. By the way how bad is it do u always gt it when you go out or
is it only sometimes??? I need as much details as possible so my friend the
skin specialst (paps) can help. Do u think u can still open the shop with
this skin problem?? Is it minor??? Or do u think u can still sort an opening
time without the skin problem worsening?????" Rauf asked whether Umar
Islam had already gone through with his rehearsal flight: "has kala done
his rapp show?????" He also proposed a change of communication: instead
of e-mail, "pls reply to my queries by text msg." As an afterthought, he
asked, "PS. Have any of the shop assistants with u also got this
infection????//"[117] Ali then drove to Slough to meet with Sarwar. After
lunch at a restaurant, they exchanged bags at Ali's car. Ali gave Sarwar
modified light bulbs in a glass jar and a videotape of wassiyas, which
Sarwar hid in the family garage.

In the evening, Ali, Hussain, Arafat, and a friend played tennis. Sarwar
called Rauf from a kiosk. Gulzar went to an Internet café, where he allegedly
tried to download software to fix his laptop, and called Rauf and Sarwar
from a public phone.[118] He then allegedly went to al Ghabra's place, but
surveillance failed to pick this up. Gulzar testified that he brought his laptop
to see what could be done to fix it. Al Ghabra allegedly gave him a USB
stick and a CD that turned out to contain radical material. Gulzar explained
that he had no television and wanted some entertainment or educational
material for his wife. He said he could not access the CD since his computer
had problems. He later returned to an Internet café and tried to download
some software to fix his computer.[119]

It seems that the conspirators lay low on 5 August. They were in contact
with each other, calling each other from phone booths and checking
Internet cafés. Sarwar looked at ads for places to rent in a shop window. In
the evening, Ali, Hussain, Arafat, and a friend again played tennis.[120]

Choosing the Airline Flights

In the late morning of 6 August, Ali e-mailed Rauf from an Internet café
that the surveillance was not so bad. "Its not all the time its here and there
usually when I link someone by my self. I aint nothing for a while now. Ill
still open shop. I dont think its so bad that I cant do work but if I feel really

ill let u know. Make isti and ask paps to make isti too. . . . Of course I dont link anyone new." He would help Sarwar find a place to concentrate the hydrogen peroxide. "Im trying to sort nabs out wid a yard." He would transfer a second wassiya videotape to him. "I also have to arrange for the printers to be picked up and stored, let me do this then ill take a back sit." He had been out of touch with Umar Islam for a week and had not yet recorded his wassiya. "Im still waiting for kala to link me and do his rap song. Everyday I send a msg to him, he is late by 7 days." Ali was now ready to work out the schedule of the flights to be blown up over the Atlantic. "I have done my prep all I have to do now is sort out opening time take and bookings. That should take a couple of days."[121] After sending this e-mail, Ali waited for a short time. He received a call on his cell phone and was heard speaking in hushed tones in a foreign language for about a minute. Presumably, Rauf gave him the go-ahead.[122]

Ali then logged on to the Heathrow Airport website, which showed a timetable, and then accessed a flight booking service website.[123] He downloaded the information on a memory stick. The stick was later found at his place; the content listed a series of planes leaving from Heathrow Airport for North America:

1415 UA 931 LHR–San Francisco (United Airlines)
1500 AC 849 LHR–Toronto (Air Canada)
1515 AC 865 LHR–Montreal (Air Canada)
1540 UA 959 LHR–Chicago (United Airlines)
1620 UA 925 LHR–Washington (United Airlines)
1635 AA 131 LHR–New York (American Airlines)
1650 AA 091 LHR–Chicago (American Airlines)[124]

At the same time, Sarwar was at another Internet café looking at hydroponics websites and stores that sold them. He left the café after five minutes and called Ali from a public phone booth. Ali, still searching for flights at his café, answered in a loud voice, telling him, "well, then, take them out of the boxes. . . . Let me know about the weight." After this brief conversation, Ali resumed his search and left the Internet café after more than two hours.[125] Gulzar and Sarwar called each other and Pakistan. After talking to Pakistan and al Ghabra, Gulzar called Sarwar back and, according to a surveillance officer nearby, told him, "I've been meaning to speak to you. There's something I've forgotten. I definitely need it to be 8 millimeters.

Can you get someone else to do it?"[126] One can only surmise that he was speaking of the wassiya videotapes.

That evening, Gulzar took a bus and Sarwar drove to Walthamstow. Ali picked them up in his car around 10 PM, parked for a while, and then went to a restaurant, with Gulzar carrying a heavy bag, the size of a laundry bag. This 45-minute meeting was the only time that the three of them met in person. Gulzar left first to call al Ghabra from a nearby public phone booth. Half an hour later, Ali dropped off Sarwar at his car and Sarwar returned home.[127] Gulzar went to al Ghabra's home to give al Ghabra the bag that he had received from Ali. Since al Ghabra's home was not searched during the wave of arrests, its content is not known. Gulzar said it was electronic equipment—a couple of iPods, a camcorder, a satellite navigation system, 36 unused Pakistani AA batteries, and some flashlights—for al Ghabra to sell on his behalf because he needed money, but the government believes it also contained a set of the wassiyas for Pakistan.[128]

Final Developments

On 7 August (Monday), Sarwar was in frequent phone contact with Ali and Gulzar. In early afternoon, he e-mailed Rauf from an Internet café, "I have sent you some new business files, and some new movies and music. You should receive them tomorrow. It should be with yaq's friend."[129] The prosecution argued that Yaq stood for Mohammed Yasar Gulzar and his friend was al Ghabra. Sarwar then an e-mail to Ali. "Hiya, my friend's uncle will be going abroad on Monday morning so I will need the film by Sunday afternoon at the latest. You still haven't gotten back to me about the yard that I need. . . . Joseph had a go at me because I haven't sorted out my things." Apparently, Rauf was upset with Sarwar because his inability to rent a place to concentrate the hydrogen peroxide was delaying the operation. Ali answered, "Okay, I'm on the case. Today I am seeing the house. The guy was unable to show it to me today." Sarwar then referred to Rauf, "I don't know why he's taking the piss. . . . I got some stuff to send with your mate so make sure we link up before that." After his e-mail session, Sarwar bought some Superglue and an expandable garden rake. Ali later texted Rauf while Gulzar called al Ghabra and Abdul Muneem from different adjacent phone booths.[130] In late evening, Gulzar made a call to someone called "Izzy" (Ismael) up north.[131]

The next day, Ali called Rauf. The conspirators called each other from various phone booths, and Ali finally connected with Umar Islam, who had been very busy at work in the previous two weeks, during which time Ali had changed his phone number. Savant made another loan application for £10,000 for the purchase of a car but it was later rejected.[132]

On the morning of 9 August, Ali and Rauf exchanged texts and Ali went to an Internet café. Gulzar took his wife to London City Airport. She flew to Brussels to see her daughters and start the registration process for her new husband. Gulzar returned home by bus. Savant kept his midday appointment for his application at the London Passport Office. Sarwar went to a local Asda store and bought five two-liter bottles of water and two one-liter bottles of Asda high juice, which he paid in cash. As he had forgotten his cell phone at home, he called several hydroponic companies from public telephones. He then bought four five-liter containers of 17.5 percent hydrogen peroxide at two stores. He returned home in late afternoon, where he found some text messages waiting for him on his cell phone.[133]

In the afternoon, Gulzar had tried to contact Sarwar no less than six times. Somewhat desperate, he called Rauf in Pakistan, who immediately called Sarwar, but without success. Gulzar continued to try to contact Sarwar and again Rauf. He also called Abdul Muneem, allegedly to ask him for money. Finally, when Sarwar turned his phone back on, he saw that he had missed a call from Rauf. He immediately called Rauf's cell phone and shortly thereafter got a text from him: "Yaq says switch your phone on. I've left you mail. I don't know of leather belts." Sarwar called Gulzar.[134]

Rauf was arrested in Pakistan shortly after this last text. He lived in Bahawalpur with his family and that evening he boarded the bus to Multan. ISID officers pulled the bus over and arrested him. The decision to arrest him has never been officially explained. Informally British officers accused U.S. authorities of putting pressure on the ISID to arrest Rauf as soon as possible for fear that he might disappear once he reached Multan. According to his report, Rauf usually took the precaution of going to an area in the FATA where he felt safe from arrest when operations were under way as he had done for the London bombings.[135] This precipitated the wave of arrests in England, lest the conspirators destroy the evidence of their impending crime. Pakistan is five hours ahead of England.

Unaware of the events unfolding in Pakistan, Ali and Islam entered the bomb factory around 6 PM and Islam recorded his carefully written out wassiya:[136]

This is an obligation on me as a Muslim to wage jihad against the kuffar. We are doing this in order to gain the pleasure of our Lord.

. . . This is revenge for the actions of the USA in the Muslim lands and their accomplices such as the British and the Jews. . . . Martyr-dom operations upon martyrdom operations will keep on raining on these kuffars until they . . . leave our lands. . . . We don't mind that, if you call us terrorists, because we will keep on terrorizing you until you learn your lesson. We love to die in the path of Allah. We love to die like you love life, so you cannot win. How can you fight against people who . . . find it an act of worship to fight against you?[137]

Off camera, a voice asked him about the kuffar, who "accuse us of being barbarians, accuse us of killing for the sake of killing. . . . What do you say about those who will be killed who the kuffar will call innocent civilians?" Islam replied, "As you [disbelievers] bomb, you will be bombed, and as you kill, you will be killed, and if you want to kill our women and children, then the same thing will happen to you. This is not a joke. If you think you can go into our lands and do what you're doing in Iraq, Afghanistan, Pales-tine and keep on supporting those who are fighting against the Muslims and think it will not come back on to your own doorstep, may you have another think coming. . . . The sons of Islam will take revenge for what you have done to us." People who paid taxes to fund an army that pillaged Muslim lands from their resources and dishonored Muslims were not inno-cent. "Even if you disagree that you've done nothing, you're just sitting there and you're still funding the army. You haven't put down your leader. You haven't pressured them enough."[138]

After recording the tape, Islam asked Ali whether it would be better for his wife to go to Sri Lanka, where he knew someone, before or after the operation. Ali suggested she should go after because if she went before people might suspect that she knew about the operation beforehand. Islam then confessed to Ali that his wife had discovered his handwritten martyr-dom script when it fell out of his pocket. She confronted him, "Is that what I think it is?" Islam relied, "Don't ask no question." Ali responded, "that's a serious lapse man. I told you to do it on the laptop, didn't I? . . . Put it in a hidden folder." Islam asked Ali how much time they had before going on the operation. Ali replied, "A couple of weeks." Islam said that he still had not been to the passport office to replace his faulty passport (with the wrong birthdate on it) and Ali urged him, "You'd better go, man." Islam agreed, "I'm going to go there in a day . . . and then book a trip." Ali explained to Islam that he had changed his phone number because "I felt some heat." Islam then told Ali that his wife was considering accompanying him on his suicide operation. Ali asked what she was going to do with their baby (she was also pregnant at the time). Islam answered, "Well, . . . obviously she's got the baby but that's all—I think, say, that she knew someone was going to be there to look after them." Ali suggested, "Maybe, she'd take them with her." Islam said, "Maybe, you know what I mean. She'd like to do it though." Islam then asked about how to assemble the bomb on the plane. When Ali told him, he said, "This is really going to happen, isn't it?" They then returned to the issue of his wife and baby coming along. Ali told him, "I know my wife wouldn't agree to it."[139] Ali and Islam left the bomb factory after an hour. Ali carried two plastic bags, one full and the other half-empty, and dropped off Islam at a bus stop.

The Arrests

Ali and Sarwar called each other from phone booths and determined to meet that evening at the Waltham Forest town hall. Sarwar arrived first and parked in the visitor parking lot. Ali arrived around 9:30 PM and carefully looped around the lot and hall. Sarwar saw him and followed him in his car. They parked in front of the town hall. Ali handed Sarwar the half-empty bag, which contained Arafat's second recording and Islam's wassiyas, the video camera, and batteries. Sarwar put them in the trunk of his car, and the two sat side by side along the wall of the town hall, where the police arrested them at 9:43 PM.[140]

This triggered a wave of 22 additional arrests, including Cossor Ali, Tanvir Hussain, Umar Islam, Arafat Khan, Ibrahim Savant, Waheed Zaman, Adam Khatib, Mohammed Gulzar, and Abdul Muneem Patel. According to Rauf, two other potential martyrs were not arrested because his contact, presumably Gulzar, had not yet reached them.[141] One of them, "Ismael," whom Gulzar had called again the evening of his arrest, has since been identified. Allegedly, Gulzar was getting ready to meet him the next day, brief him on the plot, and film his wassiya.[142]

The arrests in Britain were premature. Ali's estimate that the operation would take place in "two weeks" was wishful thinking. Sarwar had not yet started concentrating hydrogen peroxide and we saw from the previous attacks that it was the most time-consuming part of the plot. In fact, he had not yet found a place that he could use as a bomb factory. Al Qaeda, in the person of Rauf, was in constant contact with the field leaders in England: Ali, Sarwar, and Gulzar. Rauf used e-mails, texts, and voice calls. He liked e-mail and Yahoo messaging with Ali, phone calls with Sarwar, and phone voice and text with Gulzar. Sarwar used five cell phones and Gulzar and Ali four each. Hussain, Ali's lieutenant in touch with the other martyr volunteers, had six phones. The cell phones were dedicated for calling only one person. The cell phones were mostly prepaid phones, not requiring registration. All of them also used prepaid telephone cards, which they used from public telephones.[143]

The Crown Prosecution Service charged Ahmed Ali, Assad Sarwar, and Tanvir Hussain with conspiracy to cause explosions. It also charged them and Umar Islam, Ibrahim Savant, Arafat Khan, and Waheed Zaman with conspiracy to commit public nuisance. It charged these seven and Mohammed Gulzar with conspiracy to murder persons unknown and conspiracy to murder using explosives on aircraft. It also charged Adam Khatib with conspiracy to murder persons unknown and Abdul Muneem Patel with possession of a document or record containing information of a kind likely to be useful to a person committing or preparing an act of terrorism. Cossor Ali was charged with having information which might be of material assistance in preventing the commission by another person of an act of terrorism and not disclosing that information as soon as reasonably possible. Rashid Rauf was held on a British warrant related to the 2002 murder of his uncle. He was also brought on terrorism charges in connection with the British plot, but on 13 December 2006, a judge in Rawalpindi dismissed the terrorism charges as lying outside the court's jurisdiction.

Abdul Muneem Patel and Cossor Ali were released on bail. A year later, the mysterious Ismael, or AM, from Birmingham, was put under control orders.[144] Abdul Muneem Patel was the first to be tried in September 2007. He was only convicted of collecting information for a terrorist purpose and sentenced to six months in a young offenders institute on 26 October 2007.

In December 2007, Rashid Rauf managed to escape from detention during a return trip from a court hearing back to jail. Abu Ubaydah al-Masri, the alleged mastermind behind the plot, died of hepatitis in the FATA in the winter of 2008.

On 3 April 2008, Ali, Sarwar, Hussain, Islam, Savant, Arafat, Zaman, and Gulzar went on trial at Woolwich Crown Court. On 9 July, Ali, Sarwar, and Hussain pled guilty to the charge of conspiracy to cause explosions. On 10 July, these three and Islam, Savant, Arafat, and Zaman pled guilty to conspiracy to commit a public nuisance. On 8 September 2008, a jury found Ali, Sarwar, and Hussain guilty of conspiracy to murder persons unknown, but could reach no verdict on the other charge and on the other defendants. It found Gulzar not guilty of all the charges. Gulzar was immediately put under control order in connection with these charges.[145] The Crown Prosecution Service decided to retry the other seven defendants on the still outstanding charges.

Rashid Rauf was killed by a Predator missile in Ali Khel, North Waziristan, on 22 November 2008.

The retrial started on 2 March 2009. On 9 September 2009, Ali, Sarwar, and Hussain were convicted of the charge of conspiracy to murder using explosives on aircraft. Islam was found guilty of conspiracy to murder persons unknown, but, along with Savant, Arafat, and Zaman, was found not guilty of conspiracy to murder using explosives on aircraft. The jury was deadlocked for Savant, Arafat, and Zaman on the charge of conspiracy to murder persons unknown. Ali, Sarwar, Hussain, and Islam were sentenced to life in prison, with minimum terms of 40 years, 36 years, 32 years, and 22 years respectively. The Crown Prosecution Service decided to retry Savant, Arafat, and Zaman for a third time.

Adam Khatib and two others were tried at Woolwich Crown Court on 6 October 2009. They were convicted of their respective charges on 9 December 2009 and Khatib was sentenced to life in prison, with a minimum term of 18 years. Cossor Ali went on trial at the Inner London Crown Court in February 2010, but on 5 March 2010, a jury found her not guilty of the charge.

The third trial of Savant, Arafat, and Zaman on the sole charge of conspiracy to murder persons unknown started on 26 April 2010 at Woolwich Crown Court. On 8 July 2010, a jury convicted all three of the defendants. On 15 July 2010, they were all sentenced to life in prison, with a minimum term of 20 years.

CHAPTER 6

GETTING THE STORY STRAIGHT

THE PRECEDING CHAPTERS ON the Crevice, Theseus, Vivace, and Overt attacks present very different accounts of their respective plots than what the public has been told so far. It has become common among my colleagues in terrorism research to gloss over differences with previous works. Replication of findings and testing a theory with evidence are the basis of every scientific discipline, but the field of terrorism research generally avoids this type of peer review. Yet without it, the scientific enterprise cannot build on existing work. The first step is to get the facts straight. The previous narratives were built on primary-source material collected from trials where claims by the government were challenged by defendants. The emerging evidence was more valid and reliable than anonymous intelligence leaks and initial newspaper accounts. In this concluding chapter, I compare my four narratives with previous accounts and analyze how these differences emerged in order to improve future research.

Despite their importance in shaping Western counterterrorism strategy, the four attacks described in this book have not been the subject of extensive research. In contrast to the many volumes published about the 9/11 attacks in the United States, there have been only three sets of accounts about these attacks in Britain. The first one, Mitchell Silber's *The Al Qaeda Factor*, is not a narrative account of these attacks but an analysis based on functional requirements necessary to carry them out, such as recruitment of perpetrators, training, and manufacture of bombs.[1] Based on material similar to that which I used, Silber reaches similar conclusions to mine. This is not surprising as we worked together on parts of his book, which I will not address further in this chapter. The second account is an edited volume by Bruce Hoffman and Fernando Reinares, *The Evolution of the Global Terrorist Threat*, which skips over the Vivace attack and enlists Peter Neumann and Ryan Evans to write about Crevice, Hoffman about Theseus, and Paul Cruickshank about Overt.[2] The last set of accounts is Raffaello Pantucci's *We Love Death as You Love Life*.[3]

A quick glance at the accounts in my book and these other narratives shows that our respective accounts obviously differ in length and level of detail. The three accounts in the Hoffman and Reinares collection amount to 75 pages excluding the endnotes, many of which are filled with polemical arguments rather than facts. Pantucci devotes a total of 38 pages to these four attacks. Despite the claims found on their respective back covers that they are definitive accounts, they are in fact just outlines of these plots devoid of crucial details and use speculation to fill the gaps.

Crevice

Chapter 2 describes the haphazard circumstances that led to a bunch of guys pulling an all-nighter in Pakistan during which they made the fateful decision to attack their homeland because of al Qaeda's refusal to allow them to join its ranks in Afghanistan. They latched onto the throw-away comment, "if you really want to do something, then go back and you can do something there [the UK]." The driving force at first was Waheed Mahmood and then Omar Khyam. In fact, al Qaeda, in the person of Abu Munthir, was not aware of this decision for almost half a year; when he asked to speak with the conspirators, most of them had already left Pakistan. Abu Munthir probably did not think much of this plot because he did not bother to inform his own boss, Abdal Hadi al Iraqi, who did not know anything about it as late as December 2003. These facts refute the common argument that the global neojihadi attacks on Britain were the result of a carefully thought-out al Qaeda strategic decision and "the fruition of strategic, organizational decisions made by al-Qaeda years before."[4]

Chapter 2 also demonstrates that Khyam abandoned his plot to detonate a large remote-controlled bomb in Britain when he learned from Mohammed Babar that Abdal Hadi would welcome British volunteers to fight in Afghanistan. His behavior and words indicated that he shifted his priority to going to fight in Afghanistan: he no longer visited the fertilizer storage site except when summoned by an undercover policewoman; he did nothing to advance the original plot after learning of Abdal Hadi's decision (the Canadian Khawaja was not aware of this change of priority and continued with the original plot alone); his conversations in February and March 2004 never mentioned his plot. The person who had bought the fertilizer, Anthony Garcia, had abandoned the neojihad altogether by early 2004 to devote himself to sex and his modeling career. Some might argue that Garcia was simply dissimulating his intentions, but his contemporaneous diary already showed his obsession with sex in Pakistan (no need for dissimulation at the time), and his behavior in England was simply a continuation and overt expression of his libido.

The Government's Version of Crevice

In addition to the scholarly accounts, the British government provided an account of Crevice, especially in connection to the 7/7 Coroner's Inquests. British counterterrorism (CT) services detected a conspiracy by Omar Khyam, but did not realize that Khyam had abandoned it in favor of going to Afghanistan. The CT agencies and prosecutors misunderstood the evidence and misrepresented this conspiracy to the public and jury. Even though they detected Khyam's plot, they did not understand its significance, which prevented them from tracking down its most dangerous conspirators.

The length of the Crevice chapter is due to the fact that I provide the context of the government's claims and contrast the facts with its feverish imagination and interpretation of them. For instance, at trial, the prosecution played excerpts of a conversation between Jawad Akbar and Khyam. This collage strongly suggested that they were planning an attack on the Ministry of Sound nightclub. The tabloids could not resist reporting Akbar's disgust about those slags dancing around there and the fact that he would like to blow them up. I got the full transcript of this conversation, which I reproduced at length to provide the context of his words, which show that there was no such plot. Yet the government never disputed the tabloid version. In fact, Akbar was never part of Khyam's plot and Khyam assumed he was part of another plot that never existed.

There was certainly a plot in November–December 2003 to detonate a large bomb in the UK, but by January all the conspirators, except for the Canadian one isolated from the rest, had walked away from it. Akbar assumed that he was involved in a second and separate plot, a simultaneous attack against British utilities, and that his alleged leader, Waheed Mahmood, had not revealed the details of the plot to him for the sake of security. But, by March, it was clear that even that fantasized second attack was not real, as Mahmood was getting ready to immigrate to Pakistan. The Metropolitan Police Service (MPS) and the Security Service (SyS) had not appreciated the end of the two plots and still believed them to be operative and viable. The authorities worked themselves into a frenzy believing that the first plot was coming to an imminent conclusion and shared Akbar's fantasies about the second plot. Not finding any evidence for these nonexistent plots and fearing they were losing control, they arrested as many people as they believed were involved in both plots. Soon after the arrests, as they sifted through the evidence, they should have realized that both plots had long been abandoned. Instead, the Crown Prosecution Service (CPS) presented a simplistic and linear theory of the case to the jury: the conspirators trained in Pakistan together and came back to England to conduct their attack. In support of their case, they showed that the conspirators bought 600 kilograms of fertilizer (the main ingredient of the bomb), brought back aluminum powder (another ingredient) from Pakistan, and were creating a remote-control detonator.

The evidence points to a far more complicated situation. There certainly had been a plot in the fall of 2003, but it had been abandoned in favor of going to fight in Afghanistan by the time that the authorities started investigating it. By the time of the wave of arrests, there were two conspirators abroad, Khawaja in Canada and Amin in Pakistan, who were still actively participating in a now abandoned plot. They were indeed dangerous and rightly arrested, prosecuted, and convicted. The rest of the conspirators sorted themselves out in four ways. In a first group, some had switched from carrying out violence at home to fighting abroad. They were Khyam, Shujah, Azhar, and three mysterious conspirators from Leeds. Later, Akbar agreed to join Khyam and his group. A second group were followers of Mahmood, who believed that they would help him carry out an attack on utilities in England and included Akbar (before he decided to join Khyam in Pakistan) and Ali Khan. A third group had abandoned violent activism, like Gulzar and Garcia in late 2003 and probably Mahmood in March 2004. Mahmood was the most ideologically radical conspirator and had tried to inspire them to carry out terrorist attacks at home (in February 2003), but by the spring of 2004, his dedication to jihad at home or abroad had become uncertain. He remained the most radical among them as he refused to testify at his trial. Finally, a fourth group of people were associated with the above, like Hussain and probably Shujah.

A special mention should be made about the topic of torture and information derived from it. In Crevice, this pertains to Amin and Siddiqui, who were both arrested and allegedly tortured in Pakistan. Siddiqui's role was peripheral to Crevice, and the only information originating from him that I used was from his contemporaneous diary.[5] He wrote it before his arrest and so torture does not taint this information. Amin is more difficult to evaluate. He claimed he was tortured in Pakistan and that the information he provided at his post arrest police interview in England had been extracted from him by torture and was not true. He later retracted much of his post arrest statement. On appeal, the court conceded that he had been physically ill treated, meaning that it would have amounted to oppression in Britain, but not tortured during his early detention in Pakistan. He provided his confession during his police interview with his solicitor by his side. In fact, he had access to a solicitor and his advice before the interview, which was conducted impeccably. The appellate court rejected the argument that his confession was a product of Amin's ill treatment in Pakistan that had stopped at least six months before his extradition to England.[6]

I am very cautious about using information obtained under torture, as people often say anything to make it stop. However, this is not the case here. In his police interview, Amin had had ample time to recover from his mistreatment much earlier in Pakistan and his change to a country known to protect human rights, and his solicitor should have advised him to immediately claim that he had been tortured in Pakistan and his prior statements should be discarded. Instead, he very calmly provided a very detailed confession without any pressure from his interviewers (the whole process was videotaped). I treated his confession as just another piece of information for my narrative, which Babar for the most part independently corroborated. Because of this corroboration, I find his confession credible.[7]

The myth of a disrupted Crevice attack was intentionally perpetuated by the British government. The CPS at trial argued that the defendants were involved in a bombing plot that had been disrupted by the MPS and SyS. Even seven years after the arrests, the various services were questioned in the 7/7 Coroner's Inquests. They were careful to describe what they were thinking at the time of the arrests, in March 2004. At the time, when they were uncertain about the suspects' intents, it was appropriate to err on the side of caution and arrest them. What I found disturbing was that they never described the final results of their investigations, both for the trial and the inquests. By the time of the arrests, there was no longer any plot. The conspiracy at the end of 2003 involving at least Khyam, Garcia, and Khawaja had been abandoned. The alleged targets (including the Ministry of Sound nightclub and the Bluewater Shopping Centre) were just idle chat that could only be construed as targets if taken out of context. Ironically, it was the fact that the authorities found no evidence ("no visibility" as they put it) of an alleged second plot that triggered the wave of arrests of the suspects. At trial, the prosecution presented only decontextualized excerpts that were consistent with its theory of the case. In fact, the British government has yet to release the full transcript of the relevant conversations. I obtained my copy from the discovery material of the Canadian trial. This avoidance of telling the truth—especially in the face of widespread public belief that a plot had been disrupted by counterterrorism forces—amounts to wide-scale interservice (MPS, SyS, CPS) deception, whether intentional or not. A scholar must always treat government claims with some skepticism and look for corroborating evidence. I suspect that this deception persists to cover up the counterterrorism services' inability to track down all the Crevice conspirators, who were ready to go and fight in Afghanistan. This failure led to disaster.

Neumann and Evans's Account of Crevice

The other accounts of the Crevice plot have simply accepted the government's version of events uncritically. This is not surprising as Neumann and Evans rely almost exclusively on the prosecution's opening statement at trial. Despite the fact that the trial showed that the two al Qaeda leaders, Abu Munthir and Abdal Hadi, had no knowledge of the planned attack until told by Khyam and Babar, respectively, Neumann and Evans assert that the Crevice plotters sought guidance from al Qaeda "at several key junctures of the plot's evolution: at its inception, during the process of target selection, and in the course of its implementation."[8] They conclude that the plot "followed al-Qaeda's instruction and guidance." They further elaborate, "Al-Qaeda sanctioned attacks against Britain and prescribed the format—simultaneous attacks—in which they were to be carried out. It facilitated the plotters' participation in training camps, providing them with bomb-making skills, and formed them into a cohesive unit that had the drive, focus, and sense of mission that were needed in order for their plans to be realized. It helped members overcome difficulties in constructing the explosive device that was going to be used in the attacks. It failed to provide clear guidance during the implementation phase and, thus, prevented the attacks from being carried out."[9] All these claims contradict the evidence presented at the yearlong Crevice trial. Al Qaeda, through Abu Munthir, was only informed of the plot, did not approve it, train the conspirators, direct it, or guide it. To call it an al Qaeda plot is a stretch.

How did Neumann and Evans get the story so wrong? In a methodological paragraph, they explain that they "sifted through all publicly available materials and statements dealing with Crevice, which included—but were by no means limited to—trial exhibits and court records from the United Kingdom and Canada. Other important sources were a 2009 report of the British Parliament's Intelligence and Security Committee . . . as well as credible and well-sourced media reports. In addition, a first draft of this chapter was reviewed by Peter Clarke, the former head of the London Metropolitan Police Counter-Terrorism Command, who led the Crevice investigation. . . . This chapter represents our best possible account."[10] In other words, the authors relied on the government's version of events rather than primary sources. They claim to have used court records from the UK and Canada, but an analysis of their references shows that they only used the prepared text of the prosecution's opening statement of the Crevice trial, which was published in a Canadian newspaper,[11] and the judge's opinion in the Khawaja trial.[12] They also relied on the Intelligence and Security Committee report,[13] and filled in gaps in their narrative with journalistic reporting. In other words, they relied on secondhand evidence, namely government claims and journalistic reports. I understand that they had no access to the trial transcripts, which are filled with documentary evidence and are of course primary sources on what the defendants say in their own defense. So they had to accept uncritically the government's version of the plot, a secondary source on it.

Their claim that Peter Clark reviewed their chapter adds no validation for their version. As we saw, the MPS completely misinterpreted the facts of Crevice, and Clark's own understanding of the plot would have reflected this misinterpretation. Furthermore, the head of an agency is usually not an authoritative source on its investigations. The investigators on the ground brief their leader on their findings, who then briefs his or her superior. There may be several hierarchical layers between the investigators and their overall agency chief. In other words, the chief receives a watered-down version of the agency consensus, including its biases, of what happened on the ground. There is no evidence that the MPS conducted a postmortem on its understanding of what happened when all facts were in and then briefed its chief to correct any original misinterpretations, as were made here.

Neumann and Evans also did not examine the available evidence from the 7/7 Coroner's Inquests, which ended a full three years before the publication of their account and which carefully examined the links between Crevice and Theseus with primary source documents linked to the testimony of various witnesses. These documents showed the large gap between the evidence and what the government believed, namely that there were no acts in furtherance of a plot since the beginning of 2004, and that when Khyam heard that Afghanistan was open to British militants, he abandoned his plot. The trial transcripts showed that the authors' postulated al Qaeda guidance for the plot—its facilitation to access to training camp, its training the plotters in bomb making, its formation of the plotters into a cohesive unit, and its provision of a sense of mission—was just the authors' own fantasies projected unto the case. Their chapter is an example of baseless speculations, reaching conclusions contrary to the evidence. Unfortunately, I suspect that future scholars will still rely on their account since it is advertised as part of "the definitive account of al-Qaeda's plots in the post-9/11 era," and I have seen no reviews questioning the reliability of their account.

Pantucci's Account of Crevice

Pantucci seems to blame Crevice on al-Muhajiroun (the Emigrants, ALM), which created "an old boys' network" of individuals sharing similar values and beliefs and thus "willing to provide support 'once they were ready to act.' "[14] As we saw, the Crevice conspirators rejected ALM. Pantucci does not provide a narrative of the evolution of the Crevice plots but tries to stress the connections between the conspirators and al Qaeda. His account is very fragmented and relies mostly on news articles. In fact, he often chooses a secondary source for a statement rather than a primary source. For instance, he writes that "Babar identified Qayum Khan as Salahuddin Amin (the former Luton taxi driver) and Omar Khyam's 'emir' or leader. In turn, Babar states that Qayum Khan answered to Abdul Hadi al Iraqi, then head of external operations for al-Qaeda."[15] In fact, the transcripts are clear that Qayum was never a member of al Qaeda (only a supporter), did not have an emir, and was emir to no one. Nor did he answer to Abdal Hadi. He was simply helping his former friend Abu Munthir. At trial, Babar testified that he did not know Qayum and that Abdal Hadi had told him in person that he did not know any of the plotters.[16] Like this made-up chain of command, many of Pantucci's claims are taken out of context, lack nuance, or do not reflect the facts emerging from primary sources.

Pantucci does not discuss his methodology, but a quick look at his references shows that he used judgments, prosecution opening arguments, a few summaries of trial proceedings, and Rauf's report. Yet Pantucci still relied on secondary sources like Shiv Malik. For instance, Pantucci erroneously argues that the connection between the Crevice defendants was ALM[17] and suggests that Babar might have been a U.S. intelligence source when he was organizing the Gorque camp.[18] This suggestion runs counter to how intelligence and evidence are collected in the United States. While skepticism about a prosecution's case is welcomed, it is best to stick to primary sources rather than dubious speculations.

Pantucci's alleged use of trial transcripts is marred by the vagueness of his actual references: there are no citations to specific pages in the transcripts, as there are in Cruickshank or this book, just to dates of proceedings or even the trial as a whole. Furthermore, instead of referring to the original transcript, Pantucci often cites a newspaper article about the proceedings or secondary sources, like the judgment in Khawaja's trial, or Silber's book.[19] At one point, he duplicates an error by Silber about who had invited Sidique and Shakil to the Gorque camp.[20] Why not refer directly to the primary source, the transcript itself? I suspect that Pantucci never had the transcript, but rather a summary of the daily proceedings distributed to journalists by Central News, Press Room, Central Criminal Court, Old Bailey. These very short summaries are definitely not the transcripts themselves.[21]

Hoffman's References to Crevice

In his account of Theseus, Hoffman falsely claims that Abdal Hadi al Iraqi was the overall commander of operations in England and met directly with Qayum and Sidique; claims that Babar rather than Hassan Butt was the source on the nonexistent barbecue "party of hate," where "100 hardcore Islamists" allegedly raised £3,500 for Babar; and makes allegations against Mohammed al Ghabra based on unsubstantiated newspaper accounts.[22] All of these claims are refuted by the evidence presented at trial. I discuss Hoffman further, below.

Theseus

Chapter 3 on the London Bombings is not as well documented as the other empirical chapters because the London bombers committed suicide and therefore could not later give evidence at trial.[23] However, at the Coroner's Inquests in 2011, the government released many documents about the bombings and the bombers. The evidence contradicts the government's argument that the December 2004 visit to London by Ullah, Shakil, and Saleem (and Lindsay and Hussain) was a casing trip for the bombings seven months later. At the time, none knew that Sidique and Tanweer would come back to carry out an attack on the London transportation system. Rauf's report, Sidique's good-bye to his daughter, and the diary of Sidique's wife indicate that Sidique and Tanweer went to fight and die in Afghanistan: they were not expected back. Abu Ubaydah succeeded in turning them around after their departure. The jury correctly rejected the prosecution's claim and exonerated the London bombers' friends of this charge.

Hoffman's Account of Theseus

Both Hoffman and Pantucci wisely ignore the government's claim. Pantucci gives a decent summary of the attack, but Hoffman's very short narrative of Theseus is marred by dozens of factual errors. He claims that Sidique met Butt at a safehouse in Pakistan in 2002 and went on a tour of Syria and Israel in 2003; Rauf recruited Sidique and Tanweer and arranged for them to travel to Pakistan; they learned bomb making at an al Qaeda camp in the Malakand Agency; the Theseus, Vivace, and Overt conspirators trained together; and Sidique was directly linked to Vivace, Overt, and the 2003 Tel Aviv bombers. Hoffman also gives erroneous background information on Sidique and Tanweer.[24] On the basis of all these fictitious connections, Hoffman generates a mythical al Qaeda network in Britain and concludes, "the dimensions of al-Qaeda's subversion of Britain, establishment of a terrorist infrastructure in that country, effective radicalization of a sizeable element of its young Muslim population, and seamless recruitment into its ranks underscore the perils of complacency in the face of an

enemy that believes itself to have developed the ultimate 'fifth column.' "[25]
Evidence from the Theseus trial refutes this statement.

Unlike the other authors, Hoffman makes no mention of methodology
or sourcing. Much of his chapter is polemical, relies partially on the government's version of Theseus, and demonstrates his preference for press
reports making vague references to "sensitive intelligence, based on confi-
dential sources and methods, including telephone intercepts and information believed to have been derived from the interrogation of al-Qaeda
detainees."[26] His heavy reliance on sensationalistic and long discredited
newspaper articles—he cites Shiv Malik's two articles based on interviews
with Hassan Butt half a dozen times in his short chapter[27]—leads him
astray. Under oath, Butt confessed that he took Malik for a "patsy," admitted that he was a professional liar, and sold false stories at a high price to
the media.[28]

Hoffman compounds his reliance on sensational accounts with mis-
attribution of his information. He writes, "Butt had first met MSK at a
jihadi safe house in Pakistan in 2002. They had been introduced to one
another by Babar." Hoffman attributes his statement to an article by Rachel
Williams.[29] I tracked down Williams's article, which summarizes the testimony of Waheed Ali (Shippon Ullah) at the Theseus trial on 20 May 2008.[30]
I read Ullah's testimony and the article twice and nowhere are Hassan Butt,
any trip by Sidique to Pakistan in 2002, or even Mohammed Junaid Babar
ever mentioned. In fact, the alleged meeting between Butt and Sidique in
Pakistan could not have taken place, as Sidique never traveled to Pakistan
that year. In his multiple testimonies, Babar never mentioned he ever introduced Sidique to Butt. To be fair, Hoffman did not make the story up: Shiv
Malik mentioned it in his discredited article.[31] Hoffman simply gave the
wrong reference and never cross-checked his information.

Hoffman's cavalier sourcing, fondness for unsubstantiated leaks and
tabloid reporting, and failure to cross-check his information add up to poor
scholarship: in a casual reading of his chapter, I counted no less than 43
significant statements contrary to the evidence in about ten pages of actual
description—the rest is a combination of a polemic against MI5, excerpts
from the 2006 and 2009 Intelligence and Security Committee reports, and
Sidique's and Tanweer's wassiyas.

Like many counterterrorism analysts and commentators, Hoffman
relies on leaks or interviews with anonymous government officials.[32] He
even refers to a Powerpoint presentation given by the Metropolitan Police

without checking its sourcing.[33] As previously demonstrated, such information must be treated with caution, for it often comes from people who did not carry out any investigation but were just briefed on it, or simply repeated the intelligence rumor mill. Such dubious secondary information reflects what sections of government agencies believe, not what really happened on the ground. Nevertheless, despite his own practice, Hoffman knows the standards of scientific investigation, as demonstrated in his conclusion: "Success in this struggle [against al Qaeda] requires first and foremost that our assessments and analyses be anchored firmly in sound empirical judgement and not blinded by conjectures, mirror imaging, politically partisan prisms, and wishful thinking."[34] I agree.

Vivace

Chapter 4 suggests that Muktar Ibrahim's original plot was not a suicide operation at first, which might explain his decision to sever contact with Rauf. Bombs left behind did not require anyone besides the buyer of the chemicals, the people concentrating the hydrogen peroxide, and the ones transporting them to their targets. One of the conspirators, Yahya, even left to meet with his wife in Yemen and vacation with her in Ethiopia. However, the London bombings raised the bar for terrorist operations and changed Ibrahim's plans: he decided to copy the London bombers. He now needed at least three more suicide bombers besides himself. Omar was the first to volunteer. Then they asked Ramzi Mohamed and Hamdi to join them since they might have been the most radical people they knew. I disagree with the judge of the case: the evidence seems to indicate that Mohamed and Hamdi joined the attack in mid-July rather than in April as he believed. Ishmail was the last one to join the attack, but lost his nerve at the last moment.

Pantucci's Account of Vivace

Little has been written about this attack, despite the fact that a lot of evidence was presented at several trials about it. The Hoffman-Reinares collection ignores it. Pantucci believes that the Vivace attackers emerged out of Abu Hamza's network at the Finsbury Park Mosque. The evidence at trial does not support this speculation. Some of the failed bombers rarely went to listen to him at Finsbury Park. They worshipped at a closer mosque, the

Finchley Mosque: Ishmail, the most religious of the group, hung out there, and Omar came from time to time and got married there. The failed bombers were part of Mohammed Hamid's network *before* he got connected with Abu Hamza's network. Ibrahim and Omar fell out with Hamid in the fall of 2004, before Hamid became closer to Abu Hamza's network. While Mohamed and Hamdi still went to Hamid's circles in July 2005, the leaders of the Vivace attack had long rejected him.

Overt

Chapter 5 argues that there was no significant South African connection in the Transatlantic Airlines Liquid Bombs Plot. Contrary to the prosecution's claims, Mohammed Gulzar's participation in Overt was accidental, more of an opportunity than a planned decision by Rashid Rauf. The communications between the Overt plotters and Rauf clearly show that the plotters in England did not know Gulzar was coming beforehand. Indeed, the jury also rejected the prosecution's overreach that he was the mastermind of the operation but threw the baby out with the bathwater by exonerating him of any role in the operation. The prosecution's failure to convince the jury of its theory of the case forced it to try the plotters three times before a jury reached the appropriate conclusion.

Cruickshank's Account of Overt

In his otherwise excellent account of the Overt Plot, Cruickshank claims that there was a South African connection involving Rauf, Gulzar, and Haroon Rashid Aswat. He based this claim on a "senior U.S. intelligence source made privy to records of Rauf's later interrogation by Pakistani authorities, [who said that] Aswat, Gulzar, and Rauf spent time together in Pakistan before Aswat and Gulzar traveled to South Africa." Yet three sentences later, Cruickshank contradicts himself, "according to the senior U.S. intelligence source, *though Rauf made no specific mention of Aswat's involvement in his interrogation*, Aswat is suspected by U.S. intelligence of having played a role in the early stages of the airline plot."[35] Cruickshank continues, "U.S. and British security services believe that Aswat was also in contact with Rauf after he traveled to South Africa. The overlap between Aswat and Gulzar in South Africa (Aswat spent significant time there in 2004 and 2005) suggested to Western intelligence agencies they may have worked together there." However, Cruickshank later admits that "Aswat has never been charged for any role in the airline plot."[36] The name Aswat is not mentioned anywhere in the trial transcripts, by Rauf or any primary sources about Overt.

Cruickshank used part of the same sources I did. His chapter is by far the best of the lot, but he still makes some errors not because of his primary sources but his additional use of unreliable sources. Our difference on the importance of the South African connection does not come from our common sources: the trial transcript shows no connection and Rauf does not mention Gulzar or Aswat at all in his report. Instead of these reliable sources, Cruickshank refers to interviews he had with anonymous U.S. and British intelligence officials and several news reports for his erroneous claims.[37] He also relied only on the evidence presented at the first Overt trial when intercepted communications between Rauf and the Overt conspirators were not included. They were introduced at later trials and clearly demonstrate the chance nature of the Gulzar encounter with the Overt conspirators. Furthermore, Cruickshank's insinuations about the role of Aswat, based on anonymous intelligence sources, are off the mark. Of course, he did not have access to the relevant information as I did, first as an intelligence official carefully reviewing all classified information on Aswat, and second as the expert witness in the Aswat trial in New York, when I had access to all the discovery material, including the classified British material and had the opportunity to interview Aswat over two days.[38] I am of course barred from divulging any classified information or information I learned from my involvement in that case by court order. As Cruickshank notes, "British authorities did not charge him with any involvement [in Overt]"[39] and even in the United States, "Aswat has never been charged for any role in the airline plot."[40] In other words, he was not charged anywhere in relation to Overt, even in the United States despite American prosecutors' aggressiveness in charging people with terrorism offenses on flimsy evidence.

Pantucci's Account of Overt

Pantucci's account of the Overt plot is based mostly on Rauf's report, but he also believes in the government's South Africa connection. Despite his realization that "Rauf does not mention this individual [Gulzar] in his post-operation assessment documents," Pantucci still believes that Rauf did "elect to send someone [Gulzar] to oversee a plot of such complexity—with two different cells at least to coordinate on the ground."[41] This is simply Pantucci's speculation, which runs counter to the Overt testimony and the e-mail intercepts of Rauf, Sarwar, and Ali.

Getting the Story Straight

Elsewhere I have lamented the state of stagnation in terrorism research due to the fact that Western governments have not provided details about various plots to the public, leaving a significant information gap.[42] Sensationalistic speculations and theories devoid of facts filled this gap, and their traces can still be seen in most scholars' narratives of global neojihadi attacks.

The main reason for the differences between my account and those of these other scholars is methodological. I relied mostly on primary sources and carefully corroborated the defendants' testimonies—they naturally tried to minimize their involvements—with other primary sources and independent testimonies on the same events. I tried to avoid secondary sources, especially initial journalistic and sensationalistic articles. In essence, I applied the practices of good historical research. Other scholars reviewed in this chapter used secondary sources, especially anonymous leaks, rushed tabloid reporting based on defendants' former friends, relatives, and neighbors, and one-sided government reports trying to avoid blame.

The above comparison of competing accounts is actually very rare in terrorism research. Not having access to primary sources, most scholars uncritically accept the accounts of their colleagues (and cite them in their own work, creating an echo effect) and of their respective governments. Instead of primary sources, they use politicians' or service chiefs' speeches that are politically spun. In science, one cannot simply accept anyone's claim uncritically. The same stale and often meaningless debates are endlessly repeated whenever there is a new attack.

I blame the stagnation in terrorism research on Western governments' refusal to share information with trained scholars, supposedly for national security interests, to keep terrorists from knowing what the government knows. From my time in the intelligence community and as an expert witness with access to all the relevant information, I find this argument greatly exaggerated. In any case, this strategy prevents scientific peer review of government claims. Taking my point to the extreme, I quipped that this led to a situation in which untrained intelligence analysts know everything but understand nothing, while academics understand everything but know nothing.[43] The present analysis unfortunately partially supports these twin findings: that government officials, who collect facts, do not understand them, and that academics, who have the training to analyze them, still do not know what happened owing to lack of data. However, I had not fully appreciated two additional factors that further prevent learning from past experiences.

The first is government's officials' perseverance in believing preliminary findings about a plot despite mounting evidence to the contrary. Chapter 2 carefully contrasts the facts of Crevice with the British government's initial mistaken interpretations. Yet, seven years later, at the Coroner's Inquests, there was no attempt to correct these mistaken impressions. Nor were corrections presented at the Crevice trial. Instead, the CPS carefully presented selected facts of the case to suggest that the Crevice plot had not been abandoned by the time of the arrests. Likewise, highly ranked officials' autobiographies continue to ignore the fact that the Crevice plot had been abandoned. This is at best government self-deception and at worst deliberate misleading of the public. In any case, it demonstrates the need to be critical about a government's version of events, whether such versions are publicly articulated or privately leaked. Not getting the story straight prevents anyone from learning from it.

The second is the reluctance of academics in terrorist research to criticize each other. Recently, I sat on a "murder board" attempting to improve a book based on excellent research that essentially refuted another scholar's speculative notion based on very weak evidence. Despite this weak support, the original notion had been widely accepted in the field and built upon to generate theories of political violence. I found that this refutation was very significant and needed to be one of the major findings of the study. However, everyone else present disagreed for fear of offending the original scholar. This uncritical attitude in terrorism research prevents scientific progress.

Science is built on healthy disagreements among scholars, which in time eliminates erroneous claims when real facts emerge to refute untenable theories. So even getting the story straight is useless if not used to choose among competing theories. Unlike in any other field in physical or social science, I cannot recall any retraction of any article in any scholarly terrorism journal. Without critical inquiry, terrorism research scholars unwittingly become a mouthpiece of government propaganda thinly concealed under a veneer of social science. This loyalty to their government inhibits the search for truth and understanding. The public would be better served if academics helped governments understand domestic political violence to see what they could do to mitigate it. Instead, mistrust of government statements has sometimes become a sign of "radicalization" and is treated as a potential danger to society. I suspect the Catholic Church was in the same position when confronted with Galileo's assertions. Had the church prevailed long term, there would have been no age of scientific revolution and enlightenment. The field of terrorism research cannot advance and flourish if it is not put on sound scientific footing, with critical analysis of primary evidence.

Stagnation and lack of understanding in terrorism research are not just academic issues, but involve life and death. Without understanding, governments cannot generate effective policies to minimize this type of political violence and prevent unnecessary deaths. Counterterrorism services need to quickly learn from their experience and adapt to the new threat: what did they do right, what did they do wrong, and how can they improve? Lives are at stake. This book is a step in this direction, trying to get the story straight in order to formulate better preventive measures and save lives.

NOTES

Introduction

1. *Coroner's Inquests*, 2010–2011, Report under Rule 43 of the Coroner's Rules 1984: 26–37; Hayman, 2010: 15–64.

2. I have not found an elegant way to characterize this threat. It is global in the sense that its agents target what they call the "far enemy," the West, rather than the "near enemy," local despots in Muslim countries. It is "neojihad" because fighters in its cause call themselves mujahedin or jihad fighters, while the vast majority of Muslims worldwide reject the notion that it is a jihad, a war with very stringent rules about what is and is not permitted. As no one has yet to come up with a better term, I compromise between these two arguments and call it neojihad, like jihad, but not precisely jihad.

3. Hayman, 2010: 363–364.

4. I define terrorism as the characterization of outgroup political violence during domestic peacetime. See Sageman, 2016 and 2017.

5. Hoffman and Reinares, 2014: xi.

6. See Hoffman, 2008; Sciolino and Schmitt, 2008; Hoffman and Reinares, 2014: ix–xi.

7. Silber, 2012.

8. This was the argument in Sageman, 2008: al Qaeda was becoming harder to contact due to more intense state counterterrorism measures, resulting in more leaderless attacks.

9. See Sageman, 2016.

10. Likewise, there was not enough publicly available information of a later sixth plot, called Operation Pathway.

11. This is Paul Cruickshank's (2014) excellent account of the 2006 Airline Plot. The various British official reports on the London bombings (Intelligence and Security Committee, 2006 and 2009) and the *Coroner's Inquests*, 2010–2011, give a wealth of details, but do not provide a narrative easy to read. Raffaello Pantucci (2015) gives a good background to the attacks but only outlines the attacks themselves.

12. *Coroner's Inquests*, 2010–2011.

13. See O'Neal and McGrory, 2006, and Phillips, 2006, as examples of this widely accepted perspective.

14. This methodology is becoming popular among terrorist scholars. See Cruickshank, 2014; Vidino, 2014; Schuurmann, Eijkman, and Bakker, 2015; and Sageman, 2017.

15. The reason for some non-English press reporting is that some of the cases involve activities in foreign countries, especially Pakistan.

16. The *sub judice* ban does not extend to the foreign press, and sometimes the reporting in the U.S. press scoops the local press. See the Van Natta, Sciolino, and Grey, 2006, article in the *New York Times* of August 28, 2006, on Operation Overt, when reporting on it was banned in Britain. Readers in Britain could not access this article on the Internet at the time.

17. The discovery of a lessons-learned report on three of the London bombing attempts five years after their detection and drafted by their coordinator, Rashid Rauf in Pakistan, has deeply affected our understanding of these respective plots. See Robertson, Cruickshank, and Lister, 2012a and 2012b. Likewise, the proceedings of the *Coroner's Inquests into the London Bombings of 7 July 2005,* helped further our understanding of that attack, the subject of Chapter 4.

18. The difficulty of this task is compounded by the fact that intelligence agencies believe it is not their duty to educate the public as to the facts of an investigation and are satisfied to allow grossly mistaken beliefs to survive in the public domain.

Chapter 1

1. Winder, 2004.

2. Mandaville, 2010: 5.

3. See Bowen, 2014, for a snapshot of the diversity.

4. K. Malik, 2009: 36–47.

5. K. Malik, 2009: 72.

6. Kepel, 1994: 171.

7. See Gest, 2010.

8. See also Kepel, 1994: 123–220; Vidino, 2010: 114–124, for a good summary of this internal infighting within Muslim political organizations in Britain at the time. However, these authors focus on the competition among Muslim leaders. The account in this chapter, like Malik, 2009, focuses more on the developments on the street and the emergence of an Islamist counterculture hostile to the British government and society.

9. Quoted in K. Malik, 2009: 180.

10. K. Malik, 2009: xx.

11. See K. Malik, 2009, and Pantucci, 2015, for examples.

12. Sageman, 2008: 3–12; quote is from page 7. Despite HuT agitating on behalf of Bosnia, the people going to Bosnia to help out the refugees were unaffiliated with it. See also the discussion of Babar Ahmad's experiences in the Tooting Circle section below.

13. In Benedict Anderson's (1991) sense of the term.

14. Husain, 2007: 74.

15. Nawaz, 2012: 98.

16. Gest, 2010: 6; Husain, 2007: 80.

17. Wiktorowicz, 2005: 7–9.

18. See Bittner, 1963. In this definition of "radical," the vast majority of radicals are not violent, but a few may eventually become so.

19. This new "Islamic marriage" was neither Western nor Eastern, and very frequently ended in divorce (Husain, 2007: 69–70).

20. K. Malik, 2009: 45.

21. Maher, 2006; K. Malik, 2009: 108–109.

22. Wiktorowicz, 2005: 9. See also Kenney, 2018.

23. Wiktorowicz, 2005: 9–10.

24. Husain, 2007: 135.

25. Husain, 2007: 148.

26. Fandy, 2001: 115–194.

27. Lia, 2008: 117; Abdal Hakim, 2004: 20.

28. *Ministère Public c/ Ramda*, 2006: 14–27.

29. See Abdal Hakim, 2004: 30–34; Kepel, 2002: 267–271; Lia, 2008: 182–189.

30. Abdal Hakim, 2004: 21.

31. *U.S. v. Mustafa* (henceforth *Mustafa*), May 8, 2014: 3058–3070. He arrived too late to be part of the Afghan jihad, as the Soviets had already withdrawn from the country a year earlier.

32. *Mustafa*, May 8, 2014: 3086–3100.

33. *Mustafa*, May 8, 2014: 3102–3115. A few authors claim that during this last trip to Bosnia, Abu Hamza was not welcomed there and may have been expelled by the local mujahedin. See Pantucci, 2015: 114.

34. Kepel, 2002: 272–273; al Misri, 2000/2009: 169–175, explaining his reasoning for closing down the newsletter. See also *Mustafa*, May 8, 2014: 3119–3127.

35. Lambert, 2011: 82; *Mustafa*, May 8, 2014: 3169–3172.

36. Lambert, 2011: 155–217; A. Baker, 2009. Baker is a Salafi radical (in Britain in the sense defined earlier, but not in Saudi Arabia [he is in fact mainstream in that country], where he also lives) but a quietist one, strongly opposed to neojihadi violence.

37. A. Baker, 2009: 33–40; 288–294.

38. See Klausen, 2010: 18–19, 22, 24–25 (these nonexistent links are even quantified in Barbieri and Klausen, 2012!) or Simcox, Stuart, and Ahmed, 2010: 451–455, for example. They claimed that many of the convicted French global neojihadis were strongly linked to Abu Hamza. They were not. They were part of the Abu Qatada network and distributed his material throughout Europe. Abu Qatada financially supported them. They were linked not with al Qaeda but with the Abu Zubaydah/ibn al Sheikh al Libi network around the Khalden training camp in Afghanistan. See Omar Nasiri, 2006: 264–303, *Ministère Public c/ Bensakhria, Tcharek, Aknouche et autres*, 2004, and *Ministère Public c/ Daoudi, Beghal, Bounour et autres*, 2005. Only in the middle of 2000 did bin Laden gain control over this network in a hostile takeover. The alleged links to Abu Hamza and Finsbury Park Mosque were propagated by journalists Sean O'Neill and Daniel McGrory, 2006: 76–94, 116–118, without any references.

39. The United Nations and the International Criminal Tribunal for the former Yugoslavia called the Omarska Concentration Camp a death camp. According to survivors, about 30 men were nightly selected for murder for the three-month duration of the camp. See Greve, 1992, and International Court of Justice, 2007: 172 (paragraph 312).

40. Personal interview with Babar Ahmad, March 26, 2014.

41. *U.S. v. Abu Gaith* (henceforth *Abu Gaith*), March 10, 2014: 439–440.

42. *Mustafa*, April 28, 2014: 1571.

43. *U.S. v. Medunjanin*, March 29, 2012: Badat deposition transcript, government exhibit 450T; *Abu Gaith*, March 10, 2014: 416–486; March 11, 2014: 493–685; *Mustafa*, April 28, 2014: 1527–1756; April 29, 2014: 1759–1873.

44. Neither his London contact nor the trainer in Afghanistan were members of al Qaeda at the time. The non-British Muslims, mostly North African immigrants, had more of a pipeline from people around Abu Qatada to Khalden via the Algerian guesthouses in Peshawar and Jalalabad. See note 38 above.

45. These websites were forced off the Internet shortly after 9/11.

46. See Sageman, 2016: 111–161; 2017: 1–47.

47. The alleged 2003 Ricin Plot or more formally Operation Springbourne was simply not credible when tested at trial as the jury rejected the terrorism charges for the defendants. One of them, Kamel Bourgass, was convicted of conspiracy to cause a public nuisance after being convicted of murdering a policeman who had come to arrest him. The other four defendants were acquitted of all charges. See Archer and Bawdon, 2010.

48. *Regina v. Omar Khyam et al.*, 2006–2007 (henceforth *Khyam*, with either 2006 or 2007 dates), October 4, 2006: 61–68; October 6, 2006: 1–4.

49. *Khyam*, September 14, 2006: 150–151.

50. *Khyam*, September 14, 2006: 25, 27–28.

51. *Khyam*, March 24, 2006: 70. See also Harris, Wazir, and Burke, 2001; and "Taliban 'Martyr' Dies," 2001.

52. *Khyam*, September 14, 2006: 38–51.

53. *Khyam*, September 14, 2006: 56.

54. *Khyam*, September 14, 2006: 62–69.

55. *Khyam*, November 21, 2006: 41–49, 55.

56. Cobain and Vasagar, 2007.

57. *Regina v. Mohammed Shakil et al.*, 2008 (henceforth *Shakil*, with 2008 dates), June 17: 33.

58. *Khyam*, November 21, 2006: 99–100, 104.

59. *Khyam*, November 29, 2006: 35, 78. Amin testified at the trial of the conspirators that when he later met Abu Munthir in Pakistan in 2002, he was surprised because he had not thought of him as a jihadi when they had met in Luton.

60. *Khyam*, November 21, 2006: 52.

61. *Khyam*, November 21, 2006: 56.

62. *Khyam*, November 21, 2006: 62–64.

63. *Khyam*, November 21, 2006: 69–70; November 29, 2006: 84–85; December 1, 2006: 54–56. Amin had been tortured by Pakistani interrogators before being extradited to England in early 2005. He later claimed that, in his police interview at Paddington station, he had simply repeated the lies that had been previously extracted under torture. In time, he said he came to understand he would no longer be tortured in England and changed his story.

64. *Khyam*, November 21, 2006: 66–68; 99–101.

65. *Khyam*, November 21, 2006: 73–75; 101–102.

66. *Khyam*, September 25, 2006: 9–18, 25.

67. Lambert and Githens-Mazer, 2009: 35–37.

68. *Khyam*, September 25, 2006: 30–31.

69. I am only giving this nickname used by his friends since this person has never been arrested or charged with any terrorism offense.

70. *Khyam*, September 25, 2006: 32–42.

71. MacPherson, 1999: section 6.39.

72. See Report of the National Advisory Commission on Civil Disorders, 1968.

73. See Fassin, 2013.

74. Foley, 2013: 248.

75. Foley, 2013: 249; but see also Phillips, 2006; and Thomas, 2003.

76. Foley, 2013: 198–201.

77. *Terrorism Act 2000*: sections 11, 15, 39, 41, 42, 44, 57, 58, and 59.

Chapter 2

1. See Archer and Bawden, 2010.

2. *Khyam*, September 25, 2006: 47–48. At the trial, Rahman Adam testified that Kashmir and Afghanistan were different because Muslims were just defending themselves, but he insisted that there was no justification for 9/11, the 2004 bombings in Madrid, or 2005 bombings in London. Yet he had bought half a ton of fertilizer in November 2003 in a plot to carry out an explosion in Britain. Instead of completely dismissing his testimony as pure self-exonerating fabrication, I believe that he felt as he testified about 9/11 but changed his mind two years later after his experience in Pakistan and the Iraq war. He had probably changed his views again by the time of the trial three years later.

3. *Khyam*, September 14, 2006: 70–72.

4. *Khyam*, September 14, 2006: 74. Khyam later concluded that 9/11 had been tactically unwise because it had led to the loss of Afghanistan.

5. *Khyam*, September 14, 2006: 91–92.

6. *Khyam*, September 14, 2006: 89.

7. *Khyam*, December 1, 2006: 43.

8. Harris, Wazir, and Burke, 2001; *Khyam*, September 14, 2006: 90. See also the Crawley and Luton sections in Chapter 1.

9. *Khyam*, November 21, 2006: 81; December 1, 2006: 65–66.

10. *Khyam*, April 24, 2006: 84.

11. *Khyam*, November 21, 2006: 84–86, 96; December 1, 2006: 67.

12. *Khyam*, March 1, 2007: 57–58.

13. Gilbert, 2007.

14. *Khyam*, March 23, 2006: 10–20; April 25, 2006: 124.

15. *Khyam*, March 30, 2006: 65; April 25, 2006: 76–78.

16. Gilbert, 2007.

17. *Khyam*, March 23, 2006: 24–30; April 24, 2006: 10–13.

18. Nawaz, 2012: 133.

19. *Khyam*, March 24, 2006: 11.

20. *Khyam*, March 30, 2006: 60–63; April 4, 2006: 57, 59. Later to the FBI, he claimed that he had been paid by the interviewer $500 or $600 to "juice it up," but in court, he admitted that this was not true.

21. Gilbert, 2007.

22. *Khyam*, March 24, 2006: 18–26.

23. *Khyam*, March 24, 2006: 17, 21–22, 27–29.

24. This may have been Ahmed Omar Saeed Sheikh, arrested on 5 February 2002 for the kidnapping of *Wall Street Journal* reporter Daniel Pearl (Sageman, 2008: 3–12). Babar's identity card was found on the body of one of Ahmed Sheikh's co-conspirators in Karachi around that time.

25. *Khyam*, March 30, 2006: 5–6; April 5, 2006: 113–118, 128–130. The timing of the two events—the burial of the weapons and Rahman's departure—is a bit confusing as Babar gave slightly conflicting testimonies at trial. See also April 24, 2006: 23–24.

26. *Khyam*, March 24, 2006: 45–48; April 24, 2006: 17–18, 24.

27. The best description of the location of the village comes from *Regina v. Mohammed Shakil et al.*, 2009 (henceforth *Shakil*, with 2009 dates), January 9: 46–53.

28. *Khyam*, April 24, 2006: 97–100; *Shakil*, January 9, 2009: 67–68.

29. His true name is Nashwan Abdal Razzaq Abdal Baqi, born in 1961 in Iraq. He was a former Iraqi military officer, who had joined al Qaeda in the late 1990s and later became its top military commander in the Afghanistan-Pakistan theater of operations. See U.S. Department of Defense, 2007, and *U.S. v. Abdal Hadi al Iraqi*, 2014.

30. *Khyam*, November 21, 2006: 90, 99–110.

31. *Khyam*, November 21, 2006: 113–114; November 29, 2006: 34–38. At his trial, Amin retracted this statement, which he claimed had been extracted under torture. He denied he ever met Abu Munthir in Pakistan, but his original confession seems to fit with other testimonies.

32. *Khyam*, November 21, 2006: 111–116; November 29, 2006: 38–39, 67.

33. *Khyam*, November 29, 2006: 39.

34. *Khyam*, December 1, 2006: 84–85.

35. *Khyam*, March 1, 2007: 55.

36. *Khyam*, September 14, 2006: 96–99, 118.

37. *Khyam*, September 14, 2006: 99, 151–154.

38. *Khyam*, September 14, 2006: 101.

39. *Khyam*, September 14, 2006: 103; September 25, 2006: 71.

40. *Khyam*, September 25, 2006: 48–51, 75–76.

41. *Khyam*, March 24, 2006: 28–30, 51–52, 61.

42. *Khyam*, March 24, 2006: 55, 59, 62, 67–69, 73. Around that time, someone approached him and asked him to help carry out an assassination of President Musharraf in mid-February 2003. See *Khyam*, March 30, 2006: 6.

43. *Khyam*, September 25, 2006: 79.

44. *Khyam*, September 25, 2006: 52–65; June 6: 124.

45. *Regina v. Momin Khawaja*, 2005 (henceforth *Khawaja*, 2005), June 8: 395–400, 411, 515–519; *Regina v. Momin Khawaja*, 2008 (henceforth *Khawaja*, 2008), exhibit no 63: 15, 45; Reason for Judgment, October 29, 2008 (conclusion of *Khawaja*, 2008, henceforth Khawaja Judgment): 5–6.

46. *Khawaja*, 2008, exhibit no. 63: 45.

47. *Khawaja*, 2005, June 6: 145, 147–148.

48. Khawaja Judgment: 6.

49. *Khawaja*, 2005, June 8: 517–518; Khawaja Judgment: 5.

50. *Khyam*, September 14, 2006: 142.

51. *Khawaja*, 2005, June 6: 97–98.

52. *Khawaja*, 2005, June 6: 124–127; *Khyam*, September 27, 2006: 99.

53. *Khyam*, September 25, 2006: 86–92, 97.

54. *Khyam*, September 25, 2006: 93–97.

55. See *Khyam*, September 15, 2006: 146–147, for Khyam's version and September 26, 2006: 71, for Adam's version.

56. *Khyam*, September 25, 2006: 102, 108–111.

57. *Khyam*, November 21, 2006: 118–124. There were several contradictory accounts of this meeting, but the one retained here is the most consistent with other testimonies.

58. *Khyam*, September 25, 2006: 113.

59. *Khyam*, November 21, 2006: 122; November 29, 2006: 70; November 30, 2006: 80–81.

60. *Khyam*, December 12, 2006: 40–41; November 30, 2006: 116.

61. *Khyam*, March 1, 2007: 58.

62. *Khyam*, September 25, 2006: 114, 117–119. Adam called Mahmood "Hormones" because of his constant talk about women.

63. Murray and German, 2005.

64. *Khyam*, September 14, 2006: 94.

65. *Khyam*, September 25, 2006: 122–128.

66. *Khyam*, March 24, 2006: 76–79.

67. Babar did not remember seeing Khyam at that meeting and believed that he was in Karachi at the time (*Khyam*, March 24, 2006: 105). Other participants confirmed that Khyam was there all the time during that week.

68. *Khyam*, March 24, 2006: 84–87.

69. *Khyam*, March 24, 2006: 88–89; April 28, 2006: 12.

70. *Khyam*, December 12, 2006: 40–41.

71. *Khyam*, March 24, 2006: 89–90.

72. *Khyam*, September 14, 2006: 94–95.

73. *Khyam*, March 24, 2006: 90–93.

74. *Khyam*, March 24, 2006: 94–98.

75. *Khyam*, March 24, 2006: 99–105.

76. *Khyam*, October 20, 2006: 83.

77. *Khyam*, March 24, 2006: 105–110; *Shakil*, January 27, 2009: 67.

78. *Khyam*, September 25, 2006: 104, 132–139; September 26, 2006: 8.

79. Abu Mahmoud al Filastini, via Amin, did not seem to trust the British boys and tried to discourage them by raising all kinds of questions; see *Khyam*, November 29, 2006: 46.

80. *Khyam*, March 27, 2006: 7–11.

81. *Khyam*, March 27, 2006: 13–17; September 15, 2006: 22–23.

82. *Khyam*, October 20, 2006: 81.

83. *Khyam*, October 6, 2006: 5–20.

84. *Khyam*, October 20, 2006: 69.

85. *Khyam*, September 26, 2006: 13.

86. Casciani, 2007.

87. *Khyam*, September 25, 2006: 141–142.

88. *Khyam*, March 27, 2006: 18–20; September 15, 2006: 26–27.

89. *Khyam*, March 5, 2007: 96; March 27, 2006: 21–27; September 15, 2006: 10–11, 28.

90. *Khyam*, March 24, 2006: 30–31; March 27, 2006: 28–30; November 21, 2006: 131.

91. *Khyam*, September 26, 2006: 3, 8.

92. *Khyam*, September 26, 2006: 19–26.

93. *Khyam*, March 27, 2006: 31, 36; September 26, 2006: 46; March 12, 2007: 45.

94. *Khyam*, March 12, 2007: 42–43, 47, 56–58.

95. *Khyam*, March 12, 2007: 46. This was Shujah's version. Babar remembered that Shujah was present in the room during the conversation, but did not seem to pay much attention to it; see *Khyam*, March 27, 2006: 2006: 35–38.

96. *Khyam*, March 27, 2006: 41–42; 53–55.

97. This account runs counter to Shiv Malik's (2007a) article about the "Jihadi House Parties of Hate." Malik's source was Hassan Butt, who was later discredited on other matters. Babar, in his testimony, was quite careful about providing details on funding.

98. *Khyam*, March 24, 2006: 73; March 27, 2006: 22–26, 59, 61–64; April 3, 2006: 45; September 26, 2006: 73–74; March 12, 2007: 45.

99. *Khyam*, April 27, 2006: 72; November 29, 2006: 46; December 12, 2006: 48–49, 76, 83, 89–91.

100. *Khyam*, December 12, 2006: 48, 71. At trial, Amin retracted his confession to the British police. He denied he ever participated in explosive training and claimed that he had simply repeated statements allegedly extorted through torture and intimidation in Pakistan. However, the story fits the rest of the evidence.

101. *Khyam*, November 29, 2006: 47–52; November 30, 2006: 75; December 12, 2006: 46, 68.

102. *Khyam*, November 30, 2006: 44–47; December 12, 2006: 77, 80–81.

103. *Khyam*, November 30, 2006: 3, 4, 46, 76–79; December 12, 2006: 70.

104. *Khyam*, September 15, 2006: 44; September 26, 2006: 52–53.

105. *Khyam*, March 27, 2006: 77–87; September 26, 2006: 54–56.

106. *Khyam*, March 27, 2006: 88, 97, 104; September 15, 2006: 41–43; September 26, 2006: 58.

107. *Khyam*, March 27, 2006: 112–121.

108. *Khyam*, March 28, 2006: 8 – 15, 20–22. The remaining packages were recovered in Khyam's family backyard at the time of his arrest a year later.

109. *Khyam*, March 28, 2006: 23–34.

110. *Khyam*, March 27, 2006: 109, 118.

111. *Khyam*, March 28, 2006: 37–39. This was Babar's testimony. Shujah denied he ever brought the scales with him and said his cousin Ahmed Ali Khan told him to bring boots and fleece. See March 12, 2007: 47–48.

112. *Khyam*, April 3, 2006: 33, 102.

113. The legal proceedings and the press called the Gorque camp the Malakand camp. However, it is clear from its location that it was not in Malakand but in Upper Dir, about six hours north of Malakand, above the village of Gorque, where the maulana's madrassa was located. See *Shakil*, January 27, 2009: 46–53, for the best description of its location.

114. *Khyam*, March 28, 2006: 41–42, 45–54; September 28, 2006: 68.

115. *Khyam*, March 28, 2006: 55–57, 65; September 26, 2006: 62.

116. *Khawaja*, 2008, LIT Evidence Book, chapter 3: 45.

117. *Khyam*, September 26, 2006: 61–69; March 12, 2007: 50.

118. *Khyam*, March 28, 2006: 65–66, 78, 85–87; April 3, 2006: 97–100.

119. Khawaja Judgment: 13; *Khyam*, March 28, 2006: 88–94.

120. *Khyam*, March 28, 2006: 97–98.

121. *Khyam*, October 6, 2006: 36–41. This is of course Akbar's testimony at trial, where he denied knowing that there was a paramilitary training camp planned. The prosecutor

suggested that he knowingly went to Pakistan to attend the camp. Akbar admitted that Gulzar was talking to him about jihad at that time. It is hard to conceive that, if they were such close friends, Akbar had not known about the camp.

122. *Khyam*, September 15, 2006: 63; October 6, 2006: 51–55.

123. I deal more extensively with Mohammed Sidique Khan's and Mohammed Shakil's respective backgrounds in the next chapter.

124. *Shakil*, June 17, 2008: 31–39.

125. *Khyam*, March 28, 2006: 101–105; *Khawaja*, 2008, exhibit no. 9: 16–17.

126. *Khyam*, March 28, 2006: 106–110; September 15, 2006: 67; October 6, 2006: 61–74; *Shakil*, April 18, 2008: 8–9; June 17, 2008: 40; January 27, 2009: 37–63.

127. *Khyam*, March 31, 2006: 4; April 3, 2006: 101; October 6, 2008: 75–77; *Shakil*, June 17, 2008: 42.

128. *Khyam*, March 28, 2006: 111–115, 119. Babar gave the video to a friend when he left Pakistan.

129. *Khyam*, March 29, 2006: 50; *Coroner's Inquests*, 2010–2011, (henceforth *Coroner's Inquests*, with specific dates and page numbers given in subsequent citations for testimonial evidence and specific page number given for documentary evidence admitted at the inquests, as is the case here) MPS4–62, which is part of Babar's debrief by the FBI on 12 May 2004.

130. *Khyam*, March 28, 2006: 120.

131. *Khyam*, September 26, 2006: 76.

132. *Khyam*, October 6, 2006: 81–82.

133. *Khyam*, October 20, 2006: 128.

134. Although global neojihadis believe they represent the whole Muslim ummah, in fact they represent only their very small global neojihadi community, which I call the neo-ummah to distinguish it from the real ummah.

135. *Shakil*, June 17, 2008: 40.

136. Neumann and Evans, 2014: 69, describe this camp in the following way: "The technical training and oversight provided by al-Qaeda was critical to converting a group of (mostly) clueless young activists into halfway competent operators." This contradicts the multiple sworn firsthand descriptions of the camp in the various relevant trials.

137. *Khawaja*, 2008, exhibit no. 9: 19; *Khyam*, March 12, 2007: 52–53; March 28, 2006: 122–123, 127–128; March 29, 2006: 6–8; October 6, 2006: 82; March 1, 2007: 54.

138. *Khyam*, March 29, 2006: 10–11; September 14, 2006: 170–173.

139. *Khyam*, March 29, 2006: 11–13.

140. Intelligence and Security Committee (henceforth ISC), 2009: 7, 27. MI5 defined an al-Qaeda facilitation network as a group of extremists who support the al-Qaeda cause and who are involved in providing financial and logistic support rather than being directly involved in terrorist attack planning.

141. Khawaja Judgment: 13.

142. *Khyam*, March 29, 2006: 14–16.

143. *Khyam*, March 28, 2006: 127; March 29, 2006: 23–29; September 15, 2006: 80–84.

144. *Khyam*, March 29, 2006: 29–35.

145. *Khyam*, September 26, 2006: 76–80. From now on, I shall refer to Rahman Adam as Anthony Garcia, following his official change of name. On the reasons for changing his name, see *Khyam*, September 27, 2006: 69.

146. *Khyam*, September 26, 2006: 91–92.

147. *Khyam*, September 15, 2006: 108–112, 119, 154–155; March 12, 2007: 53, 55.

148. Sidique and Shakil are the subject of the next chapter.

149. *Khyam*, October 20, 2006: 130.

150. *Khyam*, October 6, 2006: 83–84, 86; October 30, 2006: 34–35; March 9, 2007: 46.

151. *Khyam*, October 6, 2006: 28, 94–95, 102–103; October 16, 2006: 2–17; October 20, 2006: 130–131; October 30, 2006: 29–30, 89; March 9, 2007: 6–7.

152. *Khyam*, March 1, 2007: 58–59.

153. *Khawaja*, 2005, June 6: 143–144.

154. *Khawaja*, 2008, exhibit no. 63: 3.

155. *Khawaja*, 2008, exhibit no. 63: 7.

156. *Khawaja*, 2008, exhibit no. 63: 8.

157. *Khawaja*, 2008, exhibit no. 63: 19.

158. *Khawaja*, 2008, exhibit no. 63: 62, 63.

159. *Khawaja*, 2008, exhibit no. 63: 82.

160. *Khawaja*, 2008, exhibit no. 63: 83–85. This very long e-mail is an excellent illustration of the model of turning to political violence presented in Sageman, 2017: 1–47.

161. *Khawaja*, 2008, exhibit no. 63: 88.

162. *Khyam*, March 29, 2006: 36, 40; *Khawaja*, 2008, exhibit no. 9: 61; Khawaja Judgment: 11–12.

163. *Khawaja*, 2008, exhibit no. 9: 61; Khawaja Judgment: 20.

164. *Khawaja*, 2008, exhibit no. 9: 123–125.

165. *Khawaja*, 2008, exhibit no. 63: 144.

166. *Khawaja*, 2008, exhibit no. 63: 42. Zeba did not forgive him. She later enthusiastically shared her e-mails with Khawaja with the Canadian authorities.

167. *Khawaja*, 2008, exhibit no. 9: 22.

168. Khawaja Judgment: 21. Siddiqui later denied he ever wanted to be a suicide bomber, but his diary suggests otherwise; see Casciani, 2007.

169. *Khawaja*, 2008, exhibit no. 9: 23–24.

170. *Khyam*, September 26, 2006: 100.

171. *Khyam*, September 26, 2006: 100–103. This of course was Garcia's version on direct examination. He knew it was an ingredient for a bomb but just thought it was another way to help the resistance in Kashmir.

172. *Khyam*, September 26, 2006: 109–110; March 1, 2007: 64.

173. *Khyam*, September 26, 2006: 111–119.

174. *Khyam*, March 9, 2007: 8–9.

175. *Khyam*, September 26, 2006: 120–135; October 16, 2006: 35–38; October 30, 2006: 129–143; March 9, 2007: 13; *Khawaja*, 2008, LIT Evidence Book, chapter 1: 2. At the trial, Hussain claimed that he thought the bag was full of sand, but I suspect that he knew that it was fertilizer.

176. *Khyam*, March 29, 2006: 35, 49; March 31, 2006: 70–72; *Khawaja*, 2008, exhibit no. 9: 26.

177. Khawaja Judgment: 21.

178. *Khyam*, March 12, 2007: 55–56. He was chanting on the police wiretaps played at trial and claimed he was often chanting when others were talking and not listening to what they were saying.

179. *Khyam*, October 6, 2006: 93–94, 111–117; March 9, 2007: 47–48.

180. Khawaja Judgment: 21.

181. *Khyam*, September 26, 2006: 136–138.

182. *Khyam*, September 15, 2006: 125–130.

183. *Khyam*, March 31, 2006: 34–36, between the last week of 2003 and the first 10 days of 2004.

184. *Khyam*, March 29, 2006: 53; March 31, 2006: 39–40; 45; April 4, 2006: 32–35.

185. *Khyam*, March 29, 2006: 52; March 31, 2006: 36.

186. *Khyam*, November 29, 2006: 91–93; November 30, 2006: 37–40; March 5, 2007: 109–110. At trial, Amin retracted his confession on this subject to the London police.

187. *Khyam*, March 29, 2006: 53.

188. *Khyam*, March 29, 2006: 53–57; April 4, 2006: 36–39.

189. *Khyam*, April 4, 2006: 37.

190. *Khyam*, March 29, 2006: 57–61.

191. *Khyam*, March 12, 2007: 59–60. The police later found a list of universities in Islamabad in his room.

192. Khawaja Judgment: 22.

193. *Khyam*, September 14, 2006: 158.

194. *Khyam*, September 15, 2006: 119; October 18, 2006: 42–44.

195. Khawaja Judgment: 23.

196. ISC, 2009: 8.

197. *Khyam*, March 1, 2007: 67.

198. *Khyam*, March 9, 2007: 15–16. This is of course Hussain's version of events at trial.

199. *Khyam*, March 8, 2007: 38. Qayum's cautiousness earned him the nickname of "Bashful Dwarf" with the police.

200. ISC, 2009: 10; *Khyam*, March 2, 2007: 15.

201. Khawaja Judgment: 23.

202. *Khyam*, March 2, 2007: 15.

203. *Khyam*, March 31, 2006: 36–37.

204. *Khawaja*, 2008, LIT Evidence Book, chapter 2: 19.

205. *Khyam*, September 15, 2006: 117.

206. *Khyam*, October 6, 2006: 42–46, 117–118.

207. *Khawaja*, 2008, LIT Evidence Book, chapter 2: 19.

208. ISC, 2009: 10.

209. *Khawaja*, 2008, LIT Evidence Book, chapter 2: 23–38; Khawaja Judgment: 24–25.

210. *Coroner's Inquests*, MPS5–15.

211. *Khawaja*, 2008, LIT Evidence Book, chapter 3: 49.

212. *Khawaja*, 2008, LIT Evidence Book, chapter 3: 59–60.

213. *Khawaja*, 2008, LIT Evidence Book, chapter 3: 63–74.

214. ISC, 2009: 11.

215. Khawaja Judgment: 26.

216. The full transcript of this long conversation was entered into evidence at the Khawaja trial.

217. *Khawaja*, 2008, LIT Evidence Book, chapter 4: 91–100.

218. *Khawaja*, 2008, LIT Evidence Book, chapter 4: 100–104.

219. *Khawaja*, 2008, LIT Evidence Book, chapter 4: 106–111.

220. *Khawaja*, 2008, LIT Evidence Book, chapter 4: 111–112.

221. *Khawaja*, 2008, LIT Evidence Book, chapter 4: 112.

222. *Khawaja*, 2008, LIT Evidence Book, chapter 4: 112–113.

223. *Khawaja*, 2008, LIT Evidence Book, chapter 4: 113–115.

224. *Khawaja*, 2008, LIT Evidence Book, chapter 4: 116.

225. *Coroner's Inquests*, SYS11080–4.

226. *Khyam*, March 2, 2007: 15–16; ISC, 2009: 10.

227. *Khyam*, October 30, 2006: 44.

228. *Khyam*, September 15, 2006: 135–143; March 2, 2007: 16–17, 33.

229. *Khyam*, October 16, 2006: 71–72; October 18, 2006: 49–50.

230. *Khyam*, March 29, 2006: 64.

231. *Khyam*, November 24, 2006: 51–53; March 5, 2007: 102–103.

232. *Khyam*, March 5, 2007: 103. Amin later repudiated in court this part of his Metropolitan Police confession.

233. *Khyam*, November 29, 2006: 48–49.

234. *Khyam*, November 24, 2006: 27–28.

235. *Khyam*, March 5, 2007: 104–107. Again, Amin later repudiated in court this part of his Metropolitan Police confession.

236. *Khyam*, November 24, 2006: 38–41.

237. See the conversation between Khyam and Akbar on March 10, 2004, reproduced below.

238. *Khyam*, October 16, 2006: 48, 54–56.

239. *Khyam*, September 27, 2006: 11; October 16, 2006: 67–68.

240. *Khawaja*, 2008, LIT Evidence Book, chapter 5: 121.

241. *Khyam*, September 26, 2006: 139–140; September 27, 2006: 55; October 18, 2006: 20–40.

242. *Khawaja*, 2008, LIT Evidence Book, chapter 6: 127–129.

243. *Khawaja*, 2008, LIT Evidence Book, chapter 6: 130–131.

244. *Khawaja*, 2008, LIT Evidence Book, chapter 6: 131–132.

245. *Khawaja*, 2008, LIT Evidence Book, chapter 6: 132–133.

246. *Khawaja*, 2008, LIT Evidence Book, chapter 6: 133–134.

247. *Khawaja*, 2008, LIT Evidence Book, chapter 6: 135–138.

248. *Khawaja*, 2008, LIT Evidence Book, chapter 6: 139–140.

249. *Khawaja*, 2008, LIT Evidence Book, chapter 6: 140, 143.

250. *Cononer's Inquests*, SYS11080–4.

251. *Khyam*, March 2, 2007: 38–41.

252. *Khyam*, March 2, 2007: 42–43.

253. *Khyam*, October 16, 2006: 74; October 19, 2006: 49. The following was of course Akbar's version of events at the trial as Mahmood refused to testify at trial.

254. *Khyam*, October 16, 2006: 75; October 19, 2006: 50–51.

255. *Coroner's Inquests*, SYS11080–4.

256. *Khyam*, September 15, 2006: 118.

257. *Khyam*, October 19, 2006: 58.

258. *Khyam*, October 16, 2006: 8; October 19, 2006: 61; March 2, 2007: 44–49; *Khawaja*, 2008, LIT Evidence Book, chapter 7: 170.

259. *Khyam*, March 12, 2007: 86.

260. *Khyam*, March 2, 2007: 50; October 19, 2006: 70.

261. *Khyam*, March 9, 2007: 21.

262. *Khyam*, October 19, 2006: 74–77; March 2, 2007: 52–54.

263. *Khyam*, March 2, 2007: 54–55.

264. *Khyam*, October 19, 2006: 83.

265. *Khyam*, March 2, 2007: 56.

266. *Khyam*, October 19, 2006: 92–93.

267. ISC, 2009: 11.

268. Khawaja Judgment: 28.

269. *Khyam*, March 2, 2007: 58, 66. The Bluewater Shopping Centre was Europe's largest shopping complex with a daily average of 74,000 visits.

270. *Khawaja*, 2008, LIT Evidence Book, chapter 8: 180. AMEC is an international project management and services company, involved in oil and gas exploration and building facilities for offices and infrastructure. It had a branch in Crawley. It was involved in rebuilding works after the 9/11 attacks in New York and Iraq and was supporting the military effort in Pakistan. There had been a lot of publicity about what the company did. See also *Khyam*, March 2, 2007: 51–52.

271. *Khawaja*, 2008, LIT Evidence Book, chapter 8: 180, 182.

272. *Khawaja*, 2008, LIT Evidence Book, chapter 8: 184–190.

273. *Khawaja*, 2008, LIT Evidence Book, chapter 8: 190.

274. *Khawaja*, 2008, LIT Evidence Book, chapter 8: 191–192.

275. *Khawaja*, 2008, LIT Evidence Book, chapter 8: 192–193.

276. *Coroner's Inquests*, SYS11080–4.

277. *Khyam*, March 9, 2007: 22–24, 81.

278. *Khyam*, September 27, 2006: 48–53.

279. *Khyam*, September 15, 2006: 112–113.

280. Khawaja Judgment: 28; *Khyam*, March 2, 2007: 67.

281. *Coroner's Inquests*, MPS5–63.

282. *Khyam*, March 2, 2007: 68–70.

283. *Khyam*, March 2, 2007: 75. This amount of aluminum powder could make an explosive device weighing a total of about one kilogram. It would also require a detonator and probably a booster. *Khyam*, March 5, 2007: 3.

284. *Khyam*, March 2, 2007: 73; March 12, 2007: 93.

285. *Khyam*, November 24, 2006: 58–62; November 29, 2006: 40.

286. *Khyam*, March 29, 2006: 66.

287. *Shakil*, January 27, 2009: 110.

288. See Hayman, 2010: 340–343.

Chapter 3

1. House of Commons, 2006: 13.

2. *Coroner's Inquests*, February 16, 2011: 4–5.

3. On his passport, his name is given as Mohammad Sidique Khan (*Coroner's Inquests*, INQ11405–10). Given the various spellings of his name, most writers use his initials MSK to refer to him. I have chosen Sidique or Sid because this is how his friends referred to him.

4. ISC, 2009: 57; Gardham, 2010b.

5. House of Commons, 2006: 13.

6. *Shakil*, June 6, 2008: 66.

7. *Shakil*, June 6, 2008: 64.

8. *Shakil*, June 17, 2008: 7–8.

9. *Shakil*, May 20, 2008: 21.

10. S. Malik, 2007b. This should be taken with a grain of salt. In the last chapter, we saw that Malik, 2007a, was erroneous and I found no other reference to the "Mullah boys."

11. *Shakil*, June 18, 2008: 23.

12. S. Malik, 2007b.

13. K. Malik, 2009: 43–45.

14. House of Commons, 2006: 14–15; *Shakil*, May 20, 2008: 20–21; June 17, 2008: 24–33.

15. *Shakil*, June 17, 2008: 10–11; June 18, 2008: 19–20.

16. S. Malik, 2007b; *Shakil*, June 11, 2008: 22; June 17, 2008: 29.

17. *Coroner's Inquests*, February 16, 2011: 5–9; *Shakil*, May 20, 2008: 27–29; June 6, 2008: 63; June 11, 2008: 7; June 16, 2008: 27.

18. *Shakil*, May 20, 2008: 29–40; May 22, 2008: 11–16.

19. *Shakil*, May 22, 2008: 8–9; ISC, 2009: 17, 57.

20. *Coroner's Inquests*, February 16, 2011: 104; February 24, 2011: 74–79; WYP11–1.

21. *Shakil*, June 17, 2008: 29. S. Malik (2007b) claims that Sidique tried to recruit Omar Sharif and Asif Hanif in Manchester in the summer of 2001. Sharif and Hanif were the suicide bombers at the Mike's Place Café in Tel Aviv on 30 April 2003. However, as mentioned earlier, Malik's reporting is not reliable.

22. *Shakil*, May 20, 2008: 39–59.

23. Martin Gilbertson, *Coroner's Inquests*, February 16, 2011: 121–122. His erroneous sensationalistic claims are still taken seriously.

24. *Shakil*, May 20, 2008: 65–65; June 11, 2008: 26–27.

25. *Shakil*, June 17, 2008: 12.

26. *Shakil*, June 22, 2008: 34.

27. *Shakil*, June 17, 2008: 13.

28. *Shakil*, May 20, 2008: 72.

29. *Shakil*, June 17, 2008: 13.

30. *Coroner's Inquests*, February 16, 2011: 108, 111, 115.

31. *Coroner's Inquests*, February 14, 2011: 69; February 16, 2011: 78–79, 91–93, 107–118.

32. *Coroner's Inquests*, February 14, 2011: 64.

33. House of Commons, 2006: 13; *Shakil*, June 17, 2008: 29; *Coroner's Inquests*, INQ5796–2.

34. *Coroner's Inquests*, February 14, 2011: 64–66, 70, 132.

35. House of Commons, 2006: 16.

36. *Coroner's Inquests*, February 16, 2011: 123–12, 127, 131, 134, 141–145. Gilbertson had previously given several misleading interviews to the press. At the inquests, he was more careful about his information.

37. *Shakil*, May 20, 2008: 64–66; June 6, 2008: 30; June 17, 2008: 26; *Coroner's Inquests*, February 16, 2011: 143, 148–149.

38. Charity Commission, 2011: 1.

39. *Coroner's Inquests*, INQ9370.

40. Charity Commission, 2011: 5, 12. The Coroner's Inquests and the Charity Commission concluded that Iqra was not a site used to facilitate the London bombings. On the basis of the evidence reviewed, I agree.

41. *Shakil*, May 20, 2008: 97–98; May 22, 2008: 5–7; *Coroner's Inquests*, February 14, 2011: 113.

42. House of Commons, 2006: 17–18.

43. *Coroner's Inquests*, February 14, 2011: 111–113.

44. Murray and German, 2005: 92–95.

45. House of Commons, 2006: 18. Lewthwaite gave a very misleading interview to a tabloid for £30,000, which became the source of much erroneous information about her husband.

46. *Coroner's Inquests*, February 14, 2011: 70; February 16, 2011: 54–55, 69–70; INQ5796–2; SYS11082–2.

47. *Shakil*, May 22, 2008: 105–106; June 17, 2008: 30. At trial, Shakil denied that he was part of this group, but he went on the outings despite the pain that such long walks caused him. He later went to Pakistan with Sidique.

48. This surveillance of McDaid was called Operation Honeysuckle and only lasted two days: 14 and 15 April 2003. See *Coroner's Inquests*, WYP11–2.

49. *Coroner's Inquests*, INQ9368–2, INQ9368–31.

50. *Coroner's Inquests*, February 14, 2011: 100–101; *Shakil*, May 22, 2008: 8–9; June 20, 2008: 43–46; June 24, 2008: 144.

51. *Coroner's Inquests*, February 14, 2011: 114; February 16, 2011: 43–45.

52. *Shakil*, June 9, 2008: 80–85.

53. *Coroner's Inquests*, SYS11076–1; February 21, 2011: 120–122.

54. *Shakil*, June 17, 2008: 32–33; June 20, 2008: 56–58.

55. *Shakil*, June 17, 2008: 30–34; June 20, 2008: 51–64.

56. ISC, 2009: 19, 58; *Coroner's Inquests*, SYS11079–1.

57. *Shakil*, June 20, 2008: 47–54.

58. *Shakil*, January 27, 2009: 19.

59. *Shakil*, April 17, 2008: 7–10; June 17, 2008: 34–35; January 27, 2009: 22–25.

60. *Shakil*, June 17, 2008: 35–37.

61. *Shakil*, January 27, 2009: 28.

62. *Shakil*, April 14, 2008: 11–14; June 17, 2008: 39–40; January 27, 2009: 30–33.

63. *Shakil*, April 18, 2008: 8–9; June 17, 2008: 40; January 27, 2009: 37–63.

64. *Shakil*, April 18, 2008: 45; June 17, 2008: 40–42; January 27, 2009: 82–94.

65. *Shakil*, June 17, 2008: 42.

66. *Shakil*, April 18, 2008: 58–59; June 17, 2008: 42–43; January 27, 2009: 97–101.

67. ISC, 2009: 19, 58, which gives 17 August as its date. However, *Coroner's Inquests*, SYS11079–1, gives 15 August as its date. Like the previous calls, this one was not investigated by the Security Service.

68. Hoffman, 2014: 205, declared, "MSK and Tanweer were hosted by Pakistani jihadi terrorists during their visit and then were trained by al-Qaeda operatives in both bomb making and countersurveillance techniques and tradecraft. They were provided with this instruction at an al-Qaeda camp in the Malakand Agency of Pakistan's North West Frontier

Province." Hoffman cited "interviews with a senior British Security Service officer, Washington, D.C., March and April 2008" and Robertson, Cruickshank, and Lister, 2012a, as his references. Robertson, Cruisckshank, and Lister does not mention the Gorque/Malakand camp at all.

69. *Shakil*, May 22, 2008: 89; June 17, 2008: 40, 45; June 20, 2008: 81–85; June 24, 2008: 126.

70. *Shakil*, June 17, 2008: 45–46; June 18, 2008: 30.

71. *Coroner's Inquests*, SYS11079–4. This was discovered after the London bombings when the investigation team analyzed Sidique's phone records.

72. House of Commons, 2006: 18; *Coroner's Inquests*, February 14, 2011: 114; February 16, 2011: 43–45.

73. *Coroner's Inquests*, February 16, 2011: 126; Charity Commission, 2011: 5.

74. ISC, 2009: 8.

75. *Khyam*, September 15, 2006: 117.

76. *Coroner's Inquests*, February 21, 2011: 153–180; ISC, 2009: 32–36; *Shakil*, May 22, 2008: 97–112.

77. *Khawaja*, 2008, LIT Evidence Book, chapter 3: 63–66. At trial, Ullah explained that Khyam was going to provide housing and everything in Pakistan, so he was the main man, which is the reason that Sidique was asking his permission. *Shakil*, May 22, 2008: 101.

78. *Khawaja*, 2008, LIT Evidence Book, chapter 3: 66–68.

79. *Khawaja*, 2008, LIT Evidence Book, chapter 3: 69.

80. *Khawaja*, 2008, LIT Evidence Book, chapter 3: 69–74.

81. ISC, 2009: 21; *Shakil*, May 22, 2008: 112–113; *Coroner's Inquests*, February 22, 2011: 15–25, 125–131; SYS11004–1 and SYS11004–2, SYS11079–6. The ISC and SYS11079–6 reported that the travelers met Qayum, but this was later found to be erroneous. See *Coroner's Inquests*, February 22, 2011: 129–130. It appeared that someone working for HFC helped them defraud the bank; see *Khyam*, March 2, 2007: 33.

82. *Coroner's Inquests*, February 22, 2011: 25–29, SYS11079–7.

83. *Coroner's Inquests*, SYS11079–8.

84. *Coroner's Inquests*, SYS11067–2.

85. Coroner's Inquests, SYS11079–8.

86. ISC, 2009: 28.

87. ISC, 2009: 22; *Coroner's Inquests*, February 22, 2011: 131–132; SYS11079–8.

88. *Coroner's Inquests*, February 14, 2011: 82, 103, 109; *Shakil*, May 22, 2008: 117.

89. Robertson, Cruickshank, and Lister, 2012a.

90. *Shakil*, June 6, 2008: 60; June 9, 2008: 88; June 16, 2008: 32, 37.

91. House of Commons, 2006: 14–15; *Coroner's Inquests*, February 14, 2011: 120–125.

92. *Coroner's Inquests*, February 14, 2011: 83–84.

93. *Shakil*, June 9, 2008: 93; June 11, 2008: 138–139; June 12, 2008: 127.

94. *Shakil*, May 20, 2008: 84; June 9, 2008: 93.

95. *Coroner's Inquests*, February 16, 2011: 45–47.

96. *Shakil*, June 17, 2008: 49–53.

97. *Shakil*, May 20, 2008: 85; *Coroner's Inquests*, February 14, 2011: 65–66.

98. *Coroner's Inquests*, February 15, 2011: 85, 95, 125; February 16, 2011: 58–59, 84.

99. *Shakil*, May 20, 2008: 85, 87; May 23, 2008: 12–13, 15.

100. *Coroner's Inquests*, February 15, 2011: 96. It had been previously and erroneously reported that this video was made on 16 November, see *Shakil*, May 23, 2008: 15.

101. My transcription of the video clips available on the Coroner's Inquests website.

102. House of Commons, 2006: 20.

103. Robertson, Cruickshank, and Lister, 2012c.

104. Moreton and Buncombe, 2008; Milmo, Herbert, Bennetto, and Huggler, 2006.

105. Not to be confused with Waseem Gulzar of Operation Crevice.

106. Fisher and Kovaleski, 2006.

107. *Regina v. Abdulla Ahmed Ali et al.* (henceforth *Ali*, all dates 2008), June 18, 2008: 21–22.

108. *Secretary of State for the Home Department and AY*, 2012: paragraph 59.

109. Milmo, Herbert, Bennetto, and Huggler, 2006; Fisher and Kovaleski, 2006.

110. *Ali*, June 19: 122–123.

111. U.S. Department of Treasury Press Center, 2006; *Secretary of State for the Home Department and AY*, 2012: paragraph 67. More on al-Ghabra in chapter 5. See also Pantucci, 2012. Cruickshank, 2014: 242–243, assigns an important role to Haroon Rashid Aswat based on anonymous intelligence sources. Aswat was just another militant, fleeing Afghanistan after the U.S. invasion, and had run into some of these leaders in order to retrieve his passport. Personal interview, July 20–21, 2015. Aswat was never charged with any action pertaining to his Pakistan stay.

112. Gall and Jamal, 2006.

113. Robertson, Cruickshank, and Lister, 2012a.

114. Pantucci, 2015: 186.

115. Robertson, Cruickshank, and Lister, 2012a.

116. *Coroner's Inquests*, February 15, 2011: 97; *Shakil*, May 23, 2008: 36.

117. *Coroner's Inquests*, February 15, 2011: 97; INQ11410–20.

118. *Shakil*, May 23, 2008: 4–6; 36–37; June 12, 2008: 141, 143.

119. *Shakil*, May 20, 2008: 92–93, 98–99; May 23, 2008: 39–42.

120. *Shakil*, May 20, 2008: 100–133; June 5, 2008: 33.

121. The *Shakil*, 2008, trial was about this trip.

122. *Shakil*, May 20, 2008: 139–140; June 5, 2008: 33–36.

123. *Shakil*, May 20, 2008: 141–145; June 5, 2008: 47–48, 51.

124. *Coroner's Inquests*, February 1, 2011: 169, 193, 197; March 3, 2011: 122.

125. Robertson, Cruiskshank, and Lister, 2012a.

126. *Shakil*, June 9, 2008: 113; June 12, 2008: 154.

127. *Shakil*, June 5, 2008: 51–54.

128. Robertson, Cruickshank, and Lister, 2012a.

129. Mohammed Sidique Khan, 2005.

130. See his video at *Coroner's Inquests*, February 15, 2011, evidence, videos.

131. *Shakil*, June 5, 2008: 58; June 9, 2008: 114–120.

132. *Shakil*, May 20, 2008: 152–153.

133. *Shakil*, June 9, 2008: 121–124; June 12, 2008: 161–162.

134. *Shakil*, May 21, 2008: 11–12; June 9, 2008: 60–62; June 17, 2008: 95.

135. *Coroner's Inquests*, February 14, 2011: 105; February 15, 2011: 70–73.

136. *Coroner's Inquests*, February 1, 2011: 134, 159, 162; INQ11005–1.

137. Robertson, Cruickshank, and Lister, 2012a.

138. *Coroner's Inquests*, February 2, 2011: 2–9; Rule 43 Report: 14.

139. *Shakil*, May 21, 2008: 13–16.

140. *Coroner's Inquests*, February 15, 2011: 48–49.

141. *Coroner's Inquests*, February 2, 2011: 16; February 15, 2011: 54–55. The date of the rental comes from the phone records.

142. *Coroner's Inquests*, February 14, 2011: 92; February 15, 2011: 55, 62.

143. House of Commons, 2006: 23; *Coroner's Inquests*, February 14, 2011: 116–117.

144. *Coroner's Inquests*, February 2, 2011: 17; Robertson, Cruickshank, and Lister, 2012a.

145. *Coroner's Inquests*, February 15, 2011: 56, 65.

146. *Coroner's Inquests*, INQ11177–14.

147. *Coroner's Inquests*, February 2, 2011: 20; Robertson, Cruiskshank, and Lister, 2012a.

148. *Coroner's Inquests*, February 14, 2011: 119; February 15, 2011: 4–45.

149. *Coroner's Inquests*, February 15, 2011: 75–79.

150. *Coroner's Inquests*, February 2, 2011: 21; February 14, 2011: 94; February 15, 2011: 58.

151. House of Commons, 2006: 23.

152. *Coroner's Inquests*, February 16, 2011: 197. The gun that Lindsay had used in his previous altercation was found after the bombing in the trunk of his car, and it did have something wrong with it.

153. *Coroner's Inquests*, February 16, 2011: 199–200.

154. House of Commons, 2006: 24.

155. *Coroner's Inquests*, February 16, 2011: 201.

156. House of Commons, 2006: 25.

157. *Coroner's Inquests*, February 16, 2011: 80–83.

158. *Coroner's Inquests*, February 14, 2011: 95, 107.

159. *Coroner's Inquests*, February 15, 2011: 51.

160. *Coroner's Inquests*, February 16, 2011: 203–204.

161. *Coroner's Inquests*, February 15, 2011: video.

162. Robertson, Cruickshank, and Lister, 2012a.

163. *Coroner's Inquests*, February 2, 2011: 40–41; INQ11177–40.

164. *Coroner's Inquests*, February 2, 2011: 63–64.

165. *Coroner's Inquests*, February 1, 2011: 171.

166. *Coroner's Inquests*, February 1, 2011: 179–181.

167. Robertson, Cruickshank, and Lister, 2012a.

168. *Shakil*, May 21, 2008: 17–18.

169. House of Commons, 2006: 3–6, 22.

Chapter 4

1. *Regina v. Mohamed Hamid et al.*, 2007–2008 (henceforth *Hamid*, with specific dates), November 21, 2007: 133–145.

2. *Hamid*, November 22, 2007: 76–77.

3. This IMA office figures prominently in Operation Overt in the next chapter.

4. *Hamid*, November 21, 2007: 141; November 22, 2007: 4.

5. *Hamid*, November 22, 2007: 7–11, 14.

6. See his interview in the BBC documentary *Don't Panic I'm Islamic* aired in May 2005.

7. *Hamid*, October 15, 2007: 27; November 22, 2007: 99.

8. *Regina v. Muktar Said Ibrahim et al.*, 2007 (henceforth *Ibrahim*), March 22: 55–66.

9. *Ibrahim*, March 20: 80.

10. *Ibrahim*, January 30: 2; March 16: 58, 61–62; *Regina v. Abdul Sherif et al.*, 2007–2008 (henceforth *Sherif*, with specific date), October 24, 2007: 15.

11. *Ibrahim*, January 17: 83–92; January 22: 4–6; May 30: 25.

12. *Ibrahim*, January 17: 80–81, 93, 106; February 13: 16; March 16: 61–64; March 19: 3, 14; May 3: 90–91, 101–104; June 1: 107.

13. *Ibrahim*, February 7: 42; February 8: 97; March 16: 65–71; March 19: 13; March 22: 67–78; April 2: 141–144.

14. *Ibrahim*, March 16: 71–72; March 19: 1–2.

15. *Hamid*, October 15, 2007: 27; November 15, 2007: 124; November 22, 2007: 99.

16. *Ibrahim*, May 18: 101–102. He was granted an indefinite leave to stay in Britain in May 2005.

17. *Ibrahim*, January 15: 40–41; *Sherif*, October 8, 2007: 96. Adus or Osman, the name under which he stood trial, refused to testify at his trial. I call him Hamdi as this is what all his friends called him.

18. *Ibrahim*, May 18: 105, 110–113; May 23: 14; *Regina v. Yeshiemebet ("Yehi") Girma et al.*, 2008 (henceforth *Girma*), April 8: 135–136; *Sherif*, October 8, 2007: 40.

19. *Ibrahim*, May 18: 111–118; *Girma*, April 8: 147–154.

20. *Hamid*, November 21, 2007: 137–138; November 22, 2007: 109; *Ibrahim*, May 18: 122–123, 142–144.

21. *Girma*, April 21: 20–22.

22. *Hamid*, January 16, 2008: 39, 118–162.

23. *Hamid*, March 19, 2008: 2; October 15, 2007: 28; November 22, 2007: 101–103.

24. *Girma*, April 17: 30; *Hamid*, October 15, 2007: 96–135 (quote on p. 106); October 16, 2007: 37–123; November 22, 2007: 99–111; December 10, 2007: 66–72; *Ibrahim*, January 17: 6–35; March 19: 5–10, May 30: 20–25.

25. *Hamid*, October 15, 2007: 84–85; November 22, 2007: 38–39; January 16, 2008: 38.

26. *Hamid*, January 16, 2008: 155–156.

27. *Ibrahim*, January 17: 151–204; January 18: 5–17; April 17: 56–114, 142–144.

28. *Ibrahim*, February 2: 32; April 17: 119–121, 150–151.

29. *Ibrahim*, May 30: 28–31; June 1: 56; June 6: 16–17.

30. *Ibrahim*, March 19: 5–9; March 20: 80–81; *Hamid*, October 15, 2007: 28–29; October 16, 2007: 37–123; November 22, 2007: 54–55.

31. *Hamid*, October 15, 2007: 46.

32. *Hamid*, October 15, 2007: 10–12, 29–30.

33. *Hamid*, October 15, 2007: 13; November 22, 2007: 113–116; November 23, 2007: 33.

34. *Hamid*, October 15, 2007: 30.

35. *Hamid*, December 4, 2007: 13–14; 57–61.

36. *Ibrahim*, March 19: 18, 21–24; May 3: 105–111.

37. *Ibrahim*, February 7: 24–30; February 9: 36–37; February 16: 2, 58–59.

38. *Ibrahim*, February 7: 37–43.

39. *Ibrahim*, February 8: 89–93; March 19: 29–30.

40. *Ibrahim*, February 7: 49–57; February 9: 24–27; February 15: 89–97.

41. *Ibrahim*, February 8: 87–89; February 9: 42; February 15: 94–96; March 30: 77–78, 86.

42. *Secretary of State for the Home Department and AH*, 2008. David Leppard (2007) identifies AH to be acting on Mohammed al Ghabra's instructions. I discuss al Ghabra further in the next chapter. I found no corroboration for this link.

43. *Ibrahim*, January 17: 45–46, 49–50, 75–76; *Secretary of State for the Home Department and AH*, 2008: paragraph 14.

44. *Ibrahim*, March 23: 38–39. Of course, al Ghabra might also have been the link to Rauf.

45. Robertson, Cruickshank and Lister, 2012a.

46. *Ibrahim*, June 20: 55–96; Robertson, Cruickshank, and Lister, 2012a.

47. Robertson, Cruickshank, and Lister, 2012a.

48. This may have been Abdulla Ahmed Ali again. See below.

49. Robertson, Cruickshank, and Lister, 2012a.

50. *Ibrahim*, March 19: 40–45.

51. *Hamid*, November 22, 2007: 117, 138–14; *Ibrahim*, March 30: 44–45.

52. *Ibrahim*, February 15: 27–28; 41–43.

53. *Ibrahim*, May 18: 156–161. They eventually married in prison after Mohamed was arrested: see *Ibrahim*, May 21: 3.

54. *Girma*, March 11: 2–23.

55. *Girma*, March 11: 100–116.

56. *Girma*, March 11: 103–104.

57. *Ibrahim*, February 7: 73; February 8: 100; February 9: 84; February 15: 44.

58. *Ibrahim*, January 17: 116–120.

59. *Ibrahim*, February 16: 52–24.

60. *Ibrahim*, March 19: 46; March 30: 44–46. The authorities' failure to note his return and realize he had missed his court date was a missed opportunity to put him under surveillance.

61. *Ibrahim*, February 7: 61; February 16: 2.

62. *Ibrahim*, February 15: 104–107.

63. *Ibrahim*, February 2: 101–142; summarized in *Sherif*, October 8, 2007: 69–74.

64. *Ibrahim*, July 11: 21–22.

65. *Ibrahim*, February 5: 24–27. See also January 15: 59.

66. *Ibrahim*, March 23: 41, 55; Robertson, Cruickshank, and Lister, 2012a. More on Ali in the next chapter.

67. *Ibrahim*, March 19: 47–49.

68. *Ibrahim*, January 18: 83–85; March 19: 56; April 17: 152–159; April 18: 10–11; June 25: 48.

69. *Ibrahim*, April 17: 161; April 20: 121–125.

70. *Ibrahim*, April 17: 162; April 18: 18–19.

71. *Manfu Asiedu and R., 2015*: paragraph 8.

72. *Ibrahim*, March 19: 67–73.

73. *Ibrahim*, March 12: 73, June 20: 59.

74. *Ibrahim*, March 19: 75–98.

75. *Ibrahim*, April 18: 22–26.

76. *Ibrahim*, May 3: 113.

77. *Ibrahim*, May 11: 100–106.

78. *Ibrahim*, January 18: 137–139.

79. *Ibrahim*, January 19: 3–11.

80. *Ibrahim*, January 22: 15–26; quote on pp. 21–23.

81. *Ibrahim*, April 18: 27–30.

82. *Ibrahim*, January 18: 99–101; April 18: 31–34.

83. *Ibrahim*, February 5: 27.

84. *Ibrahim*, January 19: 42–52; quote on p. 42.

85. *Ibrahim*, May 31: 159–169.

86. *Ibrahim*, May 30: 72–74; May 31: 157–158.

87. *Ibrahim*, April 18: 34–39.

88. *Ibrahim*, March 19: 57; March 22: 4–5; March 30: 153; April 18: 39–45; April 24: 78; April 27: 92–94. Ibrahim flunked his driving test that June; see *Ibrahim*, March 20, 2007: 75.

89. *Ibrahim*, January 19: 55, 60–70; March 30: 138, 141; April 18: 54–59.

90. *Ibrahim*, January 18: 73.

91. *Ibrahim*, March 30: 83–85.

92. *Ibrahim*, March 30: 152–154; May 16: 110–111.

93. *Ibrahim*, March 19: 68; March 30: 157; May 3: 126–127; June 20: 119–120.

94. *Hamid*, October 18, 2007: 11; November 12, 2007: 37; November 14, 2007: 45; December 4, 2007: 15.

95. *Hamid*, November 22, 2007: 31–32.

96. *Hamid*, November 14, 2007: 47, 52; November 22, 2007: 146–147; December 4, 2007: 15–16.

97. *Ibrahim*, March 19: 99–100.

98. *Ibrahim*, May 3: 130–131.

99. *Ibrahim*, April 27: 94.

100. *Ibrahim*, March 19: 104–105; May 3: 133.

101. *Ibrahim*, June 20: 81–85, 115–118.

102. See *Manfu Asiedu v. R*, 2015 for a description of this error. The court of appeal rejected a request for a retrial.

103. *Ibrahim*, March 19: 105–107; May 3: 121–122, 134–138. This might have taken place the next day. See March 19: 110–119.

104. *Ibrahim*, March 19: 101, 108–110; May 11: 205.

105. *Hamid*, November 14, 2007: 52; November 22, 2007: 147.

106. *Ibrahim*, May 21: 11–15.

107. *Ibrahim*, March 19: 120–126; April 18: 85–88; May 4: 10–12; May 21: 15–19.

108. *Ibrahim*, May 3: 80–81.

109. *Ibrahim*, January 17: 120–124.

110. *Ibrahim*, April 18: 89–90.

111. *Ibrahim*, May 4: 14.

112. *Ibrahim*, May 21: 20–21; *Sherif*, November 6, 2007: 1–2.

113. *Ibrahim*, March 22: 6.

114. *Ibrahim*, February 13: 67; April 18: 93–102; May 4: 17.

115. *Ibrahim*, March 19: 129–140.

116. *Ibrahim*, March 22: 16–36; April 19: 13–28.

117. *Ibrahim*, March 19: 141. This testimony was given before Ishmail turned on Ibrahim at the trial.

118. *Ibrahim*, April 18: 104–106; May 21: 28.

119. *Ibrahim*, March 19: 141–145; April 18: 109–110, 117–127.

120. *Ibrahim*, April 18: 129–141.

121. *Ibrahim*, March 20: 11; April 18: 149–150; May 4: 26.

122. *Ibrahim*, March 20: 16–23; April 18: 156–174.

123. *Ibrahim*, June 26: 65–76.

Chapter 5

1. *Ali*, June 2: 1–7.

2. *Ali*, June 4: 55–56; June 26: 130–138.

3. *Ali*, June 24: 140.

4. *Ali*, June 2: 9–15.

5. *Ali*, June 25: 34–38.

6. *Ali*, June 26: 143–144.

7. *Ali*, June 16: 1–7.

8. See Chapter 4.

9. *Ali*, June 2: 24; June 9: 73–74.

10. *Ali*, June 9: 119, 125.

11. *Ali*, July 2: 89–107.

12. *Ali*, June 9: 121–122; July 2: 108–109, 117–118.

13. *Ali*, June 2: 17.

14. *Ali*, June 25: 41–47, 55. This hard drive was later examined and revealed various IMA files, documents, and e-mails from March to December 2002, and photographs of injured children and IMA staff in the field.

15. *Ali*, June 2: 35; July 2: 119–120.

16. *Ali*, June 2: 30–33; June 11: 68.

17. *Ali*, June 2: 35, 37; June 9: 129

18. *BBC News*, 2010a.

19. *Ali*, June 18: 47; June 25: 47–61. Savant gave the boxes to Abdul Muneem in early 2006.

20. *Ali*, June 16: 11, 18.

21. Gardham, 2010a.

22. *Ali*, June 2: 75–77.

23. *Ali*, June 2: 78–84; quote on p. 80.

24. *Ali*, June 2: 43–50.

25. Robertson, Cruickshank, and Lister, 2012b.

26. See Chapter 4 and *Ibrahim*, March 23: 43, 53–54. When asked about it, Ibrahim pled ignorance. Rauf wrote that an intermediary said that Ibrahim would soon get back to him; see Robertson, Cruikshank, and Lister, 2012a.

27. *Ali*, April 23: 64; June 2: 54; June 9: 103.

28. *Ali*, June 2: 58–59, 62–73; Gardham, 2010a.

29. Swann, 2009.

30. Robertson, Cruickshank, and Lister, 2012b.

31. See Chapter 3, and *Secretary of State for the Home Department and AY*, 2012: paragraphs 63–64.

32. *Ali*, June 18: 23–50; June 19: 137–141.

33. *Secretary of State for the Home Department and AY*, 2012: paragraphs 74–82.

34. Gardham, 2010a.

35. *Ali*, June 2: 74; June 3: 2–3; June 16: 20; *Secretary of State for the Home Department and AY*, 2012: paragraph 64. At trial, both Ali and Hussain insisted that Hussain's first involvement in the plot was in April and not earlier to hide the fact that Hussain had gone to Pakistan for explosive training with Rauf and Abu Ubaydah.

36. *Ali*, June 2: 86–100.

37. *Ali*, June 12: 61–66.

38. Swann, 2009.

39. *BBC News*, 2009b.

40. *Ali*, June 16: 42–47.

41. *Ali*, June 3: 7–8; June 11: 129–132.

42. Robertson, Cruickshank, and Lister, 2012b.

43. *Ali*, June 3: 142–153; June 5: 2–10.

44. *Ali*, 2008: April 3: 31–36.

45. *Ali*, June 3: 22–25; June 9: 46.

46. Robertson, Cruickshank, and Lister, 2012b.

47. *Ali*, June 11: 112–116; July 14: 35–36.

48. *Ali*, April 3: 30–31; June 5: 153–163.

49. *Ali*, June 3: 26.

50. *Wall Street Journal*, 2009. The e-mail in the article is erroneously dated 6 June instead of 26 June. See also Gardham and Rayner, 2008.

51. *Ali*, 2008: June 18: 67; June 19: 151.

52. U.S. Department of Treasury Press Center, 2006.

53. U.S. Department of Defense, 2008: 5. Abu Faraj later became more involved in external operations.

54. *Secretary of State for the Home Department and AH*, 2008: paragraphs 1, 10–17 (the Iraqi refugee is AH and al Ghabra is BC in this document); Leppard, 2007; and Chapter 4. The authorities arrested this Iraqi refugee shortly after the Vivace Plot, and charged him with terrorism offenses, but he was acquitted of all charges on 29 August 2006. He was put under control orders. There is no evidence of any link between him and the London bombings.

55. *Ali*, June 11: 117–121; June 18: 64–75; June 19: 92–103.

56. *Ali*, July 14: 30; Cruickshank, 2014: 242–244; Pantucci, 2015: 220–221; Silber, 2012: 42.

57. *Ali*, June 23: 129–140.

58. *Ali*, July 14: 132.

59. *Ali*, June 23: 139–140.

60. *Ali*, June 24: 3–4, 7–8.

61. *Ali*, June 24: 17, 26.

62. *Ali*, June 19: 1–3; June 23: 1–13; June 24: 19–20.

63. *Ali*, June 19: 3–12; June 23: 8–23; June 24: 14–23.

64. The prosecution's portrait of Gulzar as the planner and superintendent of the plot was not consistent with the evidence the jury heard. This obvious overreach probably contributed to the jury acquitting Gulzar of all charges and becoming skeptical about the rest of the plot.

65. *Ali,* May 13: 105.

66. Robertson, Cruickshank, and Lister, 2012b.

67. *Wall Street Journal,* 2009.

68. *Ali,* July 2: 120–152.

69. *Ali,* June 11: 42–43, 49–50.

70. *Ali,* April 5: 2; May 13: 106.

71. *Ali,* June 26: 88–90.

72. *Ali,* June 26: 88.

73. *Ali,* June 24: 145–146.

74. *Ali,* June 30: 122–153; July 1: 16–32.

75. *Ali,* April 16: 61, 68.

76. Shamin Uddin and Nabeel Hussain, who were later tried and convicted for helping their friends.

77. *Ali,* April 4: 35–37; May 6: 47; July 14: 66–67.

78. *Ali,* June 11: 24–32.

79. *BBC News,* 2009a; *Wall Street Journal,* 2009.

80. *Ali,* April 16: 69–72; June 3: 30; June 10: 53–56. Their detected public meeting does not say much for their tradecraft as they were supposed to keep separate for Sarwar's continued operations.

81. *Ali,* May 6: 37, 40.

82. *Wall Street Journal,* 2009.

83. *Ali,* May 6: 51–55.

84. *Ali,* April 16: 78–80.

85. *BBC News,* 2009a; *Wall Street Journal,* 2009.

86. *Ali,* June 24: 27–28.

87. *Ali,* April 16: 82, 85–86; June 4: 98–99; June 12: 13, 108.

88. *Ali,* June 3: 69–74.

89. Ali, April 17: 3–6; June 5: 111–115.

90. *Secretary of State for the Home Department and AY,* 2012: paragraph 99b.

91. *Secretary of State for the Home Department and AY,* 2012: paragraph 73, 99b.

92. *Ali,* June 11: 134–135.

93. *Ali,* April 17: 9; May 6: 38, 40; May 13: 104.

94. *Ali,* April 17: 13–23; June 5: 120; June 12: 1–10.

95. *Ali,* April 17: 26–31; June 4: 66–67.

96. *Ali,* April 4: 15–17.

97. *Ali,* April 4 (morning): 22–23.

98. *Ali,* April 4 (morning): 17–19.

99. *Ali,* June 3: 79–80; June 12: 15, 112.

100. *Ali,* April 17: 49–51; June 11: 122.

101. *Ali,* April 4 (morning): 20–21.

102. *Ali,* April 17: 56–61; *Secretary of State for the Home Department and AY,* 2012: paragraph 80.

103. *Ali*, April 17: 66; June 10: 76–77; June 12: 28.

104. *Ali*, June 5: 128–130.

105. *Ali*, April 4 (morning): 23–24.

106. *Secretary of State for the Home Department and AY*, 2012: paragraph 83. However, *Ali*, April 4 (afternoon): 9, suggests it may have taken place two days earlier.

107. *BBC News*, 2009a.

108. *Ali*, April 17: 74–76; April 18: 1–6, 10–15; April 23: 62; June 10: 86.

109. *Ali*, April 4 (afternoon): 14–20 (quotes); April 18: 8, 16–24; June 17: 11–30.

110. *Ali*, April 18: 25–32; April 23: 63; May 13: 105; June 10: 88.

111. *Ali*, June 10: 89–104.

112. *Ali*, April 18: 32–47; May 13: 105.

113. *BBC News*, 2009a.

114. *Ali*, April 18: 47–59; June 10: 104–108; June 12: 124–126; June 19: 37–39; June 23: 52–55; *Secretary of State for the Home Department and AY*, 2012: paragraphs 87–89.

115. *Ali*, April 18: 49–50, 61; June 4: 144–155; June 17: 89 (quote).

116. *Ali*, April 18: 66.

117. *Wall Street Journal*, 2009.

118. *Ali*, April 18: 66–68; April 21: 1–7; June 10: 115.

119. *Ali*, June 19: 40–44.

120. *Ali*, April 21: 8–17.

121. *Wall Street Journal*, 2009.

122. *Ali*, April 23: 18.

123. *Ali*, April 23: 19.

124. *Ali*, April 22: 24–27.

125. *Ali*, April 21: 19–21; quote on p. 19.

126. *Ali*, June 23: 69–72.

127. *Ali*, April 21: 28–33

128. *Ali*, June 19: 54–57; June 23: 72; *Secretary of State for the Home Department and AY*, 2012: paragraphs 95–99.

129. *Ali*, April 21: 36; *Secretary of State for the Home Department and AY*, 2012: paragraph 99c.

130. *Ali*, April 21: 41, 43–45; June 12: 145–148.

131. *Secretary of State for the Home Department and AY*, 2012: paragraph 103.

132. *Ali*, April 21: 45–51; May 13: 105.

133. *Ali*, April 21: 52–67; May 6: 42; July 14: 97.

134. *Ali*, June 23: 97–104; quote on p. 97.

135. Robertson, Cruickshank, and Lister, 2012a and b.

136. *Ali*, April 21: 69; June 5: 106–107.

137. *Ali*, April 4 (morning): 6–9.

138. *Ali*, April 4 (morning): 9–10.

139. *Ali*, April 4 (afternoon): 21–28.

140. *Ali*, April 21: 71–77.

141. Robertson, Cruickshank, and Lister, 2012b.

142. *Secretary of State for the Home Department and AY*, 2012: paragraphs 102–109; *Secretary of State for the Home Department and AM*, 2009: paragraph 51.

143. *Ali*, May 1: 28–29.

144. *Secretary of State for the Home Department and AM*, 2009.

145. *Secretary of State for the Home Department and AY*, 2012.

Chapter 6

1. Silber, 2012: 36–54; 83–106; 107–127; 128–143.

2. Neumann and Evans, 2014; Hoffman, 2014; and Cruickshank, 2014.

3. Pantucci, 2015: 164–172; 185–199; 207–214; 214–223.

4. Hoffman and Reinares, 2014: xi.

5. Casciani, 2007.

6. *Regina v. Omar Khyam et al.*, 2008: paragraphs 62, 68.

7. Of course, I am not referring to additional but classified information that would also independently corroborate his confession.

8. Neumann and Evans, 2014: 74. They are also under the mistaken assumption that Qayum was a member of al Qaeda instead of just a supporter.

9. Neumann and Evans, 2014: 74.

10. Neumann and Evans, 2014: 76.

11. *Regina v. Omar Khyam et al.*, 2006, published in the *Ottawa Citizen*.

12. Khawaja Judgment, 2008.

13. ISC, 2009.

14. Pantucci, 2015: 165.

15. Pantucci, 2015: 170.

16. *Khyam*, April 4, 2006: 32–35.

17. Pantucci, 2015: 165.

18. Pantucci, 2015: 167, 318, endnote 33 based on S. Malik, 2011, who again bases the controversial part of his article on his discredited source, Hassan Butt.

19. See Pantucci, 2015: 318–319, endnotes 36–39.

20. Pantucci, 2015: 169, endnote 39 on page 319, duplicating the error in Silber, 2012: 99, from Khyam's (not Babar's) testimony in *Khyam*, September 15, 2006: 65.

21. In contrast to his references using the Coroner's Inquests, where Pantucci gives both date and page number, he only gives dates and no page numbers for his references in the Crevice trial. Central News did not provide page numbers of the transcripts.

22. Hoffman, 2014: 204–215.

23. Unlike in U.S. trials, where defendants are not penalized for not taking the stand, in Britain, judges instruct juries that this refusal to provide evidence at trial should be counted against them.

24. Hoffman, 2014: 204–215.

25. Hoffman, 2014: 215.

26. Hoffman, 2014: 212.

27. S. Malik, 2007a and 2007b.

28. Dodd, 2009.

29. Williams, 2008.

30. *Shakil*, May 20, 2008.

31. S. Malik, 2007a.

32. See Hoffman, 2014: endnotes 23, 62, 103, for instances.

33. Hoffman, 2014: endnotes 9, 11, 96.

34. Hoffmann, 2014: 215.

35. Cruickshank, 2014: 243, emphasis added.

36. Cruickshank, 2014: 243.

37. Cruickshank, 2014: endnotes 128, 129, 130, 132.

38. *U.S. v. Haroon Rashid Aswat*, 2015.

39. Cruickshank, 2014: 267 (endnote 129).

40. Cruickshank, 2014: 243.

41. Pantucci, 2015: 220.

42. Sageman, 2014.

43. Sageman, 2014: 576.

BIBLIOGRAPHY

Abdal Hakim, Umar (Abu Musab al Suri or Mustafa Setmariam Nasar), 2004, *My Testimony on Jihad in Algeria*, published on *Islamic al-Fallujah Forums* website, August 31, 2007, translated by the Open Source Center.

Abou el Fadl, Khaled, 2005, *The Great Theft: Wrestling Islam from the Extremists*, New York: HarperCollins.

Abu Hamza al-Misri (Mostafa Kamel Mostafa), 2009, *Khawaarij and Jihad*, Edited by Islam-Future, available at http://www.kalamullah.com/Books/The%20khawarij.pdf. Previously published by IslamFuture in London in 2000.

Anderson, Benedict, 1991, *Imagined Communities: Reflections on the Origin and Spread of Nationalism*, revised edition, London: Verso.

Archer, Lawrence, and Bawden, Fiona, 2010, *Ricin! The Inside Story of the Terror Plot That Never Was*, London: Pluto Press.

Manfu Asiedu and R., 2015, Court of Appeal (Criminal Division), [2015] EWCA Crim 714, April 30.

Baker, Abdul Haqq, 2009, "Countering Terrorism in the UK: A Convert Community Perspective," Ph.D. dissertation, University of Exeter.

Baker, Raymond, 2003, *Islam without Fear: Egypt and the New Islamists*, Cambridge, Massachusetts: Harvard University Press.

Barbieri, Eliane Tschaen, and Klausen, Jytte, 2012, "Al Qaeda's London Branch: Patterns of Domestic and Transnational Network Integration," *Studies in Conflict & Terrorism*, 35: 411–431.

Dhiren Barot and R., 2007, Supreme Court of Judicature, Court of Appeal (Criminal Division), [2007] EWCA Crim 1119, May 16.

BBC News, 2009a, "Airlines Bomb Plot: The E-mails," September 7, 2009, available at http://news.bbc.co.uk/2/hi/uk_news/8193501.stm.

———, 2009b, "Briton Guilty of Plotting 'Deadly Terror Attack,'" December 10, 2009, available at http://news.bbc.co.uk/2/hi/uk_news/8404551.stm.

———, 2010 a, "Airline Bomb Plotter's Wife Tells of Abuse," February 18, 2010, available at http://news.bbc.co.uk/2/hi/uk_news/8522474.stm.

———, 2010b, "Airline Bomb Plotter's Wife Cleared of Terror Charge," March 5, 2010, available at http://news.bbc.co.uk/2/hi/uk_news/8551761.stm.

———, 2016, "Lancashire 'Terrorist House' Row 'Not a Spelling Mistake,'" January 20, 2015, available at http://www.bbc.com/news/uk-england-lancashire-35354061.

Benjamin, Daniel, and Simon, Steven, 2002, *The Age of Sacred Terror*, New York: Random House.

Bergen, Peter, 2001, *Holy War, Inc.: Inside the Secret World of Osama bin Laden*, New York: Free Press.

———, 2006, *The Osama bin Laden I Know: An Oral History of al Qaeda's Leader*, New York: Free Press.

Bittner, Egon, 1963, "Radicalism and the Organization of Radical Movements," *American Sociological Review* 28, no. 6: 928–940.

Blair, Ian, 2009, *Policing Controversy*, London: Profile Books.

Bowen, Innes, 2014, *Medina in Birmingham, Najaf in Brent: Inside British Islam*, London: C. Hurst.

Burke, Jason, 2003, *Al-Qaeda: Casting a Shadow of Terror*, London: I. B. Tauris.

Casciani, Dominic, 2007, "Jihadi Diary: Inside the Mind," *BBC News*, 14 June 2007, available at http://news.bbc.co.uk/go/pr/fr/-/2/hi/uk_news/magazine/6750911.stm.

Charity Commission, 2011, *Inquiry Report: Iqra*, February 22, 2011, available at http://web archive.nationalarchives.gov.uk/20111005152008/http:/www.charity-commission.gov.uk/ Library/iqra.pdf.

Cobain, Ian, and Vasagar, Jeevan, 2007, "Free—the Man Accused of Being an al-Qaida Leader, aka 'Q'," *Guardian*, May 1, 2007.

Coroner's Inquests into the London Bombings of 7 July 2005, October 11, 2010-May 6, 2011, available at http://7julyinquests.independent.gov.uk/hearing_transcripts/ind ex.htm.

Cruickshank, Paul, 2014, "The 2006 Airline Plot," in Hoffman and Reinares, 2014: 224–272.

Dodd, Vikram, 2009, "Al-Qaida Fantasist Tells Court: I'm a Professional Liar," *Guardian*, February 9, 2009.

Dodd, Vikram, and Taylor, Matthew, 2017, "London Attack: 'Aggressive' and 'Strange' Suspect Vowed to 'Do Some Damage.'" *Guardian*, June 20, 2017.

Fandy, Mamoun, 2001, *Saudi Arabia and the Politics of Dissent*, New York: Palgrave.

Ahmed Raza Faraz and R., 2012, The Court of Appeal (Criminal Division), [2012] EWCA Crim 2820, December 21, 2012.

Fassin, Didier, 2013, *Enforcing Order: An Ethnography of Urban Policing*, Cambridge: Polity Press

Fisher, Ian, and Kovaleski, Serge, 2006, "In British Inquiry, a Family Caught in Two Worlds," *New York Times*, August 6, 2006.

Foley, Frank, 2013, *Countering Terrorism in Britain and France: Institutions, Norms and the Shadow of the Past*, Cambridge: Cambridge University Press

Gall, Carlotta, and Jamal, Arif, 2006, "Man at Heart of British Terrorist Plot Laid Roots in a Land Rife with Sunni Extremism," *New York Times*, August 21, 2006.

Gambetta, Diego, ed., 2005, *Making Sense of Suicide Missions*, Oxford: Oxford University Press.

Gardham, Duncan, 2010a, "Wife of Trans-Atlantic Airlines Bomb Plotter 'Wanted Him to Become a Martyr'," *Telegraph (London)*, February 16, 2010.

———, 2010b, "July 7 Ring Leader Was Arrested at Age 11, New Trawl of Records finds," *Telegraph (London)*, April 29, 2010

———, 2010c, "Trans-Atlantic Airlines Plot: The Frontline Troops," *Telegraph (London)*, July 8, 2010.

Gardham, Duncan, and Rayner, Gordon, 2008, "Airliner bomb trial: How MI5 uncovered the terror plot," *Telegraph (London)*, September 9, 2008

Gest, Justin, 2010, *Apart: Alienated and Engaged Muslims in the West*, New York: Columbia University Press.

Gilbert, Jon, 2007, "The Supergrass I Helped to Create," *Times (London)*, May 3, 2007.

Greve, Hanne, 1992, rapporteur, *Final Report of the United Nations Commission of Experts Established Pursuant to Security Council Resolution 780 (1992)*, annex 5, Prijedor report, section 8 A, available at http://www.ess.uwe.ac.uk/comexpert/ANX/V.htm#II-VIII.

Harris, Paul, Wazir, Burhan, and Burke, Jason, 2001, "We Will Replace the Bible with the Koran in Britain," *Observer (London)*, November 3, 2001.

Hayman, Andy (with Margaret Gilmore), 2010, *The Terrorist Hunters: On the Frontline of Britain's War Against Terror*, London: Corgi Books.

Hoffman, Bruce, 2006, *Inside Terrorism*, revised and expanded edition, New York: Columbia University Press.

———, 2008, "The Myth of Grass-Root Terrorism," *Foreign Affairs* 87, no. 3 (May-June): 133–138.

———, 2014, "The 7 July 2005 London Bombings," in Hoffman and Reinares, 2014: 192–223.

Hoffman, Bruce, and Reinares, Fernando, eds., 2014, *The Evolution of the Global Terrorist Threat: From 9/11 to Osama bin Laden's Death*, New York: Columbia University Press.

Horgan, John, 2005, *The Psychology of Terrorism*, Abingdon, England: Routledge.

House of Commons, 2006, *Report of the Official Account of the Bombings in London on 7th July 2005*, May 11, 2006, London: Her Majesty's Stationery Office.

Husain, Ed, 2007, *The Islamist*, London: Penguin Books.

Intelligence and Security Committee, 2006, *Report into the London Terrorist Attacks on 7 July 2005*, London: Her Majesty's Stationery Office.

———, 2009, *Could 7/7 Have Been Prevented? Review of the Intelligence on the London Terrorist Attacks on 7 July 2005*, London: Her Majesty's Stationery Office.

International Court of Justice, 2007, *Reports of Judgments, Advisory Opinions and Orders, Case Concerning Application of the Convention on the Prevention and Punishment of the Crime of Genocide (Bosnia and Herzegovina v. Serbia and Montenegro)*, judgment of 26 February 2007, available at http://www.icj-cij.org/docket/files/91/13685.pdf.

Keeble, Harry, and Hollington, Kris, 2010, *Terror Cops: Fighting Terrorism on Britain's Streets, the Inside Story of the Battle Against Extremism*, London: Pocket Books.

Kenney, Michael, 2018, *The Islamic State in Britain: Radicalization and Resilience in an Activist Network*, New York: Cambridge University Press

Kepel, Gilles, 1994, *A l'Ouest d'Allah*, Paris: Éditions du Seuil.

———, 2002, *Jihad: The Trail of Political Islam*, Cambridge, Mass.: Harvard University Press.

Khan, Mohammed Sidique, 2005, "London Bomber: Text in Full," *BBC News*, available at http://news.bbc.co.uk/2/hi/uk_news/4206800.stm.

Klausen, Jytte, 2010, *Al Qaeda-Affiliated and 'Homegrown' Jihadism in the UK: 1999–2010*, London: Institute for Strategic Dialogue

Lambert, Robert, 2009, "The London Partnerships: An Insider's Analysis of Legitimacy and Effectiveness," Ph.D. dissertation, Department of Politics, University of Exeter.

———, 2011, *Countering al-Qaeda in London: Police and Muslims in Partnership*, London: Hurst.

Lambert, Robert, and Githens-Mazer, Jonathan, 2009, "British Terrorists and Violent Extremists Directed or Inspired by al-Qaida," Department of Politics, University of Exeter, unpublished manuscript.

Lawrence, Bruce, ed., 2005, *Messages to the World: The Statements of Osama bin Laden*, London: Verso.

Leppard, David, 2007, "Fixer for 21/7 Plot Free in London," *Sunday Times (London)*, July 15, 2007.

Lia, Brynjar, 2008, *Architect of Global Jihad: The Life of al-Qaida Strategist Abu Mus'ab al-Suri*, New York: Columbia University Press.

MacPherson, Sir William of Cluny, 1999, *The Stephen Lawrence Inquiry: Report of an Inquiry*, London: Presented to Parliament by the Secretary of State for the Home Department by Command of Her Majesty, February 1999, Cm 4262-I.

Maher, Shiraz, 2006, "Campus Radicals," *Prospect*, September 24, available at http://www.prospectmagazine.co.uk/magazine/campusradicals/.

Malik, Kenan, 2009, *From Fatwa to Jihad: The Rushdie Affair and Its Legacy*, London: Atlantic Books.

Malik, Shiv, 2007a, "The Jihadi House Parties of Hate," *Sunday Times (London)*, May 6, 2007.

———, 2007b, "My Brother the Bomber," *Prospect*, June 30, available at http://www.prospectmagazine.co.uk/magazine/mybrotherthebomber/.

———, 2011, "The al-Qaida Supergrass and the 7/7 Questions That Remain Unanswered," *Guardian*, February 14, 2011, available at https://www.theguardian.com/uk/2011/feb/14/al-qaida-supergrass-77-questions.

Mandaville, Peter, ed., 2010, *Muslim Networks and Movements in Western Europe*, Pew Forum on Religious and Public Life, September 2010, Washington, D.C.: Pew Forum, available at http://www.pewforum.org/uploadedFiles/Topics/Religious_Affiliation/Muslim/Muslim-networks-full-report.pdf.

Milmo, Cahal, Herbert, Ian, Bennetto, Jason, and Huggler, Justin, 2006, "From Birmingham Bakery to Pakistani Prison, the Mystery of Rashid Rauf," *Independent (London)*, August 19, 2006.

Ministère Public c/ Bensakhria, Tcharek, Aknouche et autres, 2004, Tribunal de Grande Instance de Paris, 14eme chambre/2, No d'affaire: 0412639019, Jugement du: 16 Décembre 2004.

Ministère Public c/ Daoudi, Beghal, Bounour et autres, 2005, Tribunal de Grande Instance de Paris, 10ème chamber/1, No d'affaire: 0125339022, Jugement du: 15 mars 2005

Ministère Public c/ Ramda, 2006, Tribunal de Grande Instance de Paris, 16eme chambre/1, No d'affaire: 9527039040, Jugement du: 29 Mars 2006.

Moreton, Cole, and Buncombe, Andrew, 2008, "The Life and Death of Rashid Rauf," *Independent (London)*, November 23, 2008.

Mudd, Philip, 2013, *Takedown: Inside the Hunt for al Qaeda*, Philadelphia: University of Pennsylvania Press.

Murray, Andrew, and German, Lindsey, 2005, *Stop the War: The Story of Britain's Biggest Mass Movement*, London: Bookmarks Publications.

Abid Naseer et al. and SSHD, 2010, Special Immigration Appeals Commission, No: SC/77/80/81/82/83/09, May 18, 2010.

Nasiri, Omar, 2006, *Inside the Jihad: My Life with Al Qaeda; A Spy's Story*, New York: Basic Books.

Nawaz, Maajid, 2012, *Radical: My Journey from Islamist Extremism to a Democratic Awakening*, London: W. H. Allen.

Neumann, Peter, and Evans, Ryan, 2014, "Operation Crevice in London," in Hoffman and Reinares, 2014: 61–80.

Omand, David, 2010, *Securing the State*, New York: Columbia University Press.

O'Neill, Sean, and McGrory, Daniel, 2006, *The Suicide Factory: Abu Hamza and the Finsbury Park Mosque*, London: Harper Perennial.

Pantucci, Raffaello, 2010, "Manchester, New York and Oslo: Three Centrally Directed al-Qa'ida Plots," *CTC Sentinel* 3, no. 8 (August): 10–13.

———, 2012, "A Biography of Rashid Rauf: Al-Qa'ida's British Operative," *CTC Sentinel* 5, no. 7 (July): 12–16.

———, 2015, *"We Love Death as You Love Life": Britain's Suburban Terrorists*, London: Hurt.

Phillips, Melanie, 2006, *Londonistan*, New York: Encounter Books.

Regina v. Abdulla Ahmed Ali et al., 2008, Woolwich Crown Court, April 3, 2008, to September 8, 2008.

Regina v. Abdul Sherif et al., 2007–2008, Kingston Crown Court, October 1, 2007, to February 4, 2008.

Regina v. Mohamed Hamid et al., 2007–2008, Woolwich Crown Court, October 8, 2007, to February 26, 2008.

Regina v. Momin Khawaja, 2005, Superior Court of Justice, Ottawa, Ontario, bail hearing, June 6, 2005, to June 15, 2005.

———, 2008, Superior Court of Justice, Ottawa, Ontario, indictment No. 04-.G30282, June 23, 2008, to October 29, 2008.

Regina v. Mohammed Shakil et al., 2008, Crown Court, Kingston upon Thames, Surrey, case no: T20087141, 2008.

———, 2009, Crown Court, Kingston upon Thames, Surrey, case no: T20087141, 2009.

Regina v. Muktar Said Ibrahim et al., 2007, Woolwich Crown Court, January 11, 2007, to July 11, 2007.

Regina v. Omar Khyam et al., 2006–2007, Central Criminal Court, Old Bailey, London, March 21, 2006 to April 30, 2007.

———, 2006, "Prepared Text of Tuesday's Portion of the Crown's Opening Statement in the Trial of Seven Men Alleged to Have Plotted to Bomb London," *Ottawa Citizen*, March 21, 2006, available at http://www.canada.com/ottawacitizen/news/story.html?id=408dc2ed-d950–4ee5-a4b7-392eb5faaf34&k=75162.

———, 2008, Supreme Court of Judicature, Court of Appeal (Criminal Division), [2008] EWCA Crim 1612, July 23, 2008.

Regina v. Yeshiemebet ("Yeshi") Girma et al., 2008, Central Criminal Court, Old Bailey, London, February 25, 2008, to June 12, 2008.

Report of the National Advisory Commission on Civil Disorders, 1968, Washington, D.C.: U.S. Government Printing Office

Robertson, Nic, Cruickshank, Paul, and Lister, Tim, 2012a, "Documents Give New Details on al Qaeda's London Bombings," *CNN*, April 30, 2012, available at http://articles.cnn.com/2012-04-30/world/world_al-qaeda-documents-london-bombings_1_qaeda-s-london-operation-crevice-rashid-rauf?_s=PM:WORLD.

———, 2012b, "Document Shows Origins of 2006 Plot for Liquid Bombs on Planes," *CNN*, April 30, 2012, available at http://articles.cnn.com/2012-04-30/world/world_al-qaeda-documents_1_qaeda-assad-sarwar-abdulla-ahmed-ali?_s=PM:WORLD.

————, 2012c, "Documents Reveal al Qaeda's Plans for Seizing Cruise Ships, Carnage in Europe," *CNN*, May 1, 2012, available at http://www.cnn.com/2012/04/30/world/al-qaeda-documents-future/index.html.

Roy, Olivier, 2004, *Globalized Islam: The Search for a New Ummah*, New York: Columbia University Press.

Sageman, Marc, 2004, *Understanding Terror Networks*, Philadelphia: University of Pennsylvania Press.

————, 2008, *Leaderless Jihad: Terror Networks in the Twenty-First Century*, Philadelphia: University of Pennsylvania Press.

————, 2014, "The Stagnation in Terrorism Research," *Terrorism and Political Violence* 26, no. 4: 565–580.

————, 2016, *Misunderstanding Terrorism*, Philadelphia: University of Pennsylvania Press.

————, 2017, *Turning to Political Violence: The Emergence of Terrorism*, Philadelphia: University of Pennsylvania Press.

[Scheuer, Michael], 2004, *Imperial Hubris: Why the West Is Losing the War on Terror*, Dulles, Va.: Brassey's.

[————], 2002, *Through Our Enemy's Eyes: Osama bin Laden, Radical Islam, and the Future of America*, Washington, D.C.: Brassey's.

Schmid, Alex, 1983, *Political Terrorism: A Research Guide to Concepts, Theories, Data Bases and Literature*, Amsterdam: North-Holland.

Schuurman, Bart, Eijkman, Quirine, and Bakker, Edwin, 2015, "The Hofstadgroup Revisited: Questioning Its Status as a 'Quintessential' Homegrown Jihadist Network," *Terrorism and Political Violence* 27, no. 5: 906–926.

Sciolino, Elaine, and Schmitt, Eric, 2008, "A Not Very Private Feud over Terrorism," *New York Times*, Week in Review, June 8, 2008.

Secretary of State for the Home Department and AH, 2008, High Court of Justice, Queen's Bench Division, Administrative Court, [2008] EWHC 1018 (Admin), 5 September 2008.

Secretary of State for the Home Department and AM, 2009, High Court of Justice, Queen's Bench Division, Administrative Court, [2009] EWHC 3053 (Admin), 21 December 2009.

Secretary of State for the Home Department and AY, 2010, High Court of Justice, Queen's Bench Division, Administrative Court, [2010] EWHC 1860 (Admin), 26 July 2010.

Secretary of State for the Home Department and AY, 2012, High Court of Justice, Queen's Bench Division, Administrative Court, [2012] EWHC 2054 (Admin), 19 July 2012.

Senate Select Committee on Intelligence, 2012, *Committee Study of the Central Intelligence Agency's Detention and Interrogation Program*, available at https://www.intelligence.senate.gov/sites/default/files/press/executive-summary_0.pdf.

Silber, Mitchell, 2012, *The Al Qaeda Factor: Plots Against the West*, Philadelphia: University of Pennsylvania Press.

Silber, Mitchell, and Bhatt, Arvin, 2007, *Radicalization in the West: The Homegrown Threat*, New York: New York Police Department Intelligence Division, available at http://www.nypdshield.org/public/SiteFiles/documents/NYPD_Report-Radicalization_in_the_West.pdf.

Silke, Andrew, 1998, "Cheshire-Cat Logic: The Recurring Theme of Terrorist Abnormality in Psychological Research," *Psychology, Crime and Law* 4: 51–69.

————, ed., 2003, *Terrorists, Victims and Society: Psychological Perspectives on Terrorism and Its Consequences*, Chichester, England: John Wiley and Sons.

Simcox, Robin, Stuart, Hannah, and Ahmed, Houriya, 2010, *Islamist Terrorism: The British Connections*, London: The Centre for Social Cohesion.

Special Immigration Appeals Commission, 2010, *Open Judgment: Abid Naseer, Ahmad Faraz Khan, Shoaib Khan, Abdul Wahab Khan and Tariq ur Rehman v. Secretary of State for the Home Department*, Appeal no: SC/77/80/81/82/83/09, 18 May 2010.

Swann, Steve, 2009, "How British Muslim Adam Khatib Became a Bomb Plotter," *BBC News*, December 9, 2009, available at http://news.bbc.co.uk/2/hi/uk_news/8381192.stm.

"Taliban 'Martyr' Dies," *Crawley and Horley Observer*, October 31, 2001.

Terrorism Act 2000, London: Her Majesty's Stationery Office.

Terrorism Act 2006, London: Her Majesty's Stationery Office.

Thomas, Dominique, 2003, *Le Londonistan: La voix du jihad*, Paris: Éditions Michalon.

U.S. Department of Defense, 2007, Biographical Information on Abd al-Hadi al-Iraqi, April 27, 2007, available at http://www.defense.gov/news/Apr2007/d20070427hvd.pdf.

———, 2008, JFT-GTMO Detainee Assessment ISN US9LY-010017DP Abu Faraj al Libi, September 10, 2008, available at https://wikileaks.org/gitmo/pdf/ly/us9ly-010017dp.pdf

U.S. Department of Treasury Press Center, 2006, "Treasury Designates Individual Supporting al Qaida, Other Terrorist Organizations," December 19, 2006, available at http://www .treasury.gov/press-center/press-releases/Pages/hp206.aspx.

U.S. v. Abdal Hadi al Iraqi, 2014, U.S. Department of Defense, MC Form 458 (Jan 2007), Continuation of the Charges and Specifications, Receipt by Convening Authority, February 10, 2014.

U.S. v. Abu Gaith, 2014, U.S. District Court, Southern District of New York, No. S14 98 CR 1023 (LAK)

U.S. v. Haroon Rashid Aswat, 2015, U.S. District Court, Southern District of New York, No. 04 CR 356 (KBF).

U.S. v. Adis Medunjanin, 2012, U.S. District Court, Eastern District of New York, No. 10 CR 19 (JG)

U.S. v. Mustafa Kamel Mustafa, 2014, U.S. District Court, Southern District of New York, No. 04-CR-356 (KBF)

Van Natta Jr., Don, Sciolino, Elaine, and Grey, Stephen, 2006, "In Tapes, Receipts and a Diary, Details of the British Terror Case," *New York Times*, August 28, 2006.

Vidino, Lorenzo, 2006, *Al Qaeda in Europe: The New Battleground of International Jihad*, New York: Prometheus Books.

———, 2010, *The New Muslim Brotherhood in the West*, New York: Columbia University Press

———, 2014, *Home-Grown Jihadism in Italy: Birth, Development and Radicalization Dynamics*, Milan: Istituto per gli Studi di Politica Internazionale.

Wall Street Journal, 2009, "Explosive Emails," Europe News, September 7, 2009, available at http://online.wsj.com/article/SB125234624255890413.html?mod = googlenews_wsj.

Wiktorowicz, Quintan, 2005, *Radical Islam Rising: Muslim Extremism in the West*, Oxford: Rowman and Littlefield.

Williams, Rachel, 2008, "July 7 Plot Accused Tell of Times with Taliban," *Guardian*, May 20, 2008, available at http://www.theguardian.com/uk/2008/may/21/july7.uksecurity.

Winder, Robert, 2004, *Bloody Foreigners: The Story of Immigration to Britain*, London: Abacus.

INDEX

ACKNOWLEDGMENTS

Any book is a collective enterprise built on multiple discussions with various people along the way. I wish to thank Abdul Haqq Baker, Rachel Briggs, Sarah Connolly, Paul Cruickshank, Duncan Gardham, Thelma Gillen, Jonathan Githens-Mazer, John Horgan, Ed Husain, Bob Lambert, Brian Marcus, Chris Morris, John Mueller, Maajid Nawaz, Raffaello Pantucci, Tom Quiggin, Asim Quraishi, Faisal Qureshi, Mitch Silber, Max Taylor, Lorenzo Vidino, Mike Whine, Yu Sasaki, and several imprisoned informants, who provided background information. I also wish to thank the U.S. Air Force Research Laboratory for funding a project that ultimately contributed to this book. I also wish to thank the team at the University of Pennsylvania Press, especially Peter Agree, Noreen O'Connor-Abel, and Robert Milks. Finally and mostly, I wish to thank my wife and son for their unfailing support during this project.